# The Science of Demons

Witches, ghosts, fairies. Premodern Europe was filled with strange creatures, with the devil lurking behind them all. But were his powers real? Did his powers have limits? Or were tales of the demonic all one grand illusion? Physicians, lawyers, and theologians at different times and places answered these questions differently and disagreed bitterly.

The demonic took many forms in medieval and early modern Europe. By examining individual authors from across the continent, this book reveals the many purposes to which the devil could be put, both during the late medieval fight against heresy and during the age of Reformations. It explores what it was like to live with demons, and how careers and identities were constructed out of battles against them – or against those who granted them too much power. Together, contributors chart the history of the devil from his emergence during the 1300s as a threatening figure – who made pacts with human allies and appeared bodily – through to the comprehensive but controversial demonologies of the turn of the seventeenth century, when European witch-hunting entered its deadliest phase.

This book is essential reading for all students and researchers of the history of the supernatural in medieval and early modern Europe.

**Jan Machielsen** is Senior Lecturer in Early Modern History at Cardiff University, UK. He is the author of *Martin Delrio: Demonology and Scholarship in the Counter-Reformation* (2015).

**Routledge Studies in the History of Witchcraft, Demonology and Magic**

**The Science of Demons**
Early Modern Authors Facing Witchcraft and the Devil
*Edited by Jan Machielsen*

# The Science of Demons
Early Modern Authors Facing Witchcraft and the Devil

**Edited by Jan Machielsen**

LONDON AND NEW YORK

First published 2020
by Routledge
2 Park Square, Milton Park, Abingdon, Oxon OX14 4RN

and by Routledge
52 Vanderbilt Avenue, New York, NY 10017

*Routledge is an imprint of the Taylor & Francis Group, an informa business*

© 2020 selection and editorial matter, Jan Machielsen; individual chapters, the contributors

The right of Jan Machielsen to be identified as the author of the editorial material, and of the authors for their individual chapters, has been asserted in accordance with sections 77 and 78 of the Copyright, Designs and Patents Act 1988.

All rights reserved. No part of this book may be reprinted or reproduced or utilised in any form or by any electronic, mechanical, or other means, now known or hereafter invented, including photocopying and recording, or in any information storage or retrieval system, without permission in writing from the publishers.

*Trademark notice*: Product or corporate names may be trademarks or registered trademarks, and are used only for identification and explanation without intent to infringe.

*British Library Cataloguing-in-Publication Data*
A catalogue record for this book is available from the British Library

*Library of Congress Cataloging-in-Publication Data*
Names: Machielsen, Johannes M., 1984- editor.
Title: The science of demons : early modern authors facing witchcraft and the devil / edited by Jan Machielsen.
Description: Abingdon, Oxon ; New York, NY : Routledge Taylor & Francis, 2020. |
Series: Routledge studies in the history of witchcraft, demonology and magic | Includes bibliographical references and index.
Identifiers: LCCN 2019053680 (print) | LCCN 2019053681 (ebook) |
Subjects: LCSH: Demonology–Europe–History–17th century. | Witchcraft–Europe–History–17th century. | Supernatural–History–17th century. | Devil–History of doctrines–17th century.
Classification: LCC BF1517.E85 S36 2020 (print) |
LCC BF1517.E85 (ebook) | DDC 133.4094–dc23
LC record available at https://lccn.loc.gov/2019053680
LC ebook record available at https://lccn.loc.gov/2019053681

ISBN: 978-1-138-57181-5 (hbk)
ISBN: 978-1-138-57183-9 (pbk)
ISBN: 978-0-203-70251-2 (ebk)

Typeset in Bembo
by Swales & Willis, Exeter, Devon, UK

For Stuart

# Contents

*List of figures* x
*Notes on contributors* xii
*Acknowledgements* xvi
*Editor's note* xix

Introduction: The science of demons 1
JAN MACHIELSEN

### PART 1
### Beginnings 17

1 The inquisitor's demons: Nicolau Eymeric's *Directorium inquisitorum* 19
 PAU CASTELL GRANADOS

2 Promoter of the sabbat and diabolical realism: Nicolas Jacquier's *Flagellum hereticorum fascinariorum* 35
 MARTINE OSTORERO

### PART 2
### The first wave of printed witchcraft texts 51

3 The bestselling demonologist: Heinrich Institoris's *Malleus maleficarum* 53
 TAMAR HERZIG

4 Lawyers versus inquisitors: Ponzinibio's *De lamiis* and Spina's *De strigibus* 68
 MATTEO DUNI

viii   *Contents*

5   The witch-hunting humanist: Gianfrancesco Pico della
    Mirandola's *Strix*                                                    83
    WALTER STEPHENS

**PART 3**
**The sixteenth-century debate**                                         101

6   'Against the devil, the subtle and cunning enemy':
    Johann Wier's *De praestigiis daemonum*                              103
    MICHAELA VALENTE

7   The will to know and the unknowable: Jean Bodin's *De La
    Démonomanie*                                                          119
    VIRGINIA KRAUSE

8   Doubt and demonology: Reginald Scot's *The Discoverie
    of Witchcraft*                                                        133
    PHILIP C. ALMOND

9   Demonology and anti-demonology: Binsfeld's
    *De confessionibus* and Loos's *De vera et falsa magia*               149
    RITA VOLTMER

10  A royal witch theorist: James VI's *Daemonologie*                    165
    P. G. MAXWELL-STUART

11  Demonology as textual scholarship: Martin Delrio's
    *Disquisitiones magicae*                                              179
    JAN MACHIELSEN

**PART 4**
**Demonology and theology**                                              195

12  'Of ghostes and spirites walking by nyght': Ludwig
    Lavater's *Von Gespänsten*                                            197
    PIERRE KAPITANIAK

13  A Spanish demonologist during the French Wars of Religion:
    Juan Maldonado's *Traicté des anges et demons*                        211
    FABIÁN ALEJANDRO CAMPAGNE

14 Scourging demons with exorcism: Girolamo Menghi's
*Flagellum daemonum*  224
GUIDO DALL'OLIO

15 The ambivalent demonologist: William Perkins's *Discourse
of the Damned Art of Witchcraft*  238
LEIF DIXON

16 Piety and purification: The anonymous *Czarownica powołana*  252
MICHAEL OSTLING

## PART 5
## Demonology and law  267

17 An untrustworthy reporter: Nicolas Remy's
*Daemonolatreiae libri tres*  269
ROBIN BRIGGS

18 The mythmaker of the sabbat: Pierre de Lancre's *Tableau de
l'inconstance des mauvais anges et démons*  283
THIBAUT MAUS DE ROLLEY AND JAN MACHIELSEN

19 An expert lawyer and reluctant demonologist:
Alonso de Salazar Frías, Spanish Inquisitor  299
LU ANN HOMZA

*Critical editions and English translations of demonological texts*  313
*Index*  316

# Figures

Cover Image: *Versuchung des hl. Antonius.* (The Temptation of St Anthony). Follower of the Master of 1445 (Konstanz). Inv. Nr. M 128. © The Rosgartenmuseum, Constance.

0.1  Principal places mentioned in this volume. Map by Kirsty Harding   xx
I.1  Albrecht Dürer, *Witch Riding Backwards on a Goat* (c. 1500) [19.73.75]. Image courtesy of The Metropolitan Museum of Art, New York   3
I.2  The Witches' Sabbat at North Berwick. James Carmichael, *Newes from Scotland, Declaring the Damnable Life and Death of Doctor Fian a Notable Sorcerer…*, London: William Wright, 1592, sig. B4v [Sp Coll Ferguson Al-a.36]. Image by permission of University of Glasgow Library, Special Collections   7
5.1  Woman Copulating with Demon / Woman Riding a Goat. Fragment of Ulrich Tengler, *Der neü Layenspiegel*, Augsburg: Otmar Johann, 1511, fol. 190r [Res/2 J.pract]. Image by permission of Bayerische Staatsbibliothek, Munich   91
6.1  Fragment of title page showing a ritual magician surrounded by demons. Ludwig Milich, *Der Zauber Teuffel, das ist, Von Zauberen, Warsagung, Beschwehren, gegen Aberglauben, Hexeren, und mancherley Wercken des Teuffels*, Frankfurt: Martin Lechler, 1566 [Sp Coll Ferguson Af-e.74]. Image by permission of University of Glasgow Library, Special Collections   106
6.2  Title page showing a group of witches apparently preparing for flight. Johann Wier, *De Praestigiis …: Von den Teuffeln, Zaubrern, Schwartzkünstlern, Teuffelsbeschwerern, Hexen oder Unholden und Gifftbereitern*, trans. Johann Füglin, Frankfurt: Peter Schmidt and Sigmund Feyerabend, 1566 [Phys.m. 306 -1]. Image by permission of Bayerische Staatsbibliothek, Munich   109
8.1  Title page showing a ritual magician (or the Witch of Endor?). Reginald Scot, *Ontdecking van tovery*, trans. Thomas and Govert Basson, Beverwijk: Frans Pels, 1638 [KW 394 G 72]. Image by permission of the Koninklijke Bibliotheek, The Hague   134

| | | |
|---|---|---|
| 10.1 | Simon van de Passe, *James I, King of England* (c.1619) [09.1S849]. Engraving by permission of the Detroit Institute of Arts, gift of Mrs. James E. Scripps | 166 |
| 11.1 | Cover page showing Moses combatting the Magicians of Egypt. Martin Delrio, *Disquisitionum magicarum libri sex, in tres tomos partiti*, 3$^{rd}$ ed., Mainz: Johannes Albinus, 1603 [KW 3236 C 3]. Image by permission of the Koninklijke Bibliotheek, The Hague | 184 |
| 18.1 | Children being flown to the sabbat / A child being offered to a demon. Fragment from Jan Ziarnko's 'Description et figure du sabbat des sorciers' included in Pierre de Lancre, *Tableau de l'inconstance des mauvais anges et démons*, 2$^{nd}$ ed., Paris: Nicolas Buon, 1613 [Sp Coll Ferguson Al-x.50]. Image by permission of University of Glasgow Library, Special Collections | 284 |
| 18.2 | Village musicians performing at the sabbat/nude dancing at the sabbat. Fragment from Jan Ziarnko's 'Description et figure du sabbat des sorciers', in Pierre de Lancre, Tableau de l'inconstance des mauvais anges et démons, 2nd ed., Paris: Nicolas Buon, 1613 [Sp Coll Ferguson Al-x.50]. Image by permission of University of Glasgow Library, Special Collections | 294 |

# Notes on contributors

**Philip C. Almond** is Professor Emeritus in the History of Religious Thought in the Institute for Advanced Studies in the Humanities at the University of Queensland, Australia. He is the author of numerous monographs, including *England's First Demonologist: Reginald Scot and his Discoverie of Witchcraft* (2011), *The Devil: A New Biography* (2014), *Afterlife: A History of Life after Death* (2016), and most recently *God: A New Biography* (2018).

**Robin Briggs** is Emeritus Senior Research Fellow, All Souls College, University of Oxford, and a fellow of the British Academy. His books include *Communities of Belief: Social and Cultural Tensions in Early Modern France* (1989), *Witches and Neighbours: The Social and Cultural Context of European Witchcraft* (2nd ed., 2002), and *The Witches of Lorraine* (2007).

**Fabián Alejandro Campagne** is Associate Professor of Early Modern History at the Universidad de Buenos Aires. His main teaching and research interests are Christian superstition, Renaissance demonology, and discernment of spirits. He is the author of many books, including *Homo catholicus, homo superstitiosus* (2002), *Strix Hispanica* (2009), *Profetas en ninguna tierra* (2016), and *Bodin y Maldonado* (2018), as well as numerous articles in English and Spanish.

**Pau Castell Granados** teaches in the Department of Medieval and Early Modern History at the Universitat de Barcelona. His work focusses on the intellectual foundations of European witchcraft mythologies, as they emerged during the fourteenth and fifteenth centuries, as well as on the late medieval and early modern witch-hunts in the Iberian Peninsula. He is currently editing a collection of fifteenth-century sources which reveal the existence of entirely forgotten early witchcraft persecutions in Catalonia.

**Guido Dall'Olio** is Associate Professor of Early Modern History at the Università degli Studi di Urbino 'Carlo Bo'. His main fields of research are religious dissent in early modern Italy, the Roman Inquisition, witchcraft, demonic possession, and the struggle against 'superstition'. He is the author of *Eretici e inquisitori nella Bologna del Cinquecento* (1999) and many articles in Italian and English.

**Leif Dixon** is a lecturer in Early Modern History at Regent's Park College, University of Oxford, where he is also the director of studies. His first book, *Practical Predestinarians in England, c.1590–1640* (2014), examined the ways in which Calvinist ministers communicated complex and controversial doctrines to the wider population. His current research centres on early modern anxieties about atheism, and what this can tell us about religious identity in the era of Reformation.

**Matteo Duni** teaches history of the Italian Renaissance at both New York University's and Syracuse University's centres in Florence. He is the author of *Non lasciar vivere la malefica: Le streghe nei trattati e nei processi* (with Dinora Corsi, 2008), *Under the Devil's Spell: Witches, Sorcerers and the Inquisition in Renaissance Italy* (2007), and *Tra religione e magia: Storia del prete modenese Guglielmo Campana, 1460?–1541* (1999), among many other publications.

**Tamar Herzig** is Professor of Early Modern European History at Tel Aviv University. She is the author of *Savonarola's Women: Visions and Reform in Renaissance Italy* (2008), *Christ Transformed into a Virgin Woman: Lucia Brocadelli, Heinrich Institoris, and the Defense of the Faith* (2013), and *A Convert's Tale: Art, Crime, and Jewish Apostasy in Renaissance Italy* (2019) as well as numerous articles.

**Lu Ann Homza** is Professor of History at William & Mary, Virginia. She is the author of *Religious Authority in the Spanish Renaissance* (2000) and the editor and translator of the first English-language, primary source reader on the Spanish Inquisition (2006). She is currently finishing a revisionist study of the Basque witch-hunt of 1608–1614, entitled *Village Infernos and Witches' Advocates*.

**Pierre Kapitaniak** is Professor of Early Modern British Civilisation at the University of Montpellier. He is the author of *Spectres, ombres et fantômes: Discours et représentations dramatiques en Angleterre* (2008), the co-editor of *Fictions du diable: Démonologie et littérature* (2007), and the translator of a number of English demonological texts into French, the latest being Reginald Scot's *La Sorcellerie démystifiée* (2015). He is currently working on a French translation of Daniel Defoe's demonological treatises.

**Virginia Krause** is Professor of French Studies at Brown University. She is the author of *Witchcraft, Demonology, and Confession in Early Modern France* (2015) and co-editor with Christian Martin and Eric MacPhail of a critical edition of Jean Bodin's *De La Démonomanie des sorciers* (2016).

**Jan Machielsen** is Senior Lecturer in Early Modern History at Cardiff University. His first monograph, *Martin Delrio: Demonology and Scholarship in* *the Counter-Reformation* (2015), was shortlisted for the Royal Historical Society Gladstone Prize. He is currently working on a study of the 1609 witch-hunt conducted by the Bordeaux judge Pierre de Lancre in the French Basque country.

**P. G. Maxwell-Stuart** is Reader in History at the University of St Andrews, a fellow of the Royal Historical Society, and a fellow of the Society of Antiquities in Scotland. He is a classicist as well as an historian of the occult sciences in Europe, particularly during the early modern period, and is widely published in both fields. He is currently preparing a full English translation of the 1608 edition of Martin Delrio's *Disquisitionum magicarum libri sex*.

**Thibaut Maus de Rolley** is Associate Professor in French Renaissance Studies at University College London. He has published widely on early modern demonology, and in particular on the interactions between demonology and genres such as travel writing and narrative fiction. He is the author of *Elévations: L'Ecriture du voyage aérien à la Renaissance* (2011) and the co-editor of *Voyager avec le diable: Voyages réels, voyages imaginaires et discours démonologiques* (2008).

**Michael Ostling** is Senior Honors Faculty Fellow at Arizona State University. He is the author of *Between the Devil and the Host: Imagining Witchcraft in Early Modern Poland* (2011) and editor of *Emotions in the History of Witchcraft* (with Laura Kounine, 2017) and *Fairies, Demons and Nature Spirits* (2018). His current work attempts a revision of our understanding of Max Weber's 'disenchantment of the world'.

**Martine Ostorero** is Associate Professor of Medieval History at the Université de Lausanne. Her research focusses on demonological literature and the repression of demonic witchcraft in the fifteenth century. She is the author of *Le Diable au sabbat: Littérature démonologie et sorcellerie, 1440–1460* (2011) and *L'Énigme de la Vauderie de Lyon: Enquête sur l'essor des chasses aux sorcières entre France et Empire, 1430–1480* (with Franck Mercier, 2015), as well as the (co-)editor of influential volumes on late medieval and early modern demonology.

**Walter Stephens** is Charles S. Singleton Professor of Italian Studies at Johns Hopkins University. He has published *Giants in Those Days: Folklore, Ancient History, and Nationalism* (1989) and *Demon Lovers: Witchcraft, Sex, and the Crisis of Belief* (2002). He has co-edited a number of volumes, including *Literary Forgery in Early Modern Europe, 1450–1800* (2019). Upcoming publications are an edition of Gianfrancesco Pico's *Strix* and *De imaginatione*, and *It Is Written: How Writing Made Us Human*.

**Michaela Valente** is Associate Professor of Early Modern History at Università del Molise. She has published essays and books on Jean Bodin, on demonology, and on the Roman Inquisition. She is currently working on an English version of *Johann Wier: Agli albori della critica razionale dell'occulto e del demoniaco nell'Europa del Cinquecento* (2003), entitled: *Johann Wier: Debating the Devil and Witches in Early Modern Europe*.

**Rita Voltmer** is Senior Lecturer in Medieval and Early Modern History at University of Trier. She is the author of *Hexen: Wissen was stimmt* (2008) and *Hexen und Hexenverfolgung in der Frühen Neuzeit* (with Walter Rummel, 2012). She is the editor of several conference proceedings and has published more than 80 journal articles and book chapters in English, French, and German.

# Acknowledgements

A collaborative project such as this one accumulates many debts. I really must begin, however, by thanking the many contributors to this volume. They acted as touchstones throughout this project, commenting on everything from the book proposal to the cover image. They also, on occasion, suffered at the hands of a zealous editor keen to bring their chapters into dialogue with each other. Their support, advice, and forbearance made it possible for this project to be completed with only the most minimal of delays. Perhaps, the study of demons has brought out the better angels in our nature. Whatever the reason, I simply could not have wished for better colleagues.

I owe a great debt to the editors at Routledge – Laura Pilsworth, Morwenna Scott, and Jennifer Morrow – who perceived the value of this project and were fountains of wisdom and advice for this relative novice as a book editor. I am also glad to acknowledge the support of my own University and its School of History, Archaeology, and Religion (SHARE) for providing the funding necessary to clear permission rights for some of the images. It is a special pleasure to thank the Detroit Institute of Arts and the Special Collections of the University of Glasgow (and Niki Russell in particular) for making images available free of charge. Laura Kounine and Charlotte-Rose Millar checked the list of editions that concludes this volume for omissions. My colleague at SHARE, Kirsty Harding, created the map (Figure 0.1) that prefaces this volume. I am grateful to her not only for her professionalism as a designer and illustrator but also for her patience, as my ideas as to which places to include kept on changing.

One debt deserves special acknowledgement and relates to the origins of this project. The idea for this volume emerged in 2016, when two demonological anniversaries were approaching. Both ended up passing by with virtually no notice. The first was the forty-year anniversary of a volume with the enticing title *The Damned Art: Essays in the Literature of Witchcraft* (1977), edited by Sydney Anglo. The second was the twenty-year anniversary of Stuart Clark's magisterial *Thinking with Demons: The Idea of Witchcraft in Early Modern Europe* (1997), the only academic study, as one opinionated colleague and friend once put it, that should be permitted to be over 400 pages in length. (In fact, it comes in at just over 800 pages.)

*Acknowledgements* xvii

Both these publications remain widely influential. Routledge, the publishers of *The Damned Art*, released an electronic version in 2011. The studies of individual works of demonology gathered in that volume remain valuable and widely cited, even though taken together they cannot be said to be representative of the literature of witchcraft as a whole. (To be sure, the book never claimed as much. In his preface, Anglo noted that he had made 'no attempt to impose procedures upon anybody'.) No one, however, has done more to revitalise the academic study of demonology than Stuart Clark, whose contribution on James VI and I in the *Damned Art* already expressed the hope – at the end of the chapter's final endnote – to explore the subject 'more fully on another occasion'. Clark's 1997 monograph rescued demonology from the obligatory opening chapters of social historians of witchcraft – his was' not a book about witch-hunting' but about 'witch-hating' – and it also inspired a flurry of studies that sought to 'think with' other things. *Thinking* showed how central demons were to early modern thought. In fact, 'there was too much demonology embedded in early modern books – books of all kinds and on many subjects – for it to be attributed to one kind of writer'. *Thinking* was ground-breaking. It served as an inspiration to a great many literary scholars and historians of ideas, gender, religion, and culture who followed in its footsteps, many of whom have contributed to the present volume.

Both *The Damned Art* and *Thinking* have aged well. Many of the insights contained in their pages remain accepted wisdom. Yet, scholarship has also moved on to study other facets of the science of demons. Scholars have studied the rhetoric and gendering of demonology, and the self-fashioning and source criticism of its authors. They have situated individual contributions not only within a wider demonological corpus but also with an author's own oeuvre. They have paid attention to the versatility of the science of demons and the many, often contradictory purposes to which it could be put. They have enlarged the realm of the demonic to encompass other phenomena, such as demonic possession and magical creatures, and they have extended the emotional registers that witchcraft evoked. Demonology was no longer just an expression of fear and anxiety, it could be a form of entertainment as well. We have also learned a great deal more about how different ideas and beliefs came together to create the science of demons during the fourteenth and fifteenth centuries, as well as the way the early modern book trade allowed these ideas to spread.

With two notable anniversaries approaching, then, the idea emerged to publish a survey of the current state of the field, aimed at students and scholars alike. The format of *The Damned Art* – though led by a more anxious, or at least less laid-back editor – would allow us to capture the development and versatility of the science of demons across space and time. It would also bring the work of scholars with different interests and from different backgrounds into conversation with each other. This idea was informally workshopped with a number of eventual contributors at the edges of the

Sixteenth Century Society Conference in Bruges in 2016. Yet, the first person with whom I discussed the idea was Stuart Clark. He not only enthusiastically endorsed the project from the start, he also read and supported the book proposal although he was unable to contribute to the volume itself. My debts, intellectual and otherwise, to Stuart are many and are already evident from the acknowledgements of my previous publications. For all these reasons, it seems fitting to offer to him, as a tribute, a survey of the field of scholarship which he, more than any other person, helped to create.

Jan Machielsen
Cardiff, Wales
3 September 2019

# Editor's note

Note: The names of authors discussed in other chapters in this volume are marked with ° upon their first appearance in a contribution.

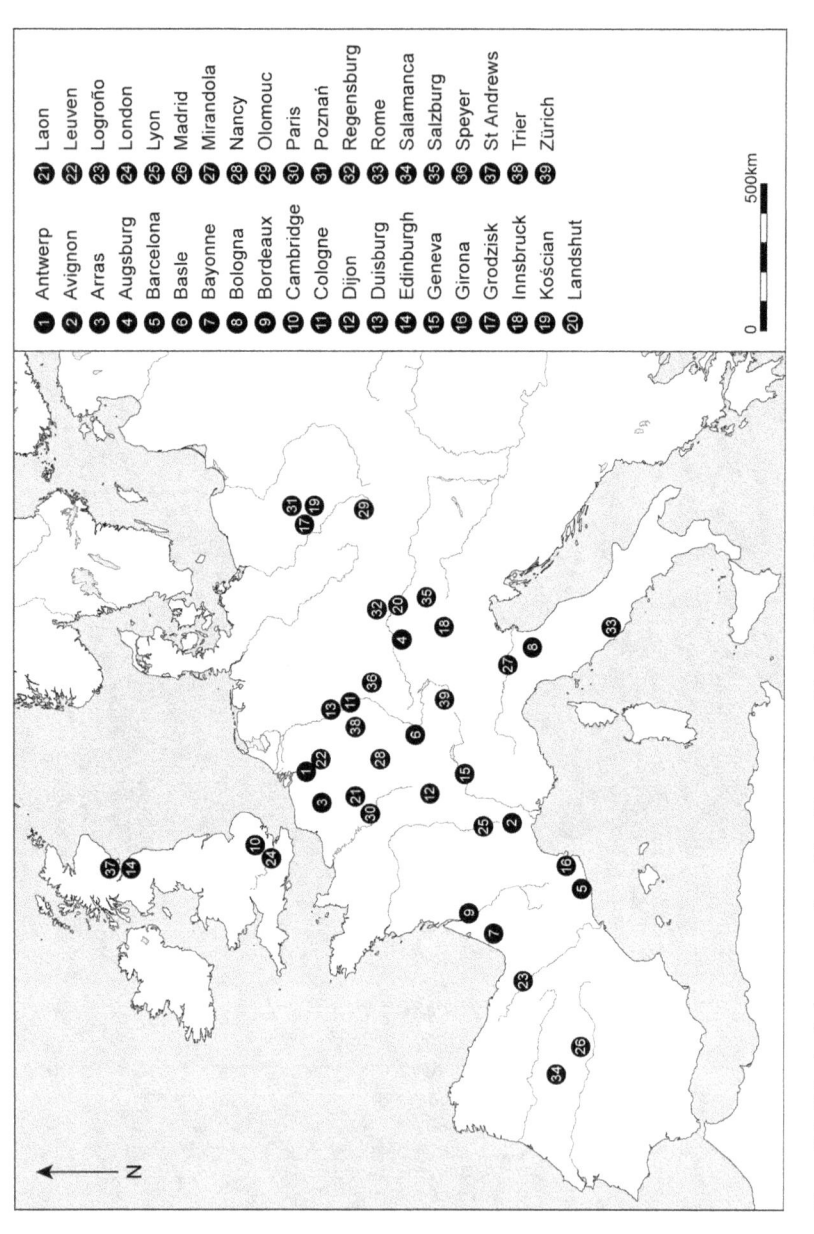

*Figure 0.1* Principal places mentioned in this volume. Map by Kirsty Harding.

# Introduction
The science of demons

*Jan Machielsen*

'What thinke yee of these strange newes, which now onelie furnishes purpose to al men at their meeting: I meane of these Witches?' asked Philomathes.[1] He was the more ignorant of the two speakers in King James VI°'s *Daemonologie* (1597) but, as his name suggests, he was keen to learn more. (Philomathes means 'someone who loves to learn things' in Ancient Greek.) His colleague Epistemon, whose name literally meant 'someone who understands what he is talking about' and who was clearly a stand-in for the Scottish king himself, was only too happy to help. James VI of Scotland and (later) I of England (1566–1625) loved word games such as these and, as we have adopted the title of his work for our own, it seems appropriate that we start with him. Demonology, a word first coined by the king, while probably intended as a conversation about demons (see P. G. Maxwell-Stuart's chapter in this volume), has come to signify nothing more or less than the science (*logos*) of demons.

By the time that Philomathes asked his question, witches were no longer 'news', not even in Scotland, which in 1563 had passed an act against them, but they may still have seemed that way. Scotland had seen a number of large-scale witch-hunts throughout the 1590s of an unprecedented scale.[2] The king had been intimately involved in the first of these (1590–91) which followed closely upon his return from Scandinavia where James had married his wife, Anne of Denmark. Having interrogated some of the accused witches himself, the king was sceptical of their powers until one of them took 'his Maiesty a little aside [and] declared unto him the very words which passed betweene the King's Maiesty and his queen at Upslo [Oslo] in Norway the first night of their mariage, with their answer each to [the] other.'[3] James was also very pleased to discover that he was the 'greatest enemy [the devil] hath in the world' but that as 'the Lord's annointed' he was under God's constant protection.[4] Witches had been unable to sink the fleet that had been transporting him across the North Sea because of 'the wonderful providence of the Almighty'.[5] A pamphlet, entitled *Newes from Scotland*, appeared in London in 1592 to spread these divine and (in a strange, inverse way) demonic testimonials among his future English subjects.

The discipline of demonology existed long before James VI and I came up with a word for it. Some of the contributions to the field included references to demons in their titles: Johann Wier°'s *De praestigiis daemonum* (On the Deceptions of Devils, 1563), Nicolas Remy°'s *Daemonolatreia* (literally, the Worship of Devils, 1595), Pierre de Lancre°'s *Tableau de l'inconstance des mauvais anges et démons* (A Tableau of the Inconstancy of Evil Angels and Demons, 1612), to list only a few. Others named their books after the devil's human allies, his witches, employing a bewilderingly large vocabulary to do so: Heinrich Institoris°'s infamous *Malleus maleficarum* (The Hammer of [Female] Witches, 1487), Gianfrancesco Pico della Mirandola°'s *Strix* (The Witch, 1523) and Reginald Scot°'s sceptical *The Discoverie of Witchcraft* (1584) are other good examples. Jean Bodin°'s *De La Démonomanie des sorciers* (On the Demon-Mania of Witches, 1580) even managed to squeeze in both the devil and the witch in close proximity. Witches, then, really were no longer 'news' in the 1590s, as James VI well knew. In fact, in a preface the king denounced Scot and Wier (or Weyer) for their scepticism and Bodin for his credulity.[6]

Neither the figure of the witch nor that of the devil were early modern inventions. Belief in the existence of witches – that is, persons who secretly harm members of their communities using mysterious (magical) means – was common to human societies across the globe. In Europe and the Middle East, often obscure references to witches, diviners, potion-makers and the like go back to the earliest written records.[7] Ethnographic comparisons can reveal striking parallels. For instance, if early modern European witches were frequently depicted as flying naked on goats, facing backwards, Zulu witches in southern Africa were said to ride baboons in the same way.[8]

Yet, the same ethnographic comparisons also bring out a wide variety of attitudes towards witches and the level of threat they posed. It depended on the society whether witches were typically gendered male or female. If witches were believed to be born with their power and *unconscious* of possessing it (the 'evil eye'), they were not generally held responsible for outcomes they could not control. One Buddhist tribe, the Shan, living on the border between Thailand and China, treated witches in the same way as 'antisocial drunks': although a danger to others and responsible for their general condition, they were not really accountable for any particular action.[9] Such global comparisons bring out the full range of witchcraft beliefs and reveal early modern European attitudes to be of a particularly nasty, virulent, and misogynistic strain.

What made these attitudes particularly deadly – causing some 40,000–50,000 women and men to lose their lives – was the way popular beliefs in witches intersected with the Christian belief in the devil.[10] Satan (Hebrew for 'adversary'; Job 2:1) had featured sporadically in the Old Testament, where he in vain tested Job's faith in God by taking away his family, health, and property, but he rose to especial prominence in the New Testament. By this time, the devil's power had clearly grown. As 'the prince of this world' (John 12:31) and 'the father of lies' (John 8:44),

*Figure I.1* Albrecht Dürer, *Witch Riding Backwards on a Goat* (c. 1500) [19.73.75]. Image courtesy of The Metropolitan Museum of Art, New York.

the devil emerged as the principal opponent of Christ and his disciples. In fact, he even sought to seduce Jesus with the offer of 'all the kingdoms of the world and the glory of them', if only Christ would worship him (Matthew 4:8). The evangelists, therefore, presented Christ's casting out of unclean spirits from the bodies of the possessed, as an important victory over the evil one, a power Christ also granted to the apostles (*e.g.* Matthew 10:1) and hence to the Church. Soon, the Greek and Roman gods were depicted as nothing other than devils in disguise.[11] Although the Bible never quite recounted the devil's origin story (nor, for that matter, that of any of the good angels), early Christians held that he had fallen as humanity had – in his case quite literally from heaven. Christians quickly identified him as the serpent in the Garden of Eden who had tempted Adam and Eve to eat from the Tree of Knowledge of Good and Evil and thus caused their expulsion from Paradise (Genesis 3).

The early modern witch-hunt was the product of an unhappy encounter between the devil, whose powers and ploys medieval theologians had discussed for centuries, and the night-flying witch of the popular imagination. It was also the product of an alliance between law and religion, which made witchcraft a crime punishable by the courts. This did not mean that witch-hunts were necessarily imposed by elites, however. In many instances, the long-suffering villagers of early modern Europe were only too quick to use the legal machinery newly at their disposal to denounce those neighbours they suspected from secretly harming them.[12] What made all this work – the beating heart of demonology, as it were – was the demonic pact a witch was alleged to have made with the devil, in which she renounced God and her baptism and pledged allegiance to God's archenemy. Of course, the devil could act without his human minions as well, for instance, by possessing and vexing the bodies of the innocent, as he was already alleged to have done in the New Testament. As Guido Dall'Olio shows in his contribution, there also existed a burgeoning early modern trade in exorcism manuals, especially in Italy.[13] Similarly, as Pierre Kapitaniak's chapter highlights, ghosts and magical creatures, such as fairies, were increasingly seen as demonic inventions and impersonations as well, especially by Protestants who had dispensed with Purgatory.[14] Witchcraft, though, was special. Christian scholars agreed that the demonic pact allowed the devil to hit two birds with one stone: not only did witches cause harm to their fellow humans, testing their faith, but they were themselves led to Hell and damnation in the process. With perfect diabolical treachery, the devil sought to ruin the souls and bodies of those who allied themselves with him.

This short survey already brings out the first two ways in which this volume will breathe new life into the study of late medieval and early modern demonology. First of all, the volume will chart its rise and elaboration from late medieval roots to the heyday of the witch-hunt (1570–1630), when perhaps as many as 90% of its victims perished.[15] The doctrine of the demonic pact developed in the early fourteenth century and was pushed mainly by Dominican inquisitors obsessed with rooting out heresy in remote regions in the Alps and Pyrenees, men like Nicolau Eymeric° and Nicolas Jacquier°, discussed by Pau Castell Granados and Martine Ostorero in this volume.[16] Their chapters highlight how for the demonic pact to succeed certain preliminary ideas had to first gain acceptance: magical practices had to be treated as forms of heresy, and encounters with the devil had to occur bodily, rather than only in the imagination. A plethora of ideas grew up around the pact: notably the witches' sabbat, where witches congregated to worship the devil and have sex with him, and the night-time flight which helped to get them there.

(Nothing shows the inherent misogyny of demonology more clearly than the fact that elite men could only conceive of women making a pact with the devil through sex.) These ideas won growing but by no means uniform support over time. In 1486, the *Malleus maleficarum* was notably silent on the existence of the sabbat; while two years later, Ulrich Molitor could still be sceptical of the possibility of demonic flight, although the engraver of his work clearly was not.[17] There was a clear chronological rhythm to this debate. A fairly active debate at the turn of the fifteenth century, still dominated by Dominican inquisitors, is surveyed here in the chapters by Tamar Herzig, Walter Stephens, and Matteo Duni. Yet, no edition of the *Malleus maleficarum* appeared between 1523 and 1574.[18] This quiet on the publishing front mirrored a decline in persecutions during the mid-sixteenth century. The peace was interrupted by the sceptical writings of Johann Wier in 1563, but the floodgates properly opened during the 1580s and 1590s, when witch-hunting began to spread into areas previously untouched by persecutions. This volume will lay bare how demonology developed over time and the shifting ways in which authors sought to persuade their audience of the reality and urgency of the threat of witchcraft.

Secondly, demonological beliefs, as they spread across the continent, also had to interact with and make sense of folkloric beliefs. The chapters in this volume show how demonologists, from Spain to Poland and from Italy to Scotland, were able to adapt demonology to the local customs and beliefs of their regions, whether they were animal familiars in England or demonic toads in the Basque country. This European perspective shows the versatility of demonology, which absorbed these beliefs and those reported by missionaries overseas with ease. The demonic pact was a surprisingly flexible and accommodating explanatory agent, because a witch could accomplish whatever the devil could, which (most thinkers agreed) was a lot. The devil, as we shall see, could appear in all forms and sizes and corrupt the imagination. Rain dances by the Indian shamans – if they were effective – could be explained as the product of a demonic pact.[19] Like the pagan gods of Greece and Rome, those worshipped by the Indians of the New World were also deemed devils in disguise. Scottish fairies were a trick played by the devil: a product of 'that imaginar[y] ravishing of the spirite foorth [*i.e.* out] of the bodie', as James VI called it, the devil both dulling the senses 'as [if] it were a sleepe' and putting physical objects in the witch's hand as a memento of that imaginary encounter.[20]

The sources for demonology were correspondingly large. They were partly textual. Although unwilling witnesses for the most part, both Scripture and the Church Fathers loom large here. (The Bible has nothing to say about the demonic pact, for instance.) For Catholic authors at least, medieval saints' lives constituted another source, because Satan tempted and vexed the saints as he once tempted Christ and vexed Job.[21] Travel reports from the New World constituted another. Upon reading Jean Bodin's *Démonomanie*, the French explorer Jean de Léry concluded that the religious ceremonies of the

Tupinamba people he had visited in Brazil resembled the witches' sabbat and that 'the master of one group was the master of the other.'[22] Two generations later, the Bordeaux judge Pierre de Lancre, discussed in a chapter in this volume by Thibaut Maus de Rolley and myself, believed that the devil was setting up shop in remote parts of France because Christian missionaries had deprived him of much of the New World.[23]

Demonology, however, was not only founded on textual authorities but on experience as well. When Henri Boguet, a judge from the Franche-Comté (now on France's border with Switzerland), wanted to know whether witches could bear children from their sex with the devil, he simply asked two of the women he had imprisoned. One replied that she was too old, the other that God would not permit it.[24] Marie Dindarte, aged 17, told Pierre de Lancre that if she had any ointment she would have been able to fly right in front of him and promised the judge to bring back some next time she went to the sabbat.[25] (Unfortunately for de Lancre, the devil foiled this plan.) A sizable number of demonologists drew on their own judicial investigations, in which the use of confessions, often extracted using torture, loomed particularly large. If Boguet and de Lancre during the occasions above might appear willing to defer to their witches, demonology's 'confessional regime' (to use Virginia Krause's phrase) on the whole reproduced orthodoxy, forcing its victims to express 'truths' predetermined by their interrogators. Crucially, however, these underpinnings were challenged at the time. The Suffragan Bishop of Trier Peter Binsfeld°, studied by Rita Voltmer in her contribution to this title, devoted an entire volume to defending the accuracy and legitimacy of the confessions of witches, and suppressed the writings of his would-be opponent Cornelius Loos°. The witchcraft sceptic Friedrich Spee, a Jesuit priest who had heard the confessions of convicted witches, wrote that

> the toughest men who were strung up in torture for the most serious crimes have solemnly affirmed to me that they could think of no crime so great that they would not immediately admit to it if their confession would free them for just a moment from such agony.[26]

What hope, he asked, did 'weak' women accused of witchcraft have?

Witches bore unwilling witness to some pretty grand theological truths because their alleged master, the devil, played a key role in the divine scheme of things, especially when the end of the world was believed to be near.[27] On the one hand, the devil was, as James VI put, it 'God's ape' (a phrase which the king, for once, did not coin himself), who sought to imitate God in all things, hence his desire to be worshipped as a god by pagans, heretics, and witches alike.[28] The devil's pact was seen as an inverse baptism or an imitation of God's covenant with the Elect, the truly faithful, while the sabbat was a black mass.[29] Taking this idea of inversion further than possibly anyone else, and pretty much to the point of blasphemy, James declared that there was no better way to study God than by studying the devil: 'For since

*Figure I.2* The Witches' Sabbat at North Berwick. James Carmichael, *Newes from Scotland, Declaring the Damnable Life and Death of Doctor Fian a Notable Sorcerer*..., London: William Wright, 1592, sig. B4v. Image by permission of University of Glasgow Library, Special Collections.

the Devill is the verie contrarie opposite to God, there is no better way to know God, then by the contrarie.'[30]

Although the idea of the devil as God's ape is late medieval in origin, it is not too far removed from the role of divine opponent and foil as set out in the New Testament. Yet, even if the devil was destined to forever play Wile E. Coyote to God's Road Runner, this still provided him with a certain amount of agency. Satan and his allies did appear to inflict actual harm on humankind, after all. It was therefore essential that everything the devil did, he did with divine permission as 'Gods hang-man'.[31] According to James, God permitted Satan to punish 'the wicked for their horrible sinnes', to waken up the faithful to their sins and infirmities, and to test 'even some of the best, [so] that their patience may bee tryed before the world, as JOBS was.'[32] (The only person exempted from demonic vexation, as we saw, was James himself, placed as a righteous king under God's protection.) Divine permission was clearly key; its absence would have made the devil God's genuine rival. Although the doctrine might make God the author of evil, it still put Him at some removal from it. In a clever form of office politics, God merely employed the devil's malice for His own divine purposes. Some demonologists even claimed that the devil wanted to commit considerably more harm than God permitted, thus using events that did *not* happen as evidence for His goodness.[33]

The great irony, of course, is that within this providential scheme there existed one group of people – those accused of witchcraft – who did not need to believe: they *knew* everything because they had witnessed it firsthand. Yet, attaining such absolute certainty (by meeting the devil and attending the sabbat) meant forsaking salvation. The inquisitors pressed witches, destined for Hell, for second-hand spiritual assurances that they could not access themselves.[34] From a twenty-first-century perspective, we might marvel at why anyone confronted with the devil – and thus given explicit assurances of the existence of Heaven, Hell and everything in between – would ever want to make a pact with His arch nemesis, but that was precisely why witches were deemed to be exceptionally wicked and stubborn.[35] Equally, we may wonder how the devil felt about his role, given that he cannot have been ignorant that his constant attempts to undermine the divine plan were, in fact, part of its execution. We might, in the devil's place, take out a particularly expansive cable TV package or, indeed, (pardon the pop culture reference) open a Los Angeles nightclub.[36] Again, the utter perversion and malice of the demons were meant to explain all.[37]

The shaky foundations of demonology, then, may be easily apparent to us who do not believe in it. We may also recall that Scripture described the devil as the 'father of lies'. Could anything touched by the devil ever be trusted? After all, his vast powers included those of deception. St Paul had even warned that Satan could appear as an 'angel of light'. (2 Corinthians 11:14) The problem of demonic deception was particularly acute because the medieval Church, in the form of a famous decree called the canon *Episcopi*, had considered claims of night-time flight to be no more than 'phantasms ... imposed on the minds of infidels ... by the malignant spirit,' a statement that early modern thinkers struggled to overturn or circumvent.[38] Divine permission offered the main answer and demonologists could use it, as Sydney Anglo once put it eloquently, 'like some invincible chess piece empowered, in moments of emergency, to remove all the opposing pieces from the board.'[39] To doubt that the devil was able to achieve something was to doubt God's ability to grant the devil the power to achieve it.

At key moments, however, God also had to keep the devil in check to allow the inquisitor to do his unseemly work. It was God who made sure that only the guilty confessed and neither the inquisitor nor any innocents were harmed in the process. Yet, the limits of God's intervention were subject to debate. Jean Bodin, whose heterodox thinking Virginia Krause explores in her chapter, was unique in holding that God might allow the devil to perform miracles – his powers, as a mere creature, were usually confined to the natural world.[40] James was virtually alone among the demonologists to defend the popular practice of the swimming of witches, claiming it was God's 'secret super-naturall signe ... that the water shal refuse to receive them in her bosom, that have shaken off them the sacred Water of Baptisme, and wilfullie refused the benefite thereof.'[41] Most authors considered it a form of testing God. A similar question mark could well be placed over the role of the witches. If they were possibly deluded by the devil *and/or* fulfilling the divine plan, how culpable exactly were they? Demonology could only function if God, devil, and witch kept each other's relative roles, responsibilities, and powers tightly in check.

The science of demons, then, may feel like the early modern equivalent of pinning jelly to a wall, but it is this very fluidity that generated the debate that is studied within the pages of this book. This brings us to the third and fourth ways this volume will contribute to our understanding of late medieval and early modern demonology. It has long been tempting to divide thinkers into two warring factions: believers versus sceptics. Stuart Clark has already taught us that there was, in fact, a whole spectrum of beliefs where witches were concerned. As Clark put it, 'in witchcraft matters belief and doubt were never simple alternatives, or fixed and separate compartments of thought.'[42] What the contributions to this volume illustrate – and this is point three – is the extent to which all discussion of witches, devils and allied beliefs, such as fairies and ghosts, was part of the same discourse. We shall show that a great deal of scepticism was generated from *within* demonology.

Scepticism came from the two factors already identified: the devil's power of deception and God's permission. Could the devil – who, after all, could masquerade as an angel of light – not transform himself into an innocent person at the witches' sabbat? Would the devil, evil as he is, not delight in the execution of people for a crime they did not commit? There is a double irony here: it was the judges (not the witches they persecuted) who were really being hoodwinked by the devil, while an *expansion* of the devil's powers increased witchcraft scepticism.[43] Insisting on God's omnipotence could destabilise demonology in the opposite direction. This was an argument that, for theological reasons, Protestant thinkers were more likely to make than Catholic ones, and they essentially argued that the devil and his witches were usurping powers that properly belonged only to God. For instance, the English Puritan Reginald Scot, whose work Philip C. Almond explores in his chapter, claimed that Christ would not permit witches to take 'upon them his office: as, to heale and cure diseases; and to worke such miraculous and supernaturall things, as whereby he himselfe was speciallie knowne, believed, and published to be God'.[44] The Calvinist theologian William Perkins°, studied by Leif Dixon in this volume, struggled to reconcile demonic agency with the will of a predestinarian deity, who was solely responsible for sending humans to Heaven or Hell.

Our volume also highlights that the impact of such scepticism was often rather slim. Johann Wier's *De praestigiis daemonum* came at the very beginning of the late-sixteenth-century surge in witch-hunting, not at the end. Because we observe demonology from the outside – because we thankfully do not believe – we perceive its weaknesses more clearly than its strengths. The latter are, of course, just as important. Because scepticism came from 'within', its arguments could be anticipated because all participants in the debate employed the same toolkit. Sceptics, whether by enlarging the power of God or altering those of the devil, were essentially redecorating rather than burning down the house, and nothing prevented their opponents from moving the furniture back. Demonology's toolkit, especially the chess piece that was 'divine permission', was flexible enough to refute sceptical arguments simply by restoring God, devil, and witch back to their original position. The sixteenth-century attacks by Gianfrancesco Ponzinibio°, Wier, and even Scot contrast with later seventeenth-century modes of witchcraft scepticism, which emerged out of the new philosophical systems developed by René Descartes, Baruch Spinoza and others, whose study would require another volume. By challenging the existence or the materiality of the spirit world, these writings attacked demonology from the outside, while as a possible bulwark against apparent atheism providing witchcraft belief with a new *raison d'être* as well.[45]

Perhaps because of these difficulties, demonology was often, and with greater success, represented as a quest for consensus or a search for common ground. This allowed authors to employ the ever-growing source base. Sure, some of the stories collected were fanciful, but enough remained to inspired to inspire belief. Invoking Homer's *Odyssey*, James sought to sail

> betuixt Charybdis and Scylla [two notorious sea monsters], in eschewing the not beleeving of them [witches] altogether on the one part ... and on the other parte in beleeving of it, make us to eschew the falling into innumerable absurdities, both monstrouslie against all Theologie divine, and Philosophie humaine.[46]

For the same reason, we should also be careful to distinguish between belief in theory and belief in practice. It was entirely possible to believe (as Lu Ann Homza and Michael Ostling's chapters demonstrate) that witchcraft was real in theory but question whether a particular person accused of witchcraft really was a witch. The slow and gradual decline of demonology during the seventeenth and eighteenth centuries owes much to this growing disconnect, which gradually made witchcraft belief unfashionable (an 'act of inurbanity' in Lord Byron's memorable phrase) among educated elites.[47] The study of demonology, then, should make us question which of our own beliefs later generations will find it difficult to fathom.

This volume's fourth part follows logically on from the third. If writers cannot easily be divided into credulous believers and heroic sceptics, then their reasons for writing also multiply and warrant consideration. Demonology was the first properly interdisciplinary science, touching not only on theology and law (which have received separate sections in this volume), but on areas of natural philosophy and medicine as well. Accordingly, contributions to demonology reflected the academic training and intellectual preoccupations of the participants. It is not surprising that the physician Johann Wier, as Michaela Valente shows in her chapter, deemed witches to be deluded because it transformed their condition into a mental illness, thus bringing it within his jurisdiction. While some authors, mostly lawyers, essentially reported case studies of witch-hunts they had personally conducted, others like Jean Bodin and the Spanish-Flemish Jesuit Martin Delrio° had little or no practical experience and based their works on their reading. A comparison of the chapters by Fabián Alejandro Campagne and Michael Ostling on two zealous Catholic texts shows that identical religious motivations, situated in different confessional and geographical contexts, could lead to fundamentally different positions on the early modern witch-hunt. Nor should we consider moral righteousness the only motivation. As Lyndal Roper has taught us, demonology could also be a form of entertainment.[48] Nicolas Remy, a prominent judge from the Duchy of Lorraine (now in Eastern France), penned his *Daemonolatreia* to entertain himself while on holiday.[49]

Implausible though it may seem (and probably is), the Scottish king's principal defender among recent historians even argued that James was a secret sceptic, who wrote the *Daemonologie* to get witchcraft 'out of his system.'[50] More likely, the king saw offering spiritual advice and correcting societal ills as a way of fulfilling (and advertising) the duties of kingship. A few years later, in his first year as James I of England, the king set his sight as 'the proper Phisician of his Politicke-body' on another group whose heathenish practices were contaminating the kingdom: tobacco smokers.[51] The king worried that people might pick up smoking just to avoid its foul smell, like the person who eats garlic so that 'he might not be troubled with the smell of it in the breath of his fellowes.'[52] Yet, as Maxwell-Stuart reminds us in his contribution to this volume, early modern authors did more than simply think with demons, they also lived with them. The *Daemonologie* has a very personal flavour because it was composed by someone who genuinely believed that witches had attempted to harm him. In a different yet related vein, Jean Bodin believed he was protected by a guardian angel who warned him against bad food, drink, and even people, and who kept him from reading bad books. Given these angelic relations, he seems to have written, at least in part, to prove that he was not a witch.[53]

All of the late medieval and early modern authors studied here were authors, who reflected on the nature, realm, and power of demons, even if the writings of one – Cornelius Loos – were suppressed, while another – the Spanish inquisitor Alonso de Salazar Frías° – would never have dreamt of publishing them. We brought these late medieval and early modern thinkers together, and into dialogue with each other, because their combined value is greater than the sum of their parts. Taken together, they allow us to tell the story of the science of demons as it developed across more than two centuries and spread across a continent. The following chapters reveal its textual and 'empirical' underpinnings, the debates that raged within, and the wide range of issues that were at stake for those who took part in them. Nevertheless, there is also value in these chapters on their own. Written by some of the world's foremost experts in the subject, they are also designed to accompany and guide the reading of demonological texts that are increasingly made available in English translation. Our hope is that these chapters will be a starting point for students and scholars wishing to study these important works and their authors further.

An explanatory note as to how we arrived at our selection of demonologists may be in order. Because of our wider ambitions, this volume could never be all-encompassing. However useful a 'Dictionary of Demonological Biography' might be, such a work of reference would not tell the larger story that we aim to present here. Perhaps controversially, we end this book at the European witch-hunt's high-water mark in the early seventeenth century, yet the reasons for such a decision seem clear and compelling. As should already have become apparent, witchcraft belief was never defeated by rational argument. There is a dreary repetition to the writings of later witchcraft theorists. With the possible exception of the struggles of Joseph Glanvill and Henry More to reconcile the science of demons with the Scientific Revolution, the later defence of the reality of witchcraft was no more than a rehash of arguments that had already been made. Perhaps the only new strategy to shore up belief in witchcraft in the face of growing scepticism was to increasingly raise the stakes. By the mid eighteenth century, John Wesley, the founder of Methodism, denounced scepticism as the 'giving up to infidels one great proof of the invisible world.' For Wesley, 'the giving up of witchcraft is in effect giving up the Bible.'[54] These high octaves were partly the response to changing sceptical tunes. If the scepticism of Wier and Scot really was part of demonological discourse, later challenges came, as we already noted, from the outside. This later history is one well worth telling, but not within the model and approach we employ here.

Of course, this early seventeenth-century end point cannot be invoked to justify the exclusion of earlier authors. Had space permitted, two authors briefly mentioned in this introduction, Henri Boguet and Friedrich Spee, could have been included with little difficulty. Our aim, however, has not been to merely reproduce an existing canon of great (or rather, Good and Bad) men but also to (re-)introduce other unjustly forgotten voices – such as the very early sceptic Giovanfrancesco Ponzinibio, the rather unorthodox Catholic demonologist Juan Maldonado°, and the exorcist Girolamo Menghi° – and to cover a wider European geography.

## Notes

1 James VI and I, 'Daemonologie in Forme of a Dialogue in Three Bookes', in James Craigie, ed., *Minor Prose Works of King James VI and I*, Edinburgh: Scottish Text Society, 1982, p. 1. I would like to thank Christopher Parry, as well as the contributors to this volume, for commenting on drafts of this introduction.
2 On the witch-hunt in Scotland, see esp. Brian P. Levack, *Witch-Hunting in Scotland: Law, Politics and Religion*, London: Routledge, 2008.

3 'News from Scotland', in Lawrence Normand and Gareth Roberts, eds, *Witchcraft in Early Modern Scotland*, Exeter: University of Exeter Press, 2000, p. 316.
4 'News from Scotland', p. 315, 323.
5 'News from Scotland', p. 324.
6 James VI and I, 'Daemonologie in Forme of a Dialogue', pp. xix–xx.
7 Norman Cohn, *Europe's Inner Demons: The Demonization of Christians in Medieval Christendom*, revised ed., London: Pimlico, 1993, p. 1–15. The Witch, Pythoness or 'a woman who has a familiar spirit' of Endor, who summoned the spirit of the prophet Samuel in the Old Testament, may be counted among those obscure early references.
8 Ronald Hutton, *The Witch: A History of Fear, from Ancient Times to the Present*, New Haven: Yale University Press, 2017, p. 23.
9 Hutton, *The Witch*, p. 20.
10 For the latest estimates, see Hutton, *The Witch*, p. 180; Julian Goodare, *The European Witch-Hunt*, London: Routledge, 2016, pp. 27–29.
11 Valerie Flint, 'The Demonisation of Magic and Sorcery in Late Antiquity', in Bengt Ankarloo and Stuart Clark, eds, *Witchcraft and Magic in Europe: Ancient Greece and Rome*, Philadelphia: University of Pennsylvania Press, 1999, p. 277–348.
12 On the local village context, see especially Robin Briggs, *Witches and Neighbours: The Social and Cultural Context of European Witchcraft*, 2nd ed., Oxford: Blackwell Publishers, 2002.
13 Brian P. Levack, *The Devil Within: Possession and Exorcism in the Christian West*, New Haven: Yale University Press, 2013.
14 Euan Cameron, 'Angels, Demons, and Everything in Between: Spiritual Beings in Early Modern Europe', in Clare Copeland and Jan Machielsen, eds, *Angels of Light? Sanctity and the Discernment of Spirits in Early Modern Europe*, Leiden: Brill, 2013, p. 17–52.
15 Good introductions to the early modern witch-hunt include: Brian P. Levack, *The Witch-Hunt in Early Modern Europe*, 4th ed., London: Routledge, 2016; Goodare, *The European Witch-Hunt*; Briggs, *Witches and Neighbours*.
16 Alain Boureau, *Satan the Heretic: The Birth of Demonology in the Medieval West*, Chicago: University of Chicago Press, 2006; Pau Castell Granados, '"Wine vat witches suffocate children": The Mythical Components of the Iberian Witch', *eHumanista*, 2014, vol. 26, pp. 170–95.
17 Natalie Kwan, 'Woodcuts and Witches: Ulrich Molitor's *De lamiis et pythonicis mulieribus*, 1489–1669', *German History*, 2012, vol. 30/4, 493–527.
18 Jan Machielsen, *Martin Delrio: Demonology and Scholarship in the Counter-Reformation*, Oxford: Oxford University Press, 2015, pp. 9–10.
19 See my contribution on Martin Delrio in this volume.
20 James VI and I, 'Daemonologie', p. 51–52.
21 See, in particular, the case of St Anthony: Stuart Clark, 'Angels of Light and Images of Sanctity', in Copeland and Machielsen, eds, *Angels of Light?* p. 279–304.
22 Jean de Léry, *Histoire d'un voyage faict en la terre du Brésil, autrement dite Amérique*, 3rd ed., [Geneva], 1585, p. 281.
23 Pierre de Lancre, *Tableau de l'inconstance des mauuais anges et démons*, Paris: Jean Berjon, 1612, p. 39.
24 Henri Boguet, *Discours exécrable des sorciers*, Rouen: Romain de Beauvais, 1606, pp. 64–65.
25 De Lancre, *Tableau*, p. 97.
26 Friedrich Spee, *Cautio Criminalis or a Book on Witch Trials*, trans. Marcus Hellyer, Charlottesville: University of Virginia Press, 2003, p. 73.

27 Andrew Cunningham and Ole Peter Grell, *The Four Horsemen of the Apocalypse: Religion, War, Famine and Death in Reformation Europe*, Cambridge: Cambridge University Press, 2000.
28 James VI and I, 'Daemonologie', p. 15; on the origins of this phrase, see Anthony Ossa-Richardson, *The Devil's Tabernacles: The Pagan Oracles in Early Modern Thought*, Princeton, NJ: Princeton University Press, 2013, p. 66.
29 James VI and I, 'Daemonologie', p. 25.
30 James VI and I, 'Daemonologie', p. 38.
31 James VI and I, 'Daemonologie', p. xx.
32 James VI and I, 'Daemonologie', p. 33.
33 Martin Delrio, *Disquisitionum magicarum libri sex*, Leuven: Gerard Rivius, 1600, vol. 2, p. 74.
34 For more on this point, see Walter Stephens, *Demon Lovers: Witchcraft, Sex, and the Crisis of Belief*, Chicago: University of Chicago Press, 2002.
35 *e.g.* Johannes Tinctor, 'Invectives against the Sect of Waldensians (Witches) (1460)', in Andrew Colin Gow et al., eds and trans., *The Arras Witch Treatises*, University Park, PA: Penn State University Press, 2016, p. 96.
36 The reference is to the DC Comics character Lucifer Morningstar, made into a television series by Fox and Netflix.
37 Tinctor, 'Invectives', p. 87.
38 Gratian, 'A Warning to Bishops: The Canon Episcopi', in Alan Kors and Edward Peters, eds, *Witchcraft in Europe, 1100–1700: A Documentary History*, Philadelphia: University of Pennsylvania Press, 1972, p. 29.
39 Sydney Anglo, 'Evident Authority and Authoritative Evidence: The Malleus Maleficarum', in Sydney Anglo, ed., *The Damned Art: Essays in the Literature of Witchcraft*, London: Routledge, 1977, p. 21.
40 See Virginia Krause's contribution to this volume, as well as Robin Briggs, 'Dubious Messengers: Bodin's Daemon, the Spirit World and the Sadducees', in Peter Marshall and Alexandra Walsham, eds, *Angels in the Early Modern World*, Cambridge: Cambridge University Press, 2006, pp. 168–90.
41 James VI and I, 'Daemonologie', p. 56.
42 Stuart Clark, *Thinking with Demons: The Idea of Witchcraft in Early Modern Europe*, Oxford: Clarendon Press, 1997, p. 182.
43 See Clare Copeland and Jan Machielsen, introduction to *Angels of Light?*, pp. 1–16.
44 Reginald Scot, *The Discoverie of Witchcraft wherein the Lewde Dealing of Witches and Witchmongers is Notabile Detected*, London: William Brome, 1584, p. 11.
45 Brian P. Levack, 'The Decline and End of Witchcraft Prosecutions' in Brian P. Levack, ed., *The Oxford Handbook of Witchcraft in Early Modern Europe and Colonial America*, Oxford: Oxford University Press, 2013, pp. 429–46.
46 James VI and I, 'Daemonologie', p. 29.
47 Ian Bostridge, *Witchcraft and Its Transformations, c.1650–c.1750*, Oxford: Clarendon Press, 1997, p. 203 (for Lord Byron's phrase). See also Euan Cameron, *Enchanted Europe: Superstition, Reason, and Religion, 1250–1750*, Oxford: Oxford University Press, 2010.
48 Lyndal Roper, 'Witchcraft and the Western Imagination', *Transactions of the Royal Historical Society*, Sixth Series, 2006, vol. 16, 117–41.
49 Nicolas Remy, *Demonolatry*, ed. Montague Summers, London: J. Rodker, 1930, p. ix.
50 Jenny Wormald, 'The Witches, the Devil and the King', in Terence Brotherstone and David Ditchburn, eds, *Freedom and Authority: Scotland c.1050–c.1650; Historical and Historiographical Essays Presented to Grant G. Simpson*, East Linton: Tuckwell Press, 2000, p. 179.

51 James VI and I, 'A Counterblaste to Tobacco', in Craigie, ed., *Minor Prose Works of King James VI and I*, p. 85. James emphasised the Indian roots of smoking on p. 88: 'Shall we … abase our selues so farre, as to imitate these beastly Indians … aliens from the holy Covenant of God? Why doe we not as well imitate them in walking naked as they doe? yea why do we not denie God and adore the Deuill, as they doe?'
52 James VI and I, 'A Counterblaste', p. 98.
53 Bodin's lyrical discussion of the guardian angel, though presented as the story of a friend, is discussed prominently almost at the outset of his treatise, see Jean Bodin, *De La Démonomanie des sorciers*, ed. Virginia Krause et al., Geneva: Droz, 2016, pp. 105–9. That Bodin considered himself a prophet is one of the principal conclusions of Howell Lloyd, *Jean Bodin, 'This Pre-eminent Man of France': An Intellectual Biography*, Oxford: Oxford University Press, 2017.
54 Cited in Owen Davies, *Witchcraft, Magic and Culture, 1736–1951*, Manchester: Manchester University Press, 1999, p. 12.

**Further reading**

Anglo, Sydney, ed., *The Damned Art: Essays in the Literature of Witchcraft*, London, 1977.
Bostridge, Ian, *Witchcraft and Its Transformations, c.1650–c.1750*, Oxford: Clarendon Press, 1997.
Boureau, Alain, *Satan the Heretic: The Birth of Demonology in the Medieval West*, Chicago: University of Chicago Press, 2006.
Briggs, Robin, *Witches and Neighbours: The Social and Cultural Context of European Witchcraft*, 2nd ed., Oxford: Blackwell Publishers, 2002.
Cameron, Euan, *Enchanted Europe: Superstition, Reason, and Religion, 1250–1750*, Oxford: Oxford University Press, 2010.
Clark, Stuart, *Thinking with Demons: The Idea of Witchcraft in Early Modern Europe*, Oxford: Clarendon Press, 1997.
Goodare, Julian, *The European Witch-Hunt*, London: Routledge, 2016.
Hutton, Ronald, *The Witch: A History of Fear, from Ancient Times to the Present*, New Haven: Yale University Press, 2017.
Levack, Brian P., ed., *The Oxford Handbook of Witchcraft in Early Modern Europe and Colonial America*, Oxford: Oxford University Press, 2013.
Levack, Brian P., *The Witch-Hunt in Early Modern Europe*, 4th ed., London: Routledge, 2016.
Roper, Lyndal, *The Witch in the Western Imagination*, Charlottesville: 2012.
Williams, Gerhild Scholz, 'Demonologies', in Levack, ed., *The Oxford Handbook of Witchcraft*, pp. 69–83.

# Part 1
# Beginnings

# 1 The inquisitor's demons
## Nicolau Eymeric's *Directorium inquisitorum*

*Pau Castell Granados*

'She heard him say that, if he wanted to, he would put the best Christian in the whole world to the flames.' These unholy words were attributed to the Catalan inquisitor Nicolau Eymeric (c.1320–1399) by a Dominican nun during a 1388 trial in Valencia, following the city's rejection of the inquisitor over his controversial anti-heretical activities.[1] Other grave accusations were also levelled against the Catalan friar, among them extortion, prevarication, violation of the order of law, requests for sexual favours, confrontations with superiors – in short, serious abuses of power. Eymeric was then acting as Inquisitor General of the Crown of Aragon, with a jurisdiction that included the principality of Catalonia and the kingdoms of Aragon and Valencia. He had been recently reinstated to his office at the order of King John I, who reversed the inquisitor's banishment issued twelve years earlier by his predecessor Peter III. Eymeric's renewed actions against the so-called Lullists – followers of the late mystic theologian Raymond Llull (1232–1316) – had set off spirited opposition from the secular, episcopal, and inquisitorial authorities of Valencia, causing the populace to rejoice that 'now the friars' filth will be revealed, thanks to the great divisions among the inquisitors.'[2] This string of accusations would lead to Eymeric's final political demise. He was again suspended from office and ultimately cast into exile in 1393 by King John himself, who went so far as to brand him a 'public enemy', commanding his subjects to expel him as one would 'a pestiferous venom' and prevent the return of 'this diabolical and depraved man, friar Nicolau Eymeric.'[3] Only the king's death three years later enabled Eymeric to return to his home-city of Girona, where he passed away soon after, roughly 80 years old.[4]

The troubled end of Nicolau Eymeric's career is in fact the result of a life marked by constant conflict and confrontation with both royal and ecclesiastical authorities. These frictions extended to other members of his own Dominican order, to the Franciscans, and (inevitably) to the 'heretical' Lullists, as well as to the cities of Barcelona, Lleida, and Valencia. During his years as inquisitor, Eymeric devoted his attention to the fields of sorcery, necromancy, errors against the faith, blasphemy, and crypto-Judaism. He also took action against the writings of authors he considered heretical. The fight against Raymond Llull's doctrines became an overriding feature of Eymeric's career, even prompting a schism within the Dominican order of his province due to his attacks on fellow Dominican (and archenemy) Bernat Ermengol. The anti-Lullist hostility would also lay at the source of many of Eymeric's enmities and – after three removals from office and two forced retreats to the papal court of Avignon, first in 1376 and again in 1393 – it turned out to be the ultimate engine of his downfall.

It was during his first exile in Avignon that Eymeric finished his influential inquisitors' manual *Directorium inquisitorum* (Guide to Inquisitors, 1376), which would become the definitive handbook on inquisitorial procedure for centuries to come and provide the judicial underpinning for all the early modern Inquisitions, especially after it was republished with a commentary by the Aragonese canonist Francisco Peña in 1578.[5] Several editions of the treatise appeared during the sixteenth century – first in Barcelona and subsequently in Rome and Venice – and they found a home in the libraries of popes and cardinals, as well as the Inquisitions of Venice and Spain.[6] Its surviving copies would later scandalize the sensibilities of Enlightenment readers such as Morellet, Voltaire, and Alembert, who saw in them the most explicit account of the horrific practices of the Inquisition and a justified foundation for the Black Legend that surrounded that institution and Spain more widely.[7]

As for Eymeric's views on demonology, these were systematized in questions 42 and 43 of the second part of the *Directorium*, in which he stated the heretical nature of 'sorcerers', 'diviners', and 'invokers of demons'.[8] The two chapters were in fact a condensed version of a work Eymeric contributed specifically to the field of demonology early in his career, *De iurisdictione inquisitorum in et contra christianos demones invocantes* (On the Inquisitors' Jurisdiction over and against Christian Invokers of Demons, 1359).[9] The *Directorium* was also preceded by another short treatise, *De iurisdictione Ecclesi[a]e et inquisitorum contra infideles demones invocantes* (On the Jurisdiction of the Church and Inquisitors against Infidel Invokers of Demons, 1370), in which Eymeric addressed the demonological practices of non-Christians in an attempt to stretch inquisitorial jurisdiction in that direction.[10] Finally, near the end of his life, he produced the *Contra astrologos imperitos atque nigromanticos* (Against Unskilled Astrologers and Necromancers, 1396), a treatise intended for King John's confessor warning secular power against the use of divination and astrology which were likened to diabolism and heresy.[11]

Eymeric's contributions to the field of demonology were based mainly on his own experience as an inquisitor, a role that not only deeply marked the friar's life, as we have already seen, but his perception of the demonic features which tainted the so-called 'heretical depravity' of his time. In fact, Eymeric's birth coincided with the major milestones in the gradual 'diabolization of heresy' and the corresponding 'hereticization of magic'. The

1320 consultations issued by Pope John XXII in Avignon on the heretical nature of sorcery and the invocation of demons, followed by Bernard Gui's *Practica inquisitionis heretice pravitatis* (1321) in nearby Toulouse, fuelled the expansion of inquisitorial jurisdiction over the practices of sorcery, divination, and necromancy – which the *Practica* defined as dangerously close to heresy and diabolism.[12] These texts had a considerable impact on inquisitorial procedure in Catalonia during Eymeric's formative years. After the final persecutions against Cathars, Fraticelli, Pseudo-Apostles, and Templars in the early fourteenth century, Catalan inquisitors started to set their sights on necromancy and practices linked to sorcery and divination, hitherto the exclusive domain of episcopal courts.[13]

Demonological features are prominent in many of the accusations Eymeric put forth against his victims from the very beginning of his inquisitorial career. In that regard, the friar's reflections on demonology did not focus so much on its doctrinal definition but rather on the role assigned to church authorities in its repression and the judicial procedure against alleged invokers of demons. Both Eymeric's writings and his controversial actions against alleged 'heretical depravity' in the Crown of Aragon would strongly contribute to this process of hereticization of magic, even anticipating some aspects of the crime of witchcraft that emerged in Europe shortly after his death.

## 1 Heresy, deception, and pain

Nicolau Eymeric was born around 1320 in the northern Catalan city of Girona, where he entered the Dominican convent at a young age. From there he would be sent to the University of Paris for his doctorate in theology, before being finally appointed Inquisitor General of the Crown of Aragon in 1357.[14] The papal inquisition had been firmly established in Eymeric's homeland since the early thirteenth century, with a profusion of trials against Waldensians and other spiritual movements.[15] Still, when Eymeric was appointed Inquisitor General the era of the great medieval heresies was already on the wane. Eymeric himself was well aware that earlier successes had left 'only a few impenitent heretics, not many relapses, and even fewer rich ones.'[16] This constituted a discouraging prospect for an ambitious young friar, who nevertheless started acting aggressively against heretical depravity. Too aggressively in the eyes of many of his contemporaries, who saw the friar as overzealous and devoid of humanity, given his constant mistreatment of the accused and his predisposition to counterfeiting evidence.

This perception derived in part from Eymeric's own ways of dealing with heresy and from his assumed role as inquisitor. As he would candidly state in his 1389 *Dialogus contra lullistas* (Dialogue against the Lullists): 'I am an inquisitor of heretics and therefore the possessor of bad faith.'[17] Acting in bad faith was, Eymeric argued, necessary when confronting heretics who, far from being passive and powerless, were seen as active and powerful agents responding to the inquisitor's questions with 'cunning', 'guile', and 'sophistries'. In other words, they were dangerous and deceitful individuals who threatened to escape the inquisitor's clutches by hiding the truth, even under torture. Faced with this perceived challenge, Eymeric suggested a new and dangerous approach that consisted of responding to such suspected duplicities by becoming duplicitous himself, as he would explain at length in the third part of his *Directorium*:

> When the inquisitor sees a cavilling, wily, and cunning heretic who does not want to uncover his error but rather circumvents the issue with cavilling responses and equivocations, then, as a nail is dislodged by another nail, the inquisitor must use ruses to catch the heretic in his error.[18]

The *Directorium* provides numerous examples of such deceptions, by advising inquisitors to always use ambiguous and deceptive speech when interrogating suspects. Thus, when the accused party requests a reprieve (*gratia*), 'they must be assured that even more will be done for them than they request, and generalities of the sort.' The inquisitor should convince the suspect that everything about their deeds is already known because others have previously confessed and incriminated them. Whereupon the inquisitor must contend:

> You see, I pity you, because you have been deluded by your own simplicity. Certainly, you are somewhat guilty, but he who instructed you in such things is much more so. Do not make the sin of another your own, nor make yourself out to be a master when you were only a disciple. Tell me the truth, since as you see, I already know everything about the matter. … Who is he, who taught you these errors, you who knew nothing of evil?[19]

Paperwork could also be used to sustain such inquisitorial theatrics. The inquisitor could ostentatiously leaf through the accused person's file and exclaim: 'It is clear that you are not speaking the truth!' If the (likely illiterate) accused rejected an allegation, the inquisitor should 'as if astonished' brandish a document from the file and exclaim: 'How can you deny it? Is it not clear enough?' The inquisitor will then 'read from the document and he will pervert it.'[20]

This long catalogue of interrogation techniques – most of which are still used in police stations around the globe – is followed by a description of the proper methods for torturing the accused. Eymeric's *Directorium* was in fact the first inquisitorial manual to refer explicitly to torture methods, a domain in which the friar showed a great knowledge as to their usefulness (and limitations) based on his own experience as inquisitor. He insisted that torture must be introduced 'only in the absence of other proof' and recommended applying it 'moderately and without effusion of blood.' The friar acknowledged that some suspects were 'so soft and faint-hearted they admit to all things under light torture, even if they are false', while others were able to resist the most compelling torture sessions, possibly because they had used magic to become insensible to pain, something which would remain a concern of demonologists for a long time to come. A sufficient amount of pain was thus needed to extract the truth that lay hidden in the accused's body, in a process described almost as a wrestling match.[21]

These interrogation methods would later shock Enlightenment *philosophes* but were justified by the Catalan friar on account of the heretics' extraordinary and maleficent agency. Both deception and pain were required to obtain the suspect's admission of guilt and repentance. Eymeric's manual thus laid out a series of actions intended to produce a sentence. The inquisitorial procedure was essentially a test of the judge's suspicions, and therefore heavily weighted against the accused. In the end, the final goal of Eymeric's efforts was none other than the salvation of the accused's soul – though often without their body – all part of a larger struggle for the preservation of the faith and the defence of the Holy Church.

## 2 The (not so) ideal inquisitor

The corpus of Eymeric's writings attests to his vision of his role as an inquisitor as one entrusted to him by the pope. Perhaps because the Dominican found his prosecutions frequently blocked by his contemporaries and because he was removed from office on various occasions, he frequently underlined the relevance and necessity of the Inquisition as well as the need for the constant presence of the inquisitor in his lands to extirpate heresies and errors, which in his absence 'sprout and grow to the great damage of the Holy Church.'[22] In one of his last works, written just before his death, Eymeric even went so far as to characterize heresy as a means by which the merit and glory of the inquisitor could be made manifest:

> The death of the sheep is the life of the lion, and the destruction of grass is the life of the sheep. Without litigations, why would there be judges? ... When and how was the patience of the martyrs revealed, if not during persecution by the tyrants? Thus, how can the inquisitors' glory manifest itself, if not for the malice of the heretics? The increase of heretics therefore reveals the faithful doctors.[23]

As this last passage suggests, Eymeric sees heresy ahistorically, as an evil that is always lying in wait. The existence of such an enemy justifies the perpetual existence of the Inquisition itself, as well as his own mission (and glory) as an inquisitor of the faith.

A collection of funeral sermons, which he composed *c*.1373 for the benefit of his fellow friars, give us a better glimpse still of Eymeric's personality and perception of himself as guardian of the faith. It included two specific sermons to be preached in the event of the death of an inquisitor.[24] As Eymeric was already an inquisitor with more than a decade of experience behind him, these texts constitute a self-portrait of sorts, with the friar leaning on the Bible to praise the inquisitorial figure through a series of revealing analogies.

The first and shortest of the sermons speaks to the inquisitor's mission as following in Adam's footsteps in defence of the Garden of Eden, whilst the second and more compelling is devoted to the inquisitor's qualities and the authority (*potestas*) conferred on him. This sermon starts with a passage from Genesis about the cherub appointed by God to stand guard, flaming sword in hand, at the entrance of the earthly Paradise. For Eymeric, the earthly Paradise represents the militant Church, irrigated by the water of the Holy Spirit, full of trees as the Church is full of saints and beautiful for its fruits as the Church is for its good deeds. In this fine tableau, the cherub represents the inquisitor himself, while the flaming sword embodies the inquisitor's power, his *potestas iudiciaria*. The sword illuminates, terrorizes, and cuts in half in order to separate truth from falsehood, heretics from Catholics, and ultimately, the body from the soul of the condemned.[25]

This worldview emerged from and thrived on opposition, not just from alleged heretics and sorcerers but also from within the church hierarchy, especially from local bishops for whom the inquisitor had little time. Such opposition started almost immediately at the outset of Eymeric's career. A series of letters sent by the bishop of Girona in 1357–1358 to the newly appointed inquisitor criticized aspects of Eymeric's approach to heresy, especially his disregard for the bishop's jurisdiction. In August 1357, he cautioned Eymeric not to prosecute blasphemers by himself, reminding him that the two men should act together against heretics in the diocese given that

> as you know, it belongs also to us and not just to you, and even to us without you, to inquire and punish blasphemers … in our diocese; and you cannot prosecute those nor any other kind of heretics in our diocese without our consent.[26]

In January 1358, after Eymeric's procedures against a group of women and men from the town of Castelló d'Empúries – among them three clerics – charged with 'heinous heretical acts' of sorcery and necromancy, the bishop summoned him to discuss the 'subtle and difficult subject'. Deciding to take the matter into his own hands, the bishop insisted on the necessity of proceeding 'properly, cautiously and safely, and not bite with excessive cruelty'. On the same day, he dispatched a letter to the council members of Castelló and reassured them that he had ordered Eymeric to desist, to not submit anyone else to torture, and bring all the suspects to him to adjudicate the matter.[27]

Eymeric's pursuit of heresy as a young inquisitor with a very extensive view of his prerogatives provoked early opposition which would only grow in subsequent years, especially when he started pursuing members of the clerical elite. As an armed cherub ready to act in bad faith in order to unnerve his hidden and deceitful enemies, Eymeric's actions would soon provoke the active resistance of many of his contemporaries, whether in the papal curia, the episcopal courts, the city councils or the royal house of Aragon. By August 1358, King Peter III was already asking the pope for a replacement, and in 1360, only three years after his appointment, Eymeric was removed from office by the Dominican order, who named a substitute more suited for its duties.[28] The Catalan friar had by then finished his first major treatise, which dealt expressly with demonology: the 1359 *De iurisdictione inquisitorum contra christianos demones invocantes*.

## 3 The inquisitor at his writing desk

The *Contra christianos* was by far the longest of Eymeric's works apart from the *Directorium*. Written during his first years as an inquisitor, it contained a series of demonological reflections that would later be systematized in questions 42 and 43 of his inquisitor's manual. As its title suggests, the treatise argued for an extension of inquisitorial jurisdiction over the practices of sorcery, necromancy, and the invocation of demons as crimes of heresy. Throughout the treatise, Eymeric mentioned the judicial confessions he had collected which allowed him, together with the magical books he had seized, to reveal the true nature of the practices of sorcerers and necromancers. According to the friar, these invokers and worshippers of demons were not simple sorcerers and diviners but actual heretics or suspects of heresy, and therefore subject to inquisitorial justice.[29]

Eymeric divided his treatise into five chapters preceded by a short prologue, in which he insisted on the need to persecute 'the wicked men, invokers and worshippers of demons.'[30] For this, he relied on a passage from the papal bull *Quod super nonnullis* issued by Alexander IV (1257). This allowed inquisitors to proceed against sorcery and divination *only if* the practices reeked of heresy. The first two chapters of the treatise, therefore, begin by defining heresy. The third turns to the fundamental question: how to determine if someone who was not a 'true' heretic (that is to say a stubborn defender of an error against the faith), could nevertheless be considered as such by the judgement of the Church. For that, Eymeric resorted to the writings of his predecessor, Gui de Terrena, to draw a crucial distinction between the 'absolute heresy' – or heresy *in re* (that is the heresy which lies within the inner consciousness) – and the 'appearance of heresy' (that is the words, facts and signs that, although fallible, could sometimes be read as its exterior manifestation).[31] Building on this distinction, the fourth chapter of *Contra christianos* discusses whether those 'who invoke demons' can be considered a *hereticus in re*. To answer that question, Eymeric sets out a series of distinctions on the different aspects that characterize the demonic invocation, regarding the demon's properties and powers, as well as the methods and purpose of invocation.[32]

Thus, if the summoner gives the demon the honour of worship, or *latria* (which is reserved for God alone), even if he does not consider the demon to be God's equal, he is still a heretic *in re*. The same goes for those who give the demon the honour of *dulia* (the veneration reserved for the saints and the good angels). But there remains a third and fundamental distinction addressed by Eymeric in the last chapter of the *Contra christianos*, regarding those cases where there was no clear sign of *latria* or *dulia* – and therefore heresy in the inner consciousness or heresy *in re* – but nonetheless, by the very practice of the invocation, they could still constitute a form of heresy. In that case, asserts Eymeric, the Inquisition must also intervene, since those behaviours could reveal sensible signs of an inner worship and belief entailing either a tacit or explicit pact with the demons. Essentially, any kind of external honour rendered to demons (whether *latria*, *dulia*, or another indistinct form of honour) indicated if not heresy *in re*, at least vehement suspicion of heresy, which ultimately required the intervention of inquisitorial justice.[33]

These demonological reflections presented in Eymeric's treatise would later be condensed in the *Directorium inquisitorum* with some substantial cuts and one revealing addition. The number of authorities is reduced to the bare minimum (Augustine, Aquinas, and a few references to canon law). The 1257 bull *Quod super nonnullis* which forbade inquisitors to deal with sorcery and divination unless they reeked of heresy – the only authority cited at the end of the *Contra christianos* prologue – also disappeared in the *Directorium*, to be replaced by another, very controversial bull *Super illius specula*, allegedly issued by Pope John XXII around 1326.[34]

The authenticity of this last bull has been the subject of much discussion among scholars, due to the fact that it is completely absent from canonical collections and papal registers, and known *only* from the manuscript and printed tradition of Eymeric's *Directorium*.[35] This is no minor issue, since its alleged content is considered the first legal embodiment of the extension of inquisitorial jurisdiction over certain magical practices involving the invocation of demons. Unsurprisingly, it argued that such practitioners should be punished as heretics. The alleged bull condemned those Christians-in-name-only who 'sacrifice and worship demons, fabricate or commission images, rings, mirrors or flasks to magically constrain demons, ask and receive responses from them, ask for their help to accomplish their evil desires', and therefore issued a general order – addressed to no one in particular but to 'competent judges' – to seize all books and material and to proceed to the confiscation of goods and excommunication of the guilty 'within eight days.'[36]

Given Eymeric's habitual deceptions, the bull *Super illius specula* could thus well be a forgery. Yet, if it was actually issued, we can also imagine our

Catalan friar's delight, since he not only discussed demonic invocations in his writings, but also, as we will see, encountered them in the field.

## 4 Eymeric in action

A register of the inquisitorial procedures carried out in some Catalan dioceses during the second half of the fourteenth century is preserved in the Bibliothèque Nationale de France, in Paris.[37] The manuscript is only a fragment of a much longer register or *memoriale* in which Eymeric and his collaborators recorded the data concerning the suspects, the state of the judicial proceedings and the interrogation of witnesses, following the exact manner prescribed in the *Directorium*.[38] The fragment still contains a total of 150 cases concerning crypto-Judaism, errors against the faith, blasphemy, sorcery, divination, necromancy, and invocation of demons, all of them gathered in the dioceses of Girona (72), Urgell (51), Vic (17), and Lleida (9). While almost no dates are indicated, some cases also survive in the episcopal archives of Girona, allowing us to confidently attribute the entire collection to the period *c.*1357–1380. A first group of cases correspond to Eymeric's first period of inquisitorial activity (1357–1360), while the larger portion overlaps with his reinstatement as Inquisitor General (1365–1375), before his first banishment by King Peter III.[39]

This invaluable source provides us with a privileged view of the influence of demonology on Eymeric's day-to-day inquisitorial practice. In that regard, the cases recorded in the *memoriale* can be divided into three main categories, according to their alleged demonic component:

- Cases unrelated to demonology
- Cases explicitly related to necromancy or invocation of demons
- Cases of sorcery, divination and blasphemy which are likened to devil worship.

Within the first category, we can find a considerable number of denunciations for crypto-Judaism. This category also includes persecutions for spreading errors against the faith, involving both clergy and laity. Heretical blasphemy was another common reason for *inquisitio* or investigation according to the register. Several persons were accused of 'making heretical oaths against God and the Blessed Virgin', often when gambling, or of blaspheming 'heretically'. Among the exterior signs of heresy, a common one concerned rejection of the sacraments of the Church, with a number of suspects flagged for not going regularly to mass or making confession, or even for lowering their eyes when the host was elevated.[40]

Aside from this first group of demon-free accusations, there is a second category of cases which appears directly related to the field of demonology. A number of men were denounced and tried for invoking or sacrificing to demons. Two men from Castelló d'Empúries tried by Eymeric in 1358, one of them a physician, were accused of invoking demons, and after being condemned they abjured publicly at Girona. A silversmith from Girona was also condemned for sacrificing to demons, while another was accused by the city's master builder of possessing 'suspicious books', which he used for invoking demons, and of saying that he would give himself to the devil if he could demolish the bridge over the river Ter.[41] The possession of books of necromancy was indeed a common reason for *inquisitio* in Eymeric's register. Two knights, a physician, a friar, and a monk, among other men of unspecified status, were tried for being necromancers, using the art of necromancy or possessing necromantic books. On several occasions, books were seized and burnt publicly, and most of the recorded trials ended with an abjuration or the excommunication of the accused, sometimes after torture.[42]

Descriptions of the rituals involved in the alleged necromantic activities are frustratingly vague. A constable employed by the bishop of Girona was seen 'making a circle, invoking the devil and reading a book', while the son (!) of the abbot of Tortosa had been trying 'to force a demon into a ring.' A prominent late medieval *experimentum* involved the placement of a child into a circle for divinatory purposes and this practice features regularly in Eymeric's register.[43] A lawyer from Vic made someone 'place a child into a circle because he had lost some silver chess pieces' which he wanted to recover. Another man used the ritual to discover the whereabouts of a captive friend. The anonymous diviners consulted by a priest from Cervera 'wanting to know certain things, specially about a theft,' reportedly made some circles and tried to force a child to step into one of them, ultimately placing a book on its head.[44]

The fullest account of a necromantic ritual is contained in the proceedings against one of the priests from Castelló d'Empúries, tried by Eymeric in 1358:

> Against Beuda, priest from the town of Castelló, friar Guillem Seguí reported that he exhumed two heads of dead people and anointed them with saffron, and he lighted candles and read a book in front of them, and he interrogated those heads and got from them responses about the manner of obtaining women and about other things. ... The said priest, in the church of Castelló, baptized a mirror and read those words that are read when a child is baptized; and the words that are usually said in God's honour, he then said them in dishonour and discredit of Jesus Christ; and the words that are usually said to the vituperation of the devil, the priest then said them in the devil's honour.[45]

We may safely assume that Eymeric's personal experience in dealing with necromancy would have greatly influenced his writings on demonology, as can be seen throughout the *Contra christianos* and the *Directorium*, as well as his *Contra astrologos imperitos atque nigromanticos* (1395–1396). In that late work, likely influenced by the divinatory rituals he had encountered,

Eymeric categorically ruled out the possibility of obtaining truthful responses about the future through demonic intervention.[46]

The third category of crimes listed in the register involved cases of sorcery and divination, which attracted the interest (and suspicion) of Eymeric and his collaborators. For the most part, they correspond to practices of folk magic performed either by lay people or by clerics; mainly healing practices, love magic, and divinatory rituals for diagnosing certain diseases. In that sense, the cases mentioned in the register do not differ from those previously attested in pastoral visitations from the early fourteenth century, aside from the fact that they were now under the jurisdiction of the inquisition. Those who performed such practices are usually branded 'diviners' (*divinator/divinatrix*) while some women are also often referred to as 'phitonisse' after the Witch or Pythoness of Endor in the Old Testament.

Among the cases in this category, we find a diviner called 'lo Rey' who was able to make a mute speak immediately. Clergy feature prominently. A monk from the monastery of Sant Pere de Galligans was reputed to cure children using nothing more than their names, while a canon from la Seu d'Urgell used a written amulet to heal the sick. Among the female accused, some were tried for diagnosing afflictions caused by magical ligatures (knots, strings, cords) and others for 'unbinding' them with holy water. The inappropriate use of the holy sacraments was obviously a supplementary cause of concern, as we can see in the trial of a woman accused of performing magical practices that included the use of the holy chrism to reconcile fighting couples.[47]

In only one recorded case are the magical-medicinal activities described in detail, perhaps because the ritual performed possessed a certain necromantic undertone. A physician from the Pyrenean town of Puigcerdà who used to 'unbind' couples afflicted with sterility or impotence, was condemned for performing a ritual in which he made them kneel, placing a stole on their necks and a book over their heads from which he read – the colour of the physician's face looking then 'almost as that of a dead man' –, before giving them something to drink in order to be completely cured.[48] Other sorcery cases bordering on necromancy included a (probably illiterate) peasant who was said to perform divinations with a book given to him 'by a fairy woman' and villages in the Barravés valley, where a young goat was consumed during Easter and its bones buried to ward off storms. Still, this sporadic mention of certain spells and objects can hardly be considered an indicator of widespread necromancy.

In addition to these accounts lacking an (explicit) component of devil worship, there is finally a crucial group of cases within this third category where accusations not only of sorcery but also of blasphemy were overtly pushed into the demonic realm. For instance, a folk healer known to cure children's fractures was investigated for 'invoking demons', while the aforementioned lo Rey confessed eventually that a Saracen (Muslim) had taught him 'the art of having a familiar demon.' Likewise, a blasphemer who exclaimed 'God dammit, the cross be burned' was accused of literally 'giving himself to the devil.' Another blasphemer from Girona, already condemned by the secular court of Peratallada for having said 'that Mary was not a virgin,' was tried again before the inquisitorial court, where he was investigated for attempting to persuade a woman to meet him at the outskirts of Girona to deny God and give her soul to the devil, a scene five craftsmen were said to have witnessed.[49]

Certainly, some of the healing practices performed in fourteenth-century Catalonia could easily resemble acts of necromancy – as in the aforementioned case of the ashen-faced physician from Puigcerdà. Yet, it is less clear how a simple affair of blasphemy could turn into an act of devil worship, or even attendance of what appears to foreshadow the sabbat. It almost appears as if, in his search for exterior signs that allegedly revealed a tacit or explicit pact with the demons, Eymeric began to combine some apparently unrelated features into a common demonological framework, even anticipating some aspects of the emerging sabbat imaginary.

In this regard, we should also note cases referring to magical transportation over great distances within short periods of time. One of the women from Castelló tried for sorcery in 1358, was flagged again ten years later for transporting a man from the island of Majorca to Castelló overnight. A similar accusation was levelled against an old woman who apparently used a plaster figure to 'bring men immediately from remote parts.' Reeds appear in a number of these magical transportation cases. For instance, a Saracen from Lleida, who also killed bats to draw circles with their blood, apparently gave two friars reeds enabling them to go from that city to Avignon in less than two days.[50] By the early modern period, reeds had become a common object used to facilitate demonic flight, as attested, among others, in Francesco Guazzo's *Compendium maleficarum* (1608, rev. ed. 1626).[51]

In addition to magical flights, one woman was also accused of wandering at night with some evil spirits popularly known as the 'good ladies' (*bones dones*), a local version of the *bonnes dammes* or *bonae res* that would play a prominent role in the formation of the witchcraft construct during the fifteenth century.[52] Last but not least, a blasphemous man from the village of Valveralla who had not gone to confession in almost twenty years was accused of transforming food into toads. During his trial, he would blame this gastronomical feat on his own wife, accusing her of being 'the worst bad Christian' and of being possessed by demons who prevented her from sitting still during mass. He then added that she worshipped demons and talked with them, and that he once saw her 'turning figs into toads.'[53]

## 5 The evil within

Despite what can be read in Eymeric's epitaph – 'truthful preacher, intrepid inquisitor, distinguished doctor' – the friar's journey was not really that of a doctor, as in a person who teaches, but more that of a judge/police officer, someone who devoted his life to extirpating heresy. It would be difficult to argue that Eymeric increased the scope of demonic agency. He stuck to a traditional paradigm without increasing the autonomy and power attributed to demons as it was conceived in the late Middle Ages. His reflections were less doctrinal and more juridical, in the sense that they were aimed at strengthening inquisitorial jurisdiction through the extension of the notion of heresy – essentially by defending the imputation of heresy to all demon-related activities.

As heresy was an act of thought and will residing in the inner consciousness, its search proved to be at the very least controversial, especially since, in his mission, Eymeric adopted Terrena's distinction between heresy *in re* and apparent heresy manifested through exterior signs. Unable to fully divine hearts and intentions, the inquisitor decided to rule primarily on 'facts', assuming that they signified or revealed the inner consciousness. Certainly, a judicial sentence based on external and fallible signs could be erroneous, but then, stated Eymeric, ecclesiastical justice had no other means but to stick to the evidence (words and facts), even if this could lead to frequent errors with regard to divine justice.[54] Christ, he noted, would ultimately correct any error in the afterlife, after the accused's death.

The procedural challenge faced by the Inquisition – and by modern secret police forces – is that the judge operates relying on a series of mental mechanisms dominated by his own subjectivity. Confronted with heresy, Eymeric acted in bad faith and assumed that heresy infected consciences. He therefore did not rest until he found it or until he obtained proof of a clean conscience. Did he thus uncover crimes or did he invent them? The inquisitor must always suspect, uncover, and ultimately extirpate heresy, either through abjuration or the elimination of the heretic himself. As much as the existence of heretics rebounded on Eymeric's own prestige as a guardian of the faith, it is also through the inquisitor's actions that the devil-worshipping heretic emerged, since without inquisitorial intervention, the accused's inner consciousness would have never been revealed.

In his search for exterior signs concealing a demonic and therefore heretical reality, Eymeric pushed the boundaries of inquisitorial justice into uncharted territories, contributing to the gradual process of hereticization of magic that would soon crystallize in the emergence of the demonic pact and the witches' sabbat. Eymeric's *Directorium* and the surviving traces of his inquisitorial activity remain a paramount example of how the determined search for evil could often leave the accused at the mercy of the inquisitor's own demons.

## Notes

1 Arxiu Municipal de València (AMV), trial from 1387, fol. 207r; Jaume de Puig, 'El procés dels lul·listes valencians contra Nicolau Eimeric en el marc del Cisma d'Occident', *Boletín de la Sociedad Castellonense de Cultura*, 1980, vol. LVI, 319–463.

2 AMV, trial from 1387, fol. 157r.
3 Arxiu de la Corona d'Aragó (ACA), Cancelleria, reg.1883, fols 73v–74r; Jaume de Puig, 'Documents inèdits referents a Nicolau Eimeric i el Lul·lisme', *Arxiu de textos catalans antics*, 1983, vol. 2, 319–46.
4 For a survey, see Claudia Heinmann, *Nicholaus Eymerich (vor 1320–1399): 'praedicator veridicus, inquisitor intrepidus, doctor egregius'; Leben und Werk eines Inquisitors*, Münster: Aschendorff, 2001.
5 Nicolau Eymeric, *Directorium inquisitorum ... cum commentariis Francisci Pegnae*, Rome: Georgius Ferrarius, 1587.
6 Edward M. Peters, 'Editing Inquisitors' Manuals in the Sixteenth Century: Francisco Peña and the *Directorium inquisitorum* of Nicholas Eymerich', *The Library Chronicle*, 1974, vol. 40, 95–107.
7 Karen Sullivan, *The Inner Lives of Medieval Inquisitors*, Chicago: University of Chicago Press, 2011, pp. 169–96.
8 Eymeric, *Directorium*, pp. 335–48.
9 Julien Véronèse, 'Nigromancie et hérésie: Le *De jurisdictione inquisitorum in et contra christianos demones invocantes* (1359) de Nicolas Eymerich (O.P.)', in Martine Ostorero and Julien Véronèse, eds, *Penser avec les demons: Démonologues et demonologies, XIIIe–XVIIe siècles*, Florence: Sismel-Edizioni del Galluzzo, 2015, pp. 5–56. On Terrena, see Alexander Fidora, ed., *Guido Terreni, O. Carm., †1342: Studies and Texts*, Barcelona: Brepols, 2015, pp. vii–xiii.
10 Josep Perarnau, 'El Tractatus brevis super iurisdictione inquisitorum contra infideles fidem catholicam agitantes de Nicolau Eimeric: Edició i estudi del text', *Arxiu de Textos Catalans Antics*, 1982, vol. 1, 79–126.
11 Julien Véronèse, 'Le *Contra astrologos imperitos atque nigromanticos* (1395–1396) de Nicolas Eymerich (O.P.): Contexte de rédaction, classification des arts magiques et divinatoires, édition critique partielle', in Martine Ostorero et al., eds, *Chasses aux sorcières et démonologie: Entre discours et pratiques, XIVe–XVIIe siècles*, Florence: Sismel-Edizioni del Galluzzo 2010, pp. 271–329.
12 Bernard Gui, *Practica inquisitionis heretice pravitatis*, ed. by Celestin Douais, Paris: Alphonse Picard, 1886, p. 150. See Michael Bailey, 'From Sorcery to Witchcraft: Clerical Conceptions of Magic in the Later Middle Ages', *Speculum*, 2001, vol. 76, 960–90; Alain Boureau, *Satan hérétique: Naissance de la démonologie dans l'Occident medieval, 1280–1330*, Paris: Odile Jacob, 2004, pp. 56–59; Isabel Iribarren, 'From Black Magic to Heresy: A Doctrinal Leap in the Pontificate of John XXII', *Church History*, 2007, vol. 76, 32–60.
13 Pau Castell Granados, 'Sortilegas, divinatrices et fetilleres: Les origines de la sorcellerie en Catalogne', *Cahiers de recherches médiévales et humanistes*, 2011, vol. 22, 217–24; Pau Castell Granados, 'Feminine Magical-Medicinal Practices in Catalan Trials for Sorcery and Witchcraft: Changing Perceptions between the Late Middle Ages and the Early Modern Times', in Alessandra Cioppi, ed., *Donne e lavoro: Attività, ruoli e complementarietà secc. XIV–XIX*, Naples: ISEM-CNR, 2019, pp. 173–92.
14 Heinmann, *Nicholaus Eymerich*, pp. 22–33.
15 Sergi Grau et al., eds., *L'herètica pravitat a la Corona d'Aragó: Documents sobre càtars, valdesos i altres heretges, 1155–1324*, Barcelona: Fundació Noguera, 2015.
16 Eymeric, *Directorium*, p. 653.
17 Jaume de Puig, 'El "Dialogus contra lullistas" de Nicolau Eimeric: Edició i estudi', *Arxiu de Textos Catalans Antics*, 2000, vol. 19, 220.
18 Eymeric, *Directorium*, p. 433. On Eymeric's methodology of interrogation, see also Sullivan, *The Inner Lives*, pp. 169–95.
19 Eymeric, *Directorium*, p. 433.
20 Eymeric, *Directorium*, p. 434.
21 Eymeric, *Directorium*, pp. 480–86.

22 Eymeric, *Directorium*, p. 460.
23 Jaume de Puig, 'La "Incantatio Studii Ilerdensis" de Nicolau Eimeric O.P.: Edició i estudi', *Arxiu de Textos Catalans Antics*, 1996, vol. 15, 46.
24 Jaume de Puig, 'Dos sermons de Nicolau Eimeric O.P.', *Arxiu de Textos Catalans Antics*, 2003, vol. 22, 223–67.
25 Puig, 'Dos sermons', 245–54.
26 Jaume de Puig, 'Documents relatius a la Inquisició del registrum litterarum de l'Arxiu Diocesà de Girona, s. XIV', *Arxiu de Textos Catalans Antics*, 1998, vol. 17, 415–16.
27 Puig, 'Documents relatius a la Inquisició', 416–17.
28 Heinmann, *Nicolaus Eymerich*, pp. 25–33.
29 For more on the *Contra christianos*, see Veronèse, 'Nigromancie et hérésie', pp. 5–56.
30 Véronèse, 'Nigromancie et hérésie', p. 12.
31 Véronèse, 'Nigromancie et hérésie', pp. 21–24.
32 Véronèse, 'Nigromancie et hérésie', pp. 24–33.
33 Véronèse, 'Nigromancie et hérésie', pp. 33–35. In addition to the fifth chapter of the *Contra christianos*, Eymeric devoted a short treatise entitled *De suspicione levi, vehementi et violenta* (1359) to the judicial treatment of invocation with no sign of *latria* or *dulia* (ms. Escorial, Biblioteca del Monasterio, Z.II.12, fols 191vb–202vb; Paris, BnF, lat. 14,533, fols 124vb–31rb).
34 Eymeric, *Directorium*, pp. 341–42.
35 Boureau, *Satan hérétique*, pp. 21–24; Véronèse, 'Nigromancie et hérésie', pp. 14–20; Martine Ostorero, *Le Diable au sabbat: Littérature démonologique et sorcellerie, 1440–1460*, Florence: SISMEL-Edizioni del Galluzzo, 2011, pp. 437–38.
36 Eymeric, *Directorium*, pp. 341–42.
37 Bibliothèque Nationale de France (BnF), Nouv. Acq. Lat. 834. See also the editions by Henry Omont, 'Mémorial de l'inquisiteur d'Aragon à la fin du XIVe siècle', *Bibliothèque de l'École de Chartes*, 1905, vol. LXVI, 261–68; Johannes Vincke, *Zur Vorgeschichte der Spanischen Inquisition: Die Inquisition in Aragon, Katalonien, Mallorca und Valencia während des 13. und 14. Jahrunderts*. Bonn: P. Hanstein 1941, pp. 162–82.
38 Eymeric, *Directorium*, p. 413.
39 Puig, 'Documents relatius a la Inquisició', pp. 384–85, 421, 434–53.
40 BnF, Nouv. Acq. Lat. 834, fols 4r–13r.
41 BnF, Nouv. Acq. Lat. 834, fols 2v–3v.
42 BnF, Nouv. Acq. Lat. 834, fols 2r–9v.
43 On this subject, see Richard Kieckhefer, *Forbidden Rites: A Necromancer's Manual of the Fifteenth Century*, University Park, PA: Pennsylvania State University Press, 1997; Jean-Patrice Boudet, *Entre Science et nigromance: Astrologie, divination et magie dans l'Occident medieval, XIIe–XVe siècle*, Paris: Publications de la Sorbonne, 2006.
44 BnF, Nouv. Acq. Lat. 834, fols 5r, 11r–16v.
45 BnF, Nouv. Acq. Lat. 834, fol. 5v.
46 Veronèse, 'Le *Contra astrologos*', p. 298.
47 BnF, Nouv. Acq. Lat. 834, fols 3v–8v, 10r, 16v.
48 BnF, Nouv. Acq. Lat. 834, fol. 8r.
49 BnF, Nouv. Acq. Lat. 834, fols 4v, 6v, 7r.
50 BnF, Nouv. Acq. Lat. 834, fols 6v–7v, 16v.
51 Francesco Maria Guazzo, *Compendium maleficarum*, Milan: ex Collegii Ambrosiani typographia, 1626, p. 85.
52 Pau Castell Granados, '"Wine Vat Witches Suffocate Children": The Mythical Components of the Iberian Witch', *eHumanista: Journal of Iberian Studies*, 2014, vol. 25, 170–95.

53  BnF, Nouv. Acq. Lat. 834, fols 7v and 13r.
54  Véronèse, 'Nigromancie et hérésie', p. 24.

**Further reading**

Heinmann, Claudia, *Nicholaus Eymerich (vor 1320–1399): 'Praedicator veridicus, inquisitor intrepidus, doctor egregius'; Leben und Werk eines Inquisitors*, Münster: Aschendorff, 2001.

Peters, Edward M., 'Editing Inquisitors' Manuals in the Sixteenth Century: Francisco Peña and the *Directorium inquisitorum* of Nicholas Eymerich', *Library Chronicle*, 1974, vol. 40/1, 95–107.

Puig i Oliver, Jaume de, 'Nicolás Eymerich, un inquisidor discutido', in Wolfram Hoyer, ed., *Praedicatores, Inquisitores, Vol. 1: The Dominicans and the Medieval Inquisition*, Rome: Istituto Storico Domenicano, 2004, pp. 545–593.

Sullivan, Karen, *The Inner Lives of Medieval Inquisitors*, Chicago: University of Chicago Press, 2011, pp. 169–196.

Véronèse, Julien, 'Nigromancie et hérésie: Le *De jurisdictione inquisitorum in et contra christianos demones invocantes* (1359) de Nicolas Eymerich (O.P.)', in Martine Ostorero and Julien Véronèse, eds, *Penser avec les demons: Démonologues et demonologies, XIIIe–XVIIe siècles*, Florence: Sismel-Edizioni del Galluzzo, 2015, pp. 5–56.

*Most manuscript material on Eymeric has been published by Jaume de Puig and Josep Perarnau in various issues of the online journal 'Arxiu de Textos Catalans Antics' ATCA*: http://revistes.iec.cat/index.php/ATCA/issue/archive.

# 2 Promoter of the sabbat and diabolical realism

Nicolas Jacquier's *Flagellum hereticorum fascinariorum*

*Martine Ostorero*
*(translated by Jan Machielsen)*

During the first half of the fifteenth century, the development of the concept of the witches' sabbat helped spread belief in the reality of a demonic conspiracy. Both male and female witches were believed to have obtained their maleficent powers through a pact with the devil, after having denied God and the Christian faith. The witch did not, however, operate alone – they were a member of a secret sect which gathered at the devil's direction. Witches constituted a form of anti-Church – frequently called a sabbat or synagogue, reflecting strong anti-Jewish sentiments in the late Middle Ages – with the aim of blaspheming and abusing the Church's sacraments. Together, they sought to destroy Christian society and the Church through the most infamous and reprehensible acts imaginable (infanticide, cannibalism, and unnatural sex). Inevitably, this new discourse on the witches' sabbat had a lasting impact on judicial practice with deadly consequences. Those accused of participating in the sabbat risked death by burning at the stake.

Several accounts, with richly detailed sabbat descriptions, were written as early as the 1430s, starting in the Western Alps before spreading into France and Italy.[1] Frequently, these texts accompanied or promoted legal proceedings against individuals suspected of witchcraft. They were written by clerics, theologians, inquisitors, or magistrates who had become convinced of the reality of the sabbat and demon-worshipping sects, a reality that they themselves had helped to forge and which they sought to defend. These accounts generally described the alleged crimes of sorcerers in all their gruesome and grisly detail, crimes which they insisted were real, despite their unbelievable horror. Although their authors still made up a minority, these sabbat 'fanatics' were becoming increasingly assertive and prominent in certain regions (the Western Alps, Western Switzerland, Savoy, Burgundy, as well as parts of France) and in certain cultural circles (the Dominican and Franciscan religious orders, as well as among those who attended the Council of Basel, 1431–1449). For the most part, these authors did not approach the subject in gendered terms, including men alongside women among the alleged devil-worshippers. The feminization of diabolical witchcraft had to await the *Malleus maleficarum* (The Hammer of [Female] Witches). Instead, their primary objective was to overturn the long-established medieval consensus that those who claimed to engage in forms of night-time worship or even flight were the victims of the deceptions or illusions of demons who had confounded their imagination.

This radical 'realist' trend is perhaps best illustrated by the *Errores gazariorum* (Errors of the Gazarii), an anonymous pamphlet written around 1436–1438, probably by Ponce Feugeyron, one of the Franciscan inquisitors charged with eradicating heresy and witchcraft in the Aosta Valley, in the Duchy of Savoy. Claude Tholosan, a judge in the Dauphiné, recorded his experiences around the same time in a treatise entitled *Ut magorum et maleficorum errores ...* (So that the Errors of Magicians and Sorcerers ... ). A very detailed sabbat description was included in *La Vauderye de Lyonois en brief* (The Vauderie of Lyon), produced by a group of Dominicans from Lyon around 1438–1440, with the aim of convincing the reader of the danger (and thus of the reality) of this 'new sect of apostates and infidels.'[2]

The work discussed in the present chapter, the *Flagellum hereticorum fascinariorum* (The Scourge of the Heretical Enchanters), written in 1458, must be placed within the same context.[3] Yet, its author, Nicolas Jacquier, was not content to describe only the witches' sabbat. He also sought to demonstrate the reality of their acts of harmful magic, of magical flight, and of the physical interactions between demons and humans. Jacquier's *Flagellum* becomes an advocate for what can be called diabolical realism in its most extreme form – there was nothing illusory or imaginary about the actions of witches and devils. The Dominican's aim, therefore, was the eradication of witches, who as 'the worst of the heretics' only deserved death. Jacquier's mission was therefore twofold: to convince his audience of the existence of sects of witches, and to convince his readers to join him in his fight against them. He considered the proliferation of diabolical witchcraft to be a sign of the end of the world. Within this apocalyptic framework, the *Flagellum* sought to defeat not only witches but sceptics as well.[4]

## 1 Nicolas Jacquier, a Dominican defending the faith

Originally from Burgundy and educated in Dijon, the Dominican Nicolas Jacquier (d. 1472) was trained in the fight against heresy at the Council of Basel. As a member of the important Commission for Faith and Church Reform, he became familiar with the dangers posed by the Hussites, the followers of Jan Hus, whom the earlier Council of Constance had burned at the stake for heresy a few years earlier. Not only had he discussed the Hussite threat with the Bishop of Prague, Jan Rokycana, a marginal annotation in one of his treatises even presents him as having 'defeated the Bohemians at the Council of Basel.'[5] Later in life, when he was sent on an embassy to Bohemia by the Duke of Burgundy he composed two works against the Hussites (1466) and utraquism, one of their principal dogmas (1470).[6]

Jacquier stayed in Basel from 1433 to 1440, leaving only when the Council began to lose credibility and political support. During the 1430s, however, the Swiss Rhine city hosted one of the largest meetings of churchmen Europe had ever seen. It also became a place for informal discussions about demonology and demonic witchcraft, even if no conciliar decree referred to the subject.[7] In fact, where the sabbat was concerned the Council was something of an echo chamber. Among those present was the Dominican observant Johannes Nider, prior of the local convent until 1434, who devoted part of his *Formicarius* (The Anthill) to witchcraft. Martin Le Franc, secretary of the Duke of Savoy Amédée VIII, elected (anti-)pope by the Council under the name of Felix V, detailed the misdeeds of witches called '*faicturieres* or *cauquemares* who are married to the devil' in his *Champion des dames* (The Champion of Women). Other texts were already circulating at the Council, including the above-mentioned *Errores gazariorum*. Nicolas Jacquier was part of a network of Council participants promoting new theories on the demonic, ideas he took further when he came to draft the *Flagellum*.

From the mid-1430s onwards, Nicolas Jacquier was chosen on several occasions by Philip the Good, the influential Duke of Burgundy, for diplomatic missions in the Holy Roman Empire (Germany, Hungary and Bohemia). Under Philip, the Duchy of Burgundy extended north from its ancestral territory in what is now eastern France to cover much of the Low Countries, and the dukes were confident enough to attempt to engage in a foreign policy independent of the Kingdom of France of which the duchy was nominally a part. Jacquier was charged, in particular, with promoting a project of the ambitious duke for a crusade against the Turks, who were then threatening Constantinople.[8] The Dominican friar would remain a ducal adviser and close to the duke's court in Dijon for the remainder of his life.

In 1451, Jacquier appears for the first time in the records as a papal (vice-)inquisitor of the faith, charged with extirpating so-called 'heretical depravity'. His presence is mainly attested in the Burgundian heartlands, as well as in the nearby Lyon region and county of Forez. It appears, however, that the inquisitor struggled to exercise his office. Much as Heinrich Institoris° a generation later, Jacquier took up his pen to prove the reality and danger of this sect of demon-worshipping witches when his inquisitorial efforts were frustrated. He first wrote a brief treatise on how to fight demons, the *De calcatione demonum*, in 1457. A year later in Lyon, at Notre-Dame de Confort, the inquisitor composed his longer *Flagellum* (1458), possibly taking inspiration from the *Vauderye de Lyonois* that had been produced at the same Dominican convent twenty years earlier.[9]

Between 1459 and 1461, a major witchcraft persecution took place in Arras, a town in present-day northern France but then also part of the Duchy of Burgundy. Although the victims were identified as 'Vaudois' or Waldensians – a late medieval heresy –, the crime of which they were accused was demonic witchcraft.[10] As we shall see, Jacquier likely provided the inspiration for those trials, because the crimes of which these 'Vaudois' were accused greatly resembled those laid out in the *Flagellum*. Yet, he certainly was not present himself. We can place Jacquier in Venice at this time for the preliminary phase of the canonization proceedings of Catherine of Siena (*c.*1347–1380), the most famous female mystic of the Middle Ages. In 1464, we find Jacquier at the Dominican Observant convent in Lille. He would preach in all the major Flemish cities (Lille, Tournai, Ghent) which were then part of Burgundy, while composing the two above-mentioned treatises against the Hussite heresy. He died in 1472 in the convent of Ghent, where he was buried.

Nicolas Jacquier was thus much more than simply an inquisitor eager to hunt witches. He was also a man pre-occupied with the problems of his time, in particular the reform of the Church and the fight against heresy. His project to eradicate demonic witchcraft was a central part of his defence of Christian orthodoxy, as was his battle against the Hussites and his involvement in the crusade against the Turks. Jacquier also participated in the reform of his own Dominican order by joining the Congregation of Holland, one of the most important groups promoting the so-called Dominican Observance in the second half of the fifteenth century.[11] From the 1460s onwards, he encouraged its development by seeking political and financial support from the dukes of Burgundy. He also worked towards the canonization of Catherine of Siena and (much less successfully) Colette of Corbie (1381–1447), two female mystics whom the Observants sought to promote as contemporary models of holiness.[12] All these activities were fundamentally linked. Historians have shown how the spread of the Observant movement was often accompanied by campaigns to eradicate magic and witchcraft, which consequently helped promote belief in the existence of the sabbat.[13]

## 2 A first reflection on demons: the *De calcatione demonum* (1457)

In 1457, one year before composing his *Flagellum*, Nicolas Jacquier offered his first reflection on demonology. His *De calcatione demonum seu malignorum spirituum* (On the Trampling of Demons or Bad Spirits) discusses not only the actions of demons on human beings but also the different means available to the faithful and priests to coerce them, expel them, or even 'trample' them (*calcare*).[14] While it was hardly an innovative work, the *De calcatione demonum* does illustrate brilliantly the apparent paradox that lies at the heart of demonology. While the devil, as a creature, is God's instrument and thus can be controlled by the ministers of the Church, he was nevertheless also at war with God and able to commit evil because of the tyrannical empire he exercises over humans since the original sin led to Adam and Eve's expulsion from Paradise. Demonic witchcraft was for Jacquier a sign of the ultimate eschatological struggle between God and Satan. Like many of his contemporaries, our Dominican could not reconcile the devil's subservient role as an instrument of the divine will with his identity as God's principal adversary.

It is within this context that we must place Jacquier's discussion of a case of demonic possession with which he was confronted as vice-inquisitor in the region of Lyon in 1452. During an exorcism, the demons, interrogated by a priest, were forced to reveal through the mouths of the possessed 'truths' relating to the alleged sect of witches. These statements challenged a heterodox Carmelite friar, Guillaume Adeline, who – doubtlessly not coincidentally – had recently preached that the sabbat was an illusion, the product of demonic deceptions on the human imagination.[15] The divine truth, as uttered by demons through the mouths of possessed women, made it possible to expose the preacher's error as heresy. Jacquier drew on a relatively recent tradition here: that of the figure of the demonically possessed person who revealed the divine truth, especially in the struggle against heresy.[16] Exorcism thus forced God's opponent to testify against his own cause, apparently squaring the circle of the devil's bipolar identity. Having thus demonstrated the existence of terrifying heretical sects of witches, Jacquier argued that exorcism no longer sufficed and that an inquisition against witchcraft was necessary. This brings us to the *Flagellum*.

## 3 The *Flagellum hereticorum fascinariorum*

### 3.1 Manuscripts and editions

The *Flagellum* survives in nine manuscripts, all dating from the second half of the fifteenth century, as well as a printed edition of 1581.[17] The text mainly circulated in clerical circles, especially in Burgundy and neighbouring Savoy.[18] The first owners were often abbeys and other religious establishments. Members of the Burgundy court, however, such as Nicolas Clopper, canon of Sainte Gudule in Brussels, and Simon van der Sluis, ducal physician, also possessed demonological writings by Jacquier. Yet, the importance – and usefulness – of the treatise is perhaps best indicated by the number of manuscripts found in regions that experienced witch hunts during the fifteenth century, such as Savoy, Valais, Lyonnais, and Artois.

Jacquier also took his *Flagellum* with him on his diplomatic missions to the Empire: during his mission against the Hussites in 1467, his treatise was copied at Wrocław, at the reformed Dominican convent of Saint Adalbert (St. Wojciech). It was also copied in Trier in 1471, at the Benedictine convent of Our Lady and the Martyrs, where a monk combined Jacquier's two treatises with that of Jean Vinet and the *Vauderye de Lyonois*. It should be noted, however, that the famous *Malleus maleficarum* never explicitly mentions Jacquier's treatise, even if some of their demonological reflections seem similar.

It was not until 1581 that the treatise was printed by the Frankfurt printer Nicolaus Bassaeus in a compendium alongside many other, mostly lesser known texts, such as those by Lambert Daneau, Johannes Trithemius, and Thomas Erastus. This volume, accompanied by a copious index, appears to have been a response to the publication of Jean Bodin°'s famous *De la Démonomanie des sorciers* (On the Demon-Mania of Witches) the year before. Its appearance coincides with the onset of Europe's largest wave of witch-hunting and it no doubt found an avid readership. Its publication also suggests that Jacquier's work still appeared relevant at the end of the sixteenth century.

### 3.2 A short outline of the treatise

Almost all versions of Nicolas Jacquier's *Flagellum* consist of twenty-eight chapters. Although there is no division into parts, we can still distinguish several sections. Chapters 1 to 6 deal with the various manifestations of demons: despite a discussion of illusion and a brief reflection on dreams, our Dominican insists on the reality of demonic apparitions. Demons were able to form real bodies which humans could sensibly perceive. Chapters 7 to 9 are, therefore, crucial. They are devoted to the canon *Episcopi*, the medieval church decree which had dismissed accounts of women flying with the pagan goddess Diana as a demonic illusion. Jacquier used a number of witchcraft trials to distinguish the demon-worshipping witches he himself had encountered from the deceived (and therefore innocent) women discussed by the canon. For the inquisitor, judicial evidence demonstrated not only the veracity of his claims but also underlined the seriousness of the crime of witchcraft: witches were not only heretics, but also idolaters, apostates, and blasphemers. Together, these opening chapters demonstrated both the reality and danger of the witchcraft sect.

The next section of the *Flagellum* broadens the demonological discussion. Chapters 10 to 17 explain the concrete actions of demons both on human beings and the wider world: how can the demon undermine the human psyche in order to incite them to sin (Chapter 11)? How can he act on their body to cause sometimes even fatal illnesses (Chapters 12 and 13)? Returning to the theme of witchcraft and the sabbat, Jacquier then shows how demons and witches collaborate to harm humans and perpetrate evil spells (Chapters 15 and 16) and how they disturb the natural elements (Chapter 17). Faced with these attacks by demons and witches, Chapter 14 provides a whole set of rituals (prayers, the sign of the cross, holy water, visits to holy places) meant to protect against demons. Jacquier underlines the importance of a daily regimen of devotional practice to ward off evil spirits.

After this distressing demonstration of the vast powers and wickedness of demons, Jacquier must remind the reader that the devil can only act with divine permission. This begs the inevitable question that all demonologists must face: why would God allow witchcraft to flourish? The third part of the treatise (Chapters 18 to 25) develops five explanations. These emphasize the pedagogical, moral, and edifying lessons that humans can draw from a divine plan that includes dangerous demon-worshipping witches. Paradoxically, the submission of demons to God also further increased their powers: with divine permission, demons can accomplish everything that God wants, and God, as Jacquier makes clear, desires a great deal from humanity.

Finally, two crucial chapters (26 and 27) deal with the legal aspects of demonology, with important consequences for the criminalization of witchcraft. The inquisitor discussed the validity of the testimony of accused witches – a subject that we will see many later authors confront as well – and an insistence that witches should not be allowed to do penance for their sins (and thus avoid judicial punishment) because of the enormity of their crimes. Chapter 28, which is not present in all the manuscripts, adds an additional argument to the discussion of the medieval canon *Episcopi*: even if the sabbat were only a dream, those who experienced it were nevertheless guilty of believing and acting according to dreams in which they were members of a demonic cult. Nicolas Jacquier thus managed to even criminalize sleep.

### 3.3 Deconstructing the canon Episcopi, a stumbling block for demonologists

By the mid fifteenth century, belief in the witches' sabbat was far from being universally accepted, while their supposed *maleficia* remained the subject of much elite debate. Sceptics relied on a famous church decree, the canon *Episcopi*, which was part of the collection of canon law compiled by Gratian in the twelfth century but believed to have been much older.[19] Why was the canon *Episcopi* such a stumbling block for demonologists and how did Jacquier try to overcome its authority?

Named after the bishops ('*episcopi*') which it addresses, the canon *Episcopi* strongly condemned the use of spells and curses. At the same time, however, it dismissed the women who claimed to ride animals at night with the pagan goddess Diana as deceived by demonic illusions. Belief in the *reality* of such nocturnal flights was thus labelled a heresy. Although clearly far removed from the sabbat concept as it emerged in the fifteenth century, the canon nevertheless served as a pretext for debating the vast issues surrounding demonic witchcraft. Some authors, notably Jacquier, tried to reduce its relevance by demonstrating that both night flight and (consequently) the sabbat were, in fact, real. Others, such as the Italian Franciscan Bernardino of Siena, accepted that such flights were demonic illusions but did not fully exonerate those who experienced them. Still others, including Jean Tinctor and, later, Heinrich Institoris, solved the puzzle by claiming that both arguments were true: witches could be physically transported by demons and they could experience flight in a dream-like state. In both cases, they deserved to be condemned.[20]

Chapters 7 to 9 of the *Flagellum* embrace the *novelty* of witchcraft in order to dismiss the relevance of the canon *Episcopi*. Jacquier differentiated the women reported by the seemingly ancient canon from his so-called 'modern witches' to prove that the canon's scepticism could not apply to the newfangled sabbat.[21] The Dominican developed four principal differences with the canon:

(1) the reality of contact with demons (as shown by the pact, sexual relations, etc.);
(2) the reality of crimes committed at the sabbat;
(3) the judicial evidence provided by witnesses; and
(4) the pact as the product of a witch's individual and voluntary act, which required her conviction as an apostate, idolater, and blasphemer.

Jacquier also questioned the authority of the canon *Episcopi* and criticized its conclusions as partial and hasty. He claimed that it neglected the reality of the physical movements of demons, denouncing the widespread ignorance among his contemporaries of demonic powers, despite the contributions that thirteenth-century Scholastic theology had already made on that topic.

The inquisitor's attack on the canon *Episcopi*, then, was not a simple formal exercise but a dire necessity. Jacquier needed to discredit the canon to remove a barrier for legal action against witches. We will return to the judicial aspect later. First, we must explore the impact of Jacquier's realism because it sent Christian demonology in new and partly unexpected directions, bringing witches physically closer to demons.

### 3.4 The diabolical realism of Nicolas Jacquier

To prove the threat posed by the sabbat, Jacquier also needed to demonstrate the reality of physical contact between witches and demons. The Dominican's largely innovative argument was that demons were not only able to influence (and thus deceive) the human imagination, they were especially capable of presenting themselves physically to human beings using 'assumed bodies'.

The theory of 'assumed bodies', developed by thirteenth-century Scholastic theologians, and especially by Thomas Aquinas, conferred on demons a certain corporeality, while preserving their essentially spiritual nature.[22] Demons, it was argued, could take on the appearance of a human or animal body from purely natural elements (air condensation, earthly vapours, corpses, etc.). They could even invent forms that do not exist. They assume, in the original literal sense of taking on (as it were like clothing), things created by God or by nature. They could simulate bodily operations, like moving, speaking and eating, but they could not endow objects with life – demons could thus animate a corpse but not resurrect the dead, a miracle that belonged only to God.[23] Humans were able to perceive a demon's 'bodily' presence through their senses, such as sight, hearing or touch.[24]

Throughout his treatise, Nicolas Jacquier strongly insists on humans' sensory perception of demons, and consequently on the 'real' character of these apparitions: 'These bodies [demons], although they are not really alive, are nevertheless perceptible, visible and palpable by the senses of those to whom demons appear. And yet [the bodies] are still fabricated, fictitious and fallacious'.[25] Like his fellow inquisitor Jean Vinet, the author of the *Tractatus contra demonum invocatores* (Treatise against Demon Invokers, *c*.1450),[26] Jacquier never failed to highlight this demonic corporeality, perceptible by the senses, in order to overcome the arguments of the sceptics. Sensory experience provided objective and indisputable evidence of the reality of the sabbat and the physical and material presence of the devil.

The carnal union between a demon and a human being – man or woman – was Jacquier's most obvious proof:

> Several of these worshippers of the cult and heretical enchanters, of both sexes, freely confessed that at their meeting which they call a "synagogue" or "council" and which demons also attended, they had sex not only amongst themselves but also so voluptuously with demons that some of them affirm that they were worn out and exhausted after one or two days by the extreme violence of these pleasures.[27]

Reports of painful physical contact with demons refuted the theory of diabolical illusion, put forth by his opponents.[28] Jacquier was the most radical of all fifteenth-century demonologists in his insistence on diabolical realism, the physical reality of interactions between humans and demons.

### 3.5 The crime of demonic witchcraft: the powerful triad of heresy, idolatry, and apostasy

The reality of human interactions with the devil helped Jacquier to define the crimes of witches in legal terms. As an inquisitor of heretical depravity, he had to demonstrate that witches were first and foremost heretics, and that their prosecution was the responsibility of the church courts. Yet, for Jacquier, witches were more than that: 'Heretical enchanters,' he stated at the outset, 'are the worst of all heretics, for they are also vile idolaters and treacherous worshippers of demons.'[29] This rhetoric was not just antiheretical polemic. In order to justify the severity of his proposed punishments, the inquisitor had to add other crimes: idolatry, understood as adoration of demons (demonolatry), as well as apostasy, that is, the denial of God, the sacraments and the Christian faith. The sabbat was thus above all devoted to devil worship. By emphasizing the crimes of apostasy and idolatry committed at their 'synagogues', Jacquier could justify the exceptionally harsh sentences imposed on them.[30]

Thus, for Jacquier, the pact with the devil marked a witch's definitive and total allegiance to Satan. Their commitment was voluntary and irredeemable. Through an initiation rite that mimicked but inverted Christian baptism, the new follower entered a sect of devil-worshipping witches, a counter-church described by Jacquier as the 'synagogue of the devil'. In this ritual, the crime of apostasy took centre stage: the devil demanded that his followers deny the faith and profane the cross or the Eucharist. As a rite directed against Christianity, whose aim was the faith's total destruction, the sabbat constituted a major threat.

Witches were also idolatrous, because they offered children to demons at their 'synagogue'. For Jacquier, these sacrifices, which recalled the idolatry of pagan and pre-Christian religions, were an offence to the divine majesty. Christ's Incarnation made the witches of Jacquier's time worse than the idolaters described in the Old Testament, making their insult to God greater and their sin more serious. Their apostasy and the idolatrous rituals they conducted at the sabbat made witches the 'worst' of heretics. Jacquier here was not alone. The same triad of heresy, apostasy, and idolatry can be found in the anonymous *Vauderye de Lyonois* and in the *De strigiis* of Bernard Rategno (*c*.1510), and it served as the basis for the death sentences pronounced in the Pays de Vaud in the fifteenth century.[31]

The severity of their crimes led Jacquier to argue that the normal procedures observed for 'traditional' heretics should be set aside. Canon law prescribed that heretics, if convicted of a first offence, should perform a penance and then be absolved. For our Dominican, this clearly would not suffice: 'Heretical enchanters arrested judicially for the crime of heresy and the use of evil spells should not be admitted [back] into the community of the faithful, as other heretics are after they have abjured their heresy.'[32] Jacquier wanted to depart from this penitential tradition, which still prevailed in the Kingdom of France, and proceed immediately to the death penalty. Jacquier argued that absolution of heresy would leave a witch's other crimes untouched. Both Roman and canon law imposed the death penalty for the crimes of idolatry, homicide and sodomy. Jacquier urged that witches be punished for all their crimes.

Jacquier's plea for the death penalty places him at the extreme fringe of the fifteenth-century fight against demonic witchcraft. In many respects, Jacquier's *Flagellum* is the inquisitorial counterpart to the *Ut magorum et maleficorum errores* by the secular judge Claude Tholosan, which we mentioned at the start of this chapter.[33] If this judge from the nearby Dauphiné developed the legal argument to punish witches in secular courts by making them guilty of the crime of lese-majesty (treason), Jacquier used the triad of heresy, apostasy, and idolatry to advocate a similar harsh approach by the ecclesiastical courts.

## 4 Conclusion: the *Flagellum* between favourable reception and harsh resistance

Both the success of Jacquier's *Flagellum* and its innovative and radical nature can only be properly understood when placed in the context of the legal traditions that it sought to overturn. Papal inquisitors like Jacquier were rarely able to act against witchcraft in the Kingdom of France in the mid fifteenth century. Sometimes authorities at the local or royal level would even block or disown their attempts to repress witchcraft, as happened in Lyon around 1440, and in Arras around 1460, as we shall presently see. For their part, episcopal courts in France were relatively lenient. A convicted witch might be excommunicated and only handed over to the secular arm in the event of a recurrence. Secular courts did more often hand down death sentences, but these may be overturned on appeal, particularly in the Parlement of Paris, or pardoned by the king.[34] By contrast, a number of areas neighbouring the kingdom, such as Western Switzerland, the Duchy of Savoy and the Dauphiné, had seen some of the earliest witch-hunts, starting in the 1430s, resulting in a great number of executions. This difference between France and the territories at its margin is essential to understanding the importance of Nicolas Jacquier's *Flagellum*.

Did Jacquier succeed? As we have seen, manuscripts of the *Flagellum* circulated in areas of intense witchcraft persecution. Above all, the so-called *Vauderie* of Arras (1459–1461), the first major witch-hunt in Burgundian lands, broke out only a year after Nicolas Jacquier's *Flagellum* was written. It can therefore be taken as a sign of the work's positive reception, at least at first. About sixty inhabitants of Arras and the surrounding area were incriminated and about twenty death sentences or life sentences were handed down between May and October 1460. Nevertheless, royal advisers in Paris acted to put an end to the hunt. From 1461 onwards, they pleaded for the annulment of the sentences and the posthumous rehabilitation of the supposed Waldensians, which would be completed in 1491. This royal disavowal was a political masterstroke. As Franck Mercier has shown, the *Vauderie* of Arras was the site of intense competition between two states, the Kingdom of France and the Duchy of Burgundy, which was attempting to escape French sovereignty but ultimately failed to go its own way.[35]

We should note the strong similarities between Jacquier's *Flagellum* and a text produced by one of the defenders of the Arras witch-hunt, the *Recollectio casus, status et condicionis Valdensium ydolatrarum* (A Recapitulation of the Case, State and Condition of the Waldensian Idolaters).[36] Its anonymous author, possibly the dean of the cathedral chapter Jacques du Bois, who had been one of the judges, seems to have relied heavily on the *Flagellum*, particularly in procedural matters. Although the treatise placed more emphasis on the reality of night flying, it posed almost the same set of questions as Jacquier's work, while its responses closely corresponded to those provided by the Dominican. The *Recollectio* justified the death in the same way as Nicolas Jacquier had, by insisting on the novelty and seriousness of the crime, on the incorrigibility of the offenders and on the need for exemplary punishment.[37] The *Recollectio*, like the *Flagellum* and *La Vauderye de Lyonois*, also defended the jurisdiction of the church over the crime of witchcraft. As a combination of the crimes of heresy, apostasy, and idolatry, witchcraft could not exclusively belong to the jurisdiction of the secular courts and required the use of extraordinary inquisitorial procedures, such as the use of denunciations and public reputation (*fama*), as well as torture.

This last claim drew a number of highly critical responses from sceptics and believers alike to demonstrate that ecclesiastical courts were not competent to judge the crime of witchcraft on their own. Both Claude Tholosan, already mentioned above, and the Lombard lawyer Ambrogio Vignati were very hostile to the intervention of the inquisition in cases of witchcraft.[38] Yet, Jacquier's radical treatise encountered equally fanatical scepticism as well. Marginal notes on one of the manuscripts by a French opponent, for instance, sought to demolish Jacquier's argument. Satisfied with a job well done, the anonymous hand concluded: 'And so his whole edifice totters and collapses.'[39]

The mid fifteenth century was a crucial period in the development of the witchcraft stereotype, laying the foundation for larger-scale witch-hunting to follow. Debates and polemics raged about witchcraft and the witches' sabbat throughout the Christian West. When the *Malleus maleficarum* appeared in print, questions relating to demonic witchcraft had already been discussed by well over a dozen, mostly manuscript, treatises. At stake were the legal definition of witchcraft, its possible reality, and the judicial procedures to be followed. Behind this lurked the prestige that princes and the Church could derive from the exercise of justice and the eradication of Satan's henchmen. Nicolas Jacquier, inquisitor and preacher, a man of practical experience but also a man of faith beset by demons, was one of the major voices in this seminal debate.

## Notes

1 Martine Ostorero et al., eds, *L'Imaginaire du sabbat: Édition critique des textes les plus anciens, 1430 c.–1440 c.*, Lausanne: Université de Lausanne, 1999.
2 Franck Mercier and Martine Ostorero, *L'Énigme de la Vauderie de Lyon: Enquête sur l'essor des chasses aux sorcières entre France et Empire, 1430–1480*, Florence: SISMEL–Edizioni del Galuzzo, 2015, chaps 1–3.
3 Martine Ostorero, *Le Diable au sabbat: Littérature démonologique et sorcellerie (1440–1460)*, Florence: SISMEL-Edizioni del Galuzzo, 2011. An important section of this book is devoted to Nicolas Jacquier and the *Flagellum*, which inspired this chapter. On Jacquier and his *Scourge*, cf. Matthew Champion, 'Scourging the Temple of God: Towards an Understanding of Nicolas Jacquier's *Flagellum haereticorum fascinariorum* (1458)', *Parergon*, 2011, vol. 28/1, 1–24.
4 Ostorero, *Le Diable au sabbat*, pp. 117–48.
5 Saint-Omer, Bibliothèque municipale, Ms. 295, fol. 1v.
6 Olivier Marin, ed., *Les Traités anti-hussites du dominicain Nicolas Jacquier, † 1472: Une Histoire du concile de Bâle et de sa postérité*, Turnhout: Brepols, 2012.
7 Stefan Sudmann, 'Hexen – Ketzer – Kirchenreform: Debatten des Basler Konzils im Vergleich', in Martine Ostorero et al., eds, *Chasses aux sorcières et démonologie: Entre discours et pratiques*, Florence: SISMEL-Edizioni del Galuzzo, 2010, pp. 169–97; Michael D. Bailey and Edward E. Peters, 'A Sabbat of Demonologists: Basel, 1431–1440', *The Historian*, 2003, vol. 65/6, 1375–95.
8 Jacques Paviot, *Les Ducs de Bourgogne, la croisade et l'Orient: Fin XIV$^e$ siècle, XV$^e$ siècle*, Paris: Presses de l'Université de Paris-Sorbonne, 2002, pp. 117–48; Anne-

Brigitte Spitzbarth, *Ambassades et ambassadeurs de Philippe le Bon, troisième duc de Valois Bourgogne, 1419–1467*, Turnhout: Brepols, 2013, pp. 107, 238, 390, 399, 447.
9 Mercier and Ostorero, *L'Énigme de la Vauderie de Lyon*, chaps 4–5.
10 Franck Mercier, *La Vauderie d'Arras: Une Chasse aux sorcières à l'Automne du Moyen Age*, Rennes: Presses Universitaires de Rennes, 2006.
11 Matthew Champion, 'Black and White: Dominican Reform and Heretical Inversion in the Fifteenth-Century Low Countries', in Cornelia Linde, ed., *Making and Breaking the Rules: Discussion, Implementation, and Consequences of Dominican Legislation*, Oxford: Oxford University Press, 2018, pp. 131–49; Albert de Meyer, *La Congrégation de Hollande ou la Réforme dominicaine en territoire bourguignon, 1465–1515*, Liège: Soledi, 1946. Daniel-Antonin Mortier, *Histoire des maîtres généraux de l'ordre des Frères Prêcheurs*, Paris: A. Picard, 1909, vol. 4, pp. 445–51.
12 Tamar Herzig, 'Female Mysticism, Heterodoxy, and Reform' in James D. Mixson and Bert Roest, eds, *A Companion to Observant Reform in the Late Middle Ages and Beyond*, Leiden: Brill 2015, pp. 255–82.
13 Marina Montesano, *Classical Culture and Witchcraft in Medieval and Renaissance Italy*, London: Palgrave MacMillan 2018; Fabrizio Conti, *Witchcraft, Superstition, and Observant Franciscan Preachers: Pastoral Approach and Intellectual Debate in Renaissance Milan*, Turnhout: Brepols, 2015; Michael D. Bailey, *Battling Demons: Witchcraft, Heresy and Reform in the Late Middle Ages*, University Park, PA: Pennsylvania University Press, 2003.
14 Martine Ostorero, 'Vérités diaboliques et puissance divine: Le *De calcatione demonum seu malignorum spirituum* (1457), une première réflexion de Nicolas Jacquier concernant les démons et la sorcellerie', in Martine Ostorero and Julien Véronèse, eds, *Penser avec les démons: Démonologues et démonologies, XIII$^e$–XVII$^e$ siècles*, Florence: SISMEL–Edizioni del Galuzzo, 2015, pp. 81–120.
15 Martine Ostorero, 'Un Prédicateur au cachot: Guillaume Adeline et le sabbat', *Médiévales*, 2003, vol. 44, 73–96; Ostorero, *Le Diable au sabbat*, pp. 649–66.
16 Florence Chave-Mahir, *L'Exorcisme des possédés dans l'Église d'Occident, X$^e$–XIV$^e$ siècle*, Turnhout: Brepols, 2011, pp. 217–41, 265–66.
17 Ostorero, *Le Diable au sabbat*, pp. 152–163. List of manuscripts: Brussels, Bibliothèque royale, MS 11,441–43, fols 85r–138r; Brussels, Bibliothèque royale, MS 733–41, fols 13v–53v; London, British Library, Add. 41,619, fols 19r–81r; Lyon, Bibliothèque municipale, MS 721, fols 1r–62r; Saint-Omer, Bibliothèque municipale, MS 295, fol. 67r–151v; Sion, Chapter Archive, MS 75, fols 1r–105v; Trier, Stadtbibliothek, MS 613, fol. 51r–73r; Vatican, Biblioteca Apostolica Vaticana, Reg. lat. 1008, fols 1r–62v; Wroclaw, Bibl. Uniw, MS I Q 97, fols 26r–103r. The 1581 printed edition appeared in Frankfurt with Nicolaus Bassaeus.
18 Martine Ostorero, 'Comment communiquer et diffuser le "crime" de sorcellerie et le sabbat au XV$^e$ siècle? L'Exemple des *Errores gazariorum* et du *Flagellum hereticorum fascinariorum* de Nicolas Jacquier', in Heinz Sieburg et al., eds, *Hexenwissen: Zum Transfer von Magie- und Zauberei-Imaginationen in interdisziplinärer Perspektive*, Trier: Paulinus-Verlag, 2017, pp. 61–83; Céline van Hoorebeeck, *Livres et lectures des fonctionnaires des ducs de Bourgogne*, Turnhout: Brepols, 2014, pp. 92–8.
19 The earliest known version is recorded by Regino of Prüm in his *Synodal Causes* (canon 371, c. 906), after which it recurs in compilations by Burchard of Worms (c. 1020) and Yves de Chartres (1091–1095), before being incorporated by Gratian in his authoritative *Decretum* in the mid twelfth century. See the Latin edition: C. 26, q. 5, c. 12, in Emil Friedberg, ed., *Corpus iuris canonici*, Leipzig: Tauchnitz, 1879–1881, vol. 1, col. 1030–1031; and the English translation in:

P. G. Maxwell-Stuart, *Witch Beliefs and Witch Trials in the Middle Ages: Documents and Readings*, London: Continuum, 2011, pp. 47–8.
20 Ostorero, *Le Diable au sabbat*, pp. 567–720.
21 Joseph Hansen, *Quellen und Untersuchungen zur Geschichte des Hexenwahns und der Hexenverfolgung im Mittelalter*, Bonn: Carl Georgi, 1901, pp. 136–40 (extracts); Ostorero, *Le Diable au sabbat*, pp. 621–34; Matthew Champion, 'Crushing the Canon: Nicolas Jacquier's Response to the Canon Episcopi in the *Flagellum haereticorum fascinariorum*', *Magic, Witchcraft, Ritual*, 2011, vol. 6/2, 183–211.
22 Thomas Aquinas, *Summa theologiae*, prima pars, q. 50–59; Aquinas, *De malo*, q. 3, art. 4 and q. 16; Aquinas, *De demonibus*, art. 1; Aquinas, *De potestate Dei*, q. 6, art. 7, resp. and sol. ad 20 art; Ostorero, *Le Diable au sabbat*, pp. 214–32, 307–23.
23 Alain Boureau, 'Le sabbat et la question scolastique de la personne', in Nicole Jacques-Chaquin et al., eds, *Le Sabbat des sorciers, XV$^e$–XVIII$^e$ siècles: Actes du colloque international de l'E.N.S. de Fontenay/Saint-Cloud (4–7 novembre 1992)*, Grenoble: Jérôme Millon, 1993, pp. 33–46; Christine Pigné, 'Du *De malo* au *Malleus Maleficarum*: Les Conséquences de la démonologie thomiste sur le corps de la sorcière', *Cahiers de recherches médiévales*, 2006, vol. 13, 2006, 195–220.
24 Nicolas Jacquier, *Flagellum*, chap. 3 (Brussels, Bibliothèque royale, MS 11,441–43, fol. 88r). Ostorero, *Le Diable au sabbat*, pp. 298–313, 342–44; Martine Ostorero, 'Meeting the Devil, Facing the Invisible: Sensory Perception and Emotions in Fifteenth-Century Swiss-French Record', in Sophie Page et al., eds, *Living in a Magical World: Inner Lives, 1300–1900*, Basingstoke: Palgrave Macmillan, forthcoming.
25 Jacquier, *Flagellum*, chap. 6 (Brussels, Bibliothèque royale, MS 11,441–43, fol. 95r).
26 Ostorero, *Le Diable au sabbat*, pp. 265–72.
27 Jacquier, *Flagellum*, chap. 6 (Brussels, Bibliothèque royale, ms 11,441–43, fol. 131v).
28 Ostorero, *Le Diable au sabbat*, pp. 387–400; Walter Stephens, *Demon Lovers: Witchcraft, Sex, and the Crisis of Belief*, Chicago: University of Chicago Press, 2002, pp. 13–26.
29 Ostorero, *Le Diable au sabbat*, pp. 755–56.
30 Ostorero, *Le Diable au sabbat*, pp. 460–70, 480–501.
31 Mercier and Ostorero, *L'Énigme de la Vauderie de Lyon*, pp. 99–100; Alessia Belli and Astrid Estuardo Flaction, *Striges et lamies en Italie du Nord: Édition critique et commentaire des traités de démonologie et sorcellerie de Girolamo Visconti, Milan, c. 1460, et de Bernard Rategno, Côme, c. 1510*, Florence, SISMEL–Edizioni del Galluzzo, 2019; Martine Ostorero, 'Crimes et sanctions dans la répression de la sorcellerie à la fin du Moyen Âge: Une Étude des sentences prononcées contre les inculpés, ACV, Ac 29', *Revue historique vaudoise*, 2010, vol. 118, 17–33.
32 Jacquier, *Flagellum*, chap. 27.
33 Ostorero et al., *L'Imaginaire du sabbat*, pp. 355–438.
34 Jean-Patrice Boudet, *Entre science et 'nigromance': Astrologie, divination et magie dans l'Occident médiéval, XII$^e$–XV$^e$ siècle*, Paris: Publ. de la Sorbonne, 2006, pp. 498–99; Claude Gauvard, *'De Grace especial': Crime, état et société en France à la fin du Moyen Age*, Paris: Publ. de la Sorbonne, 1991, pp. 895–935.
35 Mercier and Ostorero, *L'Énigme de la Vauderie de Lyon*, pp. 348–59; Franck Mercier, 'D'une Vauderie l'autre: Les Clés de la réussite ou de l'échec d'une persécution contre la sorcellerie en territoire urbain à Lyon (v. 1440) et à Arras (v. 1460)', in Antoine Follain, Maryse Simon, eds, *La Sorcellerie et la ville/ Witchcraft and the City*, Strasbourg: Presses universitaires de Strasbourg, 2018, pp. 31–50.

36 Hansen, *Quellen*, pp. 149–81; Andrew C. Gow et al., eds and trans., *The Arras Witch Treatises*, University Park, PA: Pennsylvania State University Press, 2016, pp. 19–79.
37 Mercier, *La Vauderie d'Arras*, pp. 64–66, 279–300, and *passim*; Ostorero, *Le Diable au sabbat*, pp. 480–90, 498–501.
38 Franck Mercier, 'Limiter l'hérésie? Un Discours de résistance face à l'inquisition et au sabbat des sorcières: Le *Tractatus de haeresi* d'Ambroise de Vignate (vers 1468)', in Martine Ostorero and Sylvain Parent, eds, *Résister à l'Inquisition, XIII$^e$–XV$^e$ siècle*, Rennes: Presses Universitaires de Rennes, forthcoming; Matteo Duni, 'Doubting Witchcraft: Theologians, Jurists, Inquisitors during the Fifteenth and Sixteenth Centuries', *Studies in Church History*, 2016, vol. 52, 203–31.
39 Franck Mercier and I are currently working on a study of this treatise, its development, and its dissemination.

## Further reading

Champion, Matthew, 'Crushing the Canon: Nicolas Jacquier's Response to the Canon Episcopi in the *Flagellum haereticorum fascinariorum*', *Magic, Witchcraft, Ritual*, 2011, vol. 6/2, 183–211.

Champion, Matthew, 'Scourging the Temple of God: Towards an Understanding of Nicolas Jacquier's *Flagellum haereticorum fascinariorum* (1458)', *Parergon*, 2011, vol. 28/1, 1–24.

Mercier, Franck and Martine Ostorero, *L'Énigme de la Vauderie de Lyon: Enquête sur l'essor des chasses aux sorcières entre France et Empire, 1430–1480*, Florence: SISMEL–Edizioni del Galuzzo, 2015.

Ostorero, Martine et al., eds, *L'Imaginaire du sabbat: Édition critique des textes les plus anciens, 1430 c.–1440 c.*, Lausanne: Université de Lausanne, 1999.

Ostorero, Martine, *Le Diable au sabbat: Littérature démonologique et sorcellerie, 1440–1460*, Florence: SISMEL-Edizioni del Galuzzo, 2011.

Part 2

# The first wave of printed witchcraft texts

# 3 The bestselling demonologist
## Heinrich Institoris's *Malleus maleficarum*

*Tamar Herzig*

In the latter half of the fifteenth century there was a marked proliferation of treatises specifically devoted to witchcraft, employing the great corpus of authority to establish the reality of a perverted magical conspiracy. The most important of these manuals, both in scope and practicality, was the *Malleus Maleficarum*.[1]

This claim was made in 1977, in Sydney Anglo's opening essay in *The Damned Art: Essays in the Literature of Witchcraft* – a pioneering collection of essays that, among its other merits, has served as an inspiration for the present volume. More than forty years later, the *Malleus maleficarum* (The Hammer of [Female] Witches) remains the best-known demonological tract of the premodern era.[2] Intensive research in the decades following the publication of *The Damned Art* has helped to discern the medieval roots of the main claims put forward in the *Malleus*, reinforcing Anglo's suggestion that the work's importance lies in its fatal combination of 'unoriginality, popularity, and influence.'[3] At the same time, however, the *Malleus* continues to be regarded as a work that 'became enshrined as the most popular model for demonological writings, evolving into one of the central texts of the European witchcraft prosecutions.'[4]

## 1 Biographical context

Assembled hastily in the course of about nine months in 1486, the *Malleus* was first published by the printing house of Peter Drach in Speyer, without a title page. The apologetic foreword to the 1487 edition (*Apologia auctoris in Malleum Maleficarum*) presented the tract as co-written by two Dominican inquisitors, Heinrich Kramer, better known by the Latinized name Institoris (literally, shopkeeper, d. *c.*1505), and Jakob Sprenger (*c.*1436/1438–1492).[5] Based on modern historical research, though, most scholars now agree that the Alsatian friar Institoris was the book's main author, and that he was the driving force behind the work's composition and publication.[6]

There is no certain information about the first decades of Institoris/ Kramer's life. Born in Schlettstadt (Sélestat) around 1430, he spent a considerable part of his lifetime on the Italian peninsula.[7] Nothing is known of the circumstances of his entry into the Dominican order. Nonetheless, he had no doubt been involved in refuting the heterodox tenets attributed to dissenting religious groups and individual heretics, as well as in anti-Jewish and anti-Muslim activities, already prior to his appointment as inquisitor of Upper Germany in 1479.[8]

The inquisitor first expressed his concern with diabolic witches, whom he regarded as one of several groups partaking in the devil's conspiracy to undermine Christendom, in a letter that he addressed to Pope Sixtus IV in 1484.[9] Although he later boasted of having been responsible for the public execution of more than two hundred witches, extant documentation suggests that these claims were greatly exaggerated. Institoris appears to have been personally involved only in the witch trials that erupted in Ravensburg in 1484 and in Innsbruck in 1485.[10]

In Ravensburg, the Alsatian friar enjoyed the support of the city council, but when he attempted to initiate witch-hunting elsewhere in the Rhineland he met with considerable opposition. In the winter of 1484 he journeyed to Rome, to request a papal bull in favour of himself and of his fellow inquisitor Jakob Sprenger in their prosecution of witches. Innocent VIII (r. 1484–1492) granted Institoris this request and issued the infamous 'witch bull' *Summis desiderantes affectibus* (Desiring with Greatest Ardor) which affirmed the reality of the witches' crimes and stressed inquisitors' obligation to prosecute them.[11]

Armed with the papal bull, in the summer of 1485 Institoris attempted to launch a paradigmatic witch-hunt at Innsbruck. After the local bishop dutifully published the *Summis desiderantes affectibus*, Institoris began preaching sermons urging the populace to denounce suspected witches.[12] Several women were arrested, and the inquisitor began questioning them about their sexual history, employing dubious interrogation methods that aroused criticism from local opponents of his witch-hunting crusade. Charged with procedural irregularities, the Alsatian friar was soon ordered to leave the diocese.

Institoris retired to a friary, where he consulted various classical, theological, and judicial works, including the writings of Dominican luminaries Thomas Aquinas (d. 1274), Nicolau Eymeric° (*c*.1320–1399), Johannes Nider (1380–1438), and Antonino Pierozzi (St Antoninus of Florence, 1389–1459). Relying on their authoritative works and on his own notes about the prosecution of witches at Innsbruck, Institoris composed the *Malleus maleficarum*, a handbook for judges in cases of witchcraft. The text was delivered to the printing house in late 1486. The seasoned inquisitor apparently hoped that the *Malleus* would help to prevent future debacles – like the one he had experienced in Innsbruck – by employing the new technology of printing for propagating the recently developed demonological theory, which stressed the reality of the witches' horrendous transgressions.

From May 1487 onwards, editions of the *Malleus* included the *Summis desiderantes affectibus* as well as an approval (*Approbatio*) by professors from the University of Cologne's faculty of theology. The *Approbatio* was aimed to vouch for the work's orthodoxy and certify its conformity to Scholastic theology, while the inclusion of the 'witch bull' served to create the impression that the pope himself validated the tract's main arguments. The incorporation of both texts undoubtedly increased the *Malleus*'s appeal.[13] Institoris was evidently well aware of this. Thus, when in 1501 he published another polemical tract, he likewise prefaced it with a papal bull.[14]

A bestseller by early modern standards, the *Malleus* was issued in no fewer than twelve editions before 1523. Before the end of the seventeenth century, it was reprinted more than thirty times. Circulating in large format Latin editions, the *Malleus* appealed to clergymen as well as to learned magistrates and other lay readers, shaping early modern demonological discourse and serving as an authoritative reference for witch-hunters and sceptics alike.[15]

## 2 Structure and main arguments

Institoris divided his tract into three parts and devoted the first to theological questions pertaining to witchcraft. Drawing on traditional Thomistic theology, he argues that the witches derive their power to harm from their pact with the Evil One. He insists that humans enter such pacts of their own free will, albeit with divine permission. Although witches cannot cause physical harm on their own, the diabolic entities who collaborated with them can intervene supernaturally, inflicting damage in ways that may seem to be real. Thus, even though witches might believe that they cast spells of harmful magic, this is actually performed by demons. The witches' explicit pact with the devil is the cause for their ceaseless attempts to insult God, the creator of the universe, by harming his creations.

Institoris maintains that all witches are heretics who renounce the Christian faith. Nonetheless, the *Malleus* portrays the witches' role in the diabolic plot to destroy Christendom as radically different from that played by all the other heretical groups. As Institoris contends, the devil

> [A]ttacks through these heresies at that time in particular, when the evening of the world declines towards its setting and the evil of men swells up, since he knows in great anger, as John bears witness in the Book of Apocalypse [12:12], that he has little time remaining. Hence, he has also caused a certain unusual heretical perversity to grow up in the land of the Lord – a heresy, I say, of [female] witches (*maleficarum*), since it is to be designated by the particular sex over which he is known to have power. He contrives these things through countless forms of assault, and this one is carried out in the form of individual works. This is clearly daunting to conceive of, exceedingly loathsome to God and hateful to all believers in Christ, since in accordance with their agreement with Hell

and treaty with Death they submit themselves to the foulest slavery in return for fulfilling their filthy acts of depravity. The heresy also consists of losses that are inflicted in the form of daily misfortunes on humans, domestic animals and the fruits of the earth through the permission of God with the cooperation of demons.[16]

According to the *Malleus*, then, diabolic witchcraft is a new and unique kind of heresy: one that is manifested by causing physical damage. Hence, although all heresy is essentially spiritual, the heresy of witchcraft is expressed through the physical infliction of harm. This occurs as a result of the witches' collaboration with the devil and his minions, which turns their transgressions into real crimes that justify their public execution. If other heretics are to be prosecuted only for upholding heterodox views, witches have to be punished for their alleged deeds.

Elaborating upon the notions presented in Johannes Nider's *Formicarius* (The Anthill, c.1438) and in other earlier demonological works, Institoris avers that witches submit both their bodies and their souls to the devil. Once they enter a diabolic pact, they indulge in social crimes of the worst kinds – including the unnatural and atrocious one of devouring human babies – as well as in anti-religious transgressions against the sacraments of baptism, marriage, and the Eucharist. They worship the devil and perform blasphemous rituals, in which they deny the tenets of the Christian faith, misuse sacramental materials, and tread on the Cross.[17]

Institoris holds that the devil is capable of physically transporting witches to faraway places, where they attend nocturnal meetings of their diabolic sect. In stressing the reality of their supernatural flight, the *Malleus* distinguishes the modern sect of witches from members of the ancient cult of Diana, whose purported beliefs were refuted in the part of a law known as the canon *Episcopi* from the mid-ninth century (though assumed in the fifteenth century to have been passed by the early church Council of Ancyra/Ankara in 314). The canon *Episcopi* categorized women who believed that they could traverse great distances at night, when riding with the Goddess Diana, as heretics deluded by the devil.

Institoris explains that the sect described in his own demonological tract is a new sect of dangerous, devil-worshipping heretics, and is thus different from the cult of Diana, which the canon *Episcopi* discusses. This argument echoes the repeated papal warnings about the new sects (*novas sectas*) of sorcerers promulgated earlier in the fifteenth century (in 1409, 1418, and 1435). Institoris further declares that, with diabolic assistance, witches cast spells that may transform humans into animals. Here, too, he aims to reconcile his contention with the canon *Episcopi*, which states that such metamorphoses are entirely illusory.[18]

The second part of the *Malleus* deals with practical problems concerning the witches' misdemeanours. The Alsatian friar draws on his first-hand experience as an inquisitor who interrogated accused witches, though he also refers to late fifteenth-century witchcraft prosecutions in which he was not personally involved. About 75 of the 250 examples discussed in the *Malleus* pertain to recent cases. Many of them are from the area around Speyer, where the author may have completed his witch hunters' guide, but others are from other places that Institoris had visited in the past, including the regions of Alsace, Tyrol, Swabia, and the cities of Augsburg, Salzburg, Landshut, Cologne, and Rome.

The *Malleus* surveys different types of common *maleficia*, from destructive hailstorms to harming domestic animals and causing the disease or death of adults, and especially of infants. Witches, Institoris makes clear, are particularly intent on the obstruction of sexual relations between married spouses and on impeding the conception and birth of legitimate babies. They achieve their aims by causing male impotence, virtual castration, and miscarriages. If a healthy baby is born to a married couple, the witches strive to prevent his or her baptism and offer the child to the devil. Yet, the Evil One also teaches witches the healing arts, so that they are able to profit financially from curing the illnesses that they inflict. Institoris cautions his readers not to seek the aid of sorcerers for undoing evil spells. Instead, he lists various means of protection against bewitchment, as well as orthodox methods of curing maladies caused by witchcraft.[19]

The third part of the *Malleus* contains legal advice on how to proceed against suspected witches. In discussing judicial aspects, its author draws heavily on Nicolau Eymeric's inquisitorial handbook, *Directorium inquisitorum* (Guide to Inquisitors, 1376). Institoris favours the adoption of the inquisitorial procedure in witchcraft cases and maintains that normal legal precautions should be abandoned in prosecuting alleged witches, because of witchcraft's occult and especially heinous nature. Thus, whereas the first two parts of the *Malleus* elaborated upon theological notions that fifteenth-century authors had already advocated earlier, the insistence, in the tract's third part, that witchcraft should be prosecuted as an exceptional crime (*crimen exceptum*) was quite novel.

The fiasco at Innsbruck had made it clear to the Alsatian demonologist that papal inquisitors alone were unable to deal with the complexities of pursuing accused witches, because this required the firm support of local secular authorities. He was therefore willing to turn witchcraft trials over to civil courts that would employ the inquisitorial procedure. Emphasizing the social dimensions of the witches' horrendous transgressions, Institoris thereby broke with ecclesiastical authorities' earlier insistence on the Inquisition's jurisdiction in cases of magic.[20]

## 3 The *Malleus*'s diatribe against the female sex

Arguably the most misogynistic text to appear in print in premodern times, the *Malleus* owes much of its notoriety to its virulent tirade against the female sex.[21] In the second half of the twentieth century, second-wave feminists presented the *Malleus* in their writings as the epitome of woman-hating, which they regarded as the principal motive for witch-hunting.[22] Hence, American radical feminist writer Andrea Dworkin (1946–2005) portrayed the *Malleus*'s 'frenzied and psychotic woman-hating' as emblematic of the Church's fear of female sexuality, which brought about the witch craze of the early modern era.[23]

The tract's title, *Malleus maleficarum* (The Hammer of [Female] Witches) certainly conveys its author's presumption that witchcraft is essentially a female crime. Although the existence of male witches is acknowledged in the *Malleus*, it is pointedly minimized. When referring to men who engage in magical practices, Institoris designates them as *superstitiosi* or *magi* rather than as male witches (*malefici*).[24] On the other hand, he dedicates an entire section (*Quaestio* 6 in *Pars* 1) of the *Malleus* to expounding women's predominance in the sect of witches.[25] In this section, Institoris asserts that witchcraft results mainly from women's inability to restrain their passions. He adds that the female sex is by nature weaker than the male sex not only physically, but also morally and intellectually. Echoing contemporary medical notions, the Dominican author presents women's carnal appetite not only as far greater than that of men, but also as insatiable, and argues that it accounts for women's preponderance in the diabolic sect.[26]

The mechanisms of demonic copulation, which forms part of the efforts to prove the reality of demons in the *Malleus*, are detailed at great length. Institoris states that women find having sexual intercourse with demons in the shape of men (*incubi*) as pleasurable as copulating with humans. Relying on Thomas Aquinas's treatment of demonic conception, Institoris affirms that *incubi* may impregnate female witches, by using semen obtained from humans.[27] Although he concedes the possibility of men's sexual relations with demons in the shape of women (*succubi*), Institoris insists that men are naturally not as prone to such 'filthiness' as women are.[28]

In 1978, French historian Jean Delumeau characterized Institoris's attack on women in the *Malleus* as a reflection of a chaste friar's anxiety over female sexuality.[29] While some scholars have accepted this explanation,[30] others have proposed different understandings of the *Malleus*'s apparent preoccupation with the female sex. Thus, in 1998 Walter Stephens provocatively argued that the notorious tract 'betrays no fear of feminine power, but rather a will to prove such power exists; not a simple hatred of female sexuality, but rather a desire to appropriate and exploit women's real or imagined potential.'[31] However, in a 2003 monograph devoted to the *Malleus* Hans Peter Broedel suggests:

> [b]oth masculinity and social order are defined against a rigidly controlled, powerfully sexualized notion of femininity; anxiety about the stability of these structures expresses itself … , as in the *Malleus*, in terms of fears of occult harm and deviant sexuality.[32]

The close of the twentieth century also saw a shifting of scholarly attention from Institoris's views of women as slaves to their sexual desires to the demonologist's attitude toward female spiritual powers. Specialists of medieval religious and gender history have interpreted the configuration of witchcraft in the *Malleus* as the apogee of escalating ecclesiastical anxiety over the somatic spirituality and public prestige of charismatic holy women in the last centuries of the Middle Ages. In Institoris's invective against women, so their argument goes, the apprehension of clerical men vis-à-vis the increased social and political influence of saintly female mystics in the fourteenth and fifteenth centuries reached its climax.[33]

In his discussion of the female sex in the *Malleus*, Institoris avows that women's minds are naturally more impressionable than the minds of men. As a result, the female mind is more susceptible to the influence of disembodied spirits. This assertion is based on the presumption that, because of women's moist and cool bodily humours, they receive impressions more easily, retain them better, and are not as capable of critically evaluating them as are their male counterparts.[34] The Dominican author admits that women may receive and retain impressions whose origin is not diabolical. Indeed, he even concedes that devout women use the quality of their greater impressionability *well*, remarking: '[women] are by nature more easily impressed upon to receive revelations through the impression of the disembodied spirits, and when they use this temperament well, they are very good, but when they use it badly, they are worse.'[35]

Historians have often emphasized the first part of this claim, dismissing the part in which Institoris exclaims that women tend to be *either* extremely good or very evil as mere rhetoric.[36] Nonetheless, the concerted attention that Institoris devoted to the supernatural experiences of pious women in the works that he published after the completion of the *Malleus* indicate that his acknowledgment of pious women's ability to become 'very good' when receiving the influence of a disembodied spirit was, indeed, far from rhetorical. Moreover, a close reading of his *entire* corpus, authored in the course of a long inquisitorial career, reveals that whereas Institoris held witchcraft to be a predominantly female heresy, he regarded men as the ones primarily guilty of doctrinal heterodoxy.[37]

## 4 Witchcraft, heresy, and female holiness in Heinrich Institoris's oeuvre

Institoris published his earliest known work, *Epistola contra quendam conciliistam archiepiscopem videlicet Crainensem* (Epistle against a Certain Conciliarist Archbishop, namely the Archbishop of the Craina), in 1482.[38] This brief treatise was directed against Andrea Jamometić of the Craina (d. 1484), a Dominican Archbishop who endeavoured to summon an anti-papal Church council. In his *Epistola*, Institoris stressed the threat posed by learned men such as Jamometić who espoused heretical Conciliarist views.[39] Similarly, in

1493, seven years after the publication of the *Malleus*, Institoris penned his *Tractatus novus de miraculoso eucharistie sacramento* (A New Tract Concerning the Miraculous Sacrament of the Eucharist). In this work, he condemned the doctrinal errors of Berengar of Tours (d. 1088), another man who had been accused of heresy.[40]

In a 1496 publication, *Tractatus varii contra errores adversus eucharistie sacramentum exortos* (Various Tracts against the Errors Appearing against the Sacrament of the Eucharist), Institoris explained that all heterodox groups who strayed from the Catholic faith originated with intellectual male founders, who rebelled against the Church and founded their own sects. The Alsatian witch-hunter once again decried the doctrinal errors of Berengar in his *Tractatus varii*, and also disparaged the tenets presumably held by the thirteenth-century heretic Guido Lacha of Brescia and by a few other (unnamed) male heretics.[41] Three years later, in 1499, Institoris issued his *Opusculum in errores 'Monarchie'* (Small Work against the Errors of the 'Monarchia'), in which he censured the views of another erudite man: the celebrated jurist Antonio de' Roselli (1381–1466), who had challenged papal supremacy. In the *Opusculum*, Institoris restated his anti-Conciliarist views and designated all men who attempted to detract from the pope's absolute authority – whether in spiritual or in temporal matters – as heretics. He further associated Roselli with well-known heterodox men, such as the Waldensian (and philo-Hussite) Bishop Friedrich Reiser (d. 1458).[42]

Institoris was doubtlessly aware of women's attraction to dissenting religious groups, such as the one centred around Reiser in mid-fifteenth-century Strasburg.[43] Indeed, the indefatigable inquisitor was actually involved in questioning the lay female followers of canon Johannes Molitoris (d. 1482), who in 1480 was suspected of heterodox practices while administering daily communion in Augsburg.[44] Notwithstanding these personal experiences, in his published tracts Institoris sought to downplay women's involvement in heretical sects. The Dominican friar evidently perceived doctrinal heresy – which involved learning, writing, or preaching – as inherently a male affair. As such, it was very different from diabolic witchcraft, which Institoris depicted in his writings as a physically-manifested female heresy.

Not long after the publication of his *Opusculum*, Pope Alexander VI (r. 1492–1503) charged Institoris with prosecuting Hussite groups in the Kingdom of Bohemia. The by-now elderly inquisitor was particularly concerned with the sect known as the Bohemian Brethren (*Unitas fratrum*) or 'Pikarts', regarded by Catholic authorities as a Waldensian offshoot, who had split off from the Utraquists.[45] In 1501, Institoris issued his most influential polemical work against religious dissent, titled *Sancte Romane Ecclesie fidei defensionis clippeum adversus Waldensium seu Pikardorum heresim* (A Shield to Defend the Holy Roman Church against the Heresy of the Pikards or Waldensians).[46] In this work, Institoris portrays the Bohemian Brethren as a heretical group that is closely linked to witches, because both sects partake in a diabolic conspiracy to harm the Catholic Church. According to

Institoris, the devil employs (female) witches who perform demonic deeds, but uses (male) heretics, such as the Bohemian Brethren, for propagating heterodox doctrines that undermine the true faith.[47] Although this gendered division of labour attests to the author's presumptions about women's greater propensity to witchcraft, it also reflects his enduring concern over the potential menace posed by male-led heretical movements. The distinction between the predominantly male members of dissident sects and the female practitioners of diabolic magic also represents a significant moment in the process of the feminization of witchcraft, which had begun in the early 1400s and lasted for about a century.

During the first mass witchcraft trials of the fifteenth century, the accused were prosecuted for practicing malevolent magic as well as for upholding heterodox ('Waldensian') beliefs, and were mostly male.[48] At that time and in subsequent decades, demonologists such as the Dominicans Johannes Nider and Nicholas Jacquier° (d. 1472) continued to assume that men filled roles of leadership within the witches' sect.[49] They still found the idea of women who willingly made a pact with the devil quite astonishing.[50] Thus, even though Nider noted women's greater propensity to witchcraft, the principal witches whose crimes he discussed were male – namely, the male witches Hoppo and Scavius, and another man called Staedelin.[51] Significantly, in his reworking of key episodes from the *Formicarius* in the *Malleus*, Institoris strove to impute to female witches the crimes that Nider had attributed to specific male witches.[52]

Whereas the *Formicarius* bears witness to clerical discomfort surrounding the possibility of female witches' entering into a diabolic pact – which supposedly involves both intellect and will – Institoris attempts to tone down the spiritual aspects of witchcraft.[53] To his mind, witchcraft is a unique kind of heresy; expressed primarily by means of physical damage, it is particularly suited for depraved women. The very qualities that render wicked women more prone to witchcraft, however, may also turn pious women into the privileged conduits for divine revelations that can serve to confirm Catholic dogma. Hence, twelve folio pages of Institoris's *Clippeum* were dedicated to the spiritual experiences of contemporary Italian holy women Stefana Quinzani (1457–1530), Colomba of Rieti (1467–1501), and the stigmatic Lucia Brocadelli (1476–1544), whom Institoris met in 1500 when visiting Ferrara (in northern Italy).

The three saintly women's spiritual experiences are presented in the *Clippeum* as the most potent means of warding off the doctrinal threats posed by male-led heretical sects such as the Bohemian Brethren. As far as Institoris is concerned, only women – precisely because they are incapable of critically evaluating the images that influence their minds – can reach a perfect degree of *imitatio Christi*. Thus, thinking of the Passion of Christ could leave such an impression on Lucia Brocadelli's mind that she actually received the marks of the stigmata on her own body. In a similar manner Stefana Quinzani, who used to pray in front of a Crucifix on Fridays, entered a state of ecstasy, in which she physically relived the Passion of Jesus and the suffering of his cruel death on the Cross. Contemplating the real presence of Christ in the consecrated host at Mass likewise had such a profound impact on Colomba of Rieti's mind that she immediately underwent a mystical rapture.[54]

A few months after completing the *Clippeum*, Institoris compiled his last published work. A pamphlet of nine unpaginated leaves, it was titled *Stigmifere virginis Lucie de Narnia aliarumque spiritualium personarum feminei sexus facta admiracione digna* (Deeds of the Stigmatic Virgin Lucia of Narni and of Other Spiritual Persons of the Female Sex that are Worthy of Admiration). The *Stigmifere* was issued in Olomouc on 16 September 1501 and several abridged and translated editions were printed in different parts of Europe between 1501–1502.[55] Several documents that Institoris had received from Brocadelli's admirers in Ferrara were incorporated into the *Stigmifere*, including a letter written by Cardinal Ippolito I d'Este (1479–1520). In this text, the cardinal expressed his amazement at the miracle of Brocadelli's reception of the stigmata: 'What am I saying? [That] with these holy wounds and admirable stigmata, which He suffered in His own body for the redemption of humanity, Jesus Christ transformed Himself into a virgin woman.'[56] This statement echoed the representations of both Francis of Assisi (d. 1226) and Catherine of Siena (1347–1380) as saintly individuals who had been transfigured into Jesus at the moment of their stigmatization. Just like St Francis and St Catherine, Brocadelli was portrayed as united to Christ in soul and body, becoming one and the same as Him. Interestingly, though, it was not the holy woman who was being transformed into Jesus; rather, the Saviour was the one being transformed, as He turned Himself into a virgin woman. This affirmation contrasted with the predominant late medieval notion that Jesus had been incarnated as a man, and not as a woman, because the male sex was the more honourable one.[57] It is worth noting that even though Institoris omitted other sentences from Ippolito d'Este's letter when incorporating it into the *Stigmifere*, he left this unusual statement intact.[58] Thus, by publishing the cardinal's letter, Institoris propagated the remarkable notion that a flesh and blood woman, who was still alive at the time of the pamphlet's publication, should be revered as a reincarnated Christ.

## 5 Concluding remarks

In the *Malleus*, the twofold process of the feminization and diabolization of witchcraft, which had already found an expression in the writings of earlier fifteenth-century demonologists, reached its peak. Institoris's successful employment of the new technology of print to disseminate the belief in a dangerous, diabolic sect of female witches therefore marked a significant turning point in the evolution of European demonology. The characterization of witchcraft in his bestselling tract as an essentially feminine crime played an important role in reinforcing the misogynistic stereotype of the female witch, shaping the gendering of demonological discourse throughout the sixteenth and seventeenth centuries.

As argued in this essay, though, the friar who vilified the female sex in the *Malleus* also expressed his admiration for women whose unrestrained impressionability enabled them to attain a mystical union with Christ for which no man could ever aspire. Moreover, although he is remembered today mainly as the author of a tract against female witches, most of Institoris's writings were actually directed against heretical men. Alarmed by the proliferation of male-led heterodox groups, he exalted the emaciated bodies of ascetic women mystics as important corroborations for the contested tenets of orthodox Catholicism. Institoris's documented preoccupation with women's bodies, then, cannot be explained only as the result of a chaste friar's fear of female sexuality. He unquestionably assumed that women were more carnal than men. Nonetheless, a close reading of the *Malleus* in tandem with the inquisitor's six other works shows that he perceived diabolic witchcraft and female mystical holiness to be two sides of the same coin, regarding both phenomena as closely related to women's bodies.

## Notes

1 Sydney Anglo, 'Evident Authority and Authoritative Evidence: *The Malleus Maleficarum*', in Sydney Anglo, ed., *The Damned Art: Essays in the Literature of Witchcraft*, London: Routledge, 1977, pp. 1–31, at 14.
   This chapter draws on some of the ideas elaborated in Tamar Herzig, *Christ Transformed into a Virgin Woman: Lucia Brocadelli, Heinrich Institoris, and the Defense of the Faith*, Rome: Storia e Letteratura, 2013, where readers may also find further bibliographic references pertaining to the topics discussed in the present chapter. I thank Ori Ben-Shalom for his assistance and Jan Machielsen for his helpful suggestions.
2 In 2010, National Geographic produced the documentary *Witch Hunter's Bible*, featuring interviews with leading scholars of the *Malleus* (www.natgeotv.com/int/witch-hunters-bible). See also Edward Peters, 'The Medieval Church and State on Superstition, Magic and Witchcraft: From Augustine to the Sixteenth Century', in Karen Jolly, Catharina Raudvere and Edward Peters, eds, *Witchcraft and Magic in Europe, vol. 3: The Middle Ages*, London: Athlone Press, 2002, pp. 173–245, 239; Hans Peter Broedel, 'To Preserve the Manly Form from So Vile a Crime: Ecclesiastical Anti-Sodomitic Rhetoric and the Gendering of Witchcraft in the *Malleus Maleficarum*', *Essays in Medieval Studies*, 2002, vol. 19, 136–48, at 136.
3 Anglo, 'Evident Authority', p. 14.
4 Gerhild Scholz Williams, 'Demonologies', in Brian P. Levack, ed., *The Oxford Handbook of Witchcraft in Early Modern Europe and Colonial America*, Oxford: Oxford University Press, 2013, pp. 69–83, at 74. See also Hans Peter Broedel, 'Fifteenth-Century Witch Beliefs', in ibid., pp. 32–49, at 46.
5 For Institoris's life and works, see Tamar Herzig, *Christ Transformed into a Virgin Woman: Lucia Brocadelli, Heinrich Institoris, and the Defense of the Faith*, Rome: Storia e Letteratura, 2013, pp. 3–82.
6 Wolfgang Behringer, '*Malleus Maleficarum*', in Richard M. Golden, ed., *Encyclopedia of Witchcraft: The Western Tradition*, Santa Barbara, CA: ABC-Clio, 2006, vol.

3, pp. 717–23; Günter Jerouschek and Wolfgang Behringer, '"Das unheilvollste Buch der Weltliteratur?" Zur Entstehungs- und Wirkungsgeschichte des *Malleus Maleficarum* und zu den Anfängen der Hexenverfolgung', in Heinrich Kramer (Institoris), *Der Hexenhammer: Malleus Maleficarum*, trans. Wolfgang Behringer et al., Munich: Deutscher Taschenbuch Verlag, 2000, pp. 9–98, at 22–40; cf. Christopher S. Mackay, 'General Introduction', in Henricus Institoris (Kramer), *Malleus Maleficarum*, ed. and trans. Christopher S. Mackay, Cambridge: Cambridge University Press, 2006, vol. 1, pp. 1–171, at 103–21.

7 Peter Segl, 'Heinrich Institoris: Persönlichkeit und literarisches werk', in Peter Segl, ed., *Der Hexenhammer: Entstehung und Umfeld des 'Malleus maleficarum' von 1487*, Cologne: Bohlau, 1988, pp. 103–26; André Schnyder, *Malleus Maleficarum: Kommentar zur Wiedergabe des Einstdrucks von 1487*, Göppingen: Kümmerle Verlag, 1993, pp. 33–73.

8 Herzig, *Christ Transformed into a Virgin Woman*, pp. 3–17.

9 Jürgen Petersohn, 'Konziliaristen und Hexen: Ein unbekannter Brief des Inquisitors Heinrich Institoris an Papst Sixtus IV. aus dem Jahre 1484', *Deutsches Archiv für Erforschung des Mittelalters*, 1988, vol. 44/1, 120–60.

10 Rudolf Endres, 'Heinrich Institoris, sein Hexenhammer und der Nürnberger Rat', in Segl, ed., *Der Hexenhammer*, pp. 195–215, at 207.

11 Klaus-Bernard Springer, 'Dominican Inquisition in the Archdiocese of Mainz (1348–1520)', in Wolfram Hoyer, ed., *Praedicatores, Inquisitores I: The Dominicans and the Medieval Inquisition (Acts of the 1st International Seminar on the Dominicans and the Inquisition, 23–25 February 2002)*, Rome: Istituto storico domenicano, 2004, pp. 311–93, at 344–49; Wolfgang Behringer, 'Heinrich Kramers Hexenhammer: Text und Kontext', in Andreas Schmauder, ed., *Frühe Hexenverfolgung in Ravensburg und am Bodensee*, Constance: UVK Verlagsgesellschaft, 2001, pp. 83–124, at 96–7; cf. Mackay, 'General Introduction', pp. 80–3.

12 Hartmann Ammann, 'Der Innsbrucker Hexenprozess von 1485', *Zeitschrift des Ferdinandeums für Tirol und Voralber*, 1890, vol. 34, 1–87.

13 Rainer Decker, *Witchcraft and the Papacy: An Account Drawing on the Formerly Secret Records of the Roman Inquisition*, trans. H. C. Erik Midelfort, Charlottesville, VA: University of Virginia Press, 2008, pp. 57–8; Mackay, 'General Introduction', pp. 127–35.

14 Henricus Institoris, *Sancte Romane Ecclesie fidei defensionis clippeum adversus Waldensium seu Pickardorum heresim*, Olomouc: Konrad Baumgarten, 1501, fols 1$^r$–4$^r$.

15 Behringer, '*Malleus Maleficarum*', pp. 721–22; Schnyder, *Malleus Maleficarum: Kommentar*, pp. 452–53; Lyndal Roper, 'Witchcraft and the Western Imagination', *Transactions of the Royal Historical Society*, Sixth Series, 2006, vol. 16, 117–41, at 123n13.

16 Henricus Institoris (Kramer), *Malleus Maleficarum*, ed. and trans. Christopher S. Mackay, Cambridge: Cambridge University Press, 2006, vol. 1, p. 207. I have slightly modified the English translation of this passage in ibid., vol. 2, pp. 28–9, for the reasons expounded in Tamar Herzig, 'Review of *Malleus maleficarum*, ed. and trans. Christopher S. Mackay', in *Magic, Ritual, and Witchcraft*, 2010, vol. 5/1, 135–38.

17 On the notion of witchcraft as a 'countersacrament' in the *Malleus*, see Walter Stephens, *Demon Lovers: Witchcraft, Sex, and the Crisis of Belief*, Chicago: University of Chicago Press, 2002, pp. 198–99.

18 Institoris, *Malleus Maleficarum*, ed. Mackay, vol. 1, pp. 217–29, 321–30, 362–63 (see also pp. 403–11), and see Stephens, *Demon Lovers*, pp. 125–31, 140–43.

19 Institoris, *Malleus Maleficarum*, ed. Mackay, vol. 1, esp. pp. 428–34, 455–82.

20 See Günter Jerouschek, '500 Years of the *Malleus Maleficarum*', in Günter Jerouschek, ed., *Malleus Maleficarum 1487 von Heinrich Kramer (Institoris): Nachdruck*

des Erstdruckes von 1487 mit Bulle und Approbatio, Hildesheim, Zurich, and New York: Georg Olms Verlag, 1992, pp. xxxi–liv, xxxiv–xxxviii; William E. Monter, *Witchcraft in France and Switzerland: The Borderlands during the Reformation*, Ithaca, NY: Cornell University Press, 1976, pp. 25–6; Carmen Rob-Santer, 'Le *Malleus Maleficarum* à la lumière de l'historiographie: Un *Kulturkampf?*', *Médiévales*, 2003, vol. 44, 155–72, at 158–59; Decker, *Witchcraft and the Papacy*, pp. 40–5, 53–60.

21 Hans Peter Broedel, *The 'Malleus Maleficarum' and the Construction of Witchcraft: Theology and Popular Belief*, Manchester: Manchester University Press, 2003, pp. 177–79.

22 See Alison Rowlands, 'Witchcraft and Gender in Early Modern Europe', in Brian P. Levack, ed., *The Oxford Handbook of Witchcraft in Early Modern Europe and Colonial America*, Oxford: Oxford University Press, 2013, pp. 449–67, at 451.

23 Andrea Dworkin, 'Gynocide: The Witches', in *Woman Hating*, New York: Plume, 1974, pp. 134–36.

24 See Broedel, 'To Preserve the Manly Form', p. 136; Catherine Chène and Martine Ostorero, 'Démonologie et misogynie: L'Émergence d'un discours spécifique sur la femme dans l'élaboration doctrinale du sabbat au XV$^e$ siècle', in Anne-Lisa Head-König and Liliane Mottu-Weber, eds, *Les Femmes dans la société européenne: 8$^e$ Congrès des historiennes suisses*, Geneva: Droz, 2000, pp. 171–96, at 192–96.

25 Institoris, *Malleus Maleficarum*, ed. Mackay, vol. 1, pp. 282–94.

26 Ibid. (lib. 1 quaest. 6); English translation in vol. 2, pp. 111–25.

27 Ibid., pp. 243–55.

28 Ibid., p. 292 (see also pp. 282–91).

29 Jean Delumeau, *La Peur en Occident, XIV$^e$–XVIII$^e$ siècles: Une Cité assiégée*, Paris: Fayard, 1978, pp. 308, 322–23.

30 Elaine Camerlynck, 'Féminité et sorcellerie chez les théoriciens de la démonologie à la fin du Moyen Age: Étude du *Malleus Maleficarum*', *Renaissance and Reformation*, 1983, vol. 19, 13–25; Jerouschek, '500 Years of the *Malleus Maleficarum*', p. xxxvii.

31 Walter Stephens, 'Witches Who Steal Penises: Impotence and Illusion in *Malleus Maleficarum*', *Journal of Medieval and Early Modern Studies*, 1998, vol. 28/3, 495–529, at 496. See also Stephens, *Demon Lovers*, pp. 32–57.

32 Broedel, *The 'Malleus Maleficarum'*, pp. 167–84 (quote on p. 180).

33 See Dyan Elliott, 'The Physiology of Rapture and Female Spirituality', in P. Biller and A. J. Minnis, eds, *Medieval Theology and the Natural Body*, Woodbridge: York Medieval Press, 1997, pp. 141–73, at 172–73; Gábor Klaniczay, 'Miraculum and Maleficium: Reflections Concerning Late Medieval Female Sainthood', in Ronnie Po-Chia Hsia and Robert W. Scribner, eds, *Problems in the Historical Anthropology of Early Modern Europe*, Wiesbaden: Harrassowitz, 1997, pp. 49–74, at 64–5; André Vauchez, 'Between Virginity and Spiritual Espousals: Models of Feminine Sainthood in the Christian West in the Middle Ages', *The Medieval History Journal*, 1999, vol. 2:2, pp. 349–59, 359; Nancy Caciola, *Discerning Spirits: Divine and Demonic Possession in the Middle Ages*, Ithaca, NY: Cornell University Press, 2003, pp. 274–319.

34 See Ian Maclean, *The Renaissance Notion of Woman: A Study in the Fortunes of Scholasticism and Medical Science in European Intellectual Life*, Cambridge: Cambridge University Press, 1980, p. 42; Daniel Bornstein, 'Spiritual Kinship and Domestic Devotions', in Judith C. Brown and Robert C. Davis, eds, *Gender and Society in Renaissance Italy*, Essex: Longman, 1998, pp. 173–91, at 176.

35 Institoris, *Malleus Maleficarum*, ed. Mackay, vol. 2, p. 116 (Latin original in vol. 1, p. 285).

36 See Broedel, *The 'Malleus Maleficarum'*, p. 176.

37 See Herzig, *Christ Transformed into a Virgin Woman*.

38 On Jamometić see Jakob Burckhardt, *Erzbischof Andreas von Krain und der letzte Concilsversuch in Basel 1482–84*, Basel: Schweighauser, 1852; Jürgen Petersohn, *Kaiserlicher Gestandter und Kurienbischof: Andreas Jamometić am Hof Papst Sixtus' IV. (1478–1481); Aufschlüsse aus neuen*, Hannover: Hahnsche Buchhandlung, 2004.

39 Henricus Institoris, *Epistola contra quendam conciliistam archiepiscopem videlicet Crainensem et adversus citationem et libellum infamie ipsius quem contra sanctissimum dominum nostrum dominum Sixtum papam IIII modernum summum pontificem edidit*, n.p., n.d. [Strasbourg, 1482]. For the responses to Institoris's attack on Jamometić see Peter Numagen, *Tertia editio invectiva responsalis sub nomine archiepiscopi Craynensis per Petrum Trevirensem contra Henricum Institoris formata*, printed in Johannes Heinrich Hottinger, *Historiae Ecclesiasticae Novi Testamenti seculum XV*, Zürich: Johannes Henrich Hambergeri, 1657, vol. 4, pp. 422–25.

40 Henricus Institoris, *Tractatus novus de miraculoso eucharistie sacramento*, n.p., n.d. [Augsburg, 1493], unpaginated.

41 Henricus Institoris, '*Sermones de corpore Christi modernis in temporibus plurimum perutiles contra quasdam novas hereses in mundo pullulantes*', in *Tractatus varii cum sermonibus plurimis contra quattuor errores novissime exortos adversus divinissimum eucharistie sacramentum*, Nuremberg: Anton Koberger, 1496, pars 1, sermo 1; pars 2, sermo 13; pars 2, sermo 17. See also Henricus Institoris, '*Tractatus erroneus*', in Ibid.

42 Henricus Institoris, *Opusculum in errores Monarchie*, Venice: Jacobus de Leucho, 1499, fol. 12$^v$ and passim.

43 See Herzig, *Christ Transformed into a Virgin Woman*, p. 15.

44 Albert Maria Koeniger, *Ein Inquisitionsprozess in Sachen der täglichen Kommunion*, Bonn and Leipzig: Schröder, 1923, pp. 5–57; Alfred Schröder, 'Die tägliche Laienkommunion in spätmittelalterlicher Auffassung', *Archiv für die Geschichte des Hochstifts Augsburg*, 1929, vol. 6, 609–29.

45 Romolo Cegna, 'I valdesi di Moravia nell'ultimo medioevo', *Rivista di storia e letteratura religiosa*, 1965, vol. 1, pp. 392–423, 392–95; Josef Müller, 'Bohemian Brethren', in *The New Schaff-Herzog Encyclopedia of Religious Knowledge*, Grand Rapids: Baker, 1963–1966, vol. 2, pp. 213–17, at 214; Gabriel Audisio, *The Waldensian Dissent: Persecution and Survival, c. 1170–1570*, trans. Claire Davison, Cambridge: Cambridge University Press, 1999, pp. 73–76; Euan Cameron, *Waldenses: Rejections of Holy Church in Medieval Europe*, Oxford: Blackwell, 2000, pp. 148–50, 226–31; Amedeo Molnàr, 'Autour des polémiques antivaudoises du début du XVI$^e$ siècle', in *I Valdesi e l'Europa*, Torre Pellice: Società di Studi Valdesi, 1982, pp. 115–36.

46 Schnyder, *Malleus Maleficarum: Kommentar*, pp. 64–7; Rudolf Říčan, *The History of the Unity of the Brethren: A Protestant Hussite Church in Bohemia and Moravia*, trans. C. Daniel Crews, Bethlehem, PA: The Moravian Church in America, 1992, pp. 91–4. For its circulation and influence, see Herzig, *Christ Transformed into a Virgin Woman*, pp. 113–15.

47 Institoris, *Sancte Romane Ecclesie*, fol. 88$^r$.

48 Monter, *Witchcraft in France and Switzerland*, pp. 23–4, 120–21; Bernard Andenmatten and Kathrin Utz Tremp, 'De L'Hérésie à la sorcellerie: L'Inquisiteur Ulric de Torrenté OP (vers 1420–1445) et l'affermissement de l'inquisition en Suisse romande', *Revue d'histoire ecclésiastique suisse*, 1992, vol. 86, 69–119, at 104; Martine Ostorero et al., *Inquisition et sorcellerie en Suisse romande: Le Registre Ac 29 des Archives cantonales vaudoises, 1438–1528*, Lausanne: Université de Lausanne, 2007, pp. 11–2; Georg Modestin, *Le Diable chez l'évêque: Chasse aux sorciers dans le diocèse de Lausanne (vers 1460)*, Lausanne: Université de Lausanne, 1999, p. 15, 122; Chène and Ostorero, 'Démonologie et misogynie', pp. 172–73.

49 Broedel, 'To Preserve the Manly Form', pp. 135–36; Robert Muchembled, *A History of the Devil from the Middle Ages to the Present*, trans. Jean Birrell, Cambridge: Polity, 2003, pp. 42–4.
50 This astonishment found its expression in the dialogue of Theologus and Piger in Johannes Nider's *Formicarius*, n.p., n.d. [Cologne: Ulrich Zell, c. 1475]), lib. 5, cap. 8 (noted in Michael D. Bailey, 'The Feminization of Magic and the Emerging Idea of the Female Witch in the Late Middle Ages', *Essays in Medieval Studies*, 2002, vol. 19, 120–34, at 123–28).
51 Michael D. Bailey, *Magic and Superstition in Europe: A Concise History from Antiquity to the Present*, Lanham: Rowman & Littlefield, 2007, pp. 131–33.
52 See Chène and Ostorero, 'Démonologie et misogynie', pp. 193–94.
53 Cf. Institoris, *Sancte Romane Ecclesie*, fol. 88$^r$.
54 Institoris, *Sancte Romane Ecclesie*, fols 10$^r$, 18$^r$–22$^v$, 50$^r$, 78$^r$–79$^v$.
55 For the publication and circulation of this pamphlet see Herzig, *Christ Transformed into a Virgin Woman*, pp. 157–271. See ibid., pp. 293–320 for a critical edition of the *Stigmifere*'s original Latin edition.
56 A copy of Cardinal Ippolito d'Este's letter of 24 July 1501 is kept at the Archivio Storico Diocesano, Ferrara, fondo Santa Caterina di Siena, busta 3/25 (*Processi della Beata Lucia da Narni*). The letter was published in Heinrich Institoris, ed., *Stigmifere virginis Lucie de Narnia aliarumque spiritualium personarum feminei sexus facta admiracione digna*, Olomouc: Konrad Baumgarten, 1501, unpaginated.
57 See Joan Gibson, 'Could Christ Have Been Born a Woman? A Medieval Debate', *Journal of Feminist Studies in Religion*, 1992, vol. 18/1, 65–82. Institoris echoed this notion in his discussion of women's greater propensity for witchcraft, which he concluded with declaring his gratitude to the Almighty for privileging the male sex and affirmed that God, having been born in the guise of a man, preserved men from the horrendous crimes of witches (Institoris, *Malleus Maleficarum*, ed. Mackay, vol. 1, p. 292).
58 On the discrepancies between the original letter and the version printed in the *Stigmifere* see Herzig, *Christ Transformed into a Virgin Woman*, pp. 175–82.

**Further reading**

Anglo, Sydney, 'Evident Authority and Authoritative Evidence: The Malleus Maleficarum', in Sydney Anglo, ed., *The Damned Art: Essays in the Literature of Witchcraft*, London: Routledge, 1977, pp. 1–31.
Behringer, Wolfgang, '*Malleus Maleficarum*', in Richard M. Golden, ed., *Encyclopedia of Witchcraft: The Western Tradition*, Santa Barbara, CA: ABC-Clio, 2006, vol. 3, pp. 717–723.
Broedel, Hans Peter, *The 'Malleus Maleficarum' and the Construction of Witchcraft: Theology and Popular Belief*, Manchester: Manchester University Press, 2003.
Herzig, Tamar, *Christ Transformed into a Virgin Woman: Lucia Brocadelli, Heinrich Institoris, and the Defense of the Faith*, Rome: Storia e Letteratura, 2013.
Schnyder, André, *Malleus Maleficarum: Kommentar zur Wiedergabe des Erstdrucks von 1487*, Göppingen: Kümmerle Verlag, 1993.
Segl, Peter, ed., *Der Hexenhammer: Entstehung und Umfeld des 'Malleus maleficarum' von 1487*, Cologne: Bohlau, 1988.

# 4 Lawyers versus inquisitors
## Ponzinibio's *De lamiis* and Spina's *De strigibus*

*Matteo Duni*

On the Italian peninsula the witch-hunt picked up speed rapidly towards the end of the fifteenth century, reaching its maximum intensity in the first thirty years of the sixteenth, principally at the hand of Dominican inquisitors, who authored an impressive series of texts in support of their endeavours.[1] Heinrich Institoris°'s *Malleus maleficarum*, published in 1486, is but the tallest tree overshadowing with its sinister reputation a wide forest of little-known works, all of them – except the *Malleus*, of course – written by Italian witch-hunters. In the roughly thirty years between Girolamo Visconti's *Lamiarum sive striarum opusculum* (A Booklet on Witches, 1490), the first book on witchcraft printed on the peninsula, and Bartolomeo Spina's *Quaestio de strigibus* (The Problem of Witches, c.1523), which was to be the last published by a Dominican on this topic for a very long time, Italian friar preachers wrote no fewer than seven books specifically devoted to prove that witchcraft was real, that witches truly went to the sabbat and consorted physically with devils, and that their new, nefarious heresy posed an unprecedented threat to Christianity.[2]

This remarkable output was a response to significant criticism of witchcraft theory as well as sustained (mostly elite) opposition to mass witch-hunting. Both were evidently so widespread as to be cited in several papal pronouncements.[3] Lawyers and jurists, who shared with inquisitors the task of prosecuting witches (but were also in charge defending them) had proved to be especially reluctant to accept the new demonology from as early as Ambrogio Vignati's *Tractatus de haeresi* (A Treatise on Heresy), written approximately in the 1460s (first published in 1581). Vignati argued that some of the feats ascribed to witches, such as night rides, taking part in the sabbat, and animal transformations, were unlikely, concluding that witches' testimonies were often highly unreliable and thus did not provide judges with sufficient grounds to question alleged accomplices under torture.[4]

For this reason, many Italian legal professionals would have approved of Ulrich Molitor's very popular *De lamiis et pythonicis mulieribus* (On Witches and Women Seers, 1489).[5] The German legal scholar had firmly denied the existence of the sabbat and demonic flight based on the sceptical canon

*Episcopi*. This was not, however, the only approach adopted by Italian critics of the witch-hunt, as shown by Samuele Cassini's *Questiones lamearum* (Problems Concerning Witches, 1505).[6] The author, a Franciscan friar, sought to prove that witchcraft was theologically impossible based on two interlocking arguments that would foreshadow much later scepticism. First, since demons are spirits, they do not have the power to move human bodies and therefore their aerial transportation of witches to the sabbat could take place only through direct divine intervention. At the same time, God would never perform a miracle for such a wicked purpose. The witches' sabbat was thus only a diabolical illusion, and its victims mostly old women and ignorant peasants. This position led Cassini to draw legal conclusions perfectly coinciding with Vignati's, namely that the testimony of a supposed witch accusing another of participation in the *ludus* ('game', the local name of the sabbat) is invalid, and that those who reject this type of accusations cannot be charged for protecting heretics.

Cassini's thesis was sternly refuted, still on theological grounds, by the Dominican Vincenzo Dodo who, in his *Apologia Dodi contra li defensori de le strie* (Dodo's Apology against the Defenders of Witches, 1506), argued that God could very well permit witchcraft, as He does with even greater evils, for His own inscrutable but always perfectly just reasons.[7] Cassini's work and Dodo's response were clear symptoms of the growing attention witchcraft was receiving following the eruption of witch trials across the highly urban Po river valley, from Brescia to Bologna and Piacenza.

## 1 Ponzinibio takes on the witch-hunters

Among these disputes, the polemic ignited by Giovanfrancesco Ponzinibio's *Tractatus subtilis et elegans de lamiis et excellentia utriusque iuris* (A Subtle and Elegant Treatise on Witches and on the Excellence of Civil and Canon Law, 1511) is undoubtedly the most significant.[8] Very little is known about its author, besides the fact that he was a practicing lawyer from the northern Italian city of Piacenza, admitted to the college of legal doctors and judges of his hometown in 1490. According to unverifiable information he may have been chief judge (*podestà*) and commander of the army in Reggio Emilia and Piacenza during the papal domination of those cities in the 1510s.[9] While his career does not seem to have left any traces, his book became one of the most successful early publications denying the reality of witchcraft, following in the footsteps of the only predecessor in that category, Molitor's *De lamiis et pythonicis mulieribus*, and going through many editions during the sixteenth century. On the Italian peninsula, Ponzinibio's book held also the notable record of being the first on witchcraft published by a lay author, a clear indication that the pre-eminence of inquisitors and theologians on this subject was beginning to be challenged.[10]

In his dedicatory letter to Gioffredo Carolo, the president of the Senate of Milan and a fellow jurist, Ponzinibio explains his decision to write 'on the issue of the witches' as a response to the strong increase of 'persecutions' (*persecutiones*, also meaning 'prosecutions') in Piacenza. He had judged the reasons against the witch-hunt 'true and useful' enough to be published, especially since they dealt with an issue which had provoked 'many controversies'. But an obstacle stood in his way: witchcraft appeared to be 'a matter for theologians', since the supporters of the persecutions assert that witches 'can be carried physically to the devil's game [*ludus*] and by the same devil' based on their reading of Scripture. Matthew 4:5 indeed recounts how the devil took Christ first to the pinnacle of the Temple in Jerusalem, then to a very high mountain. Now – witch-hunters claim – since the devil has been able to transport the Son of God through the air, he is unquestionably able to do the same with witches. Before Ponzinibio could tackle the issue, therefore, he had to demonstrate 'that legal canons and laws can be adduced and drawn upon for the interpretation of the holy Scriptures as well as for the discussion of, and decision about, theological problems.'[11]

Such ambitious intentions shape the first part of his book, dealing with the 'excellence of both laws' (that is, civil and canon law). Ponzinibio states that the divine origin of law fully justifies his claim that legal considerations are applicable to matters of theology. Law, he argues, is 'knowledge of things divine and human' (a quote from the famous medieval jurist Accursius), and it leads humanity to God because it eliminates the cause of many controversies and greater evils among humans. Since it preserves both the body and the soul it can be truly called 'wisdom' and, as guarantor of a peaceful earthly life as well as of the salvation of souls, it must be considered the highest human discipline. Given these premises, it follows that legal experts do not need to study theology, since the *Corpus iuris* includes everything one needs to know about religion and divine law, and therefore they enjoy a status second to no other professional category. Indeed, the norm mandating the participation of lawyers in heresy trials is the final proof that jurists may discuss issues pertaining to faith with the same authority as inquisitors.[12]

Having thus – quite daringly – established his own right to speak about witchcraft, Ponzinibio opens the second part of his text by reviewing the evidence brought forth by the proponents of the reality of demonic flight and the sabbat. First, they cite the confessions of the women who say they flew to meet the devil physically, and the experience of many witnesses of this phenomenon, both attesting to its reality. Then they point to the gospel's narrative of Christ transported by the devil as evidence of the possibility of the witches' flight. Further, they infer that since the devil wants to be worshipped as God, and at the same time wishes to insult Him as gravely as possible, the witches' experiences, including their sacrilegious acts at the sabbat, must really take place, or else their offence to the divine majesty would not be as serious as the devil desires. Finally, witch-hunters deprive sceptics of their strongest foundation by claiming that the canon *Episcopi* does not refer to the new sect of witches but to some women who, in ancient times, wrongly believed to ride at night with the pagan goddess Diana.[13]

Ponzinibio's confutation of the witch-hunters' logic starts with his refusal to accept the witches' flight and the sabbat as established facts. The thesis that women could cover immense distances so rapidly by flying, and that they would do so regularly, is 'far from likely', and to be reputed false. Canons *Episcopi* and *Nec mirum*, if read jointly and understood correctly, show that such women are under the spell of Satan's arts of deception, and indeed their confessions include things which are impossible from both a legal and natural point of view. It follows that the confessions of witches are valid only in relation to their own erroneous beliefs and do not provide reliable information about any real event or circumstance. Similarly, any independent witness of the witches' alleged deeds is likely deluded and thus untrustworthy.[14]

To the claim that Scripture proves the possibility of the witches' flight, Ponzinibio responds by underscoring the absolutely exceptional circumstances narrated in the Bible. Christ, being God and man at the same time, had given direct permission to the devil to carry him through the air. Such an extraordinary event can hardly be considered a legally valid precedent, and therefore cannot be applied in the courtrooms where the supposed crimes of very ordinary women are judged. Ponzinibio here extended Cassini's argument – that God would never allow a miraculous event such as the flight of a person to take place for a wicked purpose – by drawing out its legal consequences. If Matthew 4:5 proves anything, it is, ironically, that a witch's flight could be admitted as real only when divine permission was known with certainty – a practical impossibility. Yet, our lawyer continues with implacable logic, let us suppose for a moment that it were possible and real: why would the devil carry only a very small number of people to the sabbat, and only those of low status, if he truly could do the same with anyone and with as many people as he wanted?[15]

Concluding his tract, Ponzinibio sums up the consequences of his attack on witchcraft theory. To begin with, all the lurid details of the supposed sabbat are to be regarded as false. As far as the bewitching of children goes, it is a possibility, he admits, but it does not happen in the way witches recount, sucking the babies' blood at night thanks to the devil's help. Rather, it takes places through 'enchantments and spells', especially those working naturally, as when a 'poisonous glance' proceeding from an 'infected soul' affects a child's tender nature. The legal impact of all his considerations is threefold. First, as the supposed witches are deluded by the devil, their confessions are not only useless but positively misleading, since the devil could use them to accuse innocent people of participation in the sabbat. Second, inquisitors should oblige anyone believing in the reality of the sabbat to abjure such an opinion, as it was condemned in the canon *Episcopi*. Finally, since legal knowledge is beneficial in theological discussions, legal experts should be convoked at the beginning of a witchcraft trial, not just when it is concluded, as was the custom.[16]

## 2 The impact of Ponzinibio's challenge

Ponzinibio's *De lamiis et excellentia utriusque iuris* challenged witchcraft theorists more articulately and forcefully than any other text to that date. It propounded the idea that all aspects of witchcraft could and should be examined on the basis of legal principles, not just theological doctrines, and, further, it claimed the jurists' right to intervene with the same authority as the Dominican inquisitors it attacked. Implicitly, its author went beyond the vindication of the law by building his attack of demonology on an alternative metaphysics, such as when he affirmed that Christ's sacrifice had deprived the devil of any power over the physical world – and thus had made diabolical witchcraft impossible. In keeping with this view, Ponzinibio suggests that the sole material effect of witchcraft – bewitchment – can be blamed on purely natural causes, such as an imbalance of humours in the body. While his text does not draw full and explicit conclusions from these premises, a close reading reveals the author's true opinion also in some highly significant word choices: primarily, the fact that the combined occurrences of the words *lamia* and *strix*, both meaning witch in Latin, remain well below the double digits, while his favourite expression to refer to the alleged witches is 'istae mulieres', 'those women' (less often the neutral 'tales persone', 'those persons'). The overall message is not difficult to grasp: the downgrading of witchcraft to the status of a – feminine – delusion lacking any reality, the expulsion of the devil from the material world, and the reduction of his role to that of a purely spiritual tempter.[17]

No contemporary seems to have followed Ponzinibio's attack on witchcraft theory with the same degree of radicality, but his ideas likely influenced Andrea Alciato (1492–1550) when this promising young lawyer was asked to provide advice on a witch-hunt that had aroused strong opposition in the Valtellina (a large valley in Lombardy) in 1516.[18] Explaining the fantastical tales of demonic revelries at the sabbat as caused by the mental condition of poor women who should rather be cured than burned at the stake, Alciato rejected the opinion of those 'recent theologians' who believe that witches physically worshipped the devil. He affirmed, on the contrary, that the whole matter was just a delusion in keeping with the canon *Episcopi* and the opinion of 'Italian doctors of law'. Most prominent among these latter must have been Ponzinibio (whom Alciato does not mention explicitly), at that date the only Italian jurist who had published a book on the issue. Significantly, Alciato did not refrain from tackling the scriptural foundation for the witch-theory, Matthew 4:5, just as Ponzinibio had done, but he had a different take on the event: Christ had been carried through the air by the Holy Spirit, not by the devil, when He had decided to put Himself to the test against the tempter. Nonetheless, the two lawyers' conclusions were largely the same, that is, the overall rejection of the witch-hunt, and a vindication of the jurists' superiority over the theologians.[19]

No immediate response to Ponzinibio was forthcoming from the theologian-inquisitors. They continued to carry out the hunt for the devil's minions leading it to new heights during the 1510s, with probably as many as 160 executions throughout Italy's northern regions. The following decade, however, the pace of the prosecutions slowed down drastically, and executions plummeted to about 25.[20] It is difficult to say whether such a sharp drop reflected a more widespread resistance to witchcraft prosecutions, and, if so, whether works by sceptics played a role. What is certain is that the first theologian to react to Ponzinibio's work was Silvestro Mazzolini (or Prierias), a Dominican friar, former inquisitor of Brescia and Piacenza and Master of the Sacred (as in, Papal) Palace, who in his *De strigimagarum daemonumque mirandis* (On the Amazing Deeds of Witches and Demons, 1521) scornfully dismissed Ponzinibio's objections as having no value.[21] (Mazzolini's work on demonic possession would later inspire Girolamo Menghi°.) That Ponzinibio's arguments were far from worthless, however, is shown by the fact that, as the *De strigimagis* was being printed, Mazzolini's most brilliant disciple, Bartolomeo Spina, was preparing the thorough, meticulous, and harsh refutation he evidently thought Ponzinibio's *De lamiis* deserved.

## 3 Spina picks up his pen

Bartolomeo Spina, born in Pisa into a noble family in the 1470s, had entered the Dominican order in 1494, studied at Bologna under Mazzolini and then served as inquisitor of Modena between 1518–1520, going on to become vicar general of the Order in 1531 and finally Master of the Sacred Palace in 1545. A teacher of theology at the Dominican *studium* at Bologna and then at the university of Padua, Spina was a prolific author of texts reflecting a strictly traditional Thomistic theology. His experience as inquisitor, however, had opened his eyes to such new themes as witchcraft, to which Spina devoted *De strigibus* (On Witches, also referred to as *Quaestio de strigibus*, The Question of the Witches). The tract was probably ready as early as 1520, but its publication was delayed for unclear reasons and in the meantime Ponzinibio's book came to the attention of Spina. He then decided to refute the jurist's theses in full, writing two separate texts: the *Tractatus de preeminentia sacre theologie super alias omnes scientias et precipue humanarum legum* (A Treatise on the Pre-Eminence of Sacred Theology over All Other Sciences and Especially over Human Laws) and the *Quadruplex apologia de lamiis contra Ponzinibium* (Fourfold Defence of Witches against Ponzinibio), the former clearly meant to reject the jurist's attempt to exalt the law and its practitioners, the latter to rebuke Ponzinibio's attack on witch-hunting. These three works were first published together either in 1523 or 1525 (the title page lacks a date), and enjoyed a lasting fortune, being reprinted ten times in the course of the sixteenth century and a further three times in the seventeenth, almost always as part of larger compilations of demonological texts.[22]

The *Quaestio*'s main goal, as stated in the subtitle – *Striges ad ludum diabolicum corporaliter deferri (prout etiam vulgo fertur) amplissima questione diffinitur* – is to prove that witches are transported physically to the sabbat (*ludus*, the other name used in Northern Italy besides *cursus*).[23] In the preface to the reader, Spina recounts that at the end of the trial of a witch in Ferrara, the legal experts whom he had called to give advice were so shocked to learn of the woman's deeds, including her flight to the sabbat, that they insisted he should write about such a 'rare matter'.[24] Spina seems to suggest that their scepticism about demonic flight was actually based on ignorance, while also acknowledging that elites were reluctant to believe in the reality of witchcraft. The *Quaestio*'s ambitious goal, then, was to provide a thorough, systematic discussion of the issue from all possible angles, in the end proving beyond a reasonable doubt that almost all the feats ascribed to witches were true.

Spina thus sums up the sceptics' arguments in the first two chapters of the book. They include the – by now familiar – canon *Episcopi*'s pronouncement that the 'poor ordinary women', who think they ride at night following Diana, are deceived by the devil. Indeed, this is confirmed by the same witches, writes Spina, who draws on his Modenese experience to describe what appear as clearly delusory experiences. For example, witches confess to attending splendid banquets in the houses of the rich, but the abundant food eaten there did not satiate them, and additionally, nothing would be missing from cellars and pantries afterwards. Also, they recount killing, cooking, and eating oxen, and that these would be revived by the so-called 'mistress of the course' (*Domina cursus*), a female deity figure presiding over their meetings whom the witches in Ferrara call the 'wise Sybil' (*sapientem Sybillam*). Moreover, the unguent supposedly enabling witches to fly is completely ineffective, as demonstrated by the case of an unnamed 'prince' who, wanting to test a self-confessed witch's claims, had the woman grease herself with the unguent, only to discover that nothing strange would happen and she would remain in front of him in a deep slumber. (Later demonologists, such as Pierre de Lancre° would attempt similar experiments.) Finally, tales in which witches turned into cats in order to suck the blood of babies are delusional, since shapeshifting is impossible for humans and to believe in it is heretical. In short, critics of the witch-hunt pointed out that witchcraft was physically impossible, that it included numerous and unmistakable elements of delusion and was thus legally unprovable, and that believing in its reality meant attributing to the devil powers he did not have while ascribing cruelty and injustice to God, which was tantamount to heresy. Confronting these arguments, Spina has his work cut out. He needs to demonstrate how witchcraft's reality fit within the workings of the natural world, how it is metaphysically compatible with the idea of a just God and, finally, he needs to establish the conditions under which the crime could be prosecuted in court.[25]

Following this plan, Spina first discusses how demons may bodily interact with humans after all. His arguments are traditional: the demons' own nature as fallen angels explains how they can move material bodies (just like angels can move the heavenly spheres), appear to human senses, and have sexual contacts with men and women as *incubi* and *succubi*. Demons are also perfectly able to replace instantly and imperceptibly the food witches eat (thus explaining those full cellars and pantries), but they cannot revive a dead animal, as this would exceed the devil's power. Such an apparent feat is an illusion created by the devil's ability to deceive the senses, as are metamorphoses of witches into cats. However, the bewitching of innocent infants is certainly real, and is permitted by God to punish the sins of their parents or of their locality – especially when authorities had been reluctant to prosecute witches. Bewitchment also teaches Christians through direct experience what demons are capable of, as opposed to just holding it by faith.[26]

## 4 Spina's defence of reality

For Spina, the reality of witchcraft confirms the truth of the Church's teachings about demons (and by extension, the afterlife), but by granting the devil vast powers of deception he runs into the major problem of how to distinguish reality from fiction in witchcraft confessions, when the devil was evidently intent on deceiving his followers.[27] This was a very sensitive issue, as sceptics like Ponzinibio were claiming that courts should reject witches' testimonies against alleged accomplices altogether because of the devil's control over their imagination.

Spina's first line of defence is to emphasize that the devil's tricks cannot deprive humans of the ability of distinguishing reality from a vision or dream. In particular, witches who repented of their nefarious deeds, still believed in the truth of what they saw at their meetings, after breaking free from Satan's influence.[28] In addition, Spina provides three chapters full of authoritative courtroom testimony and other information which he claims to have gathered from trustworthy sources (most of which, however, turns out to be derivative).[29] Grouped on the basis of the social status of the witnesses, the cases include a report by the well-known Ferrarese physician Sozzino Benzi. Benzi's initial disbelief about the witches' 'absurdities' was shattered, he told Spina, by what he heard from a peasant from the surroundings of Ferrara who had witnessed a sabbat attended by 'more than six thousand people' banqueting, dancing, playing, and indulging in all sorts of licence (*lascivire*), in the end disappearing as if carried away in a cloud at a fantastic speed.[30] A string of similar stories and the unanimity of countless confessions of witches received by fellow inquisitors, all of which describe the sabbat in the same words, are such a strong indication of truthfulness, Spina contends, that those who still doubt the reality of witchcraft, for the sake of coherence should not believe in anything of which they do not have direct experiential knowledge – an attitude whose obvious absurdity is clearly meant to underscore how senseless the sceptics' stubborn refusal to admit the truth was.[31]

Still, Spina implicitly acknowledges as legitimate the doubts of those moderate sceptics (such as Vignati) who suggested that flight and the sabbat were possible in principle, but only as exceedingly rare events. To address this tricky issue Spina shifts to the theological level. Sketching a sort of history of humankind which reads more like a *historia perditionis* than a *historia salutis*, he argues that God, angry at the ever-growing wickedness of Christians, allows the devil to tempt humans in unprecedented ways – first and foremost through witchcraft. The current thriving of witches is plainly evident in the multiplication of sabbat locations, writes Spina: while in the early days their sect had only two meeting points, the banks of the Jordan river and the walnut tree of Benevento, now there is one in every diocese, as for example the Barco at Ferrara (a vast hunting ground owned by the ruling Este family north of the city), the plain around Mirandola (where a major witch-hunt did take place in 1522–1523, with the support from Gianfrancesco Pico della Mirandola°), and Mount Paterno near Bologna.[32]

While his geography of Italian witchcraft is rather original, the gist of Spina's thesis was nothing new, as Heinrich Institoris and Nicolas Jacquier°, among others, had already advanced the apparent proliferation of witches as a cause and a consequence of God's anger and proof of His decision to grant the devil exceptionally ample leeway.[33] But almost forty years after the publication of *Malleus maleficarum*, Kramer's theory created as many problems as it solved, since the sceptics' objections had become more sophisticated. Spina thus hastily clarifies that God does *not* permit some extraordinary things, such as having demons at the sabbat take on the likeness of innocent people (an argument raised by Ponzinibio, which Martin Delrio° still felt forced to address almost a century later). God would never let a guiltless person be convicted unjustly.[34] In other words, Spina claims that the validity of witchcraft testimony must be accepted as an article of faith, since arguing the opposite would mean doubting divine justice.

## 5 Spina's frontal assault on the canon

The inevitable strong delusory aspects of witchcraft clearly posed a major headache for inquisitors. As we have seen, the main foundation of legal scepticism was the canon *Episcopi*, as the authoritative church decree described feats very similar to those attributed to contemporary witches but dismissed them as false beliefs and illusions created by the devil.[35] It is no surprise, then, that Spina devotes as many as five chapters to tearing the canon *Episcopi* to pieces, adopting two main lines of attack. First, he raises doubts as to the authenticity of the council of Ancyra (314CE), which was at the time believed to have issued the canon, and the orthodoxy of the canon's doctrine.[36] Spina concludes that the canon makes several positively false statements, such as that the devil cannot transport bodies or shapeshift, which are contradicted by Scripture (remember Christ's trip to the Temple?) and the unanimous interpretation of the Church

Fathers.[37] Second, he also argues that the deluded women described in the canon are completely different from contemporary witches, since the latter make a pact with the devil and harm crops and humans, while the former were simply guilty of taking their imaginary participation in the goddess Diana's retinue to be real. While in ancient times the devil was content to be revered under the veil of the pagan gods, now he wants humans to worship him without any cover, and thus needs stronger tools of persuasions – as Christians would naturally be horrified at the prospect of honouring Satan as a deity. That is why the benefits of joining the sect – enjoying extreme (sexual) pleasures, acquiring great powers to harm enemies – must be real, unlike the fancies of the women of old.[38]

Nicolas Jacquier had formulated many of the same objections to the validity of *Episcopi*, but it is not clear whether his *Flagellum haereticorum fascinariorum* (*c*.1458) was known to Spina, as it only circulated in manuscript until the late sixteenth century.[39] In any case, the confutation of the canon opens the way for the demonstration of the falseness of the sceptics' theories (those outlined at the beginning of the book) in the final six chapters of the *Quaestio*. The nucleus of Spina's argument is that the great powers of deception and the remarkable freedom enjoyed by the devil, with God's permission, account for most of the supposed impossibilities and inconsistencies that sceptics find in the crime. In the test of the unguent attempted by the prince, for example, the eyewitnesses' account that the witch had remained fast asleep before their eyes does not invalidate her claims to having flown to the sabbat, writes Spina, since the devil could very well have taken on her appearance, thus killing two birds with one stone: enabling the witch's sin, while deceiving the prince and the other witnesses into disbelieving in the reality of witchcraft.[40]

The paradoxical conclusion of the *Quaestio de strigibus* – that it is impossible to prove that witches are *not* transported to the sabbat by Satan – highlights the difficulty Spina faced in his attempt to prove that witchcraft existed despite its many aspects evidently conflicting with common experience, law, and logic.[41] Spina's choice, resorting to a metaphysical argument – the devil's increased powers, due to God's decision – exposed him to the objections coming from a rather strong and sophisticated tradition of contradictory voices, including Molitor, Cassini, and Ponzinibio, among others. These emphasized that extending the perimeter of God's permission to the devil was highly problematic from both a theological and a legal standpoint, since it jeopardized the possibility of judging the witches' crimes according to verifiable legal standards, let alone faith in a just and loving God.

## 6 A special crime for special judges

The only solution to Spina's conundrum was to argue that witchcraft, being a crime committed by human beings with the indispensable cooperation of superhuman creatures, had to be evaluated and tried on the basis of special rules, not those applied in normal proceedings, and by judges and lawyers equipped with the necessary knowledge. This is precisely the gist of Spina's extended refutation of Ponzinibio's *De lamiis* across the *Tractatus de praeeminentia sacrae theologiae supra omnes alias scientias* and the four *Apologiae*.

The *Tractatus* aims to tackle the first part of Ponzinibio's text (*De excellentia iuris utriusque*), where the lawyer had argued that the exalted status of jurisprudence authorized 'legistae' (experts of civil law) to decide on complex matters pertaining to theology, even if this meant going against the opinions of theologians and the Doctors of the Church.[42] Spina adopts from the start a harshly polemical tone, referring to Ponzinibio most often by the epithet 'Adversarius', or 'antagonist', which was also one of the devil's names in the Bible. (In fact, Satan means 'adversary' in Hebrew.) The Dominican censures Ponzinibio's ridiculous claim, as a mere 'legista', to have a higher authority than inquisitors on theological questions, his insolence in arguing, against papal decrees, that jurists should supervise heresy trials in their entirety, as opposed to just offering advice at the end, and states that he will confute *De lamiis* to prevent such errors from leading anyone astray, and especially from thwarting the work of inquisitors (such as himself).

Spina's repeated worried references to the possible negative effects of Ponzinibio's book on the Inquisition's mission are one of the recurring themes of the *Apologiae*. The inquisitor of Modena must indeed have been worried, since his rebuttal of *De lamiis* runs to 87 pages in the 1576 edition (the original *Quaestio de strigibus* to which it was appended numbered 93). This also made it longer than Ponzinibio's original treatise (which numbered only 71 pages in the 1592 edition). The meticulous, point-by-point refutation of Ponzinibio's theses makes Spina's appendices to the *Quaestio* one of the most thoroughly argued works in favour of the witch-hunt, but also a dense, heavily repetitive text.[43] Yet, its essential message was simple. Spina's text was a forceful affirmation of the pre-eminence of theology surpassing the other sciences. Theologians (and therefore inquisitors) alone were equipped to adjudicate supernatural matters, such as witchcraft.

Particularly revealing of Spina's overall vision is his attack on Ponzinibio's statements that witness testimony about nocturnal flight to the sabbat was strongly suspect since they contained 'far from likely' elements rejected by both law and nature. The inquisitor retorts that any discourse on witchcraft must take the devil's extraordinary powers into consideration. Accordingly, Ponzinibio's claim to examine the issue based only on what is possible to humans or nature is a clear instance of the lawyer's stupidity and ignorance, since not even the miracles performed by Christ and the saints would pass this kind of test.[44] In other words, civil law cannot admit what witches confess not because it is false, but because it surpasses the limits of law's capabilities and jurisdiction, and for this reason the Church does not want witchcraft cases to be tried by 'pure jurists'.[45] Sceptical lay judges are leading 'princes', totally ignorant of theology, to doubt the reality of witchcraft and obstruct the work of the Inquisition, which in turn causes the diabolical sect to spread like wildfire.[46] Spina is particularly incensed by Ponzinibio's statement that inquisitors should have those who believe in the reality of the sabbat abjure this opinion as 'condemned'. Ponzinibio, he retorts, is alone in his 'astonishing conceit' and 'execrable folly', condemning a position supported not only by all inquisitors in Europe, but by the pope in person. Judging himself the world's only faithful Christian, the lawyer would force the entire Church to abjure this 'heresy' in a trial with himself as judge.[47] Spina's sarcasm gives soon way to threats, when he calls for inquisitors to arrest Ponzinibio and proceed against him as 'violently suspected of heresy'. If he refuses to retract his opinions, he should be burned at the stake alongside his book, 'full of ignorance and faithlessness', so as to avoid having more 'adversaries' of the Inquisition spring up in the future.[48]

Spina's aggressive language, however, does not seem to have had practical effects, since the *De lamiis* was not banned, but actually reprinted numerous times, although always in collections of demonological texts in which its message was counterbalanced by the presence of the *Quaestio de strigibus* and its appendixes. Spina and Ponzinibio were thus quite literally bound together in the same volume. With Spina by his side, Ponzinibio's ideas continued to circulate and, in the Italian context, they rapidly superseded Dominican theories, contributing to the onset of the Catholic Church's cautious stance towards witchcraft in the later decades of the sixteenth century.[49]

## Notes

1 Matteo Duni, 'Witchcraft and Witch-hunting in Italy', in Johannes Dillinger, ed., *The Routledge History of Witchcraft*, Abingdon: Routledge, 2020, pp. 81–93; Tamar Herzig, 'Witchcraft Prosecutions in Italy' in Brian P. Levack, ed., *The Oxford Handbook of Witchcraft in Europe and Colonial America*, Oxford: Oxford University Press, 2013, pp. 250–52.
2 Matteo Duni, 'I manuali inquisitoriali', in Luciano Cinelli and Alessandra Bartolomei Romagnoli, eds, *Contemplata aliis tradere: Lo specchio letterario dei frati Predicatori*, Florence: Nardini, in press. For Kramer's strong connections to Italy and Italian inquisitors, see Tamar Herzig, 'Heinrich Kramer e la caccia alle streghe in Italia', in Dinora Corsi and Matteo Duni, eds, *'Non lasciar vivere la malefica': Le streghe nei trattati e nei processi (XIV–XVII secolo)*, Florence: Firenze University Press, 2008, pp. 167–96; Tamar Herzig, *Christ Transformed into a Virgin Woman: Lucia Brocadelli, Heinrich Institoris, and the Defense of the Faith*, Rome: Edizioni di storia e letteratura, 2013. See the edition of two of these early texts in Alessia Belli and Astrid Estuardo Flaction, eds, *Les striges en Italie du Nord. Édition critique et commentaire des traités de démonologie et sorcellerie de Girolamo Visconti (Milan, c. 1460) et de Bernard Rategno (Côme, c. 1510)*, Florence: Sismel-Edizioni del Galluzzo, 2019.
3 This is the case with the briefs 'Honestis petentium votis', addressed by Leo X to inquisitors hunting witches in the Venetian territories in 1521, and 'Dudum, uti nobis', addressed by Adrian VI to the inquisitor of Como, Modesto Scrofeo, in 1523, which mentions a now-lost brief by Julius II as also condemning opponents of the witch-hunt. See Sergio Abbiati, Attilio Agnoletto et al., eds, *La stregoneria. Diavoli, streghe, inquisitori dal Trecento al Settecento*, Milan: Mondadori, 1984, pp. 342–45, and Alan C. Kors and Edward Peters, eds, *Witchcraft in Europe, 400–1700: A Documentary History*, Philadelphia: University of Pennsylvania Press, 2001, pp. 245–47. On Scrofeo's witch-hunts and its opponents, see Matteo Duni, 'Un manuale inedito per cacciatori di streghe: Il *Formularium pro exequendo*

*Inquisitionis officio* di Modesto Scrofeo (c. 1523)', *Archivio Storico Italiano*, 2013, vol. 171, 339–58.

4 Matteo Duni, 'Doubting Witchcraft: Theologians, Jurists, Inquisitors during the Fifteenth and Sixteenth Centuries', *Studies in Church History*, 2016, vol. 52, 203–31.

5 Duni, 'Doubting Witchcraft', pp. 219–22.

6 Fabrizio Conti, *Witchcraft, Superstition, and Observant Franciscan Preachers: Pastoral Approach and Intellectual Debate in Renaissance Milan*, Turnhout: Brepols, 2015, pp. 293–301.

7 Conti, *Witchcraft, Superstition, and Observant Franciscan Preachers*, pp. 301–304.

8 Giovanfrancesco Ponzinibio, *Tractatus subtilis et elegans de lamiis et excellentia utriusque iuris, cum nonnullis conclusionibus ad materiam heresis in practica utilibus*, Pavia: Jacopo Pocatela da Borgofranco, 1511.

9 Matteo Duni, 'Le streghe e i dubbi di un giurista: Il *De lamiis et excellentia iuris utriusque* di Gianfrancesco Ponzinibio (1511)', in Luisa Simonutti and Camilla Hermanin, eds, *La centralità del dubbio: Un progetto di Antonio Rotondò*, Florence: Leo S. Olschki, 2010, vol. I, pp. 3–26; Matteo Duni, 'Ponzinibio, Gianfrancesco', in Adriano Prosperi, ed., with Vincenzo Lavenia and John Tedeschi, *Dizionario storico dell'Inquisizione* (henceforth *DSI*), Pisa: Edizioni della Normale, 2010, vol. 3, s.v.; Matteo Duni, 'Law, Nature, Theology and Witchcraft in Ponzinibio's *De lamiis*', in Louise Nyholm Kallestrup and Raisa Maria Toivo, eds, *Contesting Orthodoxy in Medieval and Early Modern Europe: Heresy, Magic and Witchcraft*, Basingstoke: Palgrave MacMillan, 2017, pp. 217–34.

10 The first two editions of *De lamiis* (at Pavia, 1511 and 1513) are extremely rare. Except where otherwise noted, I will be quoting from the most readily available version, published together with Paolo Grillando's tract on incantations: *Tractatus duo: Unus de sortilegiis D. Pauli Grillandi; Alter de lamiis et excellentia iuris utriusque D. Ioannis Francisci Ponzinibii Florentini* [sic], Frankfurt: Martin Lechler, 1592 (henceforth *De lamiis*), in which Ponzinibio's text is on pp. 228–299.

11 Ponzinibio, *Tractatus subtilis et elegans*, fol. 1v; Duni, 'Law, Nature, Theology and Witchcraft', pp. 219–21.

12 Duni, 'Law, Nature, Theology and Witchcraft', pp. 221–22.

13 Ponzinibio, *De lamiis*, pp. 261–65.

14 Ponzinibio, *De lamiis*, pp. 265–70.

15 Ponzinibio, *De lamiis*, pp. 273–76; Duni, 'Law, Nature, Theology and Witchcraft', pp. 224–25.

16 Ponzinibio, *De lamiis*, pp. 279–81; Duni, 'Law, Nature, Theology and Witchcraft', pp. 225–26.

17 Ponzinibio, *De lamiis*, pp. 226–27.

18 On Alciato (or Alciati, 1492–1550, the foremost jurist in Europe in the first half of the sixteenth century) and witchcraft, see Matteo Duni, 'Alciati, Andrea', in Richard Golden, ed., *Encyclopedia of Witchcraft: The Western Tradition* (henceforth *EoW*), vol. 1, s.v.

19 Duni, 'Law, Nature, Theology and Witchcraft', pp. 222–24.

20 Duni, 'Witchcraft and Witch-hunting in Italy', p. 83.

21 Duni, 'Le streghe e i dubbi di un giurista', p. 9. On Mazzolini, see Michael Tavuzzi, *Prierias: The Life and Works of Silvestro Mazzolini da Prierio, 1456–1527*, Durham, NC: Duke University Press, 1997, and Herzig, 'Heinrich Kramer e la caccia alle streghe in Italia'.

22 Gabriella Zarri, 'Spina, Bartolomeo della', in *EoW*, vol. 4, s.v.; Matteo Duni, 'Spina, Bartolomeo', in *DSI*, vol. 3, s.v.; Maurizio Bertolotti, 'The Ox's Bones and the Ox's Hide: A Popular Myth, Part Hagiography and Part Witchcraft', in Edward Muir and Guido Ruggiero, eds, *Microhistory and the Lost Peoples of Europe*.

Selections from 'Quaderni Storici', Baltimore: Johns Hopkins University Press, 1991, 42–70.
23 Bartolomeo Spina, *De stribigus: Striges ad ludum diabolicum corporaliter deferri (prout etiam vulgo fertur) amplissima questione diffinitur*, n.p., n.d. [c.1525]. As this first edition is very rare, I will cite from *Quaestio de strigibus, una cum Tractatu de praeeminentia sacrae theologiae super alias omnes scientias et precipue humanarum legum et Quadruplex Apologia de lamiis contra Ponzinibium* (henceforth *Quaestio de strigibus*), Rome: in Aedibus Populi Romani, 1576.
24 Spina, *Quaestio de strigibus*, 'Author ad lectorem', no pagination.
25 Spina, *Quaestio de strigibus*, pp. 1–7.
26 Spina, *Quaestio de strigibus*, pp. 15–28 (chaps IV–IX).
27 This is the thesis of Walter Stephens, *Demon Lovers: Witchcraft, Sex, and the Crisis of Belief*, Chicago: University of Chicago Press, 2002.
28 Spina, *Quaestio de strigibus*, pp. 29–31 (chap. X).
29 Spina, *Quaestio de strigibus*, pp. 48–55 (chaps XVII–XIX).
30 Spina, *Quaestio de strigibus*, pp. 49–50 (chap. XVII). Benzi (c.1485–1556), from a Sienese family with a strong medical tradition, taught medicine at the University of Ferrara during 1518–1546. See Gionata Liboni, 'Sozzino Benzi, Basilio Sabazio e la corruttibilità del cielo: La controversia cosmologica in una lettera al cardinale Benedetto Accolti', *I castelli di Yale*, 2008, vol. 9, 123–69.
31 Spina, *Quaestio de strigibus*, p. 36.
32 Ibid., p. 58 (chap. XX).
33 [Henricus Institoris], *Malleus maleficarum*, ed. and trans. Christopher Mackay, Cambridge: Cambridge University Press, 2006, vol. 1, pp. 234–35 (Part I, *Quaestio* 2), and 'General introduction', pp. 60–1.
34 Spina, *Quaestio de strigibus*, pp. 41–2 (chap. XIV).
35 Edward Peters, *Canon Episcopi*, in *EoW*, vol. 1, s.v.
36 Spina, *Quaestio de strigibus*, pp. 59–62 (chap. XXI).
37 Spina, *Quaestio de strigibus*, pp. 64–8 (chap. XXIII).
38 Spina, *Quaestio de strigibus*, pp. 70–3 (chap. XXV).
39 Nicolas Jacquier, *Flagellum haereticorum fascinariorum*, Frankfurt: Nicholaus Bassaeus, 1581, pp. 62–72. On Jacquier, see Martine Ostorero's contribution to this volume.
40 Spina, *Quaestio de strigibus*, pp. 81–4 (chap. XXX). *Episcopi* was also discussed by Institoris, who refuted what he considered faulty interpretations of the text, rather than the text itself ([Institoris], *Malleus maleficarum*, vol. 1, pp. 217–29 (Part I, *Quaestio* 1).
41 Stephens, *Demon Lovers*, pp. 167–79.
42 Spina, *Tractatus de praeeminentia sacrae theologiae*, 'Prooemium', pp. 91–3.
43 Spina, *Apologia prima*, pp. 140–53 (chaps V–XII).
44 Ibid., pp. 135–37 (chap. II).
45 Spina, *Apologia secunda*, pp. 154–56 (chap. I).
46 Spina, *Apologia prima*, p. 148 (chap. IX).
47 Spina, *Apologia tertia*, pp. 175–76 (chap. III).
48 Spina, *Apologia tertia*, pp. 175–76.
49 On Ponzinibio's editorial fortune, see Duni, 'Law, Nature, Theology and Witchcraft'; Duni, 'Ponzinibio, Gianfrancesco'; on its impact see Matteo Duni, 'The Editor as Inquisitor: Francisco Peña and the Question of Witchcraft in the Late Sixteenth Century', in Machtelt Israëls and Louis Waldman, eds, *Renaissance Studies in Honor of Joseph Connors*, Florence: Villa I Tatti, 2012, vol. II, 297–303. On Spina's book, see Maurizio Bertolotti, 'Pomponazzi tra streghe e inquisitori: Il *De incantationibus* e il dibattito sulla stregoneria intorno al 1520', in Marco Sgarbi, ed., *Pietro Pomponazzi: Tradizione e dissenso; Atti del Congresso internazionale di studi su Pietro Pomponazzi*, Florence: Olschki, 2010, pp. 385–405.

## Further reading

Bever, Edward, 'Witchcraft Prosecutions and the Decline of Magic', *Journal of Interdisciplinary History*, 2009, vol. 40, 263–293.

Duni, Matteo, 'I dubbi sulle streghe', in Germana Ernst and Guido Giglioni, eds, *I vincoli della natura: Magia naturale e stregoneria nel Rinascimento*, Roma: Carocci, 2012, pp. 203–221.

Martino, Federico, *Il volo notturno delle streghe: Il Sabba della modernità*, Naples: La città del sole, 2011.

Romeo, Giovanni, *Inquisitori, esorcisti e streghe nell'Italia della Controriforma*, 2nd ed., Florence: Sansoni, 2003.

Stephens, Walter, *Demon Lovers: Witchcraft, Sex, and the Crisis of Belief*, Chicago: University of Chicago Press, 2002.

# 5  The witch-hunting humanist

Gianfrancesco Pico della Mirandola's *Strix*

*Walter Stephens*

Gianfrancesco Pico della Mirandola (1469–1533) was the ruler of Mirandola, a tiny principality near Ferrara in Northeast Italy. A lively contributor to the intellectual life of his time as author of respected literary and philosophical works, he nonetheless participated in and defended a witch-hunt that tried dozens of people between 1522 and 1523, executing at least ten of them.[1] His work *Strix* (The Witch), published in 1523, was written in part to justify his actions and is remarkable for the apparent contradiction between its humanistic literary sophistication and its extreme witch-hating fervor. *Strix* never appeared in the thousand-plus pages of Gianfrancesco's 'complete' works, yet it embodies his preoccupations more completely and spectacularly than his longer, recognizably philosophical Latin treatises. He published it with a handful of small pious works in 1523, and authorized its translation into Italian the following year, hoping to grant it wider circulation.[2]

Although he was deeply familiar with Scholastic theology and philosophy, Gianfrancesco chose not to write a Scholastic treatise on witchcraft, the favored genre of most early modern 'witch-haters' or witchcraft theorists, notably the *Malleus maleficarum*.[3] Instead, he transposed Scholastic theories into a far more accessible format, the humanistic dialogue. Like the works of Plato, Cicero, and the humanists who imitated them after 1400, Gianfrancesco's *Strix* takes the form of a freewheeling discussion, rather than a logical, hierarchical arrangement of topics. The apparent discursive flexibility is illusory, however. Underneath its humanistic exterior, *Strix* resolutely maintains the logic of Scholastic witchcraft treatises.

It may seem surprising that Gianfrancesco chose the archetypal humanist genre for the outstandingly inhumane *Strix*, even stranger that his contemporaries respected him as a humanist. But there is considerable difference between sixteenth- and twenty-first-century definitions of humanism. For Gianfrancesco and most of his contemporaries, humanism was not 'a doctrine, attitude, or way of life centered on human interests or values'. Nor was it 'a philosophy that usually rejects supernaturalism and stresses an individual's dignity and worth and capacity for self-realization through reason'[4]. At its foundation, Renaissance humanism was a *method of study* that stressed *philology*: whenever possible, humanists examined literature and the other 'humanities' (*studia humanitatis*) in the original Latin and Greek, paying careful, critical attention to the times, places, and mentalities within which individual texts arose, and their influence on subsequent works.[5] Humanism was not fundamentally about humaneness, so there is no contradiction in referring to Gianfrancesco as a humanist.

## 1 *Strix* as dialogue and as witchcraft theory

*Strix* differs from more famous Renaissance dialogues and their Platonic and Ciceronian models by not even attempting to portray an equable discussion based on multiple points of view. Instead, Gianfrancesco provides a kind of catechism: he presents only two perspectives on witchcraft and spends his time annihilating one of them. *Strix* does not debate whether witchcraft is a crime: that witchcraft is profoundly evil is a foregone conclusion. Rather, the issue is whether the crime of witchcraft is *real* or simply imaginary. *Strix* sets out to prove incontrovertibly that witchcraft is not imaginary, that it takes place in reality, through physical contact between demons and wide-awake humans, not in dreams, hallucinations, or imagination. Throughout the dialogue, the thesis 'witchcraft really exists' is argued as a double negative: 'witchcraft is not non-existent,' that is, 'witchcraft *doesn't not* exist'. Gianfrancesco's dialogue reveals this underlying double-negative logic of witchcraft theory more baldly than any previous or subsequent defense.

*Strix* takes aim at three principal opponents, one contemporary and the other two much older. To comprehend Gianfrancesco's stance regarding witchcraft, it is vital to understand his intellectual ambivalence toward his more celebrated uncle, Giovanni Pico (1463–1494), one of the most famous philosophers of the Renaissance. Like Marsilio Ficino (1433–1499), Giovanni Pico strove to reconcile Plato and other pagan philosophers with Christianity: they argued that certain pre-Christian thinkers foreshadowed biblical truths, a movement known as pious philosophy (*pia philosophia*) or ancient or natural theology (*prisca theologia*).[6] Giovanni's famous but somewhat misnamed 'Oration on the Dignity of Man' argued that religious truths compatible with Christianity were latent in Greek and Roman philosophy, as well as Jewish and Muslim religious texts, and even in works attributed to shadowy legendary figures like Pythagoras, Orpheus, the Sibyls, and the ancient Iranian prophet Zoroaster. As an advocate of religious and philosophical concord, Giovanni exploited his dynastic title, 'Prince of Mirandola and Concordia', to style himself a philosophical *princeps concordiae*. In 1486 he proposed to unify all human knowledge single-handedly by publicly debating 900 theses against all comers, with his *Oration* as a program for the debate.[7]

Such ecumenical interpretations (largely contradicted by modern historical scholarship) presupposed that God had not willfully kept pagans and 'infidels' in the dark, but allowed them imperfect glimpses of fundamental monotheistic truths, including human immortality, centuries before Christ or even Moses. Overtly presented as defenses of virtuous non-Christian thinkers against narrow-minded theologians, such arguments were simultaneously theodicies, defenses of the Christian God's fairness towards peoples deprived of the gospel message by accidents of chronology or geography. The idea was far from novel (Church Fathers, and later Dante, had proposed versions of it), but fifteenth- and sixteenth-century philosophers explored it in ever-greater detail.[8]

Pope Innocent VIII – who had endorsed the witch-hating doctrines of the *Malleus maleficarum* two years previously – quashed Giovanni's proposed debate, since theologians found several of its theses redolent of heresy.[9] Like the pope, Gianfrancesco considered his uncle's dreams of religious concord a deluded refusal to understand that Christianity superseded and overturned every other creed. As Peter Burke argued in *The Damned Art*, the younger Pico's purpose was to demonstrate that the Bible, rather than tolerant philosophical inquiry, was the unique source of truth. Truth was not multiple, nor had it evolved over time: there was one truth, partially understood by the Jews, fully revealed through Christ, but unrecognized by pagans and infidels.[10] Regarding Greco-Roman polytheism, Gianfrancesco swore by the watchword of the Psalmist and Saint Paul: all the gods of the Gentiles are demons.[11] Polytheism was idolatry, and idols were not mere images; 'Hermes Trismegistus', the 'ancient theologian' favored by Ficino and Giovanni Pico, had revealed idols as instruments of demon-worship.[12] Just as Satan 'transforms himself into an angel of light' (2 Corinthians 11:14), demons falsely masqueraded as 'gods' to seduce and betray humanity. Truth and polytheism could not coexist, so how could pagans foreshadow Christian dogma?

In attacking demonolatry, Gianfrancesco argued vehemently against a second target, much older than his uncle. With other early proponents of witch-hunting, he identified a passage in the Church's own laws as the source of the 'erroneous' belief that witchcraft was an imaginary crime. A directive from the early tenth century (but believed to be much older) ordered bishops to eradicate certain unlettered women's belief that 'Diana, the goddess of the pagans,' awakened them in the dead of night and led them on a weird cavalcade, riding immense distances on the backs of 'certain beasts'. This law, the so-called canon *Episcopi*, declared that such women simply mistook their dreams for reality: their delusions about the goddess 'Diana' were inspired by Satan, making them relapse into paganism. The Bible proved their mistake, since Ezekiel, Saint John, and Saint Paul never claimed to experience their prophetic visions 'in the body'. Because such holy men's visions happened only 'in the spirit', these deluded women simply could not experience 'Diana's cavalcades' in reality, 'in the body'.[13]

The canon *Episcopi* originally reflected the difficulties of spreading and maintaining Christianity in the Carolingian era, when beliefs and practices of Nordic paganism were a lingering reality. 'Diana' was an educated cleric's guess at the 'real' identity of a goddess-like figure in folklore who led a ghostly procession of the restless dead, sometimes called the 'furious host'.[14] As Christianization spread, churchmen discussed the canon less frequently, but from the late 1300s to the 1460s, they re-evaluated it. Spectacular societal catastrophes, from the increase of mass heresies to the Black Plague (1347–1352), the Great Papal Schism (1378–1417), and the Hundred Years War (1337–1453), indicated the world had gone astray. Nicolas Jacquier° and other clerics who had gathered at the Council of Basel (1431–1438), produced some of the earliest allegations that a formidable new 'sect' of demonolatrous heretics was subverting Christendom; their activities, including nocturnal mass meetings, demon-worship, and magical flight, were soon codified as witchcraft.[15]

Witchcraft theorists consistently opposed *Episcopi*'s declaration that night-traveling women were asleep and dreaming, and argued that some such experiences were undeniably real. Unable to oppose *Episcopi* categorically, then considered the decree of a fourth-century ecumenical council, theorists created a historical distinction, contrasting the illusory dreams of earlier times to the 'undoubtedly real' flying and demonic subversion of contemporary women. The *Malleus maleficarum* declared that after about 1400 modern women consorted with demons willingly, wakefully, and in reality, becoming witches.[16]

Gianfrancesco's third target was Aristotle. Aristotle's and Plato's works had been largely unavailable to western Christians during the early Middle Ages. But beginning around 1100, Latin translations of Aristotle's works allowed Scholastic theologians to rediscover the thinker they soon celebrated as 'The Philosopher'. Yet it was no secret that Aristotle ignored or even contradicted important Christian doctrines. He considered the world eternal, uncreated by any god, and provided no evidence to support the existence of angels and devils or the immortality of the individual human soul. By contrast, the *Timaeus*, Plato's only work known throughout the Middle Ages, resembled the Bible by asserting that a benevolent god had created the cosmos; moreover, Plato had espoused human immortality and the existence of beings resembling angels. In the late fifteenth century, Ficino's Latin translations confirmed that Plato and his ancient neo-Platonic disciples had championed ideas resembling Christian doctrines.[17]

Between 1500 and 1523, Gianfrancesco Pico evolved from a favorable view of Aristotle to an extreme enmity toward 'The Philosopher'. Gianfrancesco's reversal was closely related to his changing views on witchcraft. His treatise *On the Imagination* (1501) introduced demonology into Aristotle's theory of mind, arguing that good and bad angels could strongly influence the human imagination, and that demons 'deceive people through[18] the phantasies of men, and of women called witches'. This observation implies agreement with canon *Episcopi*, that witches' transgressions took place only 'in the spirit'. But in 1523, Gianfrancesco repudiated any such interpretation, proposing in *Strix* to demonstrate that witches interacted with demons *corporaliter* and *realiter*, 'in the body' and thus 'in reality'. In the two decades since *On the Imagination*, Gianfrancesco had decided that philosophy, particularly Aristotle's focus on natural causality, was inimical to Christian belief. In 1520 he published *An Examination of the Vanity of Pagan Doctrines and the Truth of Christianity*, an enormous treatise which exhorted Christians to abandon philosophy and accept the truth of the Bible wholeheartedly, unconditionally.[19]

## 2 *Strix* and the witch-hunt in Mirandola

A short time later, in early 1522, the witch-persecution began in Mirandola, with Gianfrancesco's knowledge and participation as secular authority. The connection between *Strix*'s defense of witch-hunting and the anti-Aristotelianism of *Examen vanitatis*, like the disagreement between *Strix* and *On the Imagination* over the reality of witchcraft, could hardly be clearer.[20] Like *Examen vanitatis*, *Strix* argues for the absolute truth of Christian doctrine, and asserts that witches demonstrate Christian truth by vainly opposing it.

Book One of *Strix* stages a dispute between two thoroughly educated humanist philosophers: Apistius, the 'Unbeliever', scorns the idea that witches exist, while Phronimus, the 'Prudent Man', accumulates familiar proofs that witchcraft is not imaginary. In the second book, another voice is added. The inquisitor Dicastes (Judge), gives both philosophical and theological arguments to buttress Phronimus's refutations of Apistius. *Strix*'s originality among defenses of witch-hunting depends less on the three men than on a fourth interlocutor: the eponymous Strix is an illiterate village woman, tried and convicted of witchcraft by Dicastes. While the men debate the learned theory of witchcraft, the condemned woman ostensibly represents the voice of lived experience, and her 'confession' saves the discussion from being aridly theoretical. Her first-hand authority, even more than the philosophy of Phronimus or the theology of Dicastes, finally convinces Apistius that witches' bodily interactions with demons are not a delusion, but happen in reality, on a massive scale.

Despite the overall 'orthodoxy' of *Strix*'s arguments, Gianfrancesco presumes a reader unusually hostile to the reality of witchcraft. Equally remarkable is *Strix*'s accurate portrayal of disparities between learned theories of witchcraft and common people's fears of magic: although Gianfrancesco does not show a modern historian's sensitivity to these differences, his treatment is far more nuanced than those of previous witchcraft theorists. Strix herself presents her motivations and experiences in everyday social terms, without reference to theology, except when she misunderstands it.

There are numerous other distinctive aspects. Peter Burke noted that Gianfrancesco's 'suspicion of classical antiquity' was based on two features we have observed: a stress on Greek and Roman polytheism as thoroughgoing demon-worship, and what Burke, along with Eugenio Garin and Charles Schmitt, aptly described as Gianfrancesco's desire 'to destroy philosophy to make more room for religion'.[21] Burke also observed that Gianfrancesco was particularly 'interest[ed] in the processes of illusion'. Indeed, the subtitle of *Strix* already advertises it as being 'on the deceptions perpetrated by demons'. Once opened, the book reveals itself as one long diatribe, obsessively recounting the manifold delusions by which Satan and other demonic impostors enticed the ancient Greeks and Romans into idolatry. Unlike *On the Imagination*, *Strix* asserts that demons do not merely disturb witches' imagination but interact with them 'in the body'.

Yet, there are seven other features that set Gianfrancesco apart as well. In the first place, Gianfrancesco differed from other witchcraft theorists, in particular the *Malleus maleficarum*, by insisting that witchcraft did not suddenly appear around 1400 but had always existed. Second, despite this disagreement, the *Malleus* clearly influenced Gianfrancesco's obsessively clinical preoccupation with modern witches' sexual interactions with demons. A third characteristic, also shared with the *Malleus*, is Gianfrancesco's insistence that belief in the reality of witchcraft is an obligatory, non-optional requirement of Christian faith: a Christian who disbelieves in the reality of witchcraft is living a contradiction.

Fourth, and perhaps most strangely to modern eyes, *Strix* shows little interest in magical harm, or empathy for witchcraft's perceived victims: details of 'spells' and 'bewitchments' are largely absent. Instead – and this is a fifth characteristic of the treatise – witches' most outrageous crimes are said to be attacks on the Catholic sacraments, particularly the desecration of Eucharistic hosts, the wafers consecrated by priests during Mass. Sixth, as previously mentioned, *Strix* portrays the condemned witch as one of its four interlocutors, rather than restricting the discussion to educated men. Seventh, the witch's participation in the discussions reflects another debt to the *Malleus*: her testimony is presented as 'empirical' proof that the experiences accused witches were forced to confess took place 'in the body', in reality.

These features reflect the real-life circumstances that motivated the witch-hunt in Mirandola. Both Gianfrancesco and his close associate, the Dominican inquisitor Leandro Alberti (1479–1552), clearly ascribe Mirandolese authorities' initial alarm to rumors of desecration.[22] Alberti's dedicatory letter to *Strix* declares that persecution began '[w]hen our brother Friar Girolamo [Armellini] of Faenza, the Inquisitor of Heretics, recently learned that at Mirandola many people were misinterpreting the faith of Christ the Lord of Lords and shamelessly performing various outrages against his most holy Body'. In other words, the Mirandolese witch-hunt was not sparked by common people's mutual accusations of magical harm, but by *the inquisitor's suspicion* that laypeople were desecrating the Eucharistic host. For centuries, clerics accused common people of surreptitiously spitting out the host, then using it for nefarious magic. Although deliberate desecrations doubtless occurred, most culprits probably intended to create folk remedies rather than anything malign: layfolk often believed that the transubstantiated wafer acquired magical properties. While Alberti does not specify the Mirandolese defendants' motives, Gianfrancesco's witch describes deliberate desecrations.

Echoing Alberti's allegation, the climax of *Strix* occurs when Apistius, who has steadfastly denied that witchcraft is real, hears the condemned witch confess that her demonic familiar advised her to sew two consecrated hosts into her skirt, as a magical charm against confessing. Once captured, she realized the charm was ineffective, removed the hosts, and threw them into her chamber-pot, breaking them up with a stick 'there amid the dung'.[23] As she watched in horror, the hosts reacted to her abuse by bleeding. Although transubstantiation was invisible by definition, generations of Catholics had told stories of hosts that bled or otherwise manifested their Eucharistic reality when abused by Jews or heretics.[24] No one in Gianfrancesco's dialogue bothers to observe that Strix's abomination confirms the Catholic doctrine that transubstantiated hosts become the literal body and blood of Christ. Nor was the point commonly belabored in outraged denunciations: everyone knew the doctrine from attending Mass. Thus, instead of commenting overtly, Apistius suddenly declares that 'just as I have never not accepted the truth of the Christian religion, so I would never agree that such impious defilers of it be spared punishment'.[25] Apistius's convoluted declaration is a double negative: not 'I have always believed' but 'I have *never not* believed'. He thereby explicitly renounces his identity as 'the Unbeliever'; consequently, when the dialogue ends, the inquisitor formally changes Apistius's name to Pisticus, 'the Believer'. In accordance with the third characteristic noted above, Apistius's conversion crowns the demonstration that Christian faith necessarily entails believing that demonic witchcraft is real. By dramatizing Apistius as 'straw man', the dialogue creates a far more vivid rhetorical presentation than the standardized, impersonal format of the Scholastic *quaestio*, which imitated an ideal classroom debate. *Strix* casts Apistius as a model for the skeptical reader, who should imitate his conversion.

Belief in the reality of transubstantiation had been controversial numerous times in the history of Christian theology and was once more a serious issue in Gianfrancesco's day. In the early 1520s, Luther's colleague Andreas Bodenstein von Karlstadt and other radicals were opposing the 'idolatry' of the Mass; by 1528, Swiss iconoclasts were scattering and destroying consecrated hosts, or feeding them to dogs and pigs amid ribald jokes about transubstantiation.[26] Gianfrancesco's inquisitor 'Dicastes' accuses a priest, Don Benedetto Berni, a real-life victim of Inquisitor Armellini, of consecrating hosts on an industrial scale and distributing them to local witches, who abused them at the sabbat, stamping or urinating on them. Armellini stripped Berni of his ecclesiastical rank, condemning him to the stake as supposed ringleader of a heretical 'sect' of Mirandolese witches.

The Mirandolese trials targeted an unusually large percentage of clerics: eight of seventy-three (11%), although apparently only Berni was executed.[27] This proportion could reflect the importance Armellini attributed to Eucharistic profanation as a witchcraft crime, and Gianfrancesco's focus on clerical desecration might help explain why the

Mirandolese trials inverted the gender proportion typical of witch-hunt victims. During roughly 300 years, women accounted for about 80% of prosecutions and defendant deaths.[28] Yet seven of the ten executed Mirandolese were men; moreover, although the records are incomplete, it appears that of all Mirandolese investigated by inquisitors, 'only' 45% (33 of 73) were women, a significant contrast to Gianfrancesco's, the *Malleus*'s, and other theorists' portrayal of women as the archetypal witches.[29] As we just saw, the turning-point of *Strix* comes when Apistius hears the female witch confess specifically to desecrating the Eucharist. He has resisted the 'evidence' of witches' other crimes during 63% of the dialogue, but suddenly begins accepting that witchcraft is real, and soon 'converts' to unconditional belief.

One of witches' most infamous crimes was infanticide, often followed by cannibalism. 'Dicastes' portrays Berni as greedy to consume the blood of little children, which demons helped him and other witches acquire. Strix herself 'confesses' that demons helped witches sneak into bedrooms unnoticed by sleeping parents, puncture infants with needles under their fingernails, and suck their blood. Nearly invisible wounds, inflicted by almost unseizable enemies, revealed why some children wasted away from mysterious ailments or died suddenly, despite their parents' vigilance. Such accusations were an implicit theodicy, explaining why God allowed terrible things to befall innocent people. Theodicy taught that God did not approve innocent suffering, but permitted it to happen, rather than obstruct oppressors' free will, who condemned themselves to Hell in the process.[30] Thus Gianfrancesco, the *Malleus* and other treatises declared that three agents were necessary for witchcraft: the witch and the devil, obviously, but also God, without whose permission neither could act.[31] Strix admits that witches swallowed only part of children's blood, reserving the rest to confect the 'flying ointment'. This horrendous concoction signalled witches' profound evil to demons, who were literally attracted to it. Thus summoned, they empowered witches' atrocious crimes, and flew them at unnatural speed to the sabbat.[32]

## 3 The science of demonic eros

The doomed Berni co-starred with Strix in Gianfrancesco's depiction of another fantastic crime, sexual intercourse between witches and demons. Most witchcraft theorists imagined that demonic familiars were the witches' paramours as well as the source of their power to perform *maleficia*, or magical harm.[33] Fantasies of copulation between 'male' demons and women were integral to early modern theories of witchcraft, enthusiastically expounded by many sophisticated intellectuals, including Jean Bodin°, whose juridical reputation has outlasted his enthusiasm for witch-hunting (Figure 5.1).[34] Men were accused less frequently of fornication with 'female' demons, but 'Dicastes' averred that Berni, 'that most wicked priest', confessed taking

*Figure 5.1* Woman Copulating with Demon / Woman Riding a Goat. Fragment of Ulrich Tengler, *Der neü Layenspiegel*, Augsburg: Otmar Johann, 1511, fol. 190r [Res/2 J. pract]. Image by permission of Bayerische Staatsbibliothek, Munich.

more delight from sleeping with the demon he called Armellina, than with all the women he had sex with. And lest you think he had only had a few of them, he even had intercourse with his sister, and they say he actually had a son by her.[35]

The succubus 'Armellina' has several noticeable aspects. First, 'her' name echoes Inquisitor Armellini's surname.[36] Second, the fictional Dicastes claims responsibility for condemning Berni and other real-life victims of Armellini. Third, Gianfrancesco explicitly claimed to include details from the real Mirandolese persecution. Thus, poor old Berni might have invented the name 'Armellina' himself, to protest that the inquisitor was ventriloquizing his entire 'confession'.

Like other witchcraft theorists, Gianfrancesco observed that classical texts portrayed *maleficia* under many forms: potions and ointments that killed humans or transformed them into beasts, charms that caused overwhelming erotic obsession, nefarious spells and chants that supposedly raised the dead or provoked catastrophic storms. Sorceresses were numerous, from Circe in the *Odyssey* to Horace's murderous Canidia and Lucan's necromantic Erichtho. The Bible itself confirmed that such phenomena were not mere literary fictions. Deuteronomy 22:18 commanded that 'thou shalt not suffer a witch to live'; the reality of necromancy was shown by the 'Witch of Endor', who called up the long-dead Samuel to prophesy King Saul's defeat. Significantly, early Christian theologians interpreted Samuel's 'ghost' as a masquerading devil, facilitating the demonological Christian definition of necromancy thereafter.[37] That demons caused witches to fly was proved by Old Testament examples, but also and pre-eminently by the temptation of Jesus, whom Satan transported atop a high mountain and onto the pinnacle of the Temple.[38]

Most details in Gianfrancesco's treatment of witchcraft are recognizable from earlier theories, but his overall explanation contradicted the early modern consensus. Between 1430 and 1450, the 'sect of demonic witchcraft' was defined as a dangerous, even apocalyptic *new* heresy.[39] As already mentioned, the *Malleus maleficarum* (1486) made that chronology explicit, declaring that witchcraft only emerged around 1400. However, despite being strongly influenced by the *Malleus*, Gianfrancesco argued that witchcraft had always existed. Invoking the fundamental Scholastic distinction between 'substance' and 'accidents', he declared that witchcraft might look new to superficial observers, but its essentials were eternal: *maleficium*, idolatrous worship of demons, and bodily interaction with them, including sex. He reminded readers that ancient texts, including Vergil's *Aeneid* and Ovid's *Metamorphoses*, depicted sexual relations and marriages between mortals and gods such as Venus and Jove. Children were often born from these couplings: Aeneas was the son of Venus and the mortal Anchises. Since Christians accepted that the so-called gods were demons in disguise, and because miscegenation between humans and demons was confirmed even by Genesis 6:4 (which declared that 'sons of god' coupled with 'daughters of men', producing giants),[40] Gianfrancesco argued that witchcraft could not be fundamentally new.

But there was a problem with demonic sexuality: the great Scholastic theologian Thomas Aquinas (d. 1274) had taught that angels lacked intrinsic bodies and thus had no gender or sex life. His view was accepted as orthodox by most theologians, including early modern witchcraft theorists, for Aquinas had also explained how fallen angels might participate in human generation. Demons could create and animate lifelike female-gendered bodies, then these succubi might have intercourse with men and steal their semen. Succubi could thereupon transgender themselves into male *incubi* and impregnate women with the stolen semen. The resulting children, erroneously considered 'offspring of gods', would be exceptional in many ways, including extraordinary stature, as in Genesis 6:4. Nonetheless, the fathers of such children would not be demons, but rather the men whose semen was stolen. Although Aquinas argued only that such human-demon miscegenation was *possible*, his bizarre sexual hypothesis was adopted as provable fact by numerous witchcraft theorists after 1430.

Until recently, scholars considered heresy and *maleficia* fundamental to the definition of witchcraft, interpreting accusations of demonic fornication as peripheral, merely a sadistic way of 'demonizing' witch-hunt defendants. Because women accounted for about 80% of victims, it seemed logical to some writers that these accusations unmasked witch-hunting as 'woman-hunting', a women's 'holocaust'.[41] But while witch-hating and witchcraft theory were expressed in fanatically misogynistic rhetoric (especially in the *Malleus*), the weird fantasy of human/demon copulation served ideological ends that were 'scientific'. It lent plausibility to angelology and demonology, a major sub-discipline of theology, the 'queen of sciences'.

*Strix* illustrates the philosophical and theological utility of demonic sexual relations more meticulously than other defenses of witch-hunting, including the *Malleus*. When questioned about her familiar 'Ludovicus', Strix declares that he flew her to the sabbat 'in the body'; she 'knows' Ludovicus's own body is real because she has touched it 'with these very hands'. Her enthusiastic 'confession' to copulating with her demon has a verve that equals or surpasses her professed horror at the desecrated, bleeding host. She readily 'confesses' that 'Ludovicus's' extraordinary sexual prowess gave her greater pleasure than she ever enjoyed 'with my man'. Gianfrancesco contrasts her naive description of 'Ludovicus's' virility to the demon's unnatural corporeality by having Apistius ask her to compare 'Ludovicus's' body to that of ordinary men. Strix replies that it seems identical, but softer, resembling mattresses stuffed with cotton. The inquisitor and Phronimus methodically explain that this characteristic, among others, reveals the demonic body's artificiality. Then the inquisitor pornographically speculates that the abnormal size of demons' 'members' causes the orgasmic pleasure witches 'confess', by stimulating 'something deep inside' the women.[42]

In itself, sex with demons was nothing new. Since antiquity, Christian theologians had discussed women who complained that predatory *incubi* sexually assaulted them while they slept.[43] A famous twelfth-century story recounted that Saint Bernard of Clairvaux successfully exorcised a desperate woman, exiling her incubus forever; others traced Merlin's magical powers to his parentage, a nun and an incubus.[44] There were also renowned biblical precedents. Saint Paul instructed women to veil their hair 'for the angels' and the demon Asmodeus killed seven husbands of Sarah, preventing her from ever consummating a marriage. But the angel Raphael taught her fiancé Tobias how to banish the demon, allowing the couple to enjoy their wedding night. Witchcraft theorists regularly cited both Paul and Asmodeus as proof that *incubi* were real. Technically, Asmodeus was not an incubus, but the implication was so traditional that Milton mentioned it in *Paradise Lost*, alluding to Satan's erotic fascination with Eve.[45]

## 4 The reality of demons

The *Malleus* conceded that stories of *incubi* portrayed them as unwelcome sexual predators before 1400. But, it argued, witchcraft arose around 1400 because women became sexually voracious paramours of *incubi*; it cited 'the expert testimony of the witches themselves' as evidence.[46] The *Malleus*'s rabid misogyny is justly infamous, but this accusation was *theologically* useful, allowing the treatise to address the 'elephant in the room' question about demons. Before demonstrating the reality of witches' experiences, one had to tackle an even more fundamental question, unforeseen by the canon *Episcopi*: the reality of demons. The tenth-century canonist took for granted that demons were real. Being unacquainted with Aristotle, he could not foresee that five centuries later, witchcraft theorists would be seriously preoccupied by Aquinas's admission that 'the Philosopher' made no room for demons.[47]

Some Scholastic theologians, notably Aquinas, asserted that angels and demons were incorporeal 'separate spirits'; Bonaventure and others consideredo angelic/demonic bodies real but too 'subtle' for human senses to detect. So how could humans couple with beings whose bodies were either nonexistent or imperceptible? Aquinas's theory of virtual, prosthetic demonic bodies resolved the conundrum. Demons 'assumed' or 'put on' such lifelike bodies that – as Gianfrancesco's Strix confirms – ordinary humans were often fooled. Numerous women – and some men – supposedly became witches after realistically-embodied demons lured them into coitus. The *Malleus maleficarum* codified this theory by declaring that 'the expert witness of the witches themselves' demonstrated infallibly that demons copulated as well or better than human paramours.[48]

Gianfrancesco argued with unusual bluntness that belief in demonic witchcraft is indispensable to Christian faith. Although most witchcraft theorists implied the correlation, *Strix* makes it baldly explicit. Not until John Wesley protested lapidarily that 'the giving up of witchcraft is the giving up of the Bible' was the connection expressed more forcefully.[49] Gianfrancesco Pico was a devout Christian, but he saw no incompatibility between hating witches and loving Christianity. Indeed, the appalling religious conflicts of the sixteenth and seventeenth centuries attest that few early modern Christians recognized an abstract duty to spread the milk of human kindness beyond confessional boundaries. Even in the eighteenth century, Wesley's Methodism lacked many humane ideals common to modern mainstream Christianity.

Witch-hating reflects a historic reversal of churchmen's consensus about the magical beliefs of illiterate folk. Before 1400, learned Christians considered witchcraft an unreal crime that existed only in ignorant people's imagination. They scoffed at cannibalistic figures inherited from ancient and early medieval paganism, such as the baby-killing, owl-like *strix*, or witches who surreptitiously consumed their victims' hearts or vitals 'from inside'.[50] But by about 1400 the consensus was shifting towards a double-negative judgment: 'it is *not* true that witchcraft does not exist, *not* true that it exists only in the unenlightened imagination; abundant proofs demonstrate that it exists in reality'. Some arguments were biblical, as mentioned above, but juridical 'proofs', often involving torture, were increasingly common. Preoccupation with mass heresies, especially Waldensianism and Hussitism, inspired closer scrutiny of common people's beliefs, including sorcery – charms and spells – and uncanny folkloric figures such as werewolves and witches. Christian intellectuals accepted the folk's testimony, but contested their belief that the power of charms and spells lay with the magician, and that mere humans could transform bodily reality. All power had spiritual sources: good power came from God, evil from the devil.[51]

Occasionally, pharmacology figured in early witchcraft theories, though psychotropic drug use among women accused as night-traveling 'witches' or 'servants of Diana' remains unproven. Between 1430 and 1440, anecdotes described women who applied certain ointments to their skin, inviting skeptical confessors or neighbors to watch them fly away to enjoy wonderful feasts and revels in remote locales. Observers reported that the ointments caused the women nothing but profound slumber and pleasant dreams, yet such stories piqued learned men's curiosity in Gianfrancesco's time. Several authorities experimented with 'witches' salves', hoping to witness the arrival of demons, but their experiments failed consistently.[52] Gianfrancesco's acquaintance, the inquisitor Bartolomeo Spina°, who operated in nearby Ferrara, complained that the devil caused such experiments to fail in order to spread skepticism about the reality of witchcraft and thwart the holy work of inquisitors like himself. After 1550, skeptical jurists and physicians increasingly took over the experiments, aiming to *disprove* the reality of witches' experiences, by tracing them to natural causes.[53]

Altogether, Gianfrancesco Pico's *Strix* was an innovative description of what witches did and why. It articulated the stereotypes of witchcraft more clearly than formal treatises like the *Malleus*, because its dialogic format enlivened their arid ratiocination. Terse, jargon-laden Scholastic theological arguments seemed illogical, self-contradictory or incomprehensible to many sixteenth-century humanists. Dramatized conversation allowed *Strix* a looser, more leisurely exposition, even for technical explanations and extended quotations. Gianfrancesco even attempted to make his theories accessible to people who only read the vernacular, or could only hear *Strix* read aloud. Leandro Alberti's 1524 translation strove to provide greater clarity through paraphase, expansion, and colloquial Italian. Nonetheless, *Strix* remained more difficult than either man foresaw for all but the best-educated readers, so its impact was relatively small until recent times: it was translated into

Italian again in 1555, Torquato Tasso read and cited it in the 1580s, and the Latin text was reprinted in 1612. In a crowning irony, Gianfrancesco is not infrequently confused with his celebrated humanist uncle, a gaffe neither man would have appreciated.[54]

## Notes

1 See Albano Biondi, 'Introduzione', in Gianfrancesco Pico, *Libro detto strega*, trans. Leandro Alberti, ed. Biondi, Venice: Marsilio, 1989, pp. 9–45. The last three defendants were executed in 1525 (ibid., 26).
2 See n. 1. Latin text in *La Sorcière: Dialogue en trois livres sur la tromperie des démons*, critical ed. and trans. Alfredo Perifano, Turnhout: Brepols, 2007. I include signature references for the first edition, *Strix, sive De ludificatione daemonum*, Bologna: Girolamo de' Benedetti, 1523. See also the valuable apparatus and interpretations in Lucia Pappalardo, *La Strega (Strix) di Gianfrancesco Pico: Introduzione, testo, traduzione, e commento*, Rome: Città Nuova, 2017.
3 Stuart Clark, *Thinking with Demons: The Idea of Witchcraft in Early Modern Europe*, Oxford: Oxford University Press, 1997, pp. vii–x at ix; Walter Stephens, *Demon Lovers: Witchcraft, Sex, and the Crisis of Belief*, Chicago: University of Chicago Press, 2002, pp. 8–9.
4 *Merriam-Webster Dictionary*, s.v. humanism. <www.merriam-webster.com/dictionary/humanism> (accessed 10 July 2019).
5 Christopher Celenza, 'Humanism', in Anthony Grafton et al., eds, *The Classical Tradition*, Cambridge, MA: Belknap Press, 2010, pp. 462–67; James Turner, *Philology: The Forgotten Origins of the Modern Humanities*, Princeton: Princeton University Press, 2014, pp. 1–64.
6 Michael Allen, 'Ficino, Marsilio', in Grafton et al., eds, *Classical Tradition*, pp. 360–61; Brian Copenhaver, 'Pico della Mirandola, Giovanni', in ibid., pp. 728–29; D. P. Walker, *The Ancient Theology: Studies in Christian Platonism from the Fifteenth to the Eighteenth Century*, London: Duckworth, 1972, pp. 1–21.
7 Pier Cesare Bori, 'The Historical and Biographical Background of the *Oration*', in Giovanni Pico della Mirandola, *Oration on the Dignity of Man*, ed. Francesco Borghesi, Michael Papio, and Massimo Riva, Cambridge: Cambridge University Press, 2012, pp. 10–36.
8 Walker, *Ancient Theology*, pp. 22–131.
9 Henricus Institoris, *The Hammer of Witches*, trans. Christopher S. Mackay, Cambridge: Cambridge University Press, 2009, pp. 71–74 [1A*-2B*]; Bori, 'Background'; Copenhaver, 'Pico'.
10 Peter Burke, 'Witchcraft and Magic in Renaissance Italy: Gianfrancesco Pico and His *Strix*', in Sydney Anglo, ed., *The Damned Art: Essays in the Literature of Witchcraft*, London: Routledge and Kegan Paul, 1977, pp. 32–52 at 43–44.
11 See *e.g.* Psalm 95:5 ('omnes dii gentium daemonia'); 1 Corinthians 10:20.
12 Brian P. Copenhaver, trans., *Hermetica*, Cambridge: Cambridge University Press, 1992, pp. 80–82; D. P. Walker, *Spiritual and Demonic Magic from Ficino to Campanella*, Notre Dame, IN: University of Notre Dame Press, 1975 [original ed. 1958], pp. 36–53.
13 For the canon *Episcopi* and related texts, see Alan Charles Kors and Edward Peters, *Witchcraft in Europe, 400–1700: A Documentary History*, Philadelphia: University of Pennsylvania Press, 2001, pp. 58–78. Gianfrancesco addresses it explicitly: Pico, *Strix*, sig. G2r–v (*La Sorcière*, ed. Perifano, 103–5) and it is implicit throughout. See Walter Stephens, 'Learned Credulity in Gianfrancesco Pico's *Strix*', in *Renaissance and Reformation/Renaissance et Réforme*, 2019, vol. 42/4, 17–40.

14 Christa Tuczay, 'Holda', in Richard Golden, ed., *The Encyclopedia of Witchcraft: The Western Tradition* [henceforth *EW*], Santa Barbara: ABC-CLIO, 2006, vol. 2, pp. 501–2. The works of Claude Lecouteux are particularly informative about the survival of northern paganism, especially *Fantômes et revenants au moyen âge*, Paris: Editions Imago, 1986, and *Chasses fantastiques et cohortes de la nuit au moyen âge*, Paris: Editions Imago, 1999.
15 Michael D. Bailey, *Battling Demons: Witchcraft, Heresy, and Reform in the Late Middle Ages*, University Park, PA: Pennsylvania State University Press, 2003; Michael D. Bailey and Edward Peters, 'A Sabbat of Demonologists, Basel, 1431–1440', *Historian*, 2003, vol. 65/6, 1375–95.
16 Institoris, *The Hammer of Witches*, pp. 307–10 [108A–109C]; it quoted one witch as testifying that witches could *occasionally* decide to attend the sabbat only 'in the spirit' by performing a certain ritual (ibid., 300–301 [105A–B]).
17 On the tradition of contrasting Plato and Aristotle, especially in regards to Christianity, see Eva Del Soldato, *Early Modern Aristotle: On the Making and Unmaking of Authority*, Philadelphia: University of Pennsylvania Press, 2020.
18 'run riot in': Gianfrancesco Pico della Mirandola, *On the Imagination*, trans. Harry Caplan (1930; Repr. Westport, CT: Greenwood, 1971), p. 57. *Illudunt* is a more neutral concept.
19 Charles B. Schmitt, *Gianfrancesco Pico della Mirandola (1469–1533) and His Critique of Aristotle*, The Hague: Martinus Nijhoff, 1967, and Gian Mario Cao, '*Inter Alias Philosophorum Sectas, et Humani, et Mites*: Gianfrancesco Pico and the Sceptics' in Gianni Paganini and José R. Maia Neto, eds, *Renaissance Scepticisms*, Dordrecht: Springer, 2009, pp. 138–42.
20 Walter Stephens, 'Skepticism, Empiricism, and Proof in Gianfrancesco Pico della Mirandola's *Strix*', *Magic, Ritual, and Witchcraft*, 2016, vol. 11/1, 6–29.
21 Burke, 'Witchcraft and Magic in Renaissance Italy', p. 44, quoting Eugenio Garin, *Italian Humanism*, New York: Harper and Row, 1965, p. 133.
22 Pico, *Strix*, sig. A2r (*La Sorcière*, ed. Perifano, p. 51). Alberti oversaw the publication of *Strix* and, as Albano Biondi observed ('Introduzione', pp. 10–11), functioned as 'the press agent of the entire affair'.
23 Editorial insertion by Leandro Alberti, *Libro detto strega*, p. 140.
24 Miri Rubin, *Gentile Tales: The Narrative Assault on Late Medieval Jews*, New Haven: Yale University Press, 1999; Stephens, *Demon Lovers*, pp. 207–40, esp. 217–21.
25 On the role of double-negative affirmations in this and the following speech (by Dicastes), see Stephens, *Demon Lovers*, pp. 142–44 and 256–60.
26 Andreas Bodenstein von Karlstadt, *The Eucharistic Pamphlets*, trans. Amy Nelson Burnett, Kirksville, MO: Truman State University Press, 2011, pp. 8–16, 160–62; Carlos M. N. Eire, *War Against the Idols: The Reformation of Worship from Erasmus to Calvin*, Cambridge: Cambridge University Press, 1986, pp. 110–21, 146.
27 Listed by Biondi, 'Introduzione', pp. 14–15.
28 Brian P. Levack, *The Witch-Hunt in Early Modern Europe*, 4th ed., London: Routledge, 2016, pp. 128–35; Julian Goodare, *The European Witch-Hunt*, London: Routledge, 2016, pp. 267–73.
29 Biondi, 'Introduzione', pp. 11–22; 217–22. The title *Malleus maleficarum* uses the female form of the word for witch.
30 Stephens, *Demon Lovers*, pp. 256–60, 277–87.
31 Institoris, *The Hammer of Witches*, p. 92 [7C].
32 Stephens, *Demon Lovers*, pp. 197–206.
33 English witches were rarely accused of demonic fornication except during the Civil Wars; instead, they supposedly allowed familiars embodied as small animals to suckle at the 'witch's teat' (Stephens, *Demon Lovers*, pp. 102–6).

34 See Virginia Krause's chapter in this volume.
35 *Strix*, sig. E3v (*La Sorcière*, ed. Perifano, p. 88). All English translations of *Strix* my own.
36 Stephens, *Demon Lovers*, pp. 98–99. For whatever reason, the texts of *Strix* and its translation never mention the inquisitor's surname.
37 Daniel Ogden, ed., *Magic, Witchcraft, and Ghosts in the Greek and Roman Worlds: A Sourcebook*, Oxford: Oxford University Press, 2002, pp. 78–145; Marguerite Johnson, 'Necromancy', in *EW*, vol. 3, pp. 808–9; Kieckhefer, *Magic in the Middle Ages*, pp. 152–53.
38 Stephens, *Demon Lovers*, pp. 149–54.
39 Goodare, *European Witch-Hunt*, pp. 39–50; Kors and Peters, *Witchcraft in Europe*, pp. 149–75.
40 On biblical giants, see Institoris, *The Hammer of Witches*, pp. 124–33 [22B–26D], and Walter Stephens, *Giants in Those Days: Folklore, Ancient History, and Nationalism*, Lincoln, NE: University of Nebraska Press, 1989, pp. 58–97.
41 Stephens, *Demon Lovers*, pp. 32–36; Diane Purkiss, *The Witch in History: Early Modern and Twentieth-Century Representations*, London: Routledge, 1996, pp. 1–29; for the historical realities, see Merry Wiesner-Hanks, 'Gender', *EW*, vol. 2, pp. 407–11.
42 Stephens, 'Skepticism, Empiricism, and Proof', pp. 12–18.
43 Augustine, *City of God*, 15.23; Christa Tuczay, 'Incubus and Succubus', in *EW*, vol. 2, pp. 546–48; Richard Firth Green, *Elf Queens and Holy Friars: Fairy Beliefs and the Medieval Church*, Philadelphia: University of Pennsylvania Press, 2016, pp. 76–84.
44 Juliette Wood, 'Merlin', *EW*, vol. 3, pp. 753–54; Green, *Elf Queens*, pp. 85–97; Stephens, *Demon Lovers*, pp. 318–20.
45 1 Corinthians 11:10; Tobit 3:7–8, 6:14–22; *Paradise Lost* 4.166–71, forecasting Satan's behavior in Books 4 and 9; cf. *Paradise Regained*, 2.151–52.
46 Stephens, *Demon Lovers*, pp. 46–50; Goodare, *European Witch-Hunt*, p. 50.
47 Institoris, *The Hammer of Witches*, pp. 92–93 [7D–8A]; Thomas Aquinas, *Treatise on Separate Substances*, ed. Francis J. Lescoe, West Hartford, CT: Saint Joseph College, 1963, pp. 54–55: 'we find that neither Aristotle nor any of his followers has made mention of demons'; cf. Stephens, *Demon Lovers*, pp. 20–26, 325–31; Stephens, 'Corporeality, Angelic and Demonic', and 'Imagination', in *EW*, vol. 1, pp. 217–19, vol. 2, pp. 538–40.
48 Stephens, 'Skepticism, Empiricism, and Proof', pp. 22–25; Stephens, *Demon Lovers*, pp. 92–96. For a very different interpretation, see Armando Maggi, *In the Company of Demons: Unnatural Beings, Love, and Identity in the Italian Renaissance*, Chicago: University of Chicago Press, 2006, pp. 25–65, at 47–54.
49 Stephens, *Demon Lovers*, pp. 366–67.
50 Lecouteux, *Fantômes et Revenants*, pp. 10–60, explains how Christian theologians gradually dismissed such figures as incorporeal, demonically-inspired phantoms between about 300 and 1200 CE; by opposing canon *Episcopi*, witchcraft theorists explicitly contested the previous consensus.
51 The *Malleus*'s and other theories of demonic power depend on the pre-Copernican idea that bodies (i.e., matter) are never able to move themselves; there must always be a mover, which must necessarily be spiritual (Institoris, *The Hammer of Witches*, pp. 91–105 [7A–13D]).
52 Michael Ostling, 'Babyfat and Belladonna: Witches' Ointments and the Contestation of Reality', *Magic, Ritual, and Witchcraft*, 2016, vol. 11/1, 30–59.
53 From ancient times, physicians considered the *incubus* – or *ephialtes* or *faunus* – as mere dreams caused by overindulgence or disease, an interpretation that early witchcraft theorists already opposed (Stephens, *Demon Lovers*, pp. 137–39).
54 Stephens, 'Skepticism, Empiricism, and Proof', pp. 7–9.

## Further reading

Burke, Peter, 'Witchcraft and Magic in Renaissance Italy: Gianfrancesco Pico and His *Strix*', in Sydney Anglo, ed., *The Damned Art: Essays in the Literature of Witchcraft*, London: Routledge and Kegan Paul, 1977, pp. 32–52.

Maggi, Armando, *In the Company of Demons: Unnatural Beings, Love, and Identity in the Italian Renaissance*, Chicago: University of Chicago Press. 2006.

Stephens, Walter, *Demon Lovers: Witchcraft, Sex, and the Crisis of Belief*, Chicago: University of Chicago Press. 2002.

——, 'Skepticism, Empiricism, and Proof in Gianfrancesco Pico della Mirandola's *Strix*', *Magic, Ritual, and Witchcraft*, 2016, vol. 11/1, 6–29.

——, 'Learned Credulity in Gianfrancesco Pico's *Strix*', *Renaissance and Reformation/Renaissance et Réforme*, 2019, vol. 42/4, 17–40.

# Part 3
# The sixteenth-century debate

## 6 'Against the devil, the subtle and cunning enemy'

Johann Wier's *De praestigiis daemonum*

*Michaela Valente*

The faithful minister of Jesus Christ will search out the sheep that has become lost by following Satan, and he will lead it back to the fold of Christ. If she has wandered astray because of false beliefs, a careful test – by an examination of the article of Faith – will reveal the fact readily. It will be clearly seen whether she struggles stubbornly against sounder doctrine (and thus deserves the brand of heresy) or whether she changes her mind and wakes from the lethargy of error and mental impairment, longing with all her heart to be accepted again as a member of the Church and begging that prayers be said on her behalf.[1]

It is hard to imagine when reading these words that the lost sheep to be brought back into the fold was a witch, a woman accused of heinous misdeeds that she was able to commit as a result of her alliance with Satan. It is even harder when we consider that this proposal was made at a time when trials and proceedings were being held for witches all over Europe. Stranger still, this essentially religious argument is made not by a trained theologian but by a physician. In the second half of the sixteenth century, Johann Wier (or Weyer), a physician to the Duke of Cleves, became the first major advocate of Europe's witches – the first who opposed the witch-hunt not only for religious reasons but for philological, philosophical, scientific, and legal ones as well.[2]

In his most important work, *De praestigiis daemonum* (On the Deceptions of Devils), Wier reminds us that, through his own example, Jesus Christ had taught that at least an attempt should be made to recover lost sheep: for the first time this message of mercy and its appeal to (re-)convert the wayward was extended to women accused of witchcraft. Aware of the implications, Wier maintained that it was only through direct contact with the accused that one could understand whether the woman was a stubborn heretic or whether she could be awoken from her errors so that she might ask to be readmitted into the Church. In addition, the entire Christian community, according to Wier, should seize the occasion of this confrontation with the witch as an opportunity to examine itself and its own behaviour.[3] Wier's contribution to the witchcraft debate was profound but the world had also changed since the publication of the *Malleus maleficarum*: the New World had been discovered, the authority of the Church of Rome had been challenged by Martin Luther and many others, and the earth was no longer at the centre of the universe, as Copernicus had shown. Wier's *De praestigiis* was responding to this altered reality. In turn, it would prompt numerous rebuttals from those who believed in the reality of witchcraft.

## 1 Wier's formation

Before undertaking a detailed examination of Wier's premises and his theory let us first reconstruct his biography. Johann Wier was born in 1515 at Grave, in Northern Brabant, in an area of mixed German and Dutch culture. His interest in demons began early, when he lived with his family, which, according to him, was protected by a *daemon* (a spiritual being intermediate between God and humanity). According to Wier, this *daemon* announced the arrival of merchants, an important family event as their father was a hop merchant. Wier claimed to have witnessed these announcements along with his brothers. Other biographies and autobiographies of scholars of the period contain similar tales involving more or less frequent visitations of such supernatural guardian angels. In addition to Jean Bodin°, the Italian astrologer Girolamo Cardano also revealed that he had had dealings with *daemons* since his early childhood.[4]

This is more than just a biographical detail because it reveals Wier's cultural background. With very few exceptions scholars have tended to obscure these supernatural beliefs as they generally preferred to ascribe more weight and importance to the rationalistic aspects of Wier's thought and work. Historians have found it easier to understand opposition to witchcraft on scientific grounds than religious ones. However, by neglecting this apparent contradiction between reason and belief in Wier's thought (which was quite obvious to his contemporary detractors) we risk underestimating and downplaying the radical nature of the challenge he put down.

Unlike other authors, Wier also tells us a great deal about his family, both the one he was born into and the one he founded himself. He was very close to his two brothers Arnold and Mathias. The latter was a religious reformer who was extremely active in contemporary confessional debates.[5] This close fraternal relationship may help explain Johann's ambiguous attitude in religious matters. The Dutch historian Hans de Waardt has identified the existence of a sister in the Wier family, Elizabeth, who was married to the humanist Charles Utenhove, and this is another important element in the physician's cultural network.[6]

His family's wealth and prosperity meant that Johann obtained a good education.[7] When he was fifteen years old, Johann became an apprentice to the great Renaissance philosopher Heinrich Cornelius Agrippa von Nettesheim (1486–1535). This encounter would change his life. For four years, he studied with this famous (and, to him, beloved) teacher, who was forced to move frequently because of his unconventional behaviour and controversial publications. Agrippa wrote in those years his main philosophical works: the *De occulta philosophia* (1533) and the *De incertitudine et vanitate scientiarum* (1530). Wier referred to Agrippa as 'my erstwhile host and revered teacher.'[8]

His devotion and debts to his master led Wier to deny several negative rumours that surrounded Agrippa. First, he sought to refute the accusations of magic and witchcraft that had arisen with the publication of *De occulta philosophia*.[9] He then dealt with the claims put forth in Paolo Giovio's *Elogia doctorum virorum* (1546) and Andreas Hondorff's *Promptuarium exemplorum* (1576) that Agrippa was a necromancer who was accompanied by the devil in the guise of a black dog.[10] Wier conceded that Agrippa was very attached to his dog from which he could not bear to be separated. While he denounced Agrippa's excessive love for his pet as sheer childishness ('Agrippa was too childishly fond of his dog'), he invoked his own personal experience ('I often walked him on the rope leash when I was studying under Agrippa') to prove there was nothing demonic about Agrippa's pet dog.[11]

These legends enjoyed belief because they echoed other rumours regarding demons in the form of animals similar to the Faust legend, the story of a scholar who sold his soul to the devil later made famous by Christopher Marlowe. The suspicion that Agrippa was a magician followed an episode in which, after shutting himself up for several days in his study in the sole company of his dog, he emerged quite abreast of the latest events that had transpired. Giovio argued that the demon-dog had been Agrippa's news source, but Wier denied this and pointed out that Agrippa could count on a vast network of friends who were keeping him up to date with their letters. Wier expressed dismay at those scholars who speak and write 'so foolishly on the basis of an idle rumour that had circulated.'[12]

At the same time, Wier adopted a critical attitude towards the practice of (ritual) magic, which Agrippa had repudiated in his *De vanitate* though he continued to be interested in it (Figure 6.1). Wier, instead, considered it a form of corruption of the human spirit. In spite of this difference, many elements in Agrippa's thought influenced Wier: bearing a clearly Agrippian stamp are Wier's polemics against Aristotle and the wider peripatetic tradition, though they also are tempered by a strong critique of certain aspects of Platonism. Yet, the most important thing Agrippa taught him was the model of an Erasmian scholar imbued with the ideals of Renaissance humanism.[13] In addition to always siding with the cause of scholarly freedom as in the case of the unjustly persecuted humanist Johann Reuchlin (1455–1522), Agrippa defended a woman in Metz accused of being a witch only because her mother had been one. Agrippa argued that the woman had been baptized and that the baptism thus annulled whatever pact there may have been between her mother and Satan. In this way he emphasized the substantial value of the sacrament of baptism.[14]

*Figure 6.1* Fragment of title page showing a ritual magician surrounded by demons. Ludwig Milich, *Der Zauber Teuffel, das ist, Von Zauberen, Warsagung, Beschwehren, gegen Aberglauben, Hexeren, und mancherley Wercken des Teuffels*, Frankfurt: Martin Lechler, 1566. Sp Coll Ferguson Af-e.74. Image by permission of University of Glasgow Library, Special Collections.

After this training with Agrippa, Wier studied medicine at the University of Paris, arriving in 1533 and taking his degree in 1537. This was an age of great ferment for universities in France thanks to Francis I's cultural policy: the leading medical scholars of the day were active in France including men like Andreas Vesalius (1514–1564), who overcame restrictions on anatomical dissection, the French physician Jean Fernel (1497–1558), and the heterodox Spanish physician Michael Servetus (c.1511–1553), who was burnt at the stake in Geneva for rejecting the Trinity.[15] Wier, already interested in medicine, had been in touch with all these men.

After his studies, he was subsequently employed as a town physician, first at Ravenstein and then in the more substantial city of Arnhem. The experience he acquired during these early years was of great importance for his transition from medical theory to practice. In 1548 he was involved in an episode of mass demonic possession. Faced with an explosion of cases, Wier examined the possessed and concluded that they were victims of hypnotic suggestion. As a result of this experience he was increasingly sceptical of what he regarded as human deceit and demonic trickery. During these years he unmasked various impostors who had taken advantage of popular credulity and superstition to extort money: unfortunately, some of these were churchmen. For example, a man persuaded an ailing woman that she needed an exorcism which had to be paid for when she could have been treated by a physician.[16] Wier saw that demonic and human trickery threatened humanity and needed to be exposed. Yet, Wier's indignation against those who ought to have helped but who used their position of strength for profit was also tinged with anti-clericalism.

During the same period Wier married Judith Wintgens who would later help him in a number of cases along with their daughter Sofia.[17] Their marriage also produced Dietrich, a jurist and ambassador at the court of the prince-elector of the Palatinate, Heinrich, a physician, Galenus, who later took up his father's post at the duke's court, and Johannes, who became an important ducal official.[18] When his wife Judith died in 1572, Wier lost a valued collaborator and careful observer. Though he remarried only two years later with Henrietta Holt, who is mentioned in the *De praestigiis*,[19] Wier long cherished the memory of his beloved first wife and paid homage to her in a later work *De ira morbo*.

## 2 Cleves: an Erasmian duchy

In 1550, Wier was appointed personal physician to the tolerant Duke William V of Cleves, Jülich, and Berg, whose father had progressively reformed religion in his duchy across the Dutch border under the influence of Erasmus. The duke had been defeated by the Holy Roman Emperor Charles V in 1543 but in Cleves the hopes of creating conditions favourable for a peaceful coexistence between different confessions and the church reform proposed by Erasmus and his followers lived on, in spite of the duke himself having chosen Catholicism. As Wier would later emphasize, the ducal territories also reformed the laws on witchcraft, increasing the burden of proof needed for a conviction. The irenic William V also wanted to attract the best scholars to his court and founded the university of Duisberg. The court welcomed the famous Hebraist Andreas Masius (1514–1573), a Catholic hardliner, and the geographer Gerhard Mercator (1512–1594), among others. The presence of so many illustrious scholars was a continuous source of stimulation for Wier and a constant intellectual challenge.[20]

The fluid confessional identity of the duchy also has implications for our understanding of Wier's own religious beliefs, which remains a subject of debate among historians. Wier himself seemed to send conflicting signals.

The conclusion of his *De praestigiis daemonum* appealed (perhaps tongue in cheek) to the Catholic Church,

> I wish to assert noting in this book which I would not submit, without reservation, to the equitable judgement of the universal Church of Christ (*catholicae Christi ecclesiae*), being ready to make amends at once with a willing retraction in any point I am convicted of error.[21]

By contrast, in the German translation he praised the Reformation (Figure 6.2). The two versions, however, were aimed at different readerships.[22]

In addition to Wier's public declarations, we also need to consider, as Gary Waite has pointed out, the question of the influence of his brother Mathias who was close to the Family of Love and corresponded with Henry Nicholis (c.1501–c.1580), its mystical founder.[23] The Family of Love was a secretive radical Protestant sect that rejected many traditional Protestant and Catholic practices, but the Familists remained members of the official church to avoid prosecution. Hans de Waardt has argued that Wier was a member of the Family of Love, which could explain his refusal to take part in an increasingly confessionalized society.[24] Recently, Vera Hoorens, drawing on Christopher Baxter's interpretation, has argued that Wier's *De praestigiis* was a denunciation of the alleged abuses of the Catholic Church.[25] However, such a denunciation on its own is not necessarily a sign that Wier had joined the Reformation given that many ecclesiastics, even those in leading positions, were critical and hoped for a reform of the Church.

There is similarly little evidence for H. C. Erik Midelfort's depiction of Wier as an Erasmian Lutheran.[26] Wier's writings contain no precise references to or praise for the writings of the reformers, with the exception of Luther's colleague, Philip Melanchthon, whose theological works Wier does not mention. Similarly, Wier does not seize the opportunity to attack the papacy and the Roman curia, a standard trope of Protestant polemics. Perhaps the safest conclusion is that Wier, based in Cleves, did not need to align himself with any one side. This was not opportunism but, as we shall see, a choice he made in order to further his main objective which was to combat Satan and it was a choice very much influenced by the political situation in the duchy.

## 3 The devil, witches, and magicians: *De praestigiis daemonum*

In 1563, Wier published his most important work, *De praestigiis daemonum, ac incantationibus*, with the well-known Basel printer Johann Oporinus. The choice was doubtless intentional. The printer had been a former pupil of the medical reformer Paracelsus. Basel had been Erasmus's home for many years, and it remained true to his spirit, a place of religious tolerance and scientific renewal, as demonstrated by its various printing houses and university.

'Against the devil' 109

*Figure 6.2* Title page showing a group of witches apparently preparing for flight. Johann Wier, *De Praestigiis …: Von den Teuffeln, Zaubrern, Schwartzkünstlern, Teuffelsbeschwerern, Hexen oder Unholden und Gifftbereitem*, trans. Johann Füglin, Frankfurt: Peter Schmidt and Sigmund Feyerabend, 1566 [Phys.m. 306–1]. Image by permission of Bayerische Staatsbibliothek, Munich. Other German editions show a witch with a cauldron apparently brewing up a storm.

The *De praestigiis* marked a shift in focus which was already apparent in the work's title. Where the *Malleus maleficarum* (The Hammer of [Female] Witches) focussed on the crimes of *witches*, the *De praestigiis daemonum* centred, as its title indicated, its attention on the deceptions of *demons*. This change in emphasis is crucial to understanding Wier's scepticism. Wier's readers and opponents recognized that the *De praestigiis* participated in traditional demonological discourse but that he upset the intricate balance between God, the devil and his witches that lay at its heart. The great paradox of Wier's scepticism as set out in the *De praestigiis* was that it actually assigned *more* power to the devil than his adversaries ever had.

Faced with the wide-spread and all-pervasive action of the devil and his army of followers, Wier sought to unravel the tangled skein and hand the reader the thread that will lead him out of what he calls the labyrinth of incantations.[27] In Wier's view, the only way out of that maze was to return to the authentic original doctrine of the Church of Christ, bring an end to the wars of religion and love one's neighbour. These were the weapons which Wier thought were needed to combat Satan.

Accordingly, Wier rejected the eternal struggle between good and evil, between God and devil, because this would make the latter, a creature, equal to the Creator.[28] Appealing to the authority of Saint Augustine, he argued that if God was indeed all powerful, this also mitigated the responsibility of witches whose actions were embedded in a pre-established divine plan. At the same time, he also shifted responsibility away from humans towards demons. Through a detailed analysis of demonology and Scripture, Wier pointed out that demons were superior to human beings because of their spiritual nature and because of their prior creation. This superiority made it impossible for demons to place themselves at the service of human beings. In this way, Wier cast doubt on the validity of the demonic pact which was central to early modern demonology. According to Wier, the world was dependent on God's will to keep the devil's power in check. Everything depended on God's will, and devils acted with divine permission:

> God, almighty and merciful though He is, sometimes (in accordance with His plan and our deserts) permits the demon to practice his mocking deceptions and tyranny over men of every social rank; but He still does not indulge him in all matters and permit him to pursue all his purposes, nor does He allow him infinite license, constrained by no limits.[29]

By contrast, witches were not responsible because they were weak, ignorant, ill, poor, and sometimes melancholic; the devil had persuaded them they could do things that were impossible and against natural and divine law. Even if some witches were guilty, Wier denied that they should be punished with death, because they were essentially victims:

> I use the term *lamia* [a figure from Greek mythology] for a woman who, by virtue of a deceptive or imaginary pact that she has entered into with the demon, supposedly perpetrates all kinds of evil-doing, whether by thought or by curse or by glance or by use of some ludicrous object unsuited for the purpose.[30]

The female *lamia* – whom, as we shall see, Wier distinguished from the culpable male magician – thus needed to be cured and re-educated. She may deserve punishment but never the death penalty. In the process, then, the physician also made a claim for the role of medicine in 'healing' the witch.

Wier's defence of the essential innocence of witches fit with his larger goal of refuting and rejecting any kind of magic as a product of superstition in order to establish a new purified kind of religion. His progressive use of philology linked him to the humanist tradition. His defence was based on a new scriptural approach. When discussing the famous biblical command 'Thou shalt not suffer a witch to live' (Exodus 22:18), Wier held that the Hebrew of the Old Testament had been mistranslated. The original term referred not to witches but to poisoners. In addition, he argued that the witch did not have the ability to choose as she was suffering from melancholy, an essentially female pathology that was believed to alter the humours and make the patient susceptible to the wiles of demons. According to Wier, the demon intervened in the woman's imaginative capacity, deceiving her into believing that she had powers which in reality she did not possess. Women due to their natural constitution were therefore more vulnerable to demonic deceptions. Because of their alleged physical and moral inferiority, they ought to be punished less severely than men, as the legal experts of the age agreed.

By contrast, male (ritual) magicians freely tried to subvert natural laws because they made a pact with demons:

> I call a magician anyone who willingly takes instruction from a demon or from other magicians or from books, who employs a formula of known or unknown exotic words (whether reciting it aloud, or muttering it, or affixing it (to some person or thing), or who employs any kind of magical signs, or exorcisms and dreadful execrations, or ceremonies and solemn rites, or many other practices in an illicit attempt of his own volition to summon forth a demon for some deluding, deceiving, or otherwise mocking task, so that the demon will reveal himself in some visible assumed form, or make himself ....[31]

Therefore, the magician was responsible because he chose to devote himself to Satan. Much like Jean Bodin° later, Wier emphasized the importance of a human being *knowingly* allying themselves with the devil. Yet, he placed the bar considerably higher, and out of reach of women. By contrast, the male magician was more aware of what a pact with the devil entailed, notwithstanding the fact that the latter would never submit to the orders of a human being who was ontologically inferior to him. Finally, the physician distinguished a third category, following Wier's re-interpretation of Exodus 22:18: only those who were guilty of poisoning ought to be punished by death because their action produced concrete effects. Satan was able to use all three figures – the *lamia* or (demonically) deluded witch, the arrogant magician, and the poisoner – in his scheme to harm mankind. Wier, however, promised solutions on how to deal with 'the tragedy in an appropriate and Christian manner.'[32]

Wier's deeper objective, however, was not simply to defend witches but to uncover deceptions and with this new interpretative approach to bring about a reform and renewal of the Christian faith, described as:

> a faith that one should embrace, a faith upon which [the Christian] should firmly take a stand. I do not propose a mere recitation of a prescribed formula of faith (which the devil too might readily utter), nor again the faith loudly vaunted by those whose hearts are far from Christ – a hidden, sluggish, dead and barren faith. I urge the faith which renews the whole man, manifesting itself with lively virtue among the members of Christ – a fruitful faith which by God's power brings safety to its possessor – the hallowed anchor, stem, and stern of our salvation – a rock set immovably against all Satan's storm and onsets.[33]

Like Bodin and the *Malleus*, Wier employed a large mass of widespread popular and cultural anecdotes to enrich his analysis, but as we have seen, he reversed the causal relationship between demonic activity and witches. Demons did not carry out the orders of human witches, rather they deceived them. Instead of setting out a radical new argument, Wier thus inverted and subverted the tropes of traditional demonology (he even borrowed the *Malleus*'s explanations for the gendering of witchcraft). Wier, therefore, did not deny the devil's powers to the intense fury of adversaries such as Bodin, who found his arguments weak and tried to demolish his contentions at considerable length.

Wier led an assault on superstition and ignorance by maintaining that witches were not in league with the devil but instead suffered from mental illness and needed medical treatment. He was undeniably the most thorough opponent of witch-hunting of his century. Yet he believed deeply in demonic activities, which seems a contradictory feature. Wier was neither temperamentally nor intellectually inclined to deny the devil's interference in the world, as the Dutch Reformed minister Balthasar Bekker (1634–1698) would do a century later, because Wier continued to share the common worldview of his contemporaries. The *De praestigiis* did not sweep away demonological discourse but participated in it. Wier agreed with the idea that the only infallible tribunal was that of Christ. He followed the Erasmian tradition, and in fact, Erasmus's role as one of the most important sources of *De praestigiis* was remarkable. Wier borrowed a large section from one of Erasmus's own works, *Apologia adversus monachos* (Defence against Monks, 1528), to assert that witches and heretics needed better religious instruction, not death sentences.[34] Drawing on his personal experience with witchcraft persecutions and demonic illusions, Wier went on to consider the legal and judicial aspects of the question and expressed his regret and concern over so much spilt blood, which he considered a success for Satan. Here lies the origin of his rejection, though a qualified one, of the death penalty. Because he considered women accused of witchcraft to be mentally ill and demonically deceived, he attached little value to those confessions extracted under torture, which were generally deemed the most conclusive evidence, just as he did not believe reports of human–animal metamorphosis.[35]

Once again, Wier's ultimate aim was not the defence of witches but rather to reveal Satan's twin deceptions at the expense of Christian Europe. The devil not only deceived and perturbed the minds of poor women, he also persuaded judges that killing these innocent women was the right solution. Wier denounced the laws requiring the death penalty for witches. It was the responsibility of princes to oppose an unjust law and reveal the deception whenever a witchcraft trial should present itself. Only then would demonic deceptions be revealed, would massacres cease, and would the faithful Christian's moral duty become clear. In this way, Wier also incorporated a political argument, emphasizing the benefits for the state of a new policy on witch-hunting.

## 4 Medical works

Throughout his life, Wier practiced medicine, and in his own lifetime and during the century after his death, his medical works found appreciative readers (his *Medicarum observationum liber* [Medical Observations, 1567] was translated into German in 1580 and frequently republished). Medicine faced dramatic challenges after the publication of Paracelsus's complete works (also by Wier's publisher, Oporinus), although Wier opposed Paracelsian medicine and defended Galen to the point of naming his son Galenus.[36] Paracelsus had violently attacked the tradition represented by Galen and Galenic medicine and this was also a reason why he was barred from teaching at universities, but his ideas circulated and were taken up by many.[37] Thus, Paracelsian medicine was at the centre of a Europe-wide controversy that also involved Wier and Thomas Erastus, a physician who defended the reality of witchcraft.[38] Wier's pseudo-medical treatise on anger *De ira morbo* (1577), along with a careful scientific analysis, attempted to prove that Europe's contemporary political and religious troubles derived from anger, and he prescribed Senecan stoicism as a cure.[39]

Wier's religious mission was not successful in his lifetime. Toward the end of his long reign, Duke William V of Cleves reinstituted torture in witchcraft cases.[40] Wier retired to his estates and his son, Galenus, inherited his position. The Duchy of Cleves suffered during the Dutch Revolt nearby and Wier's property was among those damaged by the passage of the Spanish army. He protested against the soldiers' cruelty and attempted to play a diplomatic role.[41] He died in Tecklemburg in 1588.

## 5 Wier's legacy

Wier's work went through six Latin editions, three French translations and two German ones between 1563 and 1583. In 1577 an abridged version, *De lamiis* (Concerning Witches), appeared which aimed at a still larger readership. It circulated widely throughout Europe, even in places like Italy, where papal censors restricted access to heretical works.[42]

Wier's ideas began to be read, received, and discussed in France, England, and the territories of the Holy Roman Empire. In the latter area, Wier's legacy found its way mainly into jurisprudence and legal writings dealing with the punishments to be meted out to witches. As the Jesuit Friedrich Spee ironically observed, the arbitrary use of torture would compel even the holiest of men to admit to the most horrific crimes and this meant that the number of confessions would rise inexorably and with them executions at the stake.[43] In addition, thanks to Wier the idea took root that a medical diagnosis like insanity could serve as a legal argument in witchcraft trials.[44]

His works, quickly opposed by such adversaries as Jean Bodin, King James VI of Scotland°, and his fellow physician Thomas Erastus, aroused a storm of controversy, lasting on and off until the second half of the nineteenth century. His opponents included the most forceful advocates of punishing diabolical witchcraft. Wier became notorious as a defender of witches, as Dudith Sbardellati, an imperial ambassador in Poland, defined him. Jean Bodin and Martin Delrio° implied that a defender of witches must be a witch himself. Wier was among the first to approach witchcraft with scepticism and originality. Andrea Alciato and Giovanni Francesco Ponzinibio° had made previous attempts, but Wier was radically different because he was the first to marshal four different perspectives (philosophical, legal, natural-scientific, and theological) in support of his goal. His book laid a foundation for later sceptics such as the French essayist Michel de Montaigne, who opposed executing alleged witches because the evidence against them was never sufficient to justify their death.[45] In 1584, Reginald Scot° took a more radical step than Wier ever dared to take, denying the possibility that demons could interfere with humans.

In 1660, his complete works were published in Latin in Amsterdam. Yet, Wier rather fell into oblivion after that. The new philosophical systems propounded by René Descartes, Baruch Spinoza, and others left no room for demons. Wier's scepticism seemed muted by comparison and rear-guard demonologists now had other targets. Rediscovery had to wait until the late nineteenth century, when Wier found new appreciation as a precursor of modern psychiatry. In 1885, a French translation appeared in Paris, edited by a pupil of the famous neurologist Jean Martin Charcot, Desirée Bourneville. Not too long afterward, Sigmund Freud ranked Wier's work among the ten most important books he had read and saw him as a forerunner of modern psychiatry, a physician affirming his right to cure his patients rather than burn them.[46] Gregory Zilboorg considered Wier 'the founder of medical psychiatry.'[47] Such assessments possess a kernel of truth but bestow too much praise. Wier's attempt to establish that madness and melancholy could explain some witches' confessions was tinged with misogyny.

An exponent of both humanist scepticism and Dutch theology, armed with the criticisms advanced in the procedural and legal domains, Johann Wier embraced and developed all these aspects: compared to those who had earlier argued in the defence of witches, he found himself at the centre of a wider European network of cultural ties and relationships centred around Basel.[48] His proposal triggered vehement debate which built on earlier polemics while issuing a challenge for battles to come. Wier measured himself against the limits of human knowledge: in his world Satan operated in order to disturb the boundaries between reality and illusions. This was the reason he wrote his works, in order that the truth should be re-established so that 'unity among Christian people will be more quickly reborn and more inviolably preserved.'[49]

He did not, however, possess the argumentative power of Jean Bodin, nor the intellectual daring of Reginald Scot because he was a physician and, thus, dependent on empirical data. Wier indeed wanted to end what he considered a bloodbath of innocent people, so that 'the constant shipwreck of souls might be more prudently avoided.'[50] More than that, he wanted to restore harmony among Christians by exposing the devil's lies.

## Notes

1 Johann Wier [Weyer], *Witches, Devils and Doctors in the Renaissance: Weyer's* De praestigiis daemonum, ed. and trans. George Mora et al., Binghamton, NY: Medieval and Renaissance Studies and Texts, 1991, pp. 498–99.
2 See my *Johann Wier: Agli albori della critica razionale dell'occulto e del demoniaco*, Florence: Olschki, 2003; forthcoming in a revised English translation as *Johann Wier: Debating the Devil and Witches in Early Modern Europe*, Amsterdam: Amsterdam University Press.
3 Wier, *Witches, Devils and Doctors*, p. 499.
4 Armando Maggi, *Satan's Rhetoric: A Study of Renaissance Demonology*, Chicago: Chicago University Press, 2001, p. 198; Paola Zambelli, *White Magic, Black Magic in the European Renaissance from Ficino and Della Porta to Trithemius, Agrippa, Bruno*, Leiden: Brill, 2007.
5 Mathijs Wijers, *Grondelicke onderrichtinghe*, Frankfurt [=Amsterdam]: [Harmen Jansz Muller], 1579; Roland Pietsch, 'Matthieu Weyer', in *Dictionnaire de Spiritualité ascétique et mystique doctrine et histoire*, Paris: Beauchesne, 1994, vol. 16, cols 1403–4.
6 Hans de Waardt, '"Lightning Strikes, Wherever Ire Dwells with Power": Johan Wier on Anger as an Illness', in *Diseases of the Imagination*, ed. Yasmin Haskell, Turnhout: Brepols, 2010, pp. 255–70, at 263.
7 Wier, *Witches, Devils and Doctors*, p. 28; H.C. Erik Midelfort and Benjamin G. Kohl, introduction to Johann Wier [Weyer], *On Witchcraft: An Abridged Translation of Johann Weyer's De praestigiis daemonum*, ed. and trans. Benjamin G. Kohl and H.C. Erik Midelfort, Asheville, NC: Pegasus Press, 1998, p. xvii.
8 Wier, *Witches, Devils and Doctors*, p. 111.

9 Charles G. Nauert, *Agrippa and the Crisis of Renaissance Thought*, Urbana, IL: University of Illinois Press, 1965, p. xii; Marc van der Poel, *Cornelius Agrippa: The Humanist Theologian and his Declamations*, Leiden: Brill, 1997, p. 1; Vittoria Perrone Compagni, 'Heinrich Cornelius Agrippa von Nettesheim', *The Stanford Encyclopedia of Philosophy* (Spring 2017 Edition), ed. Edward N. Zalta. https://plato.stanford.edu/archives/spr2017/entries/agrippa-nettesheim/. Accessed 19 July 2019.
10 See M. Isnardi Parente, 'Il cane di Cornelio Agrippa: Una disputa di dotti su un cane e il diavolo', in *Lo specchio oscuro: gli animali nell'immaginario degli uomini*, ed. Luisella Battaglia, Turin: Satyagrapha editrice, 1993, pp. 77–88; Van der Poel, *Cornelius Agrippa*, pp. 1–14.
11 Wier, *Witches, Devils and Doctors*, p. 113; Margherita Isnardi Parente, 'Le "vecchierelle pazze" di Johann Wier', in Johann Wier, *Le streghe*, ed. Aurora Tacus, Palermo: Sellerio, 1991, pp. 9–12.
12 Wier, *Witches, Devils and Doctors*, p. 113.
13 H. C. Erik Midelfort, 'Johann Weyer and the Transformation of the Insanity Defense', in Ronnie Po-Cha Hsia, ed., *The German People and the Reformation*, Ithaca, NY: Cornell University Press, 1988, pp. 234–61, at 238.
14 See Robin Briggs, *The Witches of Lorraine*, Oxford: Oxford University Press, 2008, pp. 36–7; Vera Hoorens and Hans Renders, 'Heinrich Cornelius Agrippa and Witchcraft: A Reappraisal', *The Sixteenth Century Journal*, 2012, vol. 43/1, 3–18.
15 Nancy Siraisi, *History, Medicine, and the Traditions of Renaissance Learning*, Ann Arbor, MI: The University of Michigan Press, 2007.
16 Vera Hoorens, 'Why Did Johann Weyer Write *De praestigiis daemonum*? How Anti-Catholicism Inspired the Landmark Plea for the Witches', *Low Countries Historical Review*, 2014, vol. 129/1, 3–24.
17 Wier, *Witches, Devils and Doctors*, pp. 416–17; Vera Hoorens, *Een ketterse arts voor de heksen: Jan Wier (1515–1588)*, Amsterdam: Bert Bakker, 2011, p. 92.
18 Charles D. Gunnoe, 'Thomas Erastus and his Circle of Anti-Paracelsians', in Joachim Telle, ed., *Analecta Paracelsica: Studien zum Nachleben Theophrast von Hohenheim im deutschen Kulturgebiet der frühen Neuzeit*, Stuttgart: Steiner, 1994, pp. 127–48, at 139.
19 'My second wife, Henrietta Holt, whose lively faith makes her a fierce opponent of diabolical trickery …': Wier, *Witches, Devils and Doctors*, p. 300.
20 See my *Johann Wier: Agli albori della critica razionale dell'occulto e del demoniaco*.
21 Wier, *Witches, Devils and Doctors*, p. 584.
22 Johann Wier, *Von Teuffelsgespenst, Zauberern und Gifftbereytern, Schwartzkünstlern, Hexen und Unholden*, trans. Johann Füglin, Franckfurt: Basse, 1586, p. 484.
23 Gary K. Waite, 'Radical Religion and the Medical Profession: The Spiritualist David Joris and the Brothers Wier', in Hans-Jürgen Goertz and James M. Stayer, eds, *Radikalität und Dissent im 16. Jahrhundert*, Berlin: Duncker und Humblot, 2002, pp. 167–85.
24 Hans de Waardt, 'Witchcraft, Spiritualism, and Medicine: The Religious Convictions of Johan Wier', *Sixteenth Century Journal*, 2011, vol. 42/2, 369–91.
25 Christopher Baxter, 'Johann Weyer's *De praestigiis daemonum*: Unsystematic Psychopathology', in Sidney Anglo, ed., *The Damned Art: Essays in the Literature of Witchcraft*, London: Routledge and Kegan Paul, 1977, pp. 53–75; Vera Hoorens, *Een ketterse arts voor de heksen*.
26 H. C. Erik Midelfort, *A History of Madness in Sixteenth-Century Germany*, Stanford: Stanford University Press, 1999, pp. 199–200.
27 Johann Wier, *Opera omnia quorum contenta versa pagina exhibet*, Amsterdam: Petrus van den Berge, 1660, sig. \*\*\*\*.

28 Stuart Clark, *Thinking with Demons*, Oxford: Clarendon Press, 1997, pp. 335–45; Charles Zika, *Exorcising Our Demons: Magic, Witchcraft, and Visual Culture in Early Modern Europe*, Leiden: Brill, 2003.
29 Wier, *Witches, Devils and Doctors*, p. 81.
30 Wier, *Witches, Devils and Doctors*, p. 166.
31 Wier, *Witches, Devils and Doctors*, p. 98.
32 Wier, *Witches, Devils and Doctors*, p. 341.
33 Wier, *Witches, Devils and Doctors*, p. 364.
34 Michaela Valente, '"Ludere stultitiam populi": Erasmo e le streghe', *Bruniana & Campanelliana*, 2013, vol. 19, 397–408; Willem Frijhoff, 'Erasmus' Heritage: Priestly Doubts of the Magical Universe', *Erasmus Studies*, 2015, vol. 35, 5–33.
35 Guido Giglioni, '"Phantastica Mutatio": Johann Weyer's Critique of the Imagination as a Principle of Natural Metamorphosis', in Ingo Gildnehard and Andrew Zissos, eds, *Transformative Change in Western Thought: A History of Metamorphosis from Homer to Hollywood*, Oxford: Legenda, pp. 307–30.
36 See H. C. Erik Midelfort, *Mad Princes of Renaissance Germany*, Charlottesville, VA: University Press of Virginia, 1994.
37 Ole Peter Grell, ed., *Paracelsus: The Man and His Reputation, His ideas and Their Transformation*, Leiden: Brill, 1998; Gerhild Scholz Williams and Charles D. Gunnoe, eds, *Paracelsian Moments: Science, Medicine and Astrology in Early Modern Europe*, Kirksville, MO: Truman State University Press, 2002 and Andrew Weeks, ed. and trans., *Paracelsus (Theophrastus Bombastus von Hohenheim, 1493–1541): Essential Theoretical Writings*, Leiden: Brill, 2008.
38 Charles D. Jr. Gunnoe, *Thomas Erastus and the Palatinate: A Renaissance Physician in the Second Reformation*, Leiden: Brill, 2010.
39 Karl A.E. Enenkel, 'Neo-Stoicism as an Antidote for Public Violence before Lipsius's *De constantia*: Johann Weyer's Therapy of Anger, *De ira morbo* (1577)', in Karl A.E. Enenkel and A. Traninger, eds, *Discourses of Anger in the Early Modern Period*, Leiden: Brill, 2015, pp. 49–96; Hans de Waardt, 'Melancholy and Fantasy: Johan Wier's Use of a Medical Concept in his Plea for Tolerance', in Jaap Grave et al., eds, *Illness and Literature in the Low Countries from the Middle Ages until the twenty-first Century*, Göttingen: V&R Unipress, 2016, pp. 33–46; Hans de Waardt, 'For the peace of man and the grace of God: Dietary Advices of Johan Wier', in Justus Nipperdey and Katharina Reinholdt, eds, *Essen und Trinken in der Europäischen Kulturgeschichte*, Berlin: LIT Verlag, 2016, pp. 69–75.
40 Rita Voltmer, 'Im Namen der Dynastie: Medizin, Astrologie und Magie, Dämonomaie und Exorzismus am jülich-klevischen Hof, 1585–1609', in Guido von Büren et al., eds, *Herrschaft, Hof und Humanismus: Wilhelm V. von Jülich-Kleve-Berg und seine Zeit*, Bielefeld: Verlag für Regionalgeschichte, 2018, pp. 403–38.
41 Michaela Valente, '"Mi Weiere, veni veni": Appunti su Johann Wier, Philip Sidney e John James', *Bibliothèque d'Humanisme et Renaissance*, 2015, vol. 77, 423–29.
42 Michaela Valente, 'Prime testimonianze della circolazione del *De praestigiis daemonum* di Johann Wier in Italia', *Bruniana & Campanelliana*, 2000, vol. 6, 561–68; Giovanni Romeo, 'Inquisizione, Chiesa e stregoneria nell'Italia della Controriforma: Nuove ipotesi', in Dinora Corsi and Matteo Duni, eds, *'Non lasciar vivere la malefica': Le streghe nei trattati e nei processi, secoli XIV–XVII*, Florence: Firenze University Press, 2008, pp. 53–64; Vincenzo Lavenia, 'Stregoneria, Italia', in Adriano Prosperi, ed., *Dizionario storico dell'Inquisizione*, Pisa: Edizioni della Normale, 2010, pp. 1523–30; Tamar Herzig, 'Witchcraft Prosecutions in Italy', in Brian P. Levack, ed., *The Oxford Handbook of Witchcraft in Early Modern Europe and Colonial America*, Oxford: Oxford University Press, 2013, pp. 249–67.

43 Friedrich Spee, *Cautio Criminalis, or a Book on Witch Trials*, trans. Marcus Hellyer, Charlottesville, VA: University of Virginia Press, 2003.
44 Clark, *Thinking with Demons*, p. 203.
45 Jan Machielsen, 'Thinking with Montaigne: Evidence, Scepticism and Meaning in Early Modern Demonology', *French History*, 2011, vol. 25/4, 427–52.
46 Jeffrey Moussaieff Masson, ed., *The Complete Letters of Sigmund Freud to Wilhelm Fliess, 1887–1904*, Cambridge MA: Harvard University Press, 1986, pp. 224–25.
47 Gregory Zilboorg, *The Medical Man and the Witch during the Renaissance*, Baltimore: Johns Hopkins University Press, 1935, p. 207.
48 De Waardt, 'Melancholy and Fantasy', pp. 33–46; Marijke Gijswijt-Hofstra, 'Witchcraft and Tolerance: The Dutch Case', *Acta Ethnographica Hungarica*, 1991–92, vol. 37, 401–12.
49 Wier, *Witches, Devils and Doctors*, p. 260.
50 Wier, *Witches, Devils and Doctors*, p. 522. See Elisa Slattery, 'To Prevent a "Shipwreck of Souls": Johann Weyer and *De praestigiis daemonum*', *Essays in History*, 1994, vol. 36, 73–88.

## Further reading

Baxter, Christopher, 'Johann Weyer's *De praestigiis daemonum*: Unsystematic Psychopathology', in Sidney Anglo, ed., *The Damned Art: Essays in the Literature of Witchcraft*, London: Routledge and Kegan Paul, 1977, pp. 53–75.
de Waardt, Hans, 'Witchcraft, Spiritualism, and Medicine: The Religious Convictions of Johan Wier', *Sixteenth Century Journal*, 2011, vol. 42/2, 369–391.
Hoorens, Vera, *Een ketterse arts voor de heksen: Jan Wier, 1515–1588*, Amsterdam: Bert Bakker, 2011.
———, 'Why Did Johann Weyer Write *De praestigiis daemonum*? How Anti-Catholicism Inspired the Landmark Plea for the Witches', *Low Countries Historical Review*, 2014, vol. 129/1, 3–24.
Midelfort, H. C. Erik, *A History of Madness in Sixteenth-Century Germany*, Stanford: Stanford University Press, 1999.
Valente, Michaela, *Johann Wier: Agli albori della critica razionale dell'occulto e del demoniaco*, Florence: Olschki, 2003; forthcoming in a revised English translation as *Johann Wier: Debating the Devil and Witches in Early Modern Europe*, Amsterdam: Amsterdam University Press.
Waite, Gary K., 'Radical Religion and the Medical Profession: The Spiritualist David Joris and the Brothers Wier', in Hans-Jürgen Goertz and James M. Stayer, eds, *Radikalität und Dissent im 16. Jahrhundert*, Berlin: Duncker und Humblot, 2002, pp. 167–185.

# 7 The will to know and the unknowable

Jean Bodin's *De La Démonomanie*

Virginia Krause

What, precisely, is a witch? And what, legally, constitutes the crime of witchcraft? Deceptively clear and straightforward, these two questions frame *De La Démonomanie des sorciers* (On the Demon-Mania of Witches, 1580). This notorious treatise advocating a hard line for the prosecution of witchcraft was a best-seller in early modern France and beyond, with 13 French editions between 1580 and 1616, along with translations into Italian, German, and Latin appearing almost immediately.[1] Its author was a respected jurist and polymath, whose expertise was exceptionally broad even for this period of encyclopedic humanism.[2] Most well-known for his work of political philosophy, *The Six Books of the Republic* (1576) which defined the key notion of sovereignty for generations to come, Jean Bodin (1529/30–1596) also composed works on historical writing, economic theory, legal studies, natural philosophy, and religion.[3] Perhaps only someone with the reputation of Jean Bodin – someone known as one of the best legal minds of his time with a keen interest in religion – could have composed the *Démonomanie*, which effectively brought witchcraft into the new era, thereby supplanting the Scholastic *Malleus maleficarum* as the go-to manual for understanding and prosecuting witchcraft.

His endeavor was at once *scientific* (understanding the clandestine world of demons and their earthly agents), *political* (responding to the threat of witchcraft, a crime of high treason against God and King), *practical* (providing a nuts and bolts guide for prosecuting witches, from arrest and interrogation to execution), and *polemical* (engaging in intellectual debates – most notably, in his refutation of Johann Wier°'s thesis that so-called 'witches' were not criminals but rather melancholics victimized by the devil). These qualities were, moreover, tightly interwoven: because witches threatened the political, social, and religious fabric of society, and because they were *multiplying*, they must be prosecuted, contrary to what Johann Wier and others maintained. To do so required using established procedures for trying an 'exceptional crime' (*crimen exceptum*) such as witchcraft – the most hidden of all crimes and also the most dangerous.[4] In short, condemning witches required understanding their secret world: Bodin's punitive agenda rested on a will to know. His first step toward this end is his definition of the witch, which must constitute our point of departure as well.

## 1 Defining the witch

> Sorcier est celuy qui par moyens Diaboliques sciemment s'efforce de parvenir à quelque chose.
> [A 'witch' is one who knowingly tries to accomplish something by diabolical means].[5]

The first thing to note about Bodin's definition above is the use of the masculine term ('le sorcier'), which testifies to his *universalizing* aspirations as well as to the distance separating the *Démonomanie* from its predecessor, the more overtly misogynistic *Malleus maleficarum*. Notwithstanding his attempt to use more neutral terminology, however, Bodin frequently falls back on the feminine form ('la sorcière') elsewhere in the treatise – tacit recognition that most witches were in fact women. And near the end of the *Démonomanie*, he even observes that there were fifty times more female witches than males.[6]

Bodin's definition further posits that the witch is someone who resorts to 'diabolical means.' In this sense, it is the means not the end that make the witch, who may or may not succeed in doing any real harm. The *Démonomanie* offers a catalogue of basic spells and magical operations (carefully withholding actual formula as Bodin did not wish to provide instruction to witches!). These range from the classic knot that causes infertility to toads and wax figurines. Bodin's conception of 'diabolical means' also includes instances of learned magic such as necromancers' rituals and invocations addressed to planetary demons, for his conception of the witch was meant to include both stereotypical female witches, believed to attend the sabbat and cast spells (such as Jeanne Harvillier, whose trial ostensibly inspired him to write), and male magicians, who practiced ceremonial magic from bookish sources (most notably, Wier's teacher, Heinrich Cornelius Agrippa, the author of *Three Books on Occult Philosophy* published in 1533).[7]

A final and decisive characteristic of Bodin's definition of the witch is the insistence on intention: witches *knowingly* attempt to accomplish something through diabolical means ('*sciemment* s'efforcent de parvenir à quelque chose'). With this caveat, he exempts admired pagan thinkers from his indictment of witchcraft. Thus, Socrates, with his familiar demon was, for Bodin, a philosopher, perhaps even a prophet, but not a 'witch' – a position not shared by all of Bodin's contemporaries.[8] Similarly, the ignorant peasant who might unwittingly seek help from a witch was not guilty of the crime of witchcraft, owing to the absence of intent. For Bodin, the witch knowingly, willfully, resorts to demonic means. For this reason, and for this reason alone, the witch is guilty – regardless of whether or not any real harm is caused. In this respect, the jurist sought to wrest the idea of witchcraft away from popular conceptions of magical acts producing real harm (*maleficium* in Latin:

literally, evil deeds). For Bodin, 'witches' are constituted by their intentions because witchcraft is, in legal terms, a matter of criminal *intent*. He further grants the juridical notion of intent a deeply moral, religious meaning, citing Deuteronomy 30:

> Puis doncques que les Anges sont bons, et les Diables mauvais, aussi les hommes ont le franc arbitre pour estre bons ou mauvais, comme Dieu dit en sa Loy: 'J'ay, dit-il, mis devant tes yeux le bien, et le mal, la vie et la mort, choisy donc le bien, et tu vivras.'
> 
> (*Démonomanie*, pp. 102–3)

> [Therefore since angels are good, and devils wicked, also men have free choice to be good, or wicked, as God says in His Law: 'I have, He states, put before your eyes good and evil, life and death, choose then the good, and you will live.']
> 
> (Scott, p. 56)

For Jean Bodin, God calls each of us to make a choice between good and evil, and witches choose evil. On the basis of this choice, on the basis of their intent, and regardless of any actual *maleficia*, witches are for Bodin guilty – and irredeemably so. The choice witches make is decisive: in the *Démonomanie*, witches are never redeemed, saved, or reformed. In the final chapter of book 4, Bodin justifies the death penalty for witches by declining witchcraft into fifteen crimes. These crimes are mostly spiritual in nature (apostasy, blasphemy, demon-worship, etc.), with the first of these being the rejection of God and of religion. This willful turning away from God – this crime of intent – is what makes the crime of witchcraft 'abominable' for Jean Bodin.

## 2 Bodin's dossier on witchcraft

The emphasis on intentions over actions in Bodin's definition is cogent, but also deceptively simple: what access can one possibly have to someone's intentions? The popular understanding of witchcraft (*maleficia*) was based on effects clear for all to see: a sudden illness with strange symptoms, a devastating storm out of nowhere, an otherwise healthy infant found dead one morning ... but what are the manifestations of intention? How does one truly know what another person desires? How can the judge determine something as elusive as intent? The primary answer to this question is to be found in juridical confession, the reigning 'queen of proofs' in a trial for witchcraft. The only way to *know*, explains Bodin, is through confession or from their accomplices ('on ne peut sçavoir que par leur confession ou de leurs complices').[9] Bodin's treatise was in this respect entirely typical: the substantial body of early modern knowledge we loosely term 'demonology' drew its truths primarily from witches' confessions – first-person narratives detailing intimate commerce with demons, pacts with the devil, and of course the most spectacular chapter in early modern witchcraft: the nocturnal sabbat, replete with its elaborate satanic rituals and other horrific acts ranging from cannibalistic feasts to incest. In early modern Europe, the notion of the sabbat was generated as a confession narrative, for demonology purported to be a science founded on experience – the experience of witches themselves, accessible to specialists primarily through their first-person accounts.[10]

Demonology's confessional regime had two sides, one practical (pursued by prosecutors in the courtroom) and the other theoretical (pursued by specialists of *scientia daemonis* in their written works). Moreover, witchcraft trials and witchcraft theory worked in tandem: the former functioned as an elaborate machinery for generating confession while the latter disseminated and interpreted witches' confessions from trials. Jean Bodin had expertise in both the practical and theoretical domains: he possessed an encyclopedic knowledge of all things related to the knowable natural world and its outer limits (including demons) combined with extensive professional experience in law (when he composed the *Démonomanie*, he was the *procureur du roi* in the town of Laon). However, it should be noted that Bodin never presided over a trial for witchcraft, although as he makes clear with the first words of the preface, he was apparently consulted in the course of the trial of Jeanne Harvillier, who serves as the quintessential witch throughout the *Démonomanie*. Promised to the devil by her own mother, Jeanne had carnal relations with the devil for many years, attended the sabbat and attempted to use witchcraft in the service of revenge before being finally brought to justice. Besides this apparently informal consultation, however, the contact Bodin had with witches was mediated and the advice he offered prosecutors was not the fruit of his own experience in trials. Notwithstanding his lack of personal experience, Bodin offers copious advice on how to effectively prosecute witches while respecting the law. Devoted to the mechanics of a trial, Book Four of the *Démonomanie* includes a catalogue of tricks and even deceit at the judge's disposal as well as the criteria for the application of torture – all with the purpose of getting 'the truth' from the witch's own mouth. In this most practical of discussions, Bodin attends meticulously to the finer points of how to extract confession 'by every means that he can imagine.'[11]

But Bodin's case is in no way limited to legal practices and trial documents. It constitutes a massive dossier culled from a broad range of bookish sources. Fragments from the confessions extracted in recent trials thus reside alongside references to ancient philosophy, history, myth, literature, medieval theology, and astrology, Roman and canon law, exegetical works, and of course Scripture itself. All of these sources concur, he insists, in their indictment of witchcraft as a capital crime. There is, he argues, a fundamental concordance among all his sources that confirms the reality of witchcraft, anticipating Martin Delrio° on this point.[12] Otherwise, how could it be possible, demands Bodin, for contemporary witches to confess to using in their spells wax figurines, the very same wax figurines one finds in Plato, and yet these witches *have never read Plato*?[13] The only explanation is that witchcraft is real and has been documented by poets, philosophers, historians, jurists, prophets, and theologians through the ages. In the process, he does not hesitate to sacrifice scholarly rigor at the altar of expediency: witchcraft was spreading, he insisted, infecting all echelons of society, from the village witch to the court of princes. Indeed, Bodin finds witches amongst the ranks of priests, former popes, princes, physicians, lawyers, and particularly those skeptics who seem rather too outspoken in seeking clemency for witches. For Jean Bodin, one must not allow the urgency of the situation to be clouded by philological nuance.

One piece in Bodin's dossier of evidence deserves particular attention: neo-Platonic philosophy, usually referenced as a list of philosophers from late antiquity: Plotinus, Proclus, Iamblichus, and Porphyry. Bodin's keen interest in (and distrust of) neo-Platonic thought is a current running through the *Démonomanie*. Here was a philosophy that placed demons (*daïmons*) at its core. Populating nearly every sphere of the cosmos, neo-Platonic demons are fundamentally ambivalent beings: some are good, some are bad, others are merely neutral, but all are engaged in the mediating activities that hold the universe together. Bodin's terminology refers to neo-Platonic *daïmons* as 'spirits' (*esprits*) rather than as 'demons', and he proves eager to avoid any possible confusion with Judeo-Christian notions of angels and demons. 'I follow the Theologians' resolution, namely that all *daïmons* are wicked,' he concludes at the end of the first chapter.[14] He nevertheless judges the pagan Neo-Platonists rather gently, reserving his righteous anger for contemporaries such as Giovanni Pico della Mirandola and Heinrich Cornelius Agrippa von Nettesheim who claim expertise in 'reformed' neo-Platonic magic. The latter have fallen into the nets Satan uses to attract philosophers, writes Bodin (*Démonomanie*, p. 151). Any form of learned magic – natural, ceremonial, hermetic – is for Jean Bodin a trap which the devil uses to ensnare intellectually ambitious men not unlike Bodin himself.

## 3 Modes of knowing

Beyond the copiousness of his corpus, with its vertiginous array of sources, Bodin puts forth a methodology, a set of tools and techniques for penetrating the secrets of witches. In the first place, he uses definition, as noted above – a tried and true method for dealing with a subject as elusive as witchcraft. In the second place, his practice of the compendium is in itself a methodology, for in gathering his source material, Bodin applies a variation of the technique known as parallel passages in search of common threads. Reading comparatively, he places one passage (from Plato, from Thomas Aquinas, from Philo, from Justinian … ) alongside another passage (from a witch's own confession, from an historian, from a poet … ). In so doing, he purports to arrive at a kernel of truth: the nature of witches – always the same, from biblical times to the present. With this exercise of transhistorical comparison, he enlists all the resources of his humanist culture to uncover the secret activities witches have long pursued. A monument of erudition with universalizing ambitions, Bodin's treatise stands out from both its predecessors and its contemporaries – works by theologians, judges, and sometimes both (as with the *Malleus maleficarum*), but always more restricted in their claims to expertise.

Bodin does not, however, place all of his sources on the same plane. Against the background of all his humanist erudition, one source stands out: the Old Testament, 'God's law,' which is in no way ambiguous when it comes to how witches must be dealt with: 'thou shalt not suffer the witch to live' (Exodus 22:18). As for those who attempted to cloud the meaning of this command, Bodin's refutation was implacable. Bodin recalls Wier's attempt to argue on philological grounds that the original Hebrew should be translated not as 'witch' but as 'poisoner'. Bodin's superior command of Hebrew allowed him to refute Wier's faulty philology in short order. Ignoring God's command comes with a heavy price, for God threatens to exterminate communities that choose to ignore or misinterpret this commandment. Bodin eventually came to believe that France's Wars of Religion (1562–1598) were the sign of God's wrath and a form of divine punishment, as it was for Juan Maldonado° as well.

With the Old Testament's injunctions against witchcraft thus functioning as a kind of master-source, Bodin constituted his dossier of evidence documenting witchcraft through the ages along with a practical 'how to' manual for prosecutors. Anecdotal evidence suggests that the *Démonomanie* was indeed consulted by judges trying witches in the lower courts.[15] His target audience was, however, situated at the highest echelons of the profession: the magistrates sitting in France's high courts of appeal (the seven Parlements), who were inclined to overturn witchcraft verdicts in the lower courts – in effect, working to restrain the zeal of judges prosecuting the crime of witchcraft. Seeking to sway these high court judges prone to clemency toward 'witches' and skepticism toward 'witchcraft', Jean Bodin dedicated his treatise to Chrestofle de Thou, President of the Parlement of Paris.[16] Bodin's attempts to persuade appear, however, to have been in vain. Despite his efforts to stem the tide, the Parlement of Paris continued to work toward the decriminalization of witchcraft.[17] In 1588, the high court sought to implement an automatic appeal process for all witchcraft cases and finally ceased to recognize witchcraft as a punishable crime altogether in 1640.[18]

## 4 Occam's razor or *lectio difficilior*?

In this rift separating the lower courts from the high courts of appeal, Bodin situated his intervention. One of the obstacles he faced in attempting to persuade elites at the highest echelons of his profession was the bizarre nature of the crimes attributed to witches, who were sent to the stake routinely for having attended the sabbat – not just in their dreams, but in reality. Night flight, feasting on human flesh, fornicating with demons … strange accusations, even if one accepts the premise that our modern notion of impossibility simply did not exist in this era.[19] Demonological high theory provided complex explanations to account for such strange occurrences and apparent inconsistencies. How were witches able to attend sabbats in distant lands? Because they rode there on the backs of demons, on a broomstick, or sometimes in a gust of wind. How could a so-called witch have been at the sabbat if her husband testified that she never left the conjugal bed? Because when witches went to the sabbat, they left decoys or true-to-life copies in their beds to allay suspicion during their absence. In regard to this theory of the demonological copy, the skeptical lawyer Andrea Alciato famously asked:

> Why do you not rather presume that the evil demon was with his fellow demons, and the woman with her husband? Why do you suppose a real body in a fictitious revel and an imaginary body in a real bed? What need is there to multiply miracles…?[20]

The famous essayist Michel de Montaigne similarly mocked the complicated scenarios typical of demonological high theory:

> My ears are battered by a thousand stories like this: 'Three people saw him on such-and-such a day in the east; three saw him the next day in the west, at such-and-such a time, in such-and-such a place, dressed thus.' Truly, I would not believe my own self about this. How much more natural and likely it seems to me that two men are lying than that one man should pass with the winds in twelve hours from the east to the west![21]

Why resort to complicated and often improbable accounts when there exists a more obvious explanation, Montaigne and Alciato both ask, each with a variation of the classic Occam's razor argument?

Bodin for his part acknowledges that the crimes committed by witches seemed fantastic: 'Often judges are puzzled by the confessions of witches and are reluctant to base a sentence on them, given the strange things that they confess, because some think that they are telling fables.'[22] His solution is to draw a firm line between physics and metaphysics, arguing that the notion of possibility has no place in matters of metaphysics. Those who apply criteria of physics to metaphysics are committing a fundamental category error.[23]

> Thus when one asserts that for a confession to be believable it must report something which is possible and true; and that it cannot be true unless it is possible; and nothing is possible in law except what is possible by nature: it is a sophistic and specious argument – and nevertheless its assumption is false. For the great works and marvels of God are impossible by nature, and nonetheless true. The actions, moreover, of Intelligences and everything that

pertains to metaphysics are impossible by nature, which is the reason why metaphysics is entirely distinct and different from physics.[24]

Inverting the logic of plausibility, Bodin insists that when it comes to witchcraft and other metaphysical matters, the truth must *always* seem strange. The stranger the crimes seem, he reasons, the truer they must be, the more they reveal hidden metaphysical truths. Bodin's justification here obeys a logic of *lectio difficilior*, literally 'the more difficult reading' – a principle used in textual criticism when there are conflicting variants. This principle serves to distinguish the correct variant from scribal error following a counter-intuitive logic: when such conflicting variants occur, the strangest variant – the variant that is the least familiar or the 'most difficult' – is assumed to be the correct one because scribal error tends to substitute the familiar for the unfamiliar.[25] While his peers writing against the witch-hunts invoked Occam's razor, Bodin countered with *lectio difficilior*.

For Jean Bodin, understanding witchcraft was in this respect a highly bookish endeavor – a reasoned and reasonable enterprise of comparing sources and resolving contradictions, proceeding from definition, that most basic operation, through the technique of parallel passages, to the most innovative techniques of textual criticism, such as *lectio difficilior*. Witchcraft was, in this sense, an elusive crime committed in secret, but it was not fundamentally unknowable. Its mysteries could be penetrated – indeed, *must be* penetrated. The demonologist thus attended to *modes of knowing* suitable to witchcraft: methods for synthesizing all that has been written about witches, strategies for extracting the truth from their very mouths, and procedures for interpreting what they confess. For all intents and purposes, Bodin's *scientia daemonis* was thus a highly rational, highly *reasoned* endeavor.

And yet these methods and principles were in some essential ways an elaborate façade masking what was precisely unknown and even unknowable at the heart of Bodin's demonology, despite his highly refined truth technologies. The *Démonomanie* was not the result of a strictly reasonable enterprise: it was perhaps first and foremost the fruit of Bodin's religious vocation and mystical experiences – his own deeply rooted conviction that he had privileged access to the spirit world, as related in Book 1, Chapter 2 'On the Association of Spirits with Humans.' As we shall see, this passage offers a key to Bodin's rather singular demonological vocation, suggesting the extent to which rationality served as a cover for his deeply felt personal heterodox beliefs.

## 5 A prophetic vocation

Book 1, Chapter 2 in the *Démonomanie* addresses the interactions between humans and spirits – both angelic and demonic. Bodin's universe is held together by a myriad of connections that unite different orders of God's creation: plants with animals, animals with humans, and – most significantly for Bodin – humans with spirits. What might initially seem to be a neo-

Platonic cosmology teaming with spiritual beings is resolved into a strictly dualistic order: the demonic versus the angelic, which correspond to two vocations, that of the witch (having commerce with demons) and that of the prophet (receiving privileged guidance from an angel). As scholars have noted, the prophet emerges as the mirror opposite of the witch.[26] Both have a privileged channel into the spirit world, although the witch's 'degeneration' is the result of free will while the prophet's elevation is an act of grace. Anyone can seemingly choose to be a witch, but few men become prophets: only those chosen by God 'by grace and a special gift' (p. 104). The witch 'knowingly, willingly' chooses the demonic while the prophet is elected – one among many. Sometimes, observes Bodin, God bestows a 'singular gift' by sending an angel who offers guidance in all matters. This is the highest privilege bestowed on any mortal being. Socrates received such a gift, but it was most frequent among the Jews, for the Hebrew Bible contains 'a thousand examples' of God assisting prophets, including Samuel, David, and Moses.

The chapter proceeds to relate the experiences of a 'friend' who received the gift of prophecy, but it is not difficult to see that this is a largely transparent conceit for relating an autobiographical account of Bodin's own experiences. Here, we read that at the age of 37, this 'friend' became aware of the presence of a spirit guiding him assiduously. The events are related in detail and in chronological order as follows. Although he had long believed that an angel accompanied him, this angel appeared initially only in dreams. Then after a period of intense prayer, contemplation, and study of Scripture – a religious quest for the one 'true' religion – he became aware of the presence of the angel. This accompanied his discovery that 'true religion' was to be found in a highly personalized version of Judaism derived largely from his study of the Hebrew Bible, Jewish philosophy and theology, prayer, and contemplation.

Bodin lived through tumultuous times in which conversions – and sometimes reconversions – were a frequent feature. Bodin's interests were, however, exceptionally heterodox, even for this period. His complete religious biography remains elusive with many abrupt twists and turns: from his early Carmelite education, to a possible (temporary) conversion to Calvinism, followed by the influence of Judaism on his quest for 'true religion,' then a decision to take sides with the radical Catholic League in 1589, and finally his last will and testament which called for a Catholic burial. Nevertheless, certain constants emerge, as Paul Rose has demonstrated. In the first place, with its emphasis on solitary meditation day and night, on prophecy, and on purity of heart, the early influence Carmelite spirituality exerted on Bodin proved to be enduring, dovetailing with his Judaizing later in life in a seemingly smooth fashion. In the second place, the Jewish ethics of Philo and Maimonides shaped his religious vision.[27] And, finally, let us recall the all-encompassing importance of the Old Testament which overshadows all other sources in the *Démonomanie*.

And so, as he relates in Book 1, Chapter 2, it was during his 37th year, after a period of intense study and continuous prayer – in particular, the recitation of Psalm 143 ('Teach me to do thy will, for thou art my God, thy spirit is good; lead me into the land of uprightness') – that Bodin began to have strange, spiritual experiences. He began first to have visions and dreams with prophetic instruction and guidance and then heard what seemed to be the voice of God, telling him 'I will save your soul; it was I who appeared to you' (Scott, p. 60). Soon after hearing this voice, he began to hear a loud knocking on his door in the middle of the night. When he would get up and open his door, however, he would see no one. These nocturnal knockings initially filled him with dread as he thought it might be some evil spirit, but he continued to pray to God to send him an angel and to sing the Psalms every day, and soon he received the reassurance that the spirit establishing contact was in fact an angel. He concludes by noting that the angel accompanied him henceforth, communicating with him using a system of signs: touching his right ear if he was in physical or moral danger and his left ear when he acted morally or when something was beneficial. These signs alerted him to plans to assassinate him; warned him if food was unsafe; guided his choice of books to study; and advised him how to proceed when he was in doubt.[28]

Bodin deciphered these events through a combination of the examples left by prophets of the Hebrew Bible who experienced similar signs on the one hand and close study of Philo and Maimonides on the other. From Philo as well as his early exposure to Carmelite spirituality, he drew the twin pillars of his thought: prophecy and purification.[29] For Bodin's spirituality did not take the form of a pursuit of the ineffable through union with the Creator, which his contemporary, the Carmelite John of the Cross, situated at the pinnacle of spirituality.[30] Nor was spiritual progress oriented along anything resembling Christian lines in relation to sin and redemption.[31] Rather, the highest order of spirituality was that obtained by the prophet. From Maimonides's *Guide of the Perplexed*, a classic of medieval Jewish philosophy, Bodin drew his understanding of the eleven degrees of prophecy, a gradual progression through ever greater communication with God mediated through an angel. The experiences that happened to Bodin's 'friend' (his younger self) and related in the *Démonomanie* follow Maimonides's eleven rungs virtually to the letter.[32]

## 6 Discerning spirits

If, as all signs seem to suggest, Bodin believed himself to be a prophet in the tradition of the Hebrew prophets, what bearing could this conviction have had on his demonology? It is not merely a question of following Jewish philosophy over Christian theology (Maimonides over Aquinas, for instance). It is not an intellectual content so much as a process – and a process that transcended a reasoned positioning within the knowable world. One of the privileges that came with prophecy was a particular skill known as the discernment of spirits, understood to be a *charism* (a gift) bestowed upon a small minority of virtuous men.³³ In the Christian tradition, Saint Anthony was believed to possess this skill conferred by God, which allowed him to distinguish between angelic and demonic beings. Theologians – from Thomas Aquinas and Jean Gerson to Martin Delrio – examined this difficult subject, glossing the two key verses of Scripture: 'Test the spirits, to see whether they are of God' (1 John 4:1), and 'Satan himself disguises himself as an angle of light' (2 Cor. 11:14). Jean Bodin displays little interest in the treatment of the question by Catholic theologians – this despite the fact that the *Démonomanie* was composed in the wake of a famous scandal that placed discernment front and center: the so-called 'Miracle of Laon' (1566) in which a young woman was initially believed to be visited by the ghost of her grandfather before it was revealed that she was in fact possessed.³⁴ Given contemporary religious polemics around ghosts and exorcism (Reformers criticized Catholic belief in Purgatory, in ghosts, and in rituals of exorcism),³⁵ scandals such as the Miracle of Laon became highly polemicized. Jean Bodin skirted these contemporary polemics, but clearly had a very personal interest in discernment. One of the rare references to the New Testament in the *Démonomanie* is in fact one of the two classic references on discernment: Paul's warning that 'Satan disguises himself as an angel of light' (2 Cor. 11:14), which Bodin paraphrases at the beginning of Book 1, Chapter 3:

> Nous avons dict que le Sorcier est celuy qui s'efforce parvenir à quelque chose par moyens Diaboliques, puis nous avons parlé de l'association des esprits avec les hommes: il faut donc sçavoir la difference des uns et des autres, pour cognoistre les enfans de Dieu d'avec les Sorciers. Ce qui est bien necessaire, pour lever le voile de pieté, et de la religion, et la masque de lumiere, que le Diable prend assez souvent, pour abuser les hommes.
>
> (*Démonomanie*, p. 113)

> [We said that a witch is one who tries to accomplish something by diabolical means. Then we spoke about the association of spirits with men. One must, therefore, learn the difference between them in order to tell the children of God from witches. This is very necessary to lift the veil of piety, of religion, and the mask of light which the devil quite often puts on to deceive men.]
>
> (Scott, p. 63)

Bodin here summarizes the unfolding of his treatise thus far: first, a definition of the witch (Chapter 1); then an exploration of the prophet (Chapter 2); and next, logically, how to distinguish the former from the latter given that the devil often hides under a mask of light (Chapter 3). As noted above, distinguishing the angelic from the demonic was one of the many problems

Bodin confronted – including in his personal experience when he wondered if the spirit knocking at his door in the darkness might, in fact, be a demon rather than an angel. Although Bodin ultimately resolved this uncertainty and felt himself to be one of the elect, his friend Claude Fauchet reached a very different conclusion. Fauchet witnessed a manifestation of the spirit accompanying Bodin, which led him to believe that Bodin was a witch and that the spirit knocking was a demon.[36] In this period of upheaval and crisis, the discernment of spirits was necessary but fraught with uncertainty.

For his part, Bodin was not plagued by uncertainty or confounded by the murkiness of the spirit world. His treatise on witchcraft is the fruit of his conviction that it is indeed possible to identify witches and, moreover, that he had been given the skill of discernment, a gift bestowed on him as one of God's elect. This conviction set him apart from demonologists preceding him as well as from his more skeptically inclined peers, such as Montaigne who acknowledged that witchcraft existed while casting doubt over any self-proclaimed expert's ability to identify a witch. Who, besides God, can say 'This is one; and that is one; but not this other'? ('Cettuy-cy en est, et celle-là, et non cet autre.'[37]) Ultimately, Bodin did not disagree fundamentally on this point: for him, discerning spirits was a divine gift conferred only to a very few, and not a practice that could be mastered through rational means. But with this gift came responsibility. Knowing that witches were multiplying, the prophet had to act accordingly, just as knowing that Jeanne Harvillier was indeed a witch required that God's law be applied. In this way, in a science that had always had gaps in understanding, had always had grey zones and its fair share of dissent and contradictions[38] – how could it be otherwise when Satan disguises himself as an angel of light? – Bodin found a path to certainty not through rational means, but through spiritual channels: through the mystical vocation of prophecy and its accompanying privileges and responsibilities, including the discernment of spirits. The *Démonomanie* was ultimately more the fruit of Bodin's prophetic vocation than of all his legal expertise and encyclopedic learning combined. It was more the result of what transcended human reason than of the scholarly methods and philosophical arguments enlisted in pursuit of *scientia daemonis*. Guided by his guardian angel more than by his humanist culture, Jean Bodin found a way into the unknown spirit world.

## Notes

1 Roland Crahay et al., 'Bibliographie critique des éditions anciennes de Jean Bodin', *Mémoire de la classe des Lettres de L'Académie Royale de Belgique*, 1992, vol. 70, pp. 221–84.
2 For a comprehensive account of Bodin's life and writings, see Howell Lloyd, *Jean Bodin: 'This Pre-Eminent Man of France'; An Intellectual Biography*, Oxford: Oxford University Press, 2017.
3 Besides the *République* (1576) and the *Démonomanie* (1580), Bodin's principal works are the *Methodus ad facilem historiarum cognitionem* (1566); *La Response au*

*Paradoxe de Monsieur de Malestroit* (1568); *Juris universi distributio* (1578); *Universae naturae theatrum* (1596); and *Colloquium Heptaplomeres*, published posthumously.
4 Christina Larner, 'Crimen Exceptum? The Crime of Witchcraft in Europe,' in Victor Gatrell, ed., *Crime and the Law*, London: Europa Publications, 1980, pp. 49–75.
5 Jean Bodin, *De La Démonomanie des sorciers*, ed. Viginia Krause et al., Geneva: Droz, 2016, p. 89. English translation: *On the Demon-Mania of Witches*, ed. Jonathan Pearl, trans. Randy Scott, Toronto: Centre for Reformation and Renaissance Studies, 2001, p. 45. Unless indicated otherwise, all subsequent references will be from these two works.
6 Bodin, *Démonomanie*, p. 448.
7 On learned magic, see D. P. Walker, *Spiritual and Demonic Magic from Ficino to Campanella*, University Park, PA: Penn State University Press, 2003 [original ed. 1958], and Richard Kieckhefer, *Magic in the Middle Ages*, Cambridge: Canto, 1989. On the merging of the magician and witch in the writings of Martin Delrio, see Jan Machielsen, *Martin Delrio: Demonology and Scholarship in the Counter-Reformation*, Oxford: Oxford University Press, 2015, p. 216.
8 Bodin's contemporary Pierre Le Loyer concluded that Socrates practiced magic: 'Socrates estoit magicien.' *Discours des spectres, ou Visions et apparitions d'esprits*, Paris: Nicolas Buon, 1608, p. 384.
9 Bodin, *Démonomanie*, p. 184; trans. Scott, p. 193; my emphasis.
10 Virginia Krause, *Witchcraft, Demonology, and Confession in Early Modern France*, New York: Cambridge, 2015.
11 '[L]e Juge par tous les moyens qu'il peut imaginer doibt tirer la verité': Bodin, *Démonomanie*, p. 382; trans. Scott, p. 191.
12 Martin Delrio also practiced demonology as a work of textual scholarship dependent upon 'editing, selecting, and grouping [texts]': Machielsen, *Martin Delrio*, p. 236.
13 Witches have been seen to 'mettre leurs images de cire aux carrefours, aux sepulchres de leurs peres, et soubz les portes, où lon voit evidemment les images de cire, dont ils usoyent du temps, et au paravant Platon, comme font nos Sorcieres, qui ne ont pas leu Platon, et par le moyen desquelles images, avec layde de Sathan elles font mourir les personnes': Bodin, *Démonomanie*, p. 444.
14 'Toutesfois nous suivirons la resolution des Theologiens, c'est à sçavoir que tous Dæmons sont malins': Bodin, *Démonomanie*, p. 99; my translation.
15 'Introduction,' in Bodin, *Démonomanie*, pp. 44–47.
16 Montaigne's response to the *Démonomanie* in the *Essais* suggests that Bodin's efforts were largely in vain. A member of the erudite milieu of magistrates Bodin sought to influence, Montaigne criticized the methods of demonology on legal, philosophical, and ethical grounds: Krause, *Witchcraft, Demonology, and Confession in Early Modern France*, chap. 3.
17 On the reception and impact of the *Démonomanie*, see Bodin, 'Introduction,' *Démonomanie*, pp. 43–52 and also Howell Lloyd, ed., *The Reception of Jean Bodin*, Leiden: Brill, 2013.
18 On the decriminalization of witchcraft, see Robert Mandrou, *Magistrats et sorciers en France au XVIIe Siècle*, Paris: Plon, 1968; Alfred Soman, *Sorcellerie et justice criminelle: Le Parlement de Paris, 16e–18e siècles*, Aldershot: Ashgate, 1992.
19 Lucien Febvre, *Le Problème de l'incroyance au XVIe siècle: La Religion de Rabelais*, Paris: Albin Michel, 2003.
20 Quoted in Johann Weyer [Wier], *Witches, Devils, and Doctors in the Renaissance* [*De praestigiis daemonum*], ed. George Mora et. al., Binghamton, NY: Medieval and Renaissance Texts and Studies, 1992, p. 537.

21 Michel de Montaigne, *The Complete Essays*, trans. Donald Frame, Stanford: Stanford University Press, 1958, p. 789.
22 Bodin, *On the Demon-Mania of Witches*, p. 190.
23 Stuart Clark, *Thinking with Demons: The Idea of Witchcraft in Early Modern Europe*, Oxford: Clarendon, 1997, p. 212.
24 Bodin, *On the Demon-Mania of Witches*, p. 193.
25 On Bodin's use of this technique, see Krause, *Witchcraft, Demonology, and Confession in Early Modern France*, pp. 85–90.
26 Rebecca Wilkin, *Women, Imagination and the Search for Truth in Early Modern France*, Aldershot: Ashgate, 2008.
27 See Paul Rose, *Bodin and the Great God of Nature: The Moral and Religious Universe of a Judaiser*, Geneva: Droz, 1980, esp. p. 11, 81–83, 191; Lloyd, *Jean Bodin*, pp. 156–58, 260–62.
28 Bodin, *Démonomanie*, pp. 106–7.
29 Rose, *Bodin and the Great God of Nature*, p. 9.
30 See Colin Thompson, 'Dangerous Visions: The Experience of Teresa of Avila and the Teaching of John of the Cross,' in Clare Copeland and Jan Machielsen, eds, *Angels of Light? Sanctity and the Discernment of Spirits in the Early Modern Period*, Leiden: Brill, 2013, pp. 71–73.
31 On Bodin's rejection of this fundamental Christian tenet, see Rose, *Bodin and the Great God of Nature*, pp. 71–86; D. P. Walker, *Spiritual and Demonic Magic*, p. 145.
32 Bodin, *Démonomanie*, n. 12–25, pp. 106–7.
33 On the discernment of spirits, see Moshe Sluhovsky, *Believe not Every Spirit: Possession, Mysticism, and Discernment in Early Modern Catholicism*, Chicago: University of Chicago Press, 2007; Copeland and Machielsen, eds, *Angels of Light?*
34 Irena Backus, *Le Miracle de Laon: Le Déraisonnable, le raisonnable, l'apocalyptique et le politique dans les récits du Miracle de Laon, 1566–1578*, Paris: Vrin, 1994.
35 Timothy Chesters, *Ghost Stories in Late Renaissance France: Walking by Night*, Oxford: Oxford University Press, 2011.
36 Janet Girvan Espiner-Scott, *Claude Fauchet: Sa Vie, son œuvre*, Geneva: Droz, 1938, p. 65
37 Michel de Montaigne, *Les Essais*, ed. Pierre Villey and V.L. Saulnier, Paris: Presses Universitaires de France, 1965, p. 1031; my translation.
38 Clark, *Thinking with Demons*, p. 184.

## Further reading

Couzinet, Marie-Dominique, *Jean Bodin*, Bibliographie des écrivains français 23, Paris: Memini, 2001.

Krause, Virginia, *Witchcraft, Demonology, and Confession in Early Modern France*, New York: Cambridge, 2015.

Lloyd, Howell, ed., *The Reception of Jean Bodin*, Leiden: Brill, 2013.

———, *Jean Bodin: 'This Pre-Eminent Man of France'; An Intellectual Biography*, Oxford: Oxford University Press, 2017.

Rose, Paul, *Bodin and the Great God of Nature: The Moral and Religious Universe of a Judaiser*, Geneva: Droz, 1980.

*Harvard University hosts the* The Bodin Project: Aids to the Study of Jean Bodin, *originally developed at the University of Hull, which includes a bibliography of post-2000 secondary sources on Jean Bodin to complement Marie-Dominique Couzinet's study*: https://projects.iq.harvard.edu/bodinproject/bibliography-secondary-sources.

# 8 Doubt and demonology

Reginald Scot's *The Discoverie of Witchcraft*

Philip C. Almond

In 1597, King James VI of Scotland° published his *Daemonologie*. It was a work that he was moved to write by his belief in what he called '[t]he fearefull aboundinge at this time in this countrie, of these detestable slaves of the Devill, the Witches or enchaunters.'[1] James himself had been the target of a plot by alleged witches in Scotland in 1590–1591, so it is little wonder that his mind was focused on witchcraft in this period. And it is not surprising that he felt that he needed to quell the doubts of many 'that such assaultes of Sathan are most certainly practized, & that the instrumentes thereof, merits most severely to be punished.'[2]

For James, one of the chief instigators of scepticism about witchcraft was Reginald Scot, 'an Englishman,' wrote James, who 'is not ashamed in publike print to deny, that ther can be such a thing as Witch-craft: and so mainteines the old error of the Sadducees, in denying of spirits.'[3] Reginald Scot (c.1538–1599) had published his work on witchcraft some thirteen years before, in 1584. He was a gentleman of Kent, an engineer, a part-time military captain and a voracious reader of witchcraft texts. Apart from a manual on the growing of hops, his book on witchcraft was his only publication.[4] As the title of this book makes clear, with the exception of natural magic, Scot was critical not only of the possibilities of witchcraft but also of the whole panoply of matters occult, divinatory, and esoteric:

> *The discoverie of witchcraft, wherein the lewde dealing of witches and witchmongers is notablie detected, the knaverie of conjurors, the impietie of inchantors, the follie of soothsaiers, the impudent falsehood of cousenors, the infidelitie of atheists, the pestilent practices of Pythonists, the curiositie of figurecasters, the vanitie of dreames, the beggerlie art of Alcumystrie, The abhomination of idolatrie, the horrible art of poisoning, the vertue and power of naturall magike, and all the conveiances of Legierdemaine and juggling are deciphered: and many other things opened, which have long lien hidden, howbeit verie necessarie to be knowne. Heereunto is added a treatise upon the nature and substance of spirits and divels, &c.*

It was England's first major work on demonology and witchcraft, and it was unashamedly and unapologetically sceptical. But paradoxically, the comprehensive account of magic, witchcraft, and legerdemain contained in *The Discoverie of Witchcraft* fostered European demonologies in England, helped the spread of indigenous witchcraft traditions, and inaugurated the English tradition of secular magic and conjuring. Translated into Dutch (in 1609), it also had an impact in the wider Protestant world as well (Figure 8.1).

*Figure 8.1* Title page showing a ritual magician (or the Witch of Endor?). Reginald Scot, *Ontdecking van tovery*, trans. Thomas and Govert Basson, Beverwijk: Frans Pels, 1638 [KW 394 G 72]. Image by permission of the Koninklijke Bibliotheek, The Hague.

As a consequence of its comprehensiveness, *The Discoverie of Witchcraft* was an invaluable source of information on magic, demonology, witchcraft, spirits, divination of many kinds, and legerdemain. In the course of its production, Scot had mined a vast array of contemporary and ancient sources. At the beginning of the work, he listed 212 Latin and 23 English authors whose views he quoted, analysed, and criticised.[5] His writing probably began in 1580 after the publication of Jean Bodin°'s *De La Démonomanie des sorciers* (On the Demon-Mania of Witches) in that year. And he continued to read fresh works right up until shortly before he completed the work.

Scot's motivation for his work was clear. It was written on behalf of the poor, the aged and the simple, country people, and those on the frontiers of poverty, not least because they, especially women, were the most likely candidates for witchcraft accusations. But it was written *to* those whom he believed had a moral obligation to ensure that such people were not unjustly persecuted. From these, Scot sought a compassionate response. 'For (God knoweth),' he wrote,

> manie of these poor wretches had more need to be releeved than chastised; and more meete were a preacher to admonish them, than a gailor to keepe them; and a physician more necessarie to helpe them, than an executioner or tormentor to hang or burne them.[6]

Scot's more immediate motivation was the prosecution of witches both in his home county of Kent and elsewhere in England of which he was personally aware. Between 1565 and the year of the publication of *The Discoverie* in 1584, there were fourteen prosecutions for witchcraft in Kent.[7] These were the result of an apparent moral panic about witches and witchcraft that had led to the Elizabethan witchcraft statute in 1563 which both legitimated and increased the panic.

## 1 *Maleficia* and melancholy

The persecution of witches that followed in the wake of the 1563 statute no doubt led Scot to begin reading the contemporary literature around witchcraft and demonology. Scot's work was peppered with around fifty marginal references to Bodin's *De La Démonomanie*. Bodin's book functioned for him as one of his two main sources for demonological theory. His references to Bodin were only exceeded by those to that most famous of demonologies, the 1486 *Malleus maleficarum* (The Hammer of [Female] Witches) by Heinrich Institoris°. Scot was a key player in introducing both of these key works to the English reading public.

The third key source for Scot was the *De praestigiis daemonum* (On the Deceptions of Devils) of Johann Wier° (or Weyer), first published in 1563 though often revised and expanded.[8] While Scot accepted the physician's beliefs that witches were deluded or ill, he did not agree with Wier that they were so, or could ever be so, as the result of the activities of demons. In the end, he was far more radical. Scot's intention in his use of Wier was a notably Protestant one. Above all, it was to deny any biblical legitimacy to the Catholic demonologists' construction of witchcraft as a Christian heresy by demonstrating that there was no relation between the demonologists' understanding of witchcraft and the various biblical understandings of the occult world.

Scot's world was indeed a Protestant one and, pre-eminently, a biblical one. He did not deny the reality of witches. But he did deny the attribution to them all of the powers that belonged only to God. 'But truelie I denie not,' wrote Scot,

> that there are witches or images: but I detest the idolatrous opinions conceived of them; referring that to Gods worke and ordinance, which they impute to the power and malice of witches; and attributing that honour to God, which they ascribe to idols.[9]

To grant to either witches or images (whether of Christ, the saints, or the Virgin) extraordinary power, as Catholics were wont to do, was to go against the doctrine of divine providence – that God alone determined the length of our lives and the number of our days. In so saying, Scot was cutting through the complex negotiations within contemporary free-will theology and demonology on the power-sharing between God, the devil and witches and locating all the power in God's hands.

Scot did not deny that there were witches in the Bible. Scripture affirmed their existence. He collapsed biblical witches into four kinds: Pharaoh's magicians, the poisoners, the diviners, and the enchanters. What these held in common, like the 'witches' or cunning men and women of Scot's own time, was that they were all 'couseners' or tricksters. In short, witches were charlatans with no supernatural powers. He was as much opposed to cunning men or women as any of his Protestant contemporaries, including English divines such as William Perkins° and George Gifford, although for quite different reasons – they, because they believed that the cunning person, whether acting with good or ill intent, was in league with the devil; he, because he believed that they were all frauds. In contrast to his peers who demonised them (quite literally), Scot disempowered them – and he offered a startlingly novel re-interpretation of the Bible in the process.

That said, Scot also recognised that the power of witchcraft was as dependent upon its customers as its suppliers. He thought of those who believed in its power as children, fools, melancholics, or papists (the standard slur for Catholics). They had been infatuated, he believed, by poets, liars, and couseners, bewitched by tales told by old doting women, their mothers' maids, and priests. It was, in short, a foundational mode of thinking about the everyday, one sustained by both suppliers and consumers of magic and witchcraft.

The elaborate explanations of the magical arts in *The Discoverie of Witchcraft* were intended to demonstrate their fraudulent nature. To assert supernatural power to be the sole prerogative of God, to deny it to the devil and witches, and to explain it all as a fake was one thing. But that witches were conjuring charlatans failed to explain how witches often deluded *themselves* into believing that they had not only magical powers but the assistance of the devil in enacting them.

To explain all this, Scot constructed another radically different narrative of witchcraft and *maleficium*, one which had at its core not a deluding and cousening magician but a deluded innocent who had mistakenly come to believe in the supernatural powers attributed to them by others and who wrongly accepted the truth of the accusations made against them by those who were 'of the basest, the unwisest, & most faithles kind of people.'[10] The accused were, as a result, he declared, 'abused, and not abusors.'[11]

This explanation was grounded in neighbourly conflict as a consequence of demands for charity, refusal, neighbourly conflict and guilt, revenge inexplicable misfortunes, suspicion and formal accusation:

> She was at my house of late, she would have had a pot of milke, she departed in a chafe because she had it not, she railed, she curssed, she mumbled and whispered, and finallie she said she would be even with me: and soone after my child, my cow, or my pullet died, or was strangelie taken. Naie (if it please your Worship) I have further proofe: I was with a wise woman, and she told me I had an ill neighbour, & that she would come to my house yer it were long, and so did she; and that she had a marke above hir waste, & and so had she: and God forgive me, my stomach hath gone against hir a great while. Hir mother before hir was counted a witch, she hath beene beaten and scratched by the face till bloud was drawne upon hir, bicause she hath beene suspected, & afterwards some of those persons were said to amend.[12]

Effectively, Scot's intent was to 'demythologise' or 'disenchant' the narratives upon which he drew in order to create a 'naturalistic' account of how witchcraft accusations arose. And he did so by imbedding them in social conflict and denying them any supernatural or magical resonances. Similarly, with regard to his image of the witch, his 'demythologised' narrative of the witch was dependent upon creating a *persona* for the witch as someone outside of the bounds of the normal – physically, mentally, morally, and religiously sufficient to inspire fear, loathing, and horror, persuading both themselves and others of their supernatural powers. 'One sort of such as are said to bee witches,' wrote Scot,

> [A]re women which be commonly old, lame, bleare-eied, pale, fowle, and full of wrinkles; poore, sullen, superstitious, and papists; or such as knowe no religion: in whose drousie minds the divell hath gotten a fine seat; so as, what mischeefe, mischance, calamitie, or slaughter is brought to passe, they are easily persuaded the same is doone by themselves; imprinting in their minds an earnest and constant imagination hereof. They are leane and deformed, shewing melancholie in their faces, to the horror of all that see them. They are doting, scolds, mad, divelish; and not much differing from them that are thought to be possessed with spirits.[13]

At the core of Scot's naturalistic reading of witchcraft was his account of melancholy, one that drew upon the standard early modern humoral account of melancholy drawn from classical resources and especially from the Greek physician Galen (second century CE). Scot was at one with his contemporaries in seeing it as a form of madness due to the dominance of 'black bile' (μέλαινα χολή) in the body unaccompanied by either fever or frenzy, more prevalent in the old than the young, especially among women, and involving the impairment of the imagination.[14] It was usually accompanied by hallucinations, and fear and sorrow with no apparent cause. Wier had also invoked melancholy in gendered terms but, unlike Scot, had invoked the devil as a plausible cause of that gendered disease.

Moreover, it was upon the hallucinatory rather than the 'depressive' features of melancholy that Scot concentrated. He aligned the delusions of melancholics with those of witches. This enabled him to suggest that, if the fantasies of melancholics were as false and impossible as those of witches, then the latter were to be classified with the former, especially since witches were old, female and, like many melancholic women, post-menstrual. His diagnosis of witches as melancholic provided an explanation of the false confessions made by those who truly believed (in their melancholic delusions) that they were indeed witches. And it demonstrated the injustice of their convictions. This melancholic humour, he declared, 'is the cause of all their strange confessions: which are so fond [silly], that I woonder how anie man can be abused thereby.'[15]

For Scot, the falsity of voluntarily-made confessions arising from melancholy was reinforced, not only by the natural impossibility of those things which witches claimed to do, but by the improbability of their having done so. Witches confessed to things done which were so against their self-interest that it was impossible to believe that any sane person would have thus acted. Thus, confessions to have acted so arose from madness: 'what creature being sound in state of mind,' asked Scot,

> would (without compulsion), make such manner of confessions as they do; or would for a trifle or nothing, make a perfect bargaine with the divell for hir soule, to be yielded up unto his tortures and everlasting flames, and that within a verie short time.[16]

Moreover, Scot argued, if the confessions of witches were true, natural, social, and political chaos would be the consequence. 'One old witch might overthrowe an armie roiall: and then what needed we any guns, or wild fire, or any other instruments of warre?'[17]

## 2 The 'demonology' of Reginald Scot

Still, Scot was aware that the falsity of confessions voluntarily made was a consequence, not only of melancholy, but also of the ideological edifice which they apparently supported – namely, demonology. Scot realised that his account of witchcraft was crucially dependent on demonstrating the feeble foundations upon which demonology was constructed. For that reason, Scot's critique of demonology was also directed at the impossibility of the European construction of witchcraft as a heretical religion based on a pact sealed with the devil, the devotees of which worshipped Satan and practiced both benevolent and malevolent magic.

Thus, particularly in Books Three, Four, and Five of *The Discoverie of Witchcraft*, Scot expounded and criticised in a fairly systematic way the key features of European demonology – the pact with the devil, the sabbat and magical transportation to it, transformation into the form of animals and sex with the devil. For his account of the demonic pact, Scot drew not only upon the *Malleus maleficarum*, but also on Dominican Bartolomeo Spina"'s 1523 *Quaestio de strigibus* (The Problem of Witches), Bodin's 1580 *Démonomanie*, and the French Calvinist Lambert Daneau's 1574 *Dialogus de veneficis* (Dialogue on Witches), translated into English in 1575. In so doing, he was the first to draw the more lurid details of European demonology to the attention of English readers.

According to Scot, and paraphrasing in part the *Malleus*, witches came together at certain assemblies at fixed times where they not only saw the devil but held familiar conversations with him. In these, the devil exhorted them to remain faithful to him, promising them prosperity and long life in return. The witches thus assembled commended a new disciple (whom they call a novice) to him. If the devil found the young witch ready to renounce the Christian faith, despise the sacraments, spit at the time of the elevation of the Host, and ignore fasting, he joined his hand with hers, and she promised to observe and keep all the devil's commandments.[18] The devil also demanded that she worship him, and that she grant him both her body and soul to be tormented in everlasting fire, an offer which as Scot argued elsewhere is, at the end of the day (or the world), not really much of a bargain. The devil also charged her to bring as many people as possible to join their society. He taught the witches how to make ointments out of the bowels and other parts of unbaptised children to fulfil all their desires.

The bargain with the devil was sealed, Scot reported, by a verbal oath or in writing, sealed with wax and often signed in blood, 'sometimes by kissing the divels bare buttocks; as did a Doctor called *Edlin*, who as (*Bodin* says) was burned for witchcraft.'[19] And he paraphrased Bodin in his telling of the dancing that was always included in the sabbat and the witches singing

> Har, Har, divell, divell, danse here, danse here, plaie here, plaie here, Sabbath, sabbath. And whiles they sing and danse, everie one hath a broome in hir hand and holdeth it up aloft. Item he [Bodin] saith that these night-walking or rather night-dansing witches, brought out of *Italie* into *France*, that danse, which is called *La volta*.[20]

Scot did not report Bodin's claim that it made men homicidally frenzied and caused women to abort.

Scot could have derived any amount of further information on the sabbat from Bodin. But he chose to supplement Bodin's account of demonic dancing with more detail derived from Lambert Daneau's *De veneficis*.[21] Although he nowhere said so, Daneau's work did at least provide him with an opportunity to demonstrate that Protestant demonologists like Daneau could be as credulous as their Catholic counterparts.

Little fresh was added to the sum of information provided to his readers by his abbreviated account of Daneau. But he did reiterate the erotic nature of the meetings with their dancing and singing of bawdy songs and their kissing of the devil's bare buttocks, and he emphasised Daneau's claim that witches 'really' travelled to the sabbat on staffs provided by the devil. In addition, he recognised the strong emphasis in Daneau on witches as poisoners, and repeated Daneau's claim that witches had to offer the devil dogs, cats, hens, or their own blood every day afterwards. Perhaps most importantly, he reminded his readers of Daneau's belief that the pact with the devil was sealed by the devil marking the witch 'either with his teeth or his claws.'[22] It was a mark, declared Daneau, which the witch

> [A]lwayes beareth about him, some under the eye liddes, others betwene their buttocks, some in the roofe of their mouthe, and in other places where it may be hid & concealed from us ... yet may I say thus more certenly and truly, that there is none of them upon whom he hath not set some note or token of his power & prerogative over them: which to thintent [sic] the judges and such as are set in aucthoritie of life and death ... let them specially provide, that when any of these shalbe convented before them, to poulie [polle] and shave them where occasion shall serve, al the body over, least haply the marke may lurke under the heare in any place.[23]

Scot, as we might now expect, was having none of all this. The impossibility of it went to the core of Scot's argument, namely, that the bargain of the sort described by the demonologists assumed that which was impossible, that is, the corporeality of the devil:

> That the joining of hands with the divell, the kissing of his bare buttocks, and his scratching and biting of them, are absurd lies; everie one having the gift of reason may plainlie perceive: in so much as it is manifest unto us by the word of God, that a spirit hath no flesh, bones, nor sinewes, whereof hands, buttocks, claws, teeth, and lips doo consist.[24]

Although Scot did not deny the existence of spirits, this sufficiently smacked of their denial for his critics, notably James VI, to accuse him of 'Sadduceeism' – as denial of the spirit world was commonly called.

He also put forward a number of other arguments, all of which went to demonstrating that the Satanic pact could not be but false: there was no evidence for it in the Scriptures, the age of miracles was over, no reasons can count as good reasons for that which is beyond reason, the visible covenant with God made in the sacrament of baptism should be of more force than the invisible covenant with the devil, and there was sheer folly in exchanging paltry profits on this side of the grave for eternal punishments in the fires of Hell on the other.

Moreover, the confessions of witches were not to be given any credence. Their confessions were, after all, to impossible crimes. They were made by persons 'diseased both in bodie and mind, wilfullie made or injuriouslie constrained,'[25] and where made voluntarily, sometimes by those in search of their own destruction:

> so doo they also (I saie) confesse voluntarilie, that which no man could proove, and that which no man would ghesse, nor yet beleeve, except he were as mad as they; so as they bring death wilfullie upon themselves: which argueth an unsound mind.[26]

Scot was never averse to turning demonology against itself and seeking justification for his arguments in Catholic sources. He was aware that, within Catholic circles, there had been a long debate about the possibility of the bodily transportation of witches to the sabbat, one that went back to the tenth-century canon *Episcopi*. The canon *Episcopi* is the oldest source for the Western notion that witches 'flew' and that they gathered together by night to attend meetings. It appealed to Scot because, in contrast to the European notion of the witch that developed after the year 1400 (as advocated by Nicolas Jacquier° and others), it declared that the nocturnal travelling of women to the sabbat was nothing but a dream or an illusion, and that the gatherings that followed were similarly imaginary.

Scot completely rejected the possibility of witches physically flying to the sabbat. He did so by invoking the authority of the Neapolitan natural magician Johannes Baptista Neapolitanus, more commonly known to us as Giambattista Della Porta (1535–1613). He was a physician and sceptic to whom Scot, as a supporter of natural magic, would have been attracted. In this work, Della Porta reported on his experiment to test the belief that

142  Philip C. Almond

witches flew by covering themselves with an ointment. Scot was no doubt delighted by Della Porta's experiment, and he translated it closely. After detailing Della Porta's two recipes for transportation, the one based on the fat of young children, the other on the blood of a flitter mouse, he gives us Della Porta's account of his experiment:

> Now (saith he) when I considered throughlie hereof, remaining doubtfull of the matter, there fell into my hands a witch, who of hir owne accord did promise me to fetch an errand out of hand from farre countries, and willed all them, whome I had brought to witnesse the matter, to depart out of the chamber. And when she had undressed hir selfe, and froted [rubbed] hir bodie with certeine ointments (which action we beheld through a chinke or little hole of the doore) she fell downe thorough the force of those soporiferous or sleepie ointments into a most sound and heavie sleepe: so as we did breake open the doore, and did beate hir exceedinglie; but the force of hir sleepe was suche, as it tooke awaie from hir the sense of feeling: and we departed for a time. Now when hir strength and powers were wearie and decaied, shee awooke of hir owne accord, and began to speake manie vaine and doting words, affirming that she had passed over both seas and mountains; delivering to us manie untrue and false reports; we earnestlie denied them, she impudentlie affirmed them.[27]

Through Della Porta, Scot was able effectively to tie the use of ointments to journeys of the imagination rather than the body. Della Porta was of help too in Scot's theory of the melancholic origins of sabbatical travelling. He was able to suggest that, according to Della Porta, such imaginary journeys were false rather than true: 'This (saith he [Della Porta]) will not so come to passe with everie one, but onlie with old women that are melancholike, whose nature is extreame cold, and their evaporation small.'[28]

Night travelling was never a part of English witchcraft beliefs before Scot's *The Discoverie of Witchcraft*. In this case he was preaching to the unconverted. It never did become so, even when other elements of continental witchcraft became part of English witchcraft in the early seventeenth century. No doubt this was a consequence of the fact that James VI in his *Daemonologie*, having one of his own more complicated sceptical moments, maintained that the devil created dreams in the minds of witches, while simultaneously deluding others to believe that they have met them, and even committing the harm to men and beasts which these witches in their imaginative state believed that they had done.[29]

Scot was just as sceptical of the possibility of the transformation of men and women into animals. The popular classical and medieval belief that a person can transform himself or be transformed by another into an animal, often a wolf (lycanthropy), was demonologised into the capacity of the devil to adopt an animal form or at least to give the illusion of so doing, of witches to change themselves into animals empowered by the devil, and of witches to turn people into animals. It was a belief that Scot described as 'this impossible, incredible, and supernaturall, or rather unnaturall doctrine of transubstantiation' – a swipe no doubt also aimed against the Catholic belief that Christ was bodily present in the Eucharist.[30]

Against the possibility of the transformation of humans into animals, Scot mounted several theological arguments. The first of these went to the fixity of species after the day of creation. Quite simply,

> God hath endued everie man and everie thing with his proper nature, substance, forme, qualities and gifts, and directeth their waies ... And therefore it is absolutelie against the ordinance of God (who hath made me a man) that I should flie like a bird, or swim like a fish, or creepe like a worme, or become an asse in shape.[31]

Further, he had no sympathy for views which, drawing on the Aristotelian distinction between substance and accidents and the doctrine of transubstantiation, made distinctions between the transformation of the accidents of the human into the animal and the preservation of the substance of the individual – the ratio or reason. Not surprisingly he was as critical of the Catholic doctrine of the transubstantiation of bread and wine into body and blood in the Mass as he was the transformation of men into animals.

His assertion of the doctrine of the fixity of species was reinforced too by that of the qualitative uniqueness of the human, both in body and soul.

> What a beastlie assertion is it, that a man, whom GOD hath made according to his owne similitude and likeness, should be by a witch turned into a beast? What an impietie is it to affirme, that an asses bodie is the temple of the Holy-ghost? Or an asse to be the childe of God, and God to be his father; as it is said of man?[32]

Much depended here on the reading of the Old Testament story of King Nebuchadnezzar's apparent transformation into a beast: 'He was driven away from human society, ate grass like oxen' (Daniel 4.33). Bodin had used the biblical text as a validation of his view that the transformation of person into animals was a real one. Scot read the text as quite simply saying no more than that Nebuchadnezzar merely lived *as if* he were a beast rather than having been transformed into one. This reading was of a piece with Scot's tendency to find metaphor in the Bible where the literal was impossible. Scot does not appear to accept the reading of Nebuchadnezzar as a mad man. Nevertheless, as for those who did think themselves to be wolves or other animals, Scot was again able to provide a unified account by looking to melancholy as the cause of their delusions. And it was in Wier that he found his explanation. For *Lycanthropia*, he wrote, 'is of the ancient physicians called *Lupina melancholia*, or *Lupina insania*. J.*Wierus* declareth verie learnedlie the cause, the circumstance, and the cure of this disease.'[33] This was one of those few points on which Wier, Scot, *and* James VI were agreed. James took it to have been produced by 'a naturall super-abundance of Melancholie, which as wee reade, hath made some thinke themselves Pitchers, and some horses, and some one kind of beast or other.'[34] And like Wier, but unlike Scot, he saw Nebuchadnezzar as a madman.[35]

At the end of Book Three of *The Discoverie of Witchcraft*, somewhat in the manner of a modern television network warning its viewers of 'adults only' material coming up, Scot advised those of his readers 'whose chaste eares cannot well endure to heare of such abhominable lecheries as are gathered out of the bookes of those witchmongers' to pass over the first eight chapters of the following Book.[36] For it is in these eight chapters of Book Four that Scot laid out the demonologists' accounts of sex with the devil, of impotence caused by witches, of penis stealing, and his own stories of bawdy priests and lecherous monks.

The *Malleus maleficarum* was Scot's key source for his account of sex with the devil and demonic impotence, and the first four chapters of Book Four in *The Discoverie of Witchcraft* summarised the relevant parts of this work.[37] Or at least it should be said, Scot paraphrased the more salacious parts, ignoring for the most part the extensive metaphysical discussions of the *Malleus* in which the teachings of Thomas Aquinas on demonic reality were adapted and refined. Scot's strategic intention is reasonably clear. For the recitation of the lurid details without the metaphysics drives the reader towards the inevitable conclusion that all this could not be true.

Witchcraft as constructed by the demonologists was ultimately dependent on the establishment of the corporeality of demons and the possibility of their corporeal interaction with humans. Sex with the devil was the ultimate form of such interaction. And it was here that Scot's key argument against the demonology of sex was to be found. Scot opposed demonology with physiology. Sex was only possible among beings essentially corporeal. Spirits were by nature incorporeal and therefore incapable of the desires of the flesh:

> Item, where the genitall members want, there can be no lust of the flesh: neither dooth nature give anie desire of generation, where there is no propagation or succession required. And as spirits cannot be greeved with hunger, so can they not be inflamed with lusts.[38]

Scot paid no attention to the complex arguments by which the *Malleus maleficarum* attempted to explain how demons can, in their *assumed* bodies, be said to speak to, see, hear, eat with, and have sex with sorceresses.[39] Its claim that, while angels in assumed bodies could both chew and swallow food, they were unable to digest and expel it but possessed 'a power by which food is immediately broken up into the previously existing matter' must have stretched the credulity of even the most sympathetic reader.[40] Scot was certainly not one of these. We may nonetheless discern a critical echo of the

*Malleus maleficarum* in Scot's declaration that a spirit 'neither dooth eate nor drinke.'[41] For him, spirits that ate and drank were the stuff of outdated superstition and fairy tales. And he was convinced that, in times to come, the belief in witches and walking spirits would be as derided and condemned as the belief in Robin good-fellow and Hob goblin was in his.[42]

At the end of the day, of course, Scot rejected all talk of assumed bodies, and thus all possibility of demonic interaction with humans. The incorporeality of spirits entailed the impossibility *in principle* of their interaction with humans. And with that, the whole edifice of witchcraft and demonology – the pact with the devil, the sabbat and magical transportation to it, transformation into the form of animals, and sex with the devil – collapsed.

## 3 Spiritual realities

Did Scot deny the reality of spirits? This was certainly the conclusion of Sydney Anglo in his important study of Scot in 1977. 'The truth of the matter is,' he concluded,

> that Scot no more accepted the reality of spirits and demons than he accepted the reality of witches ... Thus Scot's spirits and witches are defined out of existence. And in this sense Scot was, indeed, the Saddu-cee his enemies have always considered him to be.[43]

It is a position more recently endorsed by James Sharpe in his *Instruments of Darkness*. Sharpe was more attuned than Anglo to what Scot actually meant by 'spirit.' But he nonetheless still felt able to conclude that 'In effect (and despite his disavowals), the logic of Scot's arguments led to a denial of the reality of the spirit world as surely as it did to a denial of the reality of witchcraft.'[44]

However, in spite of Scot's denial of the possibility of spirits being embodied, he did not deny their *reality*. On the contrary, the reality of spirits was at the very centre of Scot's theology. Indeed, in one particular passage, in direct opposition to the sceptical Sadducees' claims that spirits and devils were only motions and affections, and that angels were but tokens of God's power, he declared,

> I will not sticke to saie, that they are living creatures, ordeined to serve the lord in their vocation. And although they abode not in their first estate, yet that they are the Lords ministers, and executioners of his wrath, to trie and tempt in this world, and to punish the reprobate in hell fier in the world to come.[45]

The consequence of the denial of embodied spirits was the limiting of the domain of the interaction between the realm of spirits (whether good or evil) and the human realm to (what we would call) the psychological realm. Thus, Scot's definition of 'spirit':

> In summe, this word [Spirit] dooth signifie a secret force and power, wherewith our minds are mooved and directed; if unto holie things, then is it the motion of the holie spirit, of the spirit of Christ and of God: if unto evill things, then is it the suggestion of the wicked spirit, of the divell, and of satan. Whereupon I inferre, by the waie of a question, with what spirit we are to suppose such to be mooved, as either practise anie of the vanities treated upon in this booke, or through credulitie addict themselves thereunto as unto divine oracles, or the voice of angels breakeing through the clouds? We cannot impute this motion unto the good spirit; for then they should be able to discerne betweene the nature of spirits, and not swarve in judgement: it followeth therefore, that the spirit of blindnes and error dooth seduce them; so that it is no mervell if in the alienation of their minds they take falshood for truth, shadowes for substances, fansies for verities, &c: for it is likewise that the good spirit of God hath forsaken them, or at leastwise absented it selfe from them: else would they detest these divelish devises of men, which consist of nothing but delusions and vaine practices, whereof (I suppose) this my booke to be a sufficient discoverie.[46]

Ironically then, for Scot himself, his *Discoverie of Witchcraft* was as much a demonology as a theology. Those whom he had criticised *were* themselves in league with the devil. He had uncovered the genuine witches, masquerading as demonologists. It was they who had been forsaken by the good spirit of God. He was, in this sense, the demonologists' demonologist, the one who had 'discovered' those in whom the spirit of evil really did work – Cornelius Loos° would make a very similar charge in a very different context a generation later.

As a consequence, Scot's theology entailed an anthropology that divided humanity into two kinds, the carnal and the spiritual. And the latter were those who, enlivened by the Holy Spirit, were able to discern spiritual things.[47] He knew the demonic when he saw it because he saw himself as a spiritual and not a carnal man, one guided by the spirit of truth.[48]

Without doubt, among his contemporaries, Scot was by far the most radically sceptical. His denial of the possibility of miracles (at least since the time of Christ), the rejection of the demonic preternatural, the medical reductionism of his account of witchcraft, his consistent questioning of the evidences for the truth of witchcraft, his denial of the possibility of the corporeality of spirits – all these pointed to a sceptical naturalism which denied the reality of the spiritual realm altogether.

But his was a radical scepticism grounded in the certainty that only a man, illuminated by the Holy Spirit, could discern the good from the evil, the true from the false, and the genuinely divine from the really demonic. And his theology entailed that such men were few and far between. He might have ended his life as a man disappointed that his ideas did not receive a sympathetic hearing, though he could hardly have been surprised at that. He would have been surprised though, had he known that his critique of witchcraft and demonology would come to be most valued in the modern world by those who, far from recognising the existence of spirits or endorsing his theology of the Spirit, would be equally sceptical of any kind of theology at all.

## Notes

1 James VI, *Daemonologie, in Forme of a Dialogue, Divided into Three Bookes*, Edinburgh: Robert Waldegrave, 1597, fol. 2r.
2 James VI, *Daemonologie*, fol. 2v.
3 James VI, *Daemonologie*, fol. 2v.
4 On Reginald Scot's life, see Philip C. Almond. *England's First Demonologist: Reginald Scot & 'The Discoverie of Witchcraft*, London: I.B. Tauris, 2014, pp. 9–12.
5 See Reginald Scot, *The Discoverie of Witchcraft*, London, 1584, sig. B6r–v. Though it should be noted that his knowledge of many of these sources was sometimes only indirect.
6 Scot, *The Discoverie*, sig. B3r.
7 See Malcolm Gaskill, 'Witches and Witchcraft Persecutions in Kent from 1565–1657,' in Michael Zell, ed., *Early Modern Kent 1540–1640*, Woodbridge: Boydell Press and Kent County Council, 2000, pp. 274–77.
8 See Johann Wier [Weyer], *Witches, Devils, and Doctors in the Renaissance: Johann Weyer, De praestigiis daemonum*, ed. and trans. George Mora et al., Binghamton, NY: Medieval and Renaissance Texts and Studies, 1991.
9 Scot, *The Discoverie*, sig. B5v.
10 Scot, *The Discoverie*, sig. A6r.
11 Scot, *The Discoverie*, sig. A4r.
12 Scot, *The Discoverie*, sig. A6v.
13 Scot, *The Discoverie*, p. 7.
14 On melancholy, see Angus Gowland, 'The Problem of Early Modern Melancholy,' *Past and Present*, 2006, vol. 191, 77–120.
15 Scot, *The Discoverie*, p. 57.
16 Scot, *The Discoverie*, p. 68.
17 Scot, *The Discoverie*, p. 63.
18 Compare Christopher S. Mackay, ed. and trans., *Malleus Maleficarum*, Cambridge: Cambridge University Press, 2009, pp. 282–83 (pt. 2, quaestio 1, chap. 2, 96C–D).
19 Scot, *The Discoverie of Witchcraft*, p. 42. See also Jean Bodin, *On the Demon-Mania of Witches*, ed. Jonathan Pearl, trans. Randy A. Scott, Toronto: Centre for Reformation and Renaissance Studies, 1995, p. 114 (bk 2, chap. 4).
20 Scot, *The Discoverie of Witchcraft*, p. 42. Compare Bodin, *On the Demon-Mania of Witches*, p. 120 (bk 2, chap. 4).
21 Scot was relying on the English translation of this work, *A Dialogue of Witches*, London, 1575.
22 Scot, *The Discoverie*, p. 43.
23 Daneau, *A Dialogue of Witches*, sig. F4v.
24 Scot, *The Discoverie*, p. 47.
25 Scot, *The Discoverie*, p. 48.

26 Scot, *The Discoverie*, p. 50.
27 Scot, *The Discoverie*, p. 185.
28 Scot, *The Discoverie*, p. 185.
29 See James, *Daemonologie*, pp. 41–42.
30 Scot, *The Discoverie*, p. 89.
31 Scot, *The Discoverie*, p. 100.
32 Scot, *The Discoverie*, p. 101.
33 Scot, *The Discoverie*, p. 102. Compare Wier, *Witches, Devils, and Doctors*, p. 343. Scot appears to be the first person in England to use the term 'lycanthropy'.
34 James, *Daemonologie*, p. 61.
35 James, *Daemonologie*, p. 62.
36 Scot, *The Discoverie*, p. 72.
37 See Mackay, ed. and trans., *Malleus Maleficarum*, pp. 302–330 (pt. 2, qn. 1, chaps 4–7).
38 Scot, *The Discoverie*, p. 86.
39 Mackay, ed. and trans., *Malleus Maleficarum*, pp. 302–6 (pt. 2, qn. 1, chap. 4, 105D–107D).
40 Mackay, ed. and trans., *Malleus Maleficarum*, p. 306 (pt. 2, qn. 1, chap. 4, 107D).
41 Scot, *The Discoverie*, p. 85.
42 Scot, *The Discoverie*, p. 131.
43 Sydney Anglo, 'Reginald Scot's *Discoverie of Witchcraft*: Scepticism and Sadduceeism', in Sydney Anglo, ed., *The Damned Art: Essays in the Literature of Witchcraft*, London: Routledge and Kegan Paul, 1977, p. 129.
44 James Sharpe, *Instruments of Darkness: Witchcraft in England 1550–1750*, London: Hamish Hamilton, 1996, p. 55.
45 Scot, *The Discoverie*, p. 540.
46 Scot, *The Discoverie*, pp. 547–48.
47 Scot, *The Discoverie*, p. 508.
48 Scot, *The Discoverie*, p. 546.

## Further reading

Almond, Philip C., *England's First Demonologist: Reginald Scot and 'The Discoverie of Witchcraft*, London: I.B. Tauris, 2014.

Anglo, Sydney, 'Reginald Scot's *Discoverie of Witchcraft*: Scepticism and Sadduceeism', in Sydney Anglo, ed., *The Damned Art: Essays in the Literature of Witchcraft*, London: Routledge and Kegan Paul, 1977, pp. 125–140.

Davies, S. F., 'The Reception of Reginald Scot's *Discovery of Witchcraft*: Witchcraft, Magic, and Radical Religion', *Journal of the History of Ideas*, 2013, vol. 74/3, 381–401.

Sharpe, James, *Instruments of Darkness: Witchcraft in England 1550–1750*, London: Hamish Hamilton, 1996.

Stephens, Walter, 'The Sceptical Tradition', in Brian P. Levack, ed., *The Oxford Handbook of Witchcraft in Early Modern Europe and Colonial America*, Oxford: Oxford University Press, 2013, pp. 101–121.

Wootton, David., 'Reginald Scot/Abraham Fleming/The Family of Love', in Stuart Clark, ed., *Languages of Witchcraft*, London: Macmillan, 2001, pp. 119–138.

# 9 Demonology and anti-demonology

Binsfeld's *De confessionibus* and Loos's
*De vera et falsa magia*

Rita Voltmer

The conflict about the reality of witchcraft between Peter Binsfeld and Cornelius Loos took place against the backdrop of some of the worst witch-hunting early modern Europe would ever see. Between 1586 and 1596, the Catholic territories in the Western part of the Holy Roman Empire, largely situated between the Rhine, Moselle, and Saar rivers, saw widespread witch-hunting, with an estimated 1,500 women and men being burned at the stake.[1] This witch-hunt had spread across three different jurisdictions: the Electorate of Trier, the city of Trier, and the territory of the Imperial Abbey of Saint Maximin. Having spread from the neighbouring duchies of Lorraine and Luxembourg, witch-hunting appears to have arrived first in the electorate's administrative districts of Grimburg, Saarburg, and Pfalzel, the last two neighboured the city of Trier itself. Ruling a sprawling and fragmented political unit, the Archbishop of Trier was one of the Prince-Electors responsible for choosing the Emperor. While most of the electorate's trial records were destroyed after 1652, one estimate puts the total number of executions in this largest and mostly rural territory at around 1,000 (or roughly 1.3% of the total population).

We know much more about the relatively small and compact territory of the Imperial Abbey of St Maximin, an entirely autonomous political and judicial entity, which was situated near the city of Trier itself.[2] Within the abbey's territory witch trials were carried out without outside legal participation and remained in the hands of popular witch-hunting committees, which were tolerated by the abbot and gained a quasi-official status. They worked together with St Maximin's local magistrates, bailiffs, and jurymen. The organization of witch-hunting attained a lethal level of perfection: at least 400 people were executed for witchcraft between 1586 and 1596, out of a population which probably did not exceed 2,500 inhabitants. Its witch-hunt thus ranks as one of Europe's deadliest. Records of more than 200 trials have survived, as well as financial accounts detailing the costs of the persecution, and lists of denunciations and executions.

Yet, of the three jurisdictions, it was the prosecutions in the city of Trier itself which most shocked contemporaries in the Holy Roman Empire, since it spared neither rich men nor Catholic clerics. A range of factors fuelled the witch-hunt: the magistrates had lost their struggle with the Elector of Trier for the city's autonomy and years of harvest failure and speculative trading had pushed up food prices, while the local Jesuits in their sermons and public exorcisms of seemingly possessed child-witches further fostered fear of witchcraft.

Other factors also came into play: the secular districts of two ecclesiastical institutions under the jurisdiction of the elector (the Benedictine abbey of St Matthias and the canon's collegiate of St Paulin) were part of Trier's urban space. The witch trials in these city districts, together with the mass hunts in the territory of St Maximin, produced many denunciations of rich male citizens and their wives. Zealous notaries brought the elaborate concept of the diabolic crime of witchcraft into the courtrooms. Imitating the witch-hunting committees on the countryside, the town guilds in the city of Trier pressed the authorities to conduct more trials. The cry for justice focussed on the rich elite, accused of profiting from the rise in food prices and money lending. Thus, the witch-hunt in the city of Trier became famous for executing wealthy mayors, senior clerics, and other members of the ruling elite, as well as (of course) women.

The so-called 'Trier super-hunts'[3] thus brought together different though connected witchcraft persecutions in judicially and politically different settings. Still, a number of commonalities are worth stressing. In all jurisdictions, the courts were manned only partly with university-educated jurists who classified demonic witchcraft as an 'exceptional crime'. This allowed for torture to be used without restraint, even if lip service was paid to the imperial legal code (the *Carolina* of 1532). Alleged witches were forced to name accomplices whom they supposedly had seen at the sabbat. These denunciations, in turn, crossed not only the borders of the three territories, but also those of gender, status, and age. In the territory of St Maximin, even children and teenagers were executed as alleged witches.

Within the city of Trier, the most dramatic moment of the witch-hunt took place on 18 September 1589, when Dr Dietrich Flade, *Stadtschultheiß* (city bailiff) of Trier and the richest man in the city, was burned as a witch. Flade's execution caused two Catholic theologians – the Trier Vice-Bishop Peter Binsfeld (*c*.1545/46–1598) and the Dutch priest Cornelius Loos (*c*.1540/45–1596/97) – to debate the devil's nature and power, the existence of witchcraft, and the legitimacy of criminal procedure during the witch-hunts, especially as it related to the validity of the confessions of witches. Accused as a heretic by an ecclesiastical tribunal, Loos was forced to revoke his work of (anti-)demonology in 1593. This did not, however, end the controversy after Loos relocated to Brussels and revived his claims. Freed from imprisonment after a second charge, only death saved Loos around 1596/1597 from a third accusation of being a *patronus sagarum* (a patron of witches). It was his death during the plague of 1598 that prevented Binsfeld from publishing another edition of one of his works on demonology, in which he was still debating the arguments of Loos. The conflict between Binsfeld and Loos precluded Catholic sceptics from founding their arguments on theological (as opposed to legal) grounds. Instead, sceptics like Adam Tanner, Paul Laymann, or Friedrich Spee had to focus their arguments on both the trustworthiness of witches' confessions and the legitimacy of torture. Loos's fate at the hand of church authorities made it impossible to doubt the material reality of demons and the existence of witches.

## 1 Peter Binsfeld: a man on a Catholic mission

Peter Binsfeld's youth is shrouded not just in mystery but in pious legends.[4] According to a convent history (written after 1674), John of Briedel, the abbot of the Cistercian abbey of Himmerod (some 50 kilometres north of Trier), had taken into his service a certain Peter (born around 1546) from the nearby village of Binsfeld, probably as a shepherd boy. Impressed with the young boy's intelligence, the abbot then facilitated the boy's education. There are good reasons to doubt this rags-to-bishopric story, however. We know that one Valentin Binsfeld was a canon of St Simeon in Trier in 1568, so Peter was not lacking clerical connections of his own. This Valentin also served as parish priest in Binsfeld. After his death in 1582, other members of the Binsfeld family acquired prebends in St Simeon, including Peter, who became its provost in 1578. We also know that Peter's mother died in Trier sometime after 1606 as a wealthy widow. Surviving her son, she donated 100 florins for requiem masses after his death.[5] The Binsfeld family was thus better off and better connected than it might appear from the myth of the shepherd boy made good.

From 1570 to 1576, Peter Binsfeld studied theology at the Jesuit-run *Collegium Germanicum* in Rome, possibly with Briedel's support, but more likely with that of Trier's Elector Jacob III of Eltz himself. It was in Rome, where Binsfeld became friends with John Gibbons, who in 1584 would become rector of the Jesuit college in Trier and play an influential role in its witch-hunt as well.[6] Both men obtained doctorates in theology. In Rome, Binsfeld also became a rigid follower of Tridentine Catholicism. Those parts of the Holy Roman Empire that had not followed Luther needed educated Catholic clergymen, able to lead the charge not only against Protestantism but also against so-called popular 'superstition'. Binsfeld's first mission as a young priest, at the behest of Trier's Elector Jacob III of Eltz, was to the town and abbey of Prüm. Its territory had recently been incorporated into the Electorate of Trier. Binsfeld's letters reveal that he had to face constant opposition in Prüm, both from the monks – who were unenthusiastic about the raising of clerical standards – and from the town-folk – who showed very little interest in his learned sermons. The monks accused Binsfeld of having plundered the convent's library, taking away several precious codices and bestowing them on the Jesuit college in Trier.

Whatever the outcome, the elector rewarded Binsfeld's missionary efforts. In 1580, Peter Binsfeld, was finally confirmed as provost of St Simeon. In the same year, he was consecrated as suffragan bishop in the archdiocese of Trier. Within Catholicism, suffragan bishops are appointed to assist diocesan bishops, which in Binsfeld's case was no less a figure than the elector (as Archbishop of Trier) himself. He was also appointed vicar general, effectively putting him in charge of the day-to-day running of the archdiocese. Binsfeld strengthened his ties with the Trier Jesuits and twice served as rector of the city's university (1582/1583, 1587/1588).

These and other offices enabled the suffragan bishop to pursue three aims of Catholic reform: firstly, to improve the education of clerics and priests according to Tridentine Catholicism; secondly, to strengthen missionary efforts, religious instruction (catechesis), and episcopal visitations; and thirdly, to battle against blasphemy, heresy, religious dissidence, superstition, magic, and witchcraft. His work as an author, however, originally focussed on the last of these aims. In 1589, Binsfeld published his *Tractatus de confessionibus maleficorum et sagarum* (Treatise on the Confessions of Male and Female Witches). This treatise saw two different German translations (1590, 1591, reprinted in 1592) and two extended versions in Latin (1591, 1596, followed by reprints).[7] In 1591, Binsfeld published his second treatise on witchcraft, magic, and superstition the *Commentarius in titulum codicis lib. 9 de maleficis & mathematicis*, as an appendix to his revised *De confessionibus*. In reaction to the sceptical arguments of Loos, Binsfeld brought out a considerable expanded version of the *Commentarius* in 1596, again as an appendix. His plan of publishing it as a revised book on its own never came to fruition.[8]

In addition to these demonological works, Binsfeld also issued his *Enchiridion theologiae pastoralis et doctrinae neccessariae sacerdotibus* (Handbook of Pastoral Theology and Doctrine Necessary for Priests, 1591), taking further the Tridentine aim of raising clerical education. The work would go through at least 16 editions before 1676 and was translated into French in 1623. In this widely acknowledged handbook, Binsfeld repeated his attacks against magic, superstition, and witchcraft in his comments on the first of the ten commandments. He also published three commentaries on canon law.[9] In 1593, he issued a second handbook on Catholic dogma, the *Liber receptarum in theologia sententiarum et conclusionum* (A Book on Accepted Opinions and Conclusions in Theology), which laid out the standard doctrines of the Catholic faith, on such issues as the Fall of Man, (demonic) temptation, free will and sin, the afterlife, and Purgatory.[10] Binsfeld's last work, the *Tractatus de tentationibus et earum remediis* (A Treatise on Temptations and Their Remedies, 1611), appeared thirteen years after his death. As the title already indicates, it discussed the five causes of humanity's temptation, predictably presenting the devil as the most powerful and omnipresent seducer. Yet, witchcraft, as well as fear of God and the devil, featured in all of these writings. There can be no doubt that Binsfeld's demonology was part of a wider effort to promote Catholic reform in the Trier archdiocese, in which he joined forces with the Jesuits who had established themselves in Trier around 1560.

Whilst the Elector and Archbishop John VII of Schönenberg lived outside the urban walls, Binsfeld had chosen as his residence the church of St Simeon, built into the city's ancient Roman city gate. (The church is no more, but parts of the collegiate's building and the gate, the *Porta Nigra*, still survive). During most of his nineteen years as suffragan bishop, St Simeon would serve as Binsfeld's home, only interrupted by visitation journeys to other parts of the archdiocese. Yet, we know little about his daily life. In letters to the rector of the *Collegium Germanicum* in the 1580s, he wrote, perhaps alluding to the original St Simeon, a hermit who had walled himself in: 'I love the solitude, but I cannot stay alone. I hate the world, but from time to time I must show it a smiling face.' He also expressed a wish to see Rome again before his death: 'My supreme desire is returning to the holy sites of Rome, afterwards death would be most welcomed.'[11] Another encounter with Binsfeld in the archives shows him considerably less contemplative, and certainly less smiling. In January 1590, the city magistrates prohibited the church of St Simeon to bring new wine from its estates onto the market for economic reasons. Enraged, Binsfeld turned to one of the elector's officials, demanding in vain a criminal investigation of the magistrates, which should strip all members of the city council from office. Binsfeld evidently saw himself as the city's true regent, who would not tolerate any slight against his honour as a high cleric and his reputation as a man of letters. He also, as we shall see, regarded Trier as a city mired in insolence, superstition, and witchcraft.[12]

A remark in the *Tractatus de confessionibus* indicates that in 1579 Binsfeld administered the Eucharist at least to one condemned person, possibly one or more witches.[13] Certainly, by that time he would have begun to witness the arrival of witchcraft trials in and near the city, accompanied by at least one lynching, the spread of rumours by students of the Jesuit college among others, and the anti-witchcraft sermons given by their Jesuit teachers. One of the prisons, where those accused of witchcraft were tortured, happened to be inside the keep of the city gate adjacent to St Simeon. Its provost, like other bystanders, might have borne witness to the interrogations. Certainly, Binsfeld would have witnessed burnings in the territories surrounding the city. At least thirteen prominent clergymen, including the provost (*Dompropst*) of the cathedral, the abbot of the Benedictine abbey of St Martin, and five canons of Binsfeld's own St Simeon were suspected of witchcraft. Two canons were executed, one died in prison. As suffragan bishop and as general vicar, Binsfeld must have been entangled in the trials of these witch-priests, at least when the clerics had to be degraded – defrocked – in advance of their execution.[14]

Binsfeld's precise role in the Trier witch-hunt was complex and remains opaque. He still exchanged letters with one canon of St Simeon who had fled ahead of his trial. In 1593, he dedicated the *Liber receptarum in theologia sententiarum et conclusionum* to the four Benedictine abbots of Trier, which included the abbot of St Martin who had often been denounced as a witch in the trials of St Maximin. We also know, however, that Binsfeld presided as keeper of the high justice in one witchcraft trial conducted in a village which belonged to St Simeon, though possibly not in person.[15] Certainly, the witch-hunt also affected other villagers living on the manors from which St Simeon drew its income, though again we do not know the number of victims nor Binsfeld's reaction. Still, as his writings will also make clear, he believed that the world was infested with the devil's machinations. Peter Binsfeld died on 24 November 1598, when the plague swept through Trier. Buried in an outside chapel of St Simeon, his grave was destroyed during the Napoleonic wars.

## 2 Cornelius Loos: another Catholic on a mission

Cornelius Loos was born as the eldest son of a distinguished Catholic citizen of the Dutch city of Gouda in the early or mid 1540s.[16] Between 1561 and 1572, he studied for an arts degree at the University of Leuven, where he would have been an almost exact contemporary of Martin Delrio°. It remains uncertain if he continued at Leuven to study theology. His family had taken part in a failed conspiracy in support of the Catholic Habsburgs and was exiled from Gouda and the increasingly Protestant Netherlands. For Loos, exile proved a formative experience. Hateful rebukes of Protestantism, which he considered the devil's most momentous invention, recur again and again throughout his many writings.

Exile also led to a peripatetic existence, with Loos struggling to find employment in order to finance his studies. For most of the 1570s, his whereabouts are known mostly from the dedications of his publications, which were themselves of course an implicit request for financial support. While he may have gone to the University of Mainz to achieve a doctorate in theology, we find him back in Leuven in 1576, working as a private teacher. Between 1576 and 1578 or 1579, he spent time at the court of the prince-countess of Arnburg (probably Margarethe von Arenberg) but left because of a lack of books. In 1578 or 1579, Loos is back in Mainz, apparently back at his theology studies. In 1579, the – by now quite radicalized – exile published two venomous anti-Protestant polemics which called for a war of extirpation against the rebellious Dutch provinces.[17]

During the 1580s, Loos appears to have been based in Mainz. For two years, he lived as a member of the household of Arnold of Bucholtz, one of the city's cathedral canons. After Loos was appointed as vicar of Mainz Cathedral (on 24 October 1582), he also worked as a librarian (from 1584), resigning the vicariate on 6 July 1590.[18] We can place Loos in Cologne in March and April 1591, although he may already have taken residence up in Trier by that time. We do not know what brought Loos to Trier. The claim that Binsfeld himself had commissioned Loos to write a refutation of Johann Wier°'s *De praestigiis* is a myth. Loos is also never listed as a member of the Trier University's theology faculty, as has been supposed. Possibly, another Dutch Catholic exile with ties to Cologne, Bartholomeus Bodeghemius, who as judicial vicar was one of the archbishopric's most senior officials, had invited Loos to Trier.

Even so, the Trier witch-hunt did not escape Loos's attention.[19] For some time, Loos stayed at one of its major centres, the Imperial Abbey of St Maximin – possibly he taught the Benedictine monks some theology. When the witch-hunts reached their peak in 1591, Loos obtained the second edition of Binsfeld's *Tractatus*, which had been revised to include fresh material from these confessions. By September 1591 at the latest, Loos had started to work on its rebuttal. Binsfeld tried hard to silence the Dutch priest's criticisms and in Cologne he found the support of the papal nuncio Ottavio Frangipani, who demanded that the Archbishop of Trier halt its publication. In a personal letter, Frangipani accused Loos of having sent his book – which allegedly contained both heretical errors and dangerous new ideas – to the printer without the censor's approval and demanded to be given a copy to examine. After the nuncio had read the text, he insisted that printing cease immediately.

Arrested and imprisoned in the Imperial Abbey of St Maximin, Loos was charged with heresy and faced an ecclesiastical tribunal.[20] To avoid a potentially deadly inquisition, Loos recanted his thesis against witchcraft on 15 March 1593. Banned from the diocese of Trier, Loos went to Brussels, where he obtained a canonry at its cathedral. According to Martin Delrio, who relished publishing Loos's recantation, the priest repeated his arguments against witchcraft belief in his sermons. In 1594, the notorious witch-hunter Jean Bacx denounced Loos for being a protector of witches, as part of a wider campaign against witchcraft. In preparing further charges against Loos, Bacx must have requested a copy of the recantation in Trier. Delrio obtained from him a certified transcript and predicted that God would reward Bacx's zealous pursuit of 'the nefarious heresy' of the witches.[21]

In 1596, Loos was arrested a second time, accused of being a 'patron of witches' (*patronus sagarum*) and put on a diet of bread and water. Released shortly thereafter, he was charged a third time but died before action could be taken against him. When Frangipani arrived in Brussels in September 1596 as the first nuncio of Flanders, Loos had likely already passed away.

## 3 Peter Binsfeld's *De confessionibus*

Binsfeld wrote the first edition of his *Tractatus de confessionibus maleficorum et sagarum* (1589), probably at the instigation of Trier's archbishop.[22] Binsfeld's preface claimed that friends who had read his manuscript had begged him to publish it. As its title suggests, his aim was to demonstrate the validity of the witches' confessions, including their denunciations of others, from a theological and legal point of view. Possibly, the work emerged out of the famous trial of Dietrich Flade, the witch-hunt's most prominent victim who had questioned the validity of testimony from the sabbat. The suffragan bishop included fragments of the former judge's confession without mentioning his name. This likely places the appearance of the first edition after Flade's execution in September. Yet, the work must have come out soon after as news of its publication had already reached Laevinus Torrentius, Bishop of Antwerp, by 5 December 1589.[23]

The narrative that Trier's suffragan bishop had written the tract as a rebuttal to Flade's opposition to witch-hunting, advocated by George Lincoln Burr and Andrew Dickson White in the nineteenth century, has its origins in Delrio's *Disquisitiones*.[24] Delrio had labelled Flade a 'patron of witches' (*patronus sagarum*) to explain why a sacrosanct judge such as Flade could have been charged with witchcraft himself. Yet archival evidence clearly shows that Flade had been no heroic opponent of the witch trials. On the contrary, he had presided over at least eight witch trials (1577–1588), in which he tried to force the accused women to confess, using both material evidence and torture.[25]

In the *Tractatus*, Binsfeld drew on a wide range of sources including the *Malleus maleficarum*, Paolo Grillando, Bartolomeo Spina°, and Jean Bodin°, treating the latter's rather heterodox demonology with care and sometimes dissent.[26] The ongoing witch trials in Trier, which aimed from the outset at higher-ranking women and men, received powerful legitimation from Binsfeld's treatise, which – both in its Latin original and in two German translations – called for the inquisition to never end. To Binsfeld, witches waged war against Christendom as part of Satan's army. In this respect, the *Tractatus* resembled the political demonology of Juan Maldonado°. Binsfeld set out his demonological argument and survey of the proper conduct of witch trials in two parts. In a Scholastic fashion, the first part opened with fourteen *praeludia*, in which witchcraft was labelled both a material crime (*maleficium*) and a spiritual one (heresy), which accordingly had to be treated by both the ecclesiastical and secular courts. While the devil could not act without God's permission, he continually sought to seduce Christians with his evil machinations, which included powerful illusions. Binsfeld adduced no fewer than nine causes for witchcraft, essentially a list of reasons for divine permission given the devil's inherent wickedness: the ignorant spiritual authorities, the ignorant secular authorities, superstition, curiosity, greed, lechery, cursing, female melancholy, and scepticism about the possibility of reconciliation with God (after a pact with the devil).

Unsurprisingly, with this set-up, all forms of witchcraft and magic were diabolic in origin, based on an explicit or implicit pact with the devil. Since the devil had the ability to assume a bodily form, both sexual intercourse with humans and demons at the sabbat happened as real physical events. Likewise, witches' flight was possible. The devil could also appear in the guise of specific persons who had given him their consent. Thus, illusions, for instance at the sabbat, were possible, but only when the person in question was a witch. Unlike Bodin, but in line with most of his peers, Binsfeld rejected the possibility of human–animal metamorphosis. He also argued against the water ordeal. Yet, while he rejected the swimming or ducking of witches, he strongly maintained that God would never allow the shedding of innocent blood, which allowed him to evaluate the confessions of witches and their denunciations of accomplices as real evidence. Only a single denunciation, if combined with other evidence, sufficed to permit the torture of a suspect. Two denunciations were sufficient, if no other evidence was present. Binsfeld justified the validity of the witches' denunciations with a list of arguments, including the claim that witches plainly were criminals as poisoners, blasphemers, church robbers, traitors of the fatherland, and heretics. In all these crimes, the law demanded the culprit to be questioned about his or her accomplices. Binsfeld permitted the use of children and adolescents as witnesses, especially if they had been seduced by witches or possessed by devils.[27] As a manual for further judicial action against witchcraft, written by one of the archbishopric's most senior clergymen, the *Tractatus* would bolster the territory's witchcraft trials with arguments taken from theology, law (ecclesiastical and secular), physics, and even etymology.

The success of the *Tractatus* prompted Binsfeld to start work on an expanded second edition, mostly aimed at refuting Johann Wier and other sceptics. The suffragan bishop equipped his demonology with additional confessions from newly condemned witches, partly from the jurisdiction of the electorate, but mostly from St Maximin. For Binsfeld, this evidence extracted out of the mouth of witches themselves confirmed the reality of the devil's machinations. Particularly important was the testimony of the Meisenbein family, as the mother Anna was executed as a 'super-witch', accused of being a ringleader of the sabbat, of having murdered her husband, of having forced her eldest son to commit incest with her, and – most of all – of having introduced both her daughters, Maria and Margret, and her sons, Hans Cuno and Hans Jacob, to the devil and to witchcraft. Except for young Margret, who was given to Jesuits for spiritual instruction, the entire family died at the stake (1590–1592).

## 4 Cornelius Loos's *De vera et falsa magia*

The second Latin edition of Binsfeld's *Tractatus* appeared in September 1591, after which it soon fell in the critical hands of Cornelius Loos. Whether the Dutch priest had read the first edition during his time as librarian in Mainz, or whether he had already begun work on his own (anti-)demonology before his arrival in Trier, cannot be determined. Yet, we do know that it was this second edition, including the Meisenbein testimony, which Loos attacked with mocking sarcasm.[28] While he mentioned neither Binsfeld nor Flade by name, he referred to the Meisenbeins by their first names. Drawing almost exclusively on the Bible, the Church Fathers, and classical authorities, Loos did not deny the existence of Satan, but he argued that the devil could not adopt any material corporeal form. Even his spiritual powers were weak; they lingered only in the minds of the confused. Having thus recast the devil's abilities, none of the witches' crimes, which Binsfeld had considered real events, could ever have taken place. While Loos must have known Wier's arguments, he does not mention him.

Like other sceptics before him and after, the Dutch priest was particularly sceptical about the validity of confessions and denunciations made by accused witches, which either came from mentally disturbed individuals or were the result of horrible torture. Yet, Loos's rhetoric was noticeably more strident. Witch-hunting had become a new alchemy, transforming human blood into gold and silver, while witch-hunters were the devil's true minions. Showing off his humanist learning, the Dutch theologian took great delight in parading Binsfeld's mistakes, who, for instance, had confused Saint Cyprian, Bishop of Carthage, with the magician Cyprian of Antioch.

It appears that Loos wanted to challenge Binsfeld to a public debate. Perhaps he hoped that – after the high-profile execution of Flade – other high-ranking men among the clerical and secular elite would rally to his side. If so, the Abbot of St Maximin, to whose household Loos belonged, was not one of them, since Reiner Biwer tolerated the massive witch-hunts in his own territory. In personal conversations and in letters to the magistrates of Trier, to high churchmen, and to other unnamed individuals, the Dutch priest questioned both the legality of the witch trials and the belief in witches in general. Specifically, he accused the authorities (including implicitly the Elector of Trier) of acting like tyrants in shedding innocent blood, a charge once made by Wier. None of these pleas were successful, since the men he had addressed were either themselves denounced as witches, feared that they themselves might be suspected, or were acting as judges in the urban and rural witchcraft trials.

## 5 Binsfeld's victory

We do not know whether Loos also contacted Binsfeld directly or whether the suffragan bishop got wind of Loos's book project some other way. It was rather easy for the suffragan bishop to rally his own formidable forces, including the papal nuncio Frangipani, the Archbishop of Trier, and the Abbot of St Maximin. The nuncio himself expressed the utmost anxiety in a letter to the Archbishop of Trier, dated 13 July 1592. If published, the book could ruin the Catholic Church, already weakened by the Reformation, and Loos's ideas must be condemned for the sake of the Catholic faith. In a personal letter to Loos the next day, Frangipani demanded and received a copy of this dangerous book. The printing of *De vera et falsa magia* was stopped. Only the first half of the manuscript (the first two out of a projected four books) has survived, probably in Loos's handwriting, in the library of the Trier Jesuit college. It is likely that the already-mentioned Bartholomeus Bodeghemius, who as judicial vicar served as a member of the tribunal, possessed this manuscript, which was bequeathed together with his library to the Society of Jesus. Bodeghemius wrote a prefatory poem praising the first edition of Binsfeld's *De confessionibus*.

Frangipani ordered Loos's incarceration in St Maximin to face an ecclesiastical tribunal, presided over by the abbot, and staffed by Binsfeld, Bodeghemius, and two canons from St Simeon, who were doctors in canon law. Loos's recantation was taken down by a notary and signed by the Dutch priest himself.[29] The sixteen statements retract his original views that the flight of witches and the sabbat were mere fantasy; that neither early modern nor biblical witches existed; that demons could not assume bodies and could therefore neither make a pact nor have sexual intercourse with human beings; and that weather magic – a recurrent accusation in the Trier and St Maximin witch-hunts – was an impossibility. Finally, in March 1593 Loos retracted his claim that popes had never issued any bulls on the subject of witchcraft, and that they only had ordered inquisitions against witches to avoid being suspected of it themselves.

Given the stridency of his views, Loos must also have enjoyed some strong protection, since he was permitted to leave for Brussels. Perhaps, there still existed trust in him as an ardent fighter against Protestantism. However, Binsfeld must have felt a further edition of his works on witchcraft, magic, and superstition was needed to answer his critics, to correct his embarrassing mistakes, and to warn his audience about any remnants of Loos's dangerous manuscript possibly still in circulation. In 1596, the suffragan bishop published a third edition of the *Tractatus*, together with a second edition of the *Commentarius*. In his preface, Binsfeld reported Loos's recantation, whom he anonymously (and ironically) called his censor. While the main body of the *Tractatus* remained mostly unchanged (except for correcting the Cyprian story), the *Commentarius* was extended not only to discuss the proper methods of torture but also to reject cruel methods and brutal judges.[30] Moreover, Binsfeld added papal bulls dealing with magic and witchcraft to disprove Loos's claims about the papacy. The suffragan bishop also turned to the confessions included in Nicolas Remy°'s recently published *Daemonolatria* (1595), which presented more case stories and thus more proof of the reality of witchcraft. His death in 1598 prevented the suffragan bishop from publishing a third, stand-alone edition of the *Commentarius*.

Meanwhile, nothing remained of the printed *De vera et falsa magia* except a few publisher's proofs which were only re-discovered in 1888. The Jesuit Martin Delrio included a copy of Loos's recantation in his *Disquisitiones* to demonstrate the incredible errors and blasphemies of this *patronus sagarum*. Both Binsfeld and Delrio feared that versions or fragments of *De vera et falsa magia* might still be circulating. Ironically, by publishing Loos's recantation, it was Delrio himself who enabled the survival of his ideas. Only in 1886 did George Lincoln Burr discover what remained of the original Loos manuscript in the city library of Trier, where it had arrived after the suppression of the Jesuits in the late eighteenth century.[31]

## 6 A study in contrasts

For all their differences on the subject of witchcraft, the biographies of Peter Binsfeld and Cornelius Loos have some elements in common. Both were of a similar age, both had studied at renowned institutions, both saw themselves as ardent fighters for Tridentine Catholicism, both died nearly in the same year. Yet the similarities end there. Loos was born into a wealthy urban family, Binsfeld had first been educated at a rural monastery. The Dutch Catholic promoted humanist learning, while Binsfeld still clung to the Scholastics. Loos had been forced by the Dutch Revolt to leave his homeland and seek new patrons in Germany, while Binsfeld was forced to leave Papal Rome to return to the superstitious peasants and unlearned priests of his native land. Loos nourished implacable hatred of Protestants. For him, witchcraft belief and witch trials were Satanic inventions, to distract authorities from eradicating the true demonic threat of Protestantism. Binsfeld, on the other hand, believed witches and demons were swarming around him, the latter constantly leading humanity towards temptation and sin. A 'patron of witches' like Loos (or Wier) therefore had to be fought with the utmost strength. Beyond the devil and his minions, Binsfeld's main enemies were ignorant, badly educated priests and superstitious lay people.

There remains much we do not know about the lives and personalities of our two protagonists. Loos clearly possessed a quick wit – one can almost feel the sarcasm drip off the pages. He was certainly not free of ambition, employing highly stylized Latin, which still makes aspects of his thinking difficult to decipher. Binsfeld's tone was more serious, and his learning more book-bound, rooted in more traditional modes of scholarship. We know of only one personal meeting between the two clerics: the tribunal that tried Loos at St Maximin. Yet, they may well have met in advance, even on the streets – Trier was a small city after all. If they debated in person, however, not a trace has remained.

Still, with Loos's forced recantation, Binsfeld had won the battle, with important implications for Catholic demonology. Loos's attempt failed to reduce the power of the devil to that of a spiritual entity only. His recantation made it impossible for any Catholic to fundamentally criticize the belief in a corporeal devil and the existence of witches on theological grounds. New forms of opposition to witch trials, thus, had to be devised, founded upon legal arguments, such as those presented by the Jesuits Adam Tanner, Paul Laymann, and especially Friedrich Spee in his *Cautio Criminalis* (A Warning on Criminal Justice, 1631). Binsfeld had clearly seen the danger of questioning the materiality of angels and demons, still articulated by Christians of all stripes into the eighteenth century and beyond, since denying the reality of the spirit world might lead to denying the existence of God.

Following the suppression of Loos's *De vera et falsa magia*, Binsfeld's demonology found widespread reception. Both the *Tractatus* and the *Commentarius* were used as legal manuals in Bavaria and in the Franconian prince-bishoprics, the latter of which saw a great deal of witch-hunting. Martin Delrio often drew on Binsfeld and referred more than once to the cases of Flade and the Meisenbein family. The suffragan bishop's arguments were even welcomed by Protestant ministers, as evidence for the urgent need for witch trials. Indeed, his work was used – sometimes indirectly through Delrio and others – by Protestant judges in Germany, Scandinavia, England, and New England.

While the history of Binsfeld's long-term impact remains to be written, we know more about the debate between Binsfeld and Loos, which cannot be understood without taking into account the complex geography in which it occurred, with different forms of witch-hunting affecting three different jurisdictions. The suffragan bishop legitimated these trials, one of the earliest 'super-hunts', and urgently demanded more. His call, ironically, was not answered in Trier, but by the Franconian witch-hunts in the seventeenth century. Loos wanted to save the lives of the innocent, yet his witchcraft scepticism did not make him into a proto-Enlightenment figure. He had no trouble in calling for the bloody extirpation of Dutch Protestants. In short, neither man wrote their tracts as intellectual exercises, but as guides to spur on concrete action. The battle between Binsfeld and Loos bears witness both to the alliance between demonology and witch trials, and to the interplay between words and deeds.[32]

## Notes

1 Georg L. Burr, *The Fate of Dietrich Flade*, New York: G.P. Putnam's Sons, 1891; Rita Voltmer, 'Zwischen Herrschaftskrise, Wirtschaftsdepression und Jesuitenpropaganda: Hexenverfolgungen in der Stadt Trier, 15.–17. Jahrhundert', *Jahrbuch für westdeutsche Landesgeschichte*, 2001, vol. 27, 37–107; Rita Voltmer, 'Witch-Finders, Witch-Hunters or Kings of the Sabbath? The Prominent Role of Men in the Mass Persecutions of the Rhine-Meuse Area, 16th–17th centuries', in Alison Rowlands, ed., *Witchcraft and Masculinities in the Early Modern World*, Palgrave: Basingstoke 2009, pp. 74–99; Rita Voltmer, 'Die Hexenverfolgungen im Raum des Erzbistums, 15.–17. Jahrhundert', in Bernhard Schneider, ed., *Geschichte des Bistums Trier*, vol. 3: Kirchenreform und Konfessionsstaat 1500–1801, Trier: Paulinus, pp. 709–49.
2 Rita Voltmer, 'St. Maximin, Prince-Abbey of', in Richard M. Golden, ed., *The Encyclopedia of Witchcraft: The Western Tradition*, Santa Barbara, CA: ABC-Clio, 2006, pp. 1082–83.
3 Rita Voltmer, 'Germany's First "Superhunt"? Rezeption und Konstruktion der so genannten Trierer Verfolgungen, 16.–21. Jahrhundert' in Katrin Moeller and Burghart Schmidt, eds, *Realität und Mythos: Hexenverfolgung und Rezeptionsgeschichte*, Hamburg: Dobu Verlag, 2003, pp. 225–58.
4 Rita Voltmer, 'Peter Binsfeld', *Internetportal Rheinische Geschichte* (www.rheinische-geschichte.lvr.de/Persoenlichkeiten/peter-binsfeld-/DE-2086/lido/57c582746257

b3.70094282); Johannes Dillinger, 'Binsfeld, Peter' in Golden, ed., *Encyclopedia*, pp. 122–25.
5 Franz-Josef Heyen, *Das Stift St. Simeon in Trier*, Berlin: de Gruyter, 2002, pp. 123, 134, 154, 162–163, 181, 191, 205, 280–82, 357, 359, 383, 423, 439, 767–77, 801–05, 828–29, 842–43, 855–56, 940–41, 944.
6 Voltmer, 'Zwischen Herrschaftskrise', pp. 40–41, 68–71, 77–102; Rita Voltmer, 'Jesuiten und Kinderhexen: Thesen zur Entstehung, Rezeption und Verbreitung eines Verfolgungsmusters', in Wolfgang Behringer and Claudia Opitz-Belakhal, eds, *Hexenkinder, Kinderbanden, Straßenkinder*, Bielefeld: Verlag für Regionalgeschichte, 2016, pp. 201–32.
7 For an edition (without critical apparatus) of the German version (1590): Petrus Binsfeld, *Tractat von Bekanntnuß der Zauberer unnd Hexen*, ed. Hiram Kümper, Vienna: Mille Tre Verlag Robert Schächter, 2004. For an English summary, see Arthur C. Howland, ed., *Materials toward a History of Witchcraft, collected by Henry Charles Lea*, Philadelphia: University of Pennsylvania Press, 1939, vol. 3, pp. 576–90.
8 For an English summary of the *Commentarius*: Howland, *Materials*, vol. 3, pp. 590–600.
9 *Commentarius theologicus et iuridicus in titulum iuris canonici de usuris*, Trier: Bock, 1593; *Commentarius in titulum iuris canonici de iniuriis de damno dato*, Trier: Bock, 1597; *Commentarius in titulum iuris canonici de simonia*, Trier: Bock, 1604.
10 Ralf-Peter Fuchs, 'Hexen aus freiem Willen: Peter Binsfeld und das tridentische Liberum-Arbitrium-Dogma', *Rheinische Vierteljahrsblätter*, 2019, vol. 83, 1–20.
11 Andreas Heinz, 'Ein Eifeler als Reformator der Eifelabtei Prüm: Dr. Peter Binsfeld, seine römischen Studienjahre und sein Wirken in Prüm', *Jahrbuch des Kreises Prüm*, 1968, vol. 9, 71–75.
12 Protocols of the sessions of the Trier City Council: Stadtarchiv Trier, TA 100/1, fols 102v–103v.
13 Binsfeld, *Tractat*, ed. Kümper, p. 285.
14 Voltmer, 'Zwischen Herrschaftskrise', pp. 95–96.
15 Voltmer, 'Die Hexenverfolgungen', pp. 736–37.
16 Rita Voltmer, 'Loos, Cornelius (1540-1596?)', in Golden, ed., *Encyclopedia*, 666–67; P.C. Van der Eerden, 'Cornelius Loos und die *magia falsa*', in Hartmut Lehmann and Otto Ulbricht, eds, *Vom Unfug des Hexen-Processes: Gegner der Hexenverfolgungen von Johann Weyer bis Friedrich Spee*, Wiesbaden: Harrasowitz, 1992, pp. 139–69; P.C. van der Eerden, 'Der Teufelspakt bei Petrus Binsfeld und Cornelius Loos', in Gunther Franz and Franz Irsigler, eds, *Hexenglaube und Hexenprozesse im Raum Rhein-Mosel-Saar*, Trier: Paulinus, 1996, pp. 51–71; Othon Scholer, *Der Hexer war's, die Hexe, ja vielleicht der Dämon höchstpersönlich!*, Trier: Paulinus, 2007, pp. 291–319.
17 Between 1579 and 1596, Loos published twelve books, see: Cornelius Loos, *De vera et falsa magia: Kommentierte lateinisch-deutsche Edition*, trans. Othon Scholer, Trier: Paulinus, forthcoming.
18 Frank Sobiech, *Torture and Confession: Jesuit Prison Ministry during the Witch Trials in the Holy Roman Empire and the Cautio Criminalis by Friedrich Spee SJ, 1591–1635*, Rome: Institutum Historicum Societatis Iesu, 2019.
19 Scholer, *Der Hexer war's*, pp. 291–319; and my forthcoming introduction to Loos, *De vera et falsa magia*.
20 See Howland, *Materials*, pp. 602–3.
21 Martin Delrio, *Disquisitionum magicarum libri sex in tres tomos partiti*, vol. 3, Mainz: Jacob König, 1606, p. 315. On Bacx (1530–1608) and his efforts to launch a witch-hunt in the Spanish Netherlands, Eril Aerts et al., eds, *Les Sorcières dans les Pays-Bas méridionaux, XVIe–XVIIe siècles*, Brussels: Archives générales du Royaume, 1989, pp. 21–22, 32; Alfons K.L. Thijs, 'Toverij in contrareformatorisch

Antwerpen', in Alfons Roeck, ed., *Liber Amicorum Prof. Dr. Joszef Van Haver*, Langemark: Vonksteen, 1991, pp. 391–400, at 396–97. On Bacx and Loos my forthcoming introduction to Loos, *De vera et falsa magia*.
22 Johannes Dillinger, '*Evil People': A Comparative Study of Witch Hunts in Swabian Austria and the Electorate of Trier*, Charlottesville, VA: University of Virginia Press, 2009, p. 108.
23 Marie Delcourt and Jean Hoyoux, eds, *Laevinus Torrentius: Correspondance*, Paris: Les Belles Lettres, 1953, vol. 2: période anversoise, 1587–1589, p. 585.
24 Rita Voltmer, 'Ein Amerikaner in Trier: George Lincoln Burr (1857–1938) und sein Beitrag zu den Sammelschwerpunkten "Hexerei und Hexenverfolgungen" an der Cornell University (Ithaca/New York) sowie an der Stadtbibliothek Trier; Mit einem Inventar', *Kurtrierisches Jahrbuch*, 2007, vol. 47, 447–89.
25 See Burr, *Flade*; Voltmer, 'Zwischen Herrschaftskrise', pp. 77–85; Voltmer, 'Germany's First "Superhunt"', pp. 251–57; Frank Baron, *Der Mythos des faustischen Teufelspaktes: Geschichte, Legende, Literatur*, Berlin: De Gruyter, 2019, pp. 121–41 (on the Flade case).
26 See Howland, *Materials*, pp. 576–90; André Schnyder, 'Der "Malleus Maleficarum": Fragen und Beobachtungen zu seiner Druckgeschichte sowie zur Rezeption bei Bodin, Binsfeld und Delrio', *Archiv für Kulturgeschichte*, 1992, vol. 74, 323–64.
27 Voltmer, 'Jesuiten und Kinderhexen', pp. 211–19.
28 See Van der Eerden, 'Cornelius Loos'; Van der Eerden, 'Der Teufelspakt'; Howland, *Materials*, pp. 601–4; Mabel Elisabeth Hodder, 'Peter Binsfeld and Cornelius Loos: An Episode in the History of Witchcraft', PhD dissertation, Ithaca, NY, 1911, and my forthcoming introduction to Loos, *De vera et falsa magia*.
29 Delrio, *Disquisitiones*, vol. 3, pp. 314–19; Howland, *Materials*, pp. 601–3.
30 Howland, *Materials*, pp. 590–600.
31 George L. Burr, 'On the Loos' Manuscript', in Roland H. Bainton and Louis Oliphant Gibbons, eds, *George Lincoln Burr: His Life; Selections from His Writings*, Ithaca, NY: Cornell University Press, 1943, pp. 147–55; Burr, *The Fate of Dietrich Flade*, pp. 20–21.
32 Rita Voltmer, 'Demonology and the Relevance of the Witches' Confessions', in Julian Goodare et al., eds, *Demonology and Witch-Hunting in Early Modern Europe*, London: Routledge, forthcoming.

## Further reading

Briggs, Robin, 'Witchcraft and the Local Communities: The Rhine-Moselle Region', in Brian P. Levack, ed., *The Oxford Handbook of Witchcraft in Early Modern Europe and Colonial America*, Oxford: Oxford University Press, 2013, pp. 199–217.

Monter, William, 'Witch Trials in Continental Europe, 1560–1660', in Bengt Ankarloo et al., eds, *The Athlone History of Witchcraft and Magic in Europe: The Period of Witch Trials*, London: Bloomsbury, 2002, pp. 1–52.

Smith, William Bradford, 'The Persecution of Witches and the Discourse on Toleration in Early Modern Germany', in Marjorie Elizabeth Plummer and Victoria Christmann, eds, *Topographies of Tolerance and Intolerance: Responses to Religious Pluralism in Reformation Europe*, Leiden: Brill, 2018, pp. 50–77.

Voltmer, Rita, 'The Judge's Lore? The Politico-Religious Concept of Metamorphoses in the Peripheries of Western Europe', in Willem de Blécourt, ed., *Werewolf Histories*, Basingstoke: Palgrave, 2015, pp. 159–184.

———, 'The Witch Trials', in Owen Davies, ed., *The Oxford Illustrated History of Witchcraft and Magic*, Oxford: Oxford University Press, 2017, pp. 97–133.

———, 'Debating the Devil's Clergy: Demonology and the Media in Dialogue with Trials (14th to 17th Century)', *Religions*, 2019, vol. 10/12. www.mdpi.com/2077-1444/10/12.

# 10  A royal witch theorist
## James VI's *Daemonologie*

### P. G. Maxwell-Stuart

James VI was born on 19 June 1566. His head was still covered with a membrane when he appeared and to contemporaries this was a good sign, an indication that in later life he would be protected from drowning and the attacks of fairies and maleficent magicians. His caul may have worked, since when he returned to Scotland from Denmark in 1589 with his new bride, Queen Anne, witches both in Copenhagen and East Lothian were said to have tried to drown him by sending a storm to wreck his ship, and it was alleged that a company of witches and magicians had met in a church in North Berwick that same year under the devil's aegis to plan further attempts to assassinate him by poison and image-magic (see Figure I.2 in the introduction). Yet he survived all their machinations. Even before that, however, his childhood and youth had been riven by religious controversy and political danger. His mother eloped with the Earl of Bothwell less than a year after James's birth, fled to England, and was put in prison. Thereafter relations between the son and mother were somewhat distant. Scotland at the time was riven by religious faction and gang warfare among the nobility and the Crown, worn by a child, was scarcely respected. James's health was never good and in a highly masculine court, where braggadocio and virility went hand in hand, this cannot have been good for his *amour propre*. Nor could his self-confidence have remained unaffected by several acts of violence against his person over the years and, indeed, more than one assassination attempt. His education, however, while conducted by a strict Presbyterian, was excellent, and he mastered the regime of Greek, Latin, history, music, mathematics, geography, astronomy, and the principles of rhetoric exceptionally well (Figure 10.1).[1]

Behind all this, however, lay general belief in the reality of the devil and magic, and the potentially malign efficacy of witchcraft in particular. Satan was taking advantage of the troubled times and recruiting followers, witches, and practitioners of magic who would help him draw people away from the Christian faith and fall into his hands. Such belief was common among all ranks of society and the establishment felt obliged to inveigh against all three, yet it took until 1563 for a Witchcraft Act to be passed and even then, trials for witchcraft were not particularly common. There were flurries of

*Figure 10.1* Simon van de Passe, *James I, King of England* (c.1619) [09.1S849]. Engraving by permission of the Detroit Institute of Arts, gift of Mrs. James E. Scripps. The royal authorship of the *Daemonologie* has often been emphasized at the expense of its highly personal nature.

prosecution from time to time, but no pogroms, in spite of the Kirk's including witchcraft in a general list of sins which, as its General Assembly said in 1583, 'daily some increases and provockes the wrath of God against the haill [*whole*] country'.[2] But magicians and witches were not the only contact with more-than-human powers and entities. Largely unseen fairies made their presence felt alongside human beings and belief that fairies interacted with them was almost universal, continuing to be so, in spite of the Kirk's strong disapproval, until the social and economic changes of the eighteenth century largely put paid to this notion. King James, then, lived in a society that took for granted the intermingling of human and non-human beings – not that it was unique in this, since the same could be said for most of the countries of Europe at the time. None of this, therefore, need have caused King James to pay the preternatural any special heed or spur him to write a short treatise condemning magic, witchcraft, and fairy belief. It took the very specific and very personal alleged attempts to kill him by magical means to rouse his particular interest and cause him to involve himself in the examinations of those accused and the aftermath of the trials.

## 1 The so-called North Berwick episode

In 1589 King James went to Denmark and married the Danish king's second daughter, Anne. On their way back to Scotland their ship was lashed by a storm said to have been raised by witches in Copenhagen and East Lothian. But this was only the first of several dangerous episodes, because Scottish witches were busy with further treason. There were two other separate, though interconnected, plots to murder James – the first by enchanting a wax image made to represent him, which would then be destroyed, and the king along with it, the second by having poison drawn from various 'magical' sources, which would then be introduced into the royal palace and placed where it could drop on his person. When the details of these plots came to light, it was also revealed that many of the accused had met the devil in a church in North Berwick where they had received instruction in evil-doing and had dug up a grave for body-parts to use in further magic. Naturally enough, since he had been the alleged target of some of this activity, James took a personal interest, and indeed part, in the subsequent interrogations of those arrested. Some of this was simple curiosity. When told one of the witches had played a pipe at a recent witches' gathering, James sent for her and had her play it for him. But when the name of James's cousin, the Earl of Bothwell, started to appear as the alleged force behind and leader of these treasonous conspiracies, James's mood changed, and he became badly frightened. Interrogations and trials continued throughout 1590, and Bothwell himself came to trial in the spring of 1591.

## 2 *Daemonologie*

It seems to have been out of this heightened and intense atmosphere that the *Daemonologie* took shape and was written down. This short treatise – and it is very short in comparison with many others written at about the same kind of time or a bit later – is remarkable in several ways among the essays and volumes on magic and allied subjects that were published during the latter part of the sixteenth century. The fact that its author was a monarch is interesting enough in itself, but there are several features that are intriguing, since right from the start, the *Daemonologie* achieves the unusual combination of being both entirely conventional in its material and highly personal in the use to which it puts that material. The exact date of its composition is uncertain, but there is good reason to think that it was written in 1591, very soon after, if not during, the trials of those accused of aiming at the king's life by magical means. Until then James's interest in witchcraft had not been great, but these personal attacks had woken both his fear and curiosity: hence his putting pen to paper. Yet, having done so, he seems to have put the manuscript on one side, since he did not have it published until 1597, when the immediacy of the trials had disappeared.[3] Pressure of time while the trials were still going on may well account for his not undertaking much research before he wrote or dictated his manuscript. The reading list he gives is not a long one and none of the books he mentions were hot off the press, so it is clear his motive in writing was not to join in a scholarly debate on the subject of magic as a whole or witchcraft in particular. His choice of the Scots vernacular rather than Latin, in any case, would have limited his hope of an international audience considerably. Two further questions about the *Daemonologie*, therefore, apart from when did James write it and why did he not publish it until several years after the event, are why did he write it and for whom did he intend it?

In his preface, James implies personal knowledge of treatises by Johann Wier°, Jean Bodin°, and Reginald Scot° in particular. If he had actually read them himself, he would probably have read Wier and Bodin in Latin and Scot in English. What none of these authors has in common with James, however, is direct, personal, and targeted experience of witchcraft, and while their motives for picking up their pens seems to have been a second-hand indignation at some aspect of the conduct of witch-trials they had either heard about or attended, or some doubts about the validity of some of the accusations against the accused, James was convinced that he himself had been a target, and the haste of composition he acknowledges in his preface – 'the fearful abounding at this time in this country of these detestable slaves of the devil ... . has moved me ... to dispatch in post [*haste*] this following treatise of mine' – suggests he may have dashed it off soon after many of those trials had finished early in 1591.[4] His savage command anent one of the accused – 'Let the doctors test whether Barbara Napier is with child or not. Accept no attempt at procrastination. If you find she is not, to the fire with her straight away and disembowel her at once' – shows how very badly frightened he had been, but his overt motives for writing are expressed in the preface to the *Daemonologie*: 'to press [*endeavour*] thereby so far as I can do to resolve the doubting hearts of many, both that such assaults of Satan are most certainly practised, and that the instruments thereof merit most severely to be punished', and he repeats this only a few lines further on.

Who were these doubters? James goes on to rail against Scot and Wier for their apparent scepticism, but it may be worth noting that he wrote in Scots, not Latin, 'to make this treatise the more pleasant and facile' [*easy to understand*], which must suggest he was aiming his remarks at home-grown and English-speaking sceptics, people who were not necessarily sceptical of witchcraft itself, of course, (although his adding that such devilish arts '*have been and are*' may suggest otherwise), but sceptical of the general reality or the specific details of the alleged conspiracies against his person.

His choice of dialogue as the form in which to cast what he wanted to say, while perfectly 'Classical' as a literary mode of discussion and teaching, was suited to his choice of the vernacular and also allowed him to adopt, at least in appearance, a less didactic, more conversational tone with which to engage his readership. His choice of 'pleasant and facile' Scots, however, does not imply that the *Daemonologie* was aimed at the general reading-public. It is expressed in full, if not dry, didactic mode, with a scattering of Latin phrases – '*homo pictus non est homo*', (Book 1, Chapter 7), '*spectra et umbrae mortuorum*' (3, 1), '*aniles fabulae*' (3, 3) – and one or two technical phrases or terms in logic – '*secundum quid*' (1, 3), '*abusivē*' (1, 7), '*affirmativē*' (2, 1) – which leads one to suppose he was addressing a well-educated, but not necessarily learned audience: lay rather than clerical readers, in other words, members of the nobility. The title, *Daemonologie*, appears to be one of James's own devising and is, perhaps deliberately, ambiguous, since it may mean either 'A Discussion of Evil Spirits', or 'A Discussion of the Evil Spirit', i.e. Satan. The conversation, such as it is, takes place between two speakers who are anonymous in one manuscript but are given names in the printed version: Philomathes ('someone who loves to learn things') and Epistemon, ('someone who understands what he is talking about') who is obviously meant to stand for James himself.

## 2.1 Book One: ritual magic

The treatise is divided into three 'books' and several short 'chapters', with each 'book' dealing with a separate, though connected theme. Book One starts with an allusion to the recent confessions of witches, but then rapidly turns to its principal concern which is that of ritual magic, and necromancy in particular which James illustrates by the well-known biblical story of the divineress of Endor's raising Satan in the guise of the dead prophet Samuel at the behest of King Saul. All necromancers, enchanters, or witches are guilty of abandoning their duty and allegiance to God, but some do so in the full knowledge that this is their deliberate intention. Curiosity is what allures magicians and necromancers to this sin; eagerness to avenge wrongs or to acquire possessions are the motives of 'sorcerers' or 'witches'. James then offers the standard etymologies of the words *magic* and *necromancy* and suggests that the popularly accepted differences between magicians and witches – that the latter are Satan's servants, while the former are his masters – may have something in it. Learned men, who belong to the category 'magician-necromancer', are led astray by practising such arts as judicial astrology, which leads step by step to ritual magic and the conjuration of spirits. At this point (Chapter 4) James throws in mention of such charms 'as commonly daft wives use', before returning to make a distinction between astrology and astronomy, the latter being 'most necessary and commendable', the former being acceptable in medicine but otherwise 'utterly unlawful to be trusted in or practised amongst Christians'.

Astrology is also responsible for giving birth to other illicit practices, such as chiromancy, geomancy, hydromancy, and so forth. Here Philomathes objects that many of these have long been in use by men and women who mean no harm by them, but Epistemon (James) counters this by saying that anyone who practises the simple rudiments of ritual magic puts himself in thrall to the devil, 'and so cometh plainly to a contract with him, wherein is specially contained forms and effects' (Chapter 5). In Chapter 6, James elaborates his remarks on this contract and points out that there is a big difference between what magicians can effect and God's miracles, and he brings this Book to a close in the final chapter by explaining why magic is illicit and maintaining that ritual magicians should actually be punished rather more severely than 'sorcerers' or witches.

Why this emphasis on ritual magic as opposed to 'sorcery' and witchcraft, which James – rather than regarding them as more or less the same, which is an elision made by several contemporary writers on the subject – clearly regards as different? It may be that Book One betrays the effect Richard Graham and the Earl of Bothwell in particular had had upon the king. Graham was a ritual magician on familiar terms with important members of the king's government, including the earl himself who was Graham's patron. Bothwell was not only accused of being part of three separate conspiracies to kill the king by magic between 1589 and 1590, but was also said to have consulted Graham about his changing relationship with James, questions Graham answered after he himself had consulted a spirit which he raised by 'devilish incantations, prayers, and invocation ... . by making a triangle.' Mention of the triangle makes it clear that this was ritual magic, and the 'raising' of the spirit may suggest necromancy, or at least something akin to it. Bothwell himself was also said to have taken a practical interest in ritual magic, since we are told that during his later exile to Europe he was known to travel in company with three magicians, 'the greatest sorcerers in the world', and an English traveller to Naples was told that the earl was 'in these parts famous for suspected negromancie.'[5] In addition to condemning ritual magic, James spends time here on warning his readers against judicial astrology which he also clearly associates with learned men (rather than the 'daft wives' who commonly employ charms for a number of practical, but un-learned purposes). Indeed, his mention of charms at this point is slightly odd because, although he gives them as examples of the devil's 'entrances to the art of magic', the magic he has been describing and continues to concentrate on in this Book is not that of the daft wives at all, but that of men such as Richard Graham and possibly the Earl of Bothwell.

### 2.2 Book Two: reflecting on witchcraft

Book Two begins with three observations from Philomathes relating to 'sorcery or witchcraft', which he calls 'a short digression': (i) people say that examples in

Scripture refer to ritual magic or necromancy, not to witchcraft; (ii) some people think that witches' confessions are mere ravings; (iii) if witches' power was real, there would be no good people left in the world. James answers that: (i) God's law condemns anyone who practises magic of any kind; (ii) 'a natural melancholic humour', on which witchcraft is sometimes blamed, makes people thin, whereas many of those convicted of witchcraft are rich, or fat, or given to the pleasures of the flesh; and (iii) witches usually have to be tortured before they confess, whereas melancholics cannot stop talking about themselves. Moreover, the devil's power has always been limited and he operates in the world only with God's permission. (James's first and third points are entirely conventional. His second, however, clearly shows he has his personal experiences at the forefront of his mind because in the margin of a manuscript of the *Daemonologie*, the initials EM, RG, and BN almost certainly refer to three of those allegedly involved in the conspiracies against him: Euphame MacCalzean (rich and worldly-wise), Richard Graham (fat or corpulent), and Barbara Napier (given to the pleasures of the flesh)).[6]

James then continues with a definition of the word sorcery – 'casting lots' – but fails to define 'witchcraft', saying merely that 'it is nothing but a proper name given in our language'. He could not have done this had he been writing in Latin. Latin offers an extensive technical vocabulary, based partly upon people's everyday experience or expectations and partly upon learned linguistic construction, which differentiates, as English 'witch' or French 'sorcier/sorcière' do not, between what were seen as the predominant activities or claimed abilities of magical practitioners. On the whole, writers in Latin tended to make full use of this terminological range, and so when James chose to write on the subject in Scots, he was immediately hampered by the relative paucity of terms available to him. This paucity, too, means it becomes easier for those terms to diminish the people they describe, blur the important differences between them, and treat them as though they were more or less one and the same – the notorious slippage of 'cunning person' into 'witch' is a prime example of this – and this kind of slippage seems to be what is happening at this point in James's treatise.

Epistemon (James) goes on to identify witches as poor people enticed by Satan into surrendering to feelings of revenge and desire for worldly goods. The devil meets them, makes them renounce Christianity, and sets his mark on them. Witches worship Satan as God and often confess 'not only his convening of the pulpit', but also 'their form of adoration to be the kissing of his hinder parts', (Chapter 3) – conventional enough but, under the circumstances, a fairly clear reference to the alleged convention of conspirator-witches in North Berwick. Witches, says James, say they come to these meetings by flying or being transported through the air. He thinks that on this point the witches are deluded, although they may believe that what they are confessing is true. At this point, Philomathes asks why so many witches are women and James says simply that they are more susceptible than men to Satan's snares – an utterly conventional remark – before going on to list some of the practices usually attributed to witches, noticeably spending time and emphasis on the method of killing someone by melting a wax image of them at a fire, raising storms at sea, making people ill, and sending spirits to frighten them in their houses, or even take possession of their persons. (Most of these accusations were levied against John Fian, one of the accused in James's case). God allows this in order to punish the wicked, rouse the godly, and test the patience of the elect. No one is immune and no one is permitted to use witchcraft to counter witchcraft. Magistrates, however, have a privileged position and may be protected by God if they root out and punish witches as they ought. When witches are arrested and imprisoned by a magistrate, their power begins to diminish, although the devil may continue to visit them in prison to prevent their confessing their sin and returning to God. Other people may or may not see Satan at this time. Before the Reformation, however, he appeared to people much more frequently than he does now, although this does not mean to say he does not appear at all.

With this, the second Book, in which echoes of James's recent experiences are frequent and clearly affect Epistemon's account of who witches are and what they do, comes to an end. James's eliding of sorcery with witchcraft as though the two were the same – in spite of his correct etymology of 'sorcery' – is by no means unusual. Scot, for example, gives a very clear picture of the English terminology used in his day. 'Sometimes jugglers [i.e. conjurors in the modern sense] are called witches. Sometimes also they are called sorcerers … . Sometimes a murtherer with poison is called a witch [i.e. the Latin *venefica*] and at this daie it is indifferent to saie in the English toong, She is a witch, or, She is a wise woman', and so he goes on. Anyone, it appears, male or female, who claimed to divine from dreams or animals' behaviour, or to do anything beyond the ordinary, or was simply 'old, lame, curst, or melancholike', was called a witch.[7] George Gifford, on the other hand, whose sceptical *Dialogue Concerning Witches and Witchcrafts* appeared in 1593, constantly refers to witches, sorcerers, and 'conjurers', (by which he probably means ritual magicians), not to mention cunning men and cunning women, as separate categories, although he does not seek to offer his readers a definition of any of them.[8] English (and, it seems, Scots) usage was thus apparently not conducive to exact expression of what writers in these languages were trying to explain to their readers and warn them to shun and punish and this, it may be thought, may have implications. Lumping magical practitioners together creates a single category of offender and makes prosecution potentially easier, whereas distinction of categories (which Latin, for example, encourages) makes the task of prosecution potentially more difficult. Hence, perhaps, the more subtle approach of the Inquisition, working in Latin, as opposed to that of secular courts working principally in the vernacular.

### 2.3 Book Three: talk of spirits

Book Three picks up the talk of spirits and James says there are four kinds that Satan uses to frighten and harm people physically: (i) those that haunt places; (ii) those that trouble human beings; (iii) those that actually take possession of people; and (iv) fairies. The first, he says, can enter people's houses either as a dead body resurrected for the purpose by the devil or by witches, or in spirit form, and the devil uses these wraiths to frighten ignorant Christians who do not realise that the dead cannot return and that angels are not producing this phenomenon. Werewolves, however, are merely human beings labouring under a delusion. The second and third kinds of spirit are permitted by God in order to punish the wicked or to test and strengthen someone's faith. Philomathes asks about some spirits who appear to help human beings and forewarn them of danger, but James explains that all spirits are evil, in support of which he reiterates the Protestant view that 'since the coming of Christ in the flesh ... all miracles, visions, prophecies, and appearances of angels or good spirits are ceased' (Chapter 2). Philomathes asks about *incubi* and *succubi* and is told that these, along with the idea that monsters can be born of a union between humans and spirits, are old wives' tales. Nature is against it, and even if it did happen, the resulting child would be a normal human being, not a monster. Explanations are given to account for the devil's role in the process, but James does not believe them. The phenomenon called 'nightmare' is a natural illness, and so sometimes is demonic possession. Three signs, however, mark this out when it is diabolical in origin – the sufferer's unnatural strength, extraordinary physical contortion, and speaking in languages the sufferer does not actually know; and the cure is not the one offered by Catholics, but the Protestant one of prayer and fasting.

Fairies, says James, are more or less fantasies which were rife when Scotland was a Catholic country. Witches confess to dealing with them because the devil has deluded them, and the same is true of others who say they have seen them. The variety of names given to fairies is misleading. Satan is the reality behind all of them. James may have dismissed fairies as papist nonsense arising from diabolically inspired illusion, but fairies sometimes played a major role in the lives of a number of Scots who were brought before the courts on a charge of witchcraft. In 1568, for example, the Lyon King of Arms, Sir William Stewart, was tried for magically attempting the life of the Regent, of raising and worshipping a spirit called 'Obirion', and of conducting magical ceremonies on Arthur's Seat in Edinburgh, so called because of the fairy arrow-heads that were found there. Janet Boyman, brought to trial in 1569, went there, too, and consulted the king and queen of the fairies. Alison Pearson, tried in 1588, had a kind of spirit-guide called William Simpson who was either a fairy himself or closely associated with the fairy kingdom, and in 1590 Isobel Watson confessed to having given her own child to the fairies in return for their curing her husband of a long illness, and of becoming a servant to the fairies who then marked her on the forehead. The case of Sir William Stewart shows that active fairy belief was not confined to the lower classes, as does that of Alison Pearson, since she and two other witches had been hired by Patrick

Adamson, Archbishop of St Andrews (not a Catholic), for purposes which are not altogether clear.⁹

Philomathes wants to know more, but James dismisses his inquisitiveness, saying, 'I have framed my whole discourse only to prove that such things are and may be, by such number of examples as I show to be possible by reason, and keeps me from dipping any further', and this brings the dialogue to its last discussion, one which gives the impression of being somewhat hastily tacked on to it – 'to make an end of our conference, since I see it draws late' (Chapter 6). How are witches and magicians to be punished? By death, according to the law and custom of each country. No exceptions should be made, except in the case of children, and those who consult witches and magicians and use their services are equally guilty. Princes and judges may postpone their execution, but should not reprieve the guilty because witchcraft, magic, and the use of them, constitute treason against God, and treason should always be punishable by death. Witches' confessions are sufficient in law to condemn them and others whom they name. God will not allow the truly innocent to be accused. Finding a witch's mark and testing it for insensitivity is useful to establish a person's guilt, as is the swimming test. Why is witchcraft rife at this time? Because of people's wickedness and the approach of the end of the world. The witch-mark was not universally accepted as a reliable or legitimate way to detect a witch – William Perkins°, for example, rejected it – but there is evidence that by the seventeenth century Scots had gained something of a reputation of being specialists in this form of detection, although it would be going too far to say that this was a result of James's recommendation; and when it comes to the swimming-test, James is very much in the minority, since most writers on magic and witchcraft, while acknowledging it was frequently used, questioned it validity and often condemned it outright. Nor was it common practice in Scotland itself, since there is only one recorded instance of its official use there although, of course, that does not preclude its being employed unofficially.¹⁰

## 3 Summary: emotionally charged

So what kind of a treatise is the *Daemonologie*, and how does it compare with others written in the last decade or so of the sixteenth century? The first thing that strikes the reader (as it has struck others before) is that while not saying anything out of the ordinary about magic or witchcraft or, indeed, offering any new or incisive arguments to combat the limited scepticism of such people as Scot or Wier, James speaks with a highly personal voice and it is this, rather than his being a royal author, that makes him noticeable among writers of this genre.¹¹ His tone is at once didactic and emotionally charged. Contrast this with the chattiness of George Gifford's *Dialogue Concerning Witches and Witchcrafts* which was published in 1593 and draws upon English examples for its illustrative references, as James does upon Scottish. James may have chosen the dialogue form 'to make this treatise more pleasant and facile', and Gifford 'to make it the fitter for the capacity of the simpler sort', and both may have had an instructive end in view, but their voices could not be more different.[12] Gifford is, to an extent, reassuring. The danger to people from witches and cunning folk, he says, is spiritual rather than physical, and God is in complete control of everything. James, on the other hand, is keen to assure his readers that witches do what they are accused of doing. They do not imagine their powers; their power to inflict physical harm as well as spiritual is real. Gifford wrote and published his *Dialogue* against the background of a case of witchcraft local to his own parish, Maldon, when one Margaret Wiseman was accused. Her magic, however, was not, it seems, directed against Gifford personally and so Gifford is able to maintain a distance between himself and his discussion of the dangers to people from witchcraft, what witches actually do, and how society should respond to its presence in their community.[13] James, however, as we have seen, is almost entirely caught up in the recent personal danger to himself, and the *Daemonologie* is shot through with oblique references to some of the individuals who had allegedly conspired to kill him.

John Fian (or Cunningham), for example, was a schoolmaster, and James may have been thinking of him when he referred to 'the Devil's school and his rudiments. The learned have their curiosity wakened up and fed by that which I call his school' (Book 1, Chapter 3). Fian deponed on 26 December 1590 that the devil marked him 'with a rod' – i.e. as though with a magic wand – which seems to cast the devil in the role of a ritual magician, and that he (John) 'was stricken in great ecstasies and trances ... his spirit taken, and suffered himself to be carried and transported to many mountains', which is how James describes witches 'lying still as in an ecstasy, their spirits ... carried to such places'.[14] Agnes Sampson is a prime example of James's remark that some witches know from 'the form of prayers, or suchlike tokens, if a person deceased should live or die';[15] and Euphame MacCalzean is another because of his noting that 'to some [the devil] gives such stones or powders as will help to cure or cast on diseases', and that sometimes Satan answered a witch's call 'by voice only'.[16] Under the circumstances, one cannot help wondering about James's savage reaction to a question about the execution of witches – 'It is commonly used by fire' (Book 3, Chapter 6). Perfectly true, perhaps, of other countries but not, as James must have known, of Scotland where garrotting was the actual cause of death, the dead body being burned afterwards. Moreover, no one is to be spared. 'Philomathes: But ought no sex, age, nor rank, to be exempted? Epistemon [i.e. James]: None at all'. (To be sure, he retracts at once the idea that children should be executed, but the fact that he has to do so points to the personal intensity of his immediate reaction to the question).

The *Daemonologie*, then, is a deeply personal piece of writing, as opposed to one that simply contains personal references or anecdotes. Many writers of demonologies included such material as 'When I was in (town) X in (year)

Y, I saw', or 'I heard', or 'I was told that', etc. But the tone is almost always impartially anecdotal, since the reminiscence is being produced to bolster and illustrate an intellectual or religious point which the author is discussing or expounding with relative calm. Not so James, whose choice of topics is somewhat more relevant to his own experiences than would be required by the lecture-room or even the pulpit in their exposition or condemnation of magic and witchcraft as religio-social phenomena. James's choice of Scots, too, indicates the quite small, quite limited audience he wanted to address. So the contrast with other publications is clear, and while Lizanne Henderson, for example, is perfectly correct in pointing to 'striking parallels between the structure and basic content of *Daemonologie* and other such tracts from the period, such as Lambert Daneau's treatise *De veneficis*', I suggest that the parallels are seeming rather than real, since the voices of their respective authors are startlingly different.[17]

One might be tempted to suppose that because James wrote about magic and witchcraft with a degree of intensity, he would be, or at least turn into, a persecutor of their practitioners. In fact, he did not. His later history as King of England shows a rapidly growing scepticism on his part regarding the truth of cases brought to his attention,[18] but his failure to pursue witches more forcefully after the trials of 1590–1593 may owe something to the increasingly fraught and dangerous relationship between himself and his cousin, the Earl of Bothwell, who was finally tried in 1593 for his alleged part in the 'North Berwick' conspiracy. Bothwell was both violent and unstable and rapidly passing beyond James's control. In December 1591, he actually broke into Holyroodhouse and tried to take James prisoner, and it is probably no accident that James equates witchcraft with treason (Book 3, Chapter 6). This attempted coup failed, but another in 1593 did not and it was in this year that Bothwell was finally acquitted of the charges relating to 1589–1590. The volatility of Scottish politics enabled James to regain control in 1595 and send Bothwell into permanent exile, and these events may account for his putting *Daemonologie* on one side in 1591 instead of committing it to print as soon as he had finished it. In 1597, however, we find witchcraft coming to the fore again. A number of trials were held in Aberdeenshire and Fife, with James himself spending several days in St Andrews to deal with the problem, one of the reasons for his renewed interest seeming to have been rumours of further attempts by witches against his life – the treason motif again – and this may account for his deciding to publish *Daemonologie* in 1597.[19]

James's apparent Calvinist credentials seem to have attracted the interest of Dutch translators and publishers after he acceded to the English throne, probably as a result of the flourishing state of magic and witchcraft in the Low Countries at the end of the sixteenth and beginning of the seventeenth century and the increasingly heated fulminations of the Dutch Reformed Church against them. Hence the versions of Vincent Meusvoet in 1603 and an anonymous version printed in Dordrecht. A Latin version (1604, reprinted

1607) from a German publishing house was in fact based on these Dutch translations.[20] Thereafter, however, publishers' interest in James's opinions on the subject disappeared, and although some of the English continued to make occasional approbatory references to it, as in Sir Robert Filmer's *Advertisement to the Jury-Men of England, Touching Witches* (1653), others were not so kind; and indeed Thomas Ady acidly, (and oddly, in the light of James's Calvinism), opined that 'whether this work was composed by King James or by the Bishop [of Winton] may very well be suspected'. Perhaps it was written 'by some Scottish man … who desired to set forth his own tenets for the upholding of Popish errors.'[21]

## Notes

1 There are many biographies of James's life and kingship. An especially good survey is Antonia Fraser, *King James VI of Scotland, I of England*, 1st ed., 1974, London: Weidenfeld & Nicolson, 1994.
2 Alexander Peterkin, ed., *The Booke of the Universall Kirk of Scotland*, Edinburgh: The Edinburgh Printing and Publishing Company, 1839, p. 281.
3 It was first printed in Edinburgh in 1597 and then reprinted in London in 1603 at James's accession to the English throne. There was a Dutch translation in 1603 and a Latin version in 1604, which was then republished in 1607, 1619, and 1689. James's spelling has been updated in this chapter.
4 Lawrence Normand and Gareth Roberts, eds, *Witchcraft in Early Modern Scotland: James VI's Demonology and the North Berwick Witches*, Exeter: University of Exeter Press, 2000, pp. 327–28.
5 P. G. Maxwell-Stuart, *Satan's Conspiracy: Magic and Witchcraft in Sixteenth-Century Scotland*, East Linton: Tuckwell Press, 2001, pp. 153–54, 169; Edward J. Cowan, 'The Darker Vision of the Scottish Renaissance: The Devil and Francis Stewart', in Ian B. Cowan and Duncan Shaw, eds, *The Renaissance and Reformation in Scotland*, Edinburgh: Scottish Academic Press, 1983, pp. 125 40, at 139.
6 The initials may have been added, as Rhodes Dunlap suggests, by James Carmichael who is the probable author of *Newes from Scotland*, a pamphlet about the North Berwick trials probably written and published in 1591 and thus more or less contemporary with the writing of the *Daemonologie*. See Normand and Roberts, eds, *Witchcraft in Early Modern Scotland*, pp. 328, 290–93.
7 Reginald Scot, *The Discoverie of Witchcraft*, London: William Brome, 1584, p. 110 (bk 5, chap. 9).
8 See, for example, George Gifford, *Dialogue Concerning Witches and Witchcrafts*, Brighton: Puckrel Publishing, 2007, p. 8, 34, 36, 40, 47.
9 See further Maxwell-Stuart, *Satan's Conspiracy*, pp. 57–59, 63–64, 102–106, 115–17.
10 William Perkins, *A Discourse of the Damned Art of Witchcraft*, Cambridge: Cantrel Legge, 1608, p. 203; P. G. Maxwell-Stuart, *Witch Hunters*, Stroud: Tempus Publishing 2003, pp. 98–117; Brian P. Levack, *Witch-Hunting in Scotland: Law, Politics and Religion*, London: Routledge, 2008, pp. 44–45.
11 Lizanne Henderson, however, quite rightly points out that the book was original in a Scottish context, and she also makes the valuable point that the fact it was published by the monarch may have discouraged others from writing on the subject, especially if their opinions did not altogether chime with those of James: Lizanne Henderson, *Witchcraft and Folk Belief in the Age of Enlightenment: Scotland, 1670–1740*, Basingstoke: Palgrave Macmillan, 2016, pp. 156, 162.

12 Both, indeed, are a long way from the stiff and ponderous didacticism of the Calvinist Lambert Daneau's dialogue, *De veneficis ... dialogus*, Geneva: Eustace Vignon, 1574, in which 'Theophilus' stolidly answers questions put to him by a straw man, Antoine.
13 See further Scott McGinnis, 'Subtiltie Exposed: Pastoral Perspectives on Witch Belief in the Thought of George Gifford', *Sixteenth Century Journal*, 2002, vol. 33, 665–86.
14 Document 19 in Normand and Roberts, eds, *Witchcraft in Early Modern Scotland*, p. 226; James, *Daemonologie*, p. 39 (bk 2, chap. 4).
15 James, *Daemonologie*, p. 31 (bk 2, chap. 2); Document 20 in Normand and Roberts, eds, *Witchcraft in Early Modern Scotland*, p. 233: 'Item 11, filed that she had foreknowledge by her witchcraft of diseased persons if they would live or not, or who was witched persons; to wit, that if she stopped once in her prayer, the sick person was bewitched, and if the prayer stopped twice, the diseased person would die'.
16 James, *Daemonologie*, p. 44 (bk 2, chap. 5); Document 23 in Normand and Roberts, eds, *Witchcraft in Early Modern Scotland*, pp. 266, 265.
17 Henderson, *Witchcraft and Folk Belief*, pp. 155–56.
18 For example, two women from Cambridge (1605), Anne Gunter (1606), a boy called Smith (1616), a boy from Bilston (1620).
19 See further Julian Goodare, ed., *The Scottish Witch-Hunt in Context*, Manchester: Manchester University Press, 2002, pp. 57–64; Stuart Macdonald, *The Witches of Fife: Witch-hunting in a Scottish Shire, 1560–1710*, East Linton: Tuckwell Press 2002, pp. 59–62.
20 Astrid Stilma, *A King Translated: The Writings of King James VI and I and their Interpretation in the Low Countries, 1593–1603*, Farnham: Ashgate, 2012, pp. 248–67. The Bishop of Winton is a reference to the Bishop of Winchester who styled himself thus on the title-page of his 1616 edition of James's collected works.
21 Thomas Ady, *A Candle in the Dark*, London: Robert Ibbitson, 1655, p. 140 (bk 3).

## Further reading

Fraser, Antonia, *King James VI of Scotland, I of England*, 1st ed., 1974. London: Weidenfeld & Nicolson, 1994.

Levack, Brian P., *Witch-Hunting in Scotland: Law, Politics and Religion*, London: Routledge, 2008.

Maxwell-Stuart, P. G., *Satan's Conspiracy: Magic and Witchcraft in Sixteenth-Century Scotland*, East Linton: Tuckwell Press, 2001.

Normand, Lawrence and Roberts, Gareth, eds, *Witchcraft in Early Modern Scotland: James VI's Demonology and the North Berwick Witches*, Exeter: University of Exeter Press, 2000.

Robertson, David M., *Goodnight, My Servants All: The Sourcebook of East Lothian Witchcraft*, Glasgow: The Grimsay Press, 2008.

Watson, Godfrey, *Bothwell and the Witches*, London: Robert Hale, 1975.

Willis, Deborah, *Malevolent Nurture: Witch-Hunting and Maternal Power in Early Modern England*, Ithaca: Cornell University Press, 1995, chap. 4 'James among the Witch-Hunters'.

# 11 Demonology as textual scholarship
## Martin Delrio's *Disquisitiones magicae*

*Jan Machielsen*

The closest that Martin Delrio (1551–1608) ever came to being threatened by witchcraft was in the spring of 1578. As a young magistrate, he had taken part in the capture of Leuven, a small university town in the Low Countries, by forces loyal to the Catholic King Philip II of Spain. Among the papers of one of the university graduates who fled was found a book 'full of magical characters' and 'a small box shaped like a coffin' which contained a mandrake root that resembled a little man, 'black and covered with mould and filth, with a large head of hair but no beard.' Such a root was 'generally believed to be wonderfully effective for divination, for profit, and for many other things.' When Delrio received the book, the capsule and 'the fictitious cadaver', he instantly tore off its arms, astonishing all those who were present.

> They said that great danger would come to me and mine. I laughed and ordered those who were afraid to go away. When they had left, I threw it in the nearby fireplace and noticed nothing other than the smell of burning roots.[1]

This anecdote, told in passing in Delrio's compendious *Disquisitionum magicarum libri sex* (Six Books of Magical Investigations, 1599–1600) illustrates three important aspects both of that influential work and its author, all of which we shall be exploring in this chapter.[2] The passage demonstrates, first of all, how the science of witches and demons could offer a platform for self-fashioning. Delrio's encounter with a mandrake root imitated an often repeated story (told by Peter Binsfeld° among others) of a king of France who similarly threw a waxen image meant to harm him into the fire without fear or consequence.[3] The idea that demonology was a field in which a scholarly reputation could be made may feel distasteful to us today and this may explain why this aspect of demonology has long been ignored.

Secondly and relatedly, this implicit invocation of a well-known demonological story suggests that the book was no mere witch-hunter's manual. Written in polished Latin, the *Disquisitiones* was more than a work of demonology alone; it was a work of literature, rich in allusions, and part of the world of Renaissance humanism, to which it sought to make a rather partisan

Catholic contribution. Its literary qualities have paradoxically made the *Disquisitiones* less accessible to historians than many of its more plain-spoken contemporary rivals.[4] This is more than just an issue of linguistic competence. It reflects the fact that the world of textual scholarship of which the *Disquisitiones* was a part is worlds away from the trial records most witchcraft historians work on. Underneath the layer of the king-of-France story, for instance, we may detect yet another layer of meaning. Delrio was, in fact, well-known for rescuing the library and possessions of a friend who fled Leuven ahead of the arrival of the Spanish army in which he was serving. Justus Lipsius (1547–1606) was one of the greatest humanist scholars of the late sixteenth century, the editor of a famous edition of the Roman historian Tacitus and instrumental in reviving the ideas of the philosopher Seneca. The two men had been friends since their shared university days, but Lipsius was also a rival, whose loyalty to the Catholic Church Delrio once had to vouch for and which he vigilantly guarded. In a published letter, Lipsius had thanked Delrio for rescuing his books: 'You have defended me and mine in my absence; you exposed yourself not only to trouble and even to danger but threw yourself into the flames of things.'[5] Given that public context, Lipsius could well have been the university graduate in question. When Delrio reported the story of the mandrake in the library, he was also making a not terribly subtle swipe at an old friend with whom he had an exceedingly complicated relationship.

Thirdly, if the *Disquisitiones* should be understood within this world of book-based learning – complete with scholarly backbiting – then it further underscores just how limited its author's encounter with witchcraft really was. The *Disquisitiones* was emphatically not the sort of demonological text based on personal experience. As far as magical encounters go, confrontations with a mandrake root must rank among the least consequential. There is no evidence that Delrio ever met a witch, let alone that he played any direct role in their persecution. The *Disquisitiones* was not a report of a witch-hunt, as the books by Nicolas Remy°, Pierre de Lancre°, and Henri Boguet were. Yet, in terms of its longevity it was much more successful than all of these works. In terms of the total number of editions it almost rivalled the *Malleus maleficarum*. Delrio's *magnum opus* was last reprinted in Venice in 1746 and in Cologne in 1755, when witchcraft persecutions had ceased across almost all of Europe.[6] If we want to explore why the *Disquisitiones* outlasted its rivals, then the types of scholarship and authorship it flaunted offer valuable clues. To understand the extraordinary success of this unusual work of demonology and to explain how it came to be written, we must begin with the author's early life and the changing world of scholarship in which he sought to make his name.

## 1 A turbulent early life

Martinus Antonius Delrio (or if you prefer, Martín Antonio del Río) was born in Antwerp on 17 May 1551, Whitsunday, as the eldest son of the wealthy Spanish merchant Antonio del Río and his wife Eleonora López de

Villanova. It is difficult to underestimate the long-term impact of Delrio's Netherlandish birth and Spanish parentage although it hardly seemed significant at the time. Antwerp in the 1550s was a vibrant metropolis, the largest city north of Paris, with more inhabitants than either Amsterdam or London. It was home to large contingents of merchants from across Europe but especially Spain. In 1516, Spain and the Habsburg Netherlands (an area covering the present-day Netherlands, Belgium, Luxembourg and parts of northern France) were united under a single ruler, Charles of Ghent, known to all as Charles V, when he also succeeded his grandfather as Holy Roman Emperor in 1519.

From an early age, Martin Delrio was ordained for a career in service of the Spanish crown. His Netherlandish birth and Spanish parentage offered a bridge between different parts of the empire and towards his family's political advancement. As a native of the Low Countries, Delrio was eligible for local political offices from which Spaniards were excluded. The family thus invented a coat of arms and Antonio bought a noble title both for himself and for his eldest son, who at 10 years of age became the lord of the small village of Aartselaar.

Aristocratic titles did not suffice, however. What the Spanish crown had prized most since the days of Isabella and Ferdinand was a university education, especially in law. Delrio arrived at the University of Leuven in 1563, at the young age of 12.[7] After his death, a devoted disciple would represent Delrio as a child prodigy, who had read 1,100 authors by the age of 19, and he would later be included in a 1688 collection entitled *Enfans devenus celebres par leurs études* (Children Made Famous by Their Studies).[8] Delrio's youth was not that unusual, however, but he did move in the same circles as high-flying young students who were a few years older than him, including Lipsius who lent him the manuscript of the fourth-century geographer Solinus that would become the basis of his first publication in 1572. After Leuven, stays at other universities followed, culminating in a law degree from Salamanca, Spain's oldest university, in 1574.

Delrio's ambitions were apparent throughout his studies. In 1567, the 16-year-old Delrio drew his coat of arms in the *album amicorum* (a friendship book, the sixteenth-century equivalent of a Facebook page) and added as his personal motto: 'I will die for my religion and for my king.' He dedicated his edition of Solinus to Cardinal Granvelle, one of Philip II's most influential advisers.[9] In his edition of Senecan tragedy, he chastized the lines in one of the plays – 'let my own land/hide me in a safe and secluded home' (*Hercules* 197–98) as 'pusillanimous':

> He, who from adolescence persuaded himself that nothing in life is more greatly to be sought than praise and honours and that in pursuing those every bodily harm, every danger of death and exile are to be thought small; he, by Hercules, will not hesitate to throw himself into many terrible fights, in daily battles against depraved men, for the salvation of the fatherland, for the advantage and benefit of his king.[10]

This edition, which appeared in 1576, was styled as a public goodbye to the world of humanist letters and classical scholarship. A preface supposedly written by his younger brother Gerónimo was dedicated to a cousin, Luís or Louis, who had already risen up in royal service. The letter claimed that Martin 'blinded by the splendour of jurisprudence, began to disdain the study of the good letters long ago' and that the work, supposedly completed years earlier, had to be published against the author's will. The letter was a forgery. In fact, Delrio wrote it himself so that he could claim to have completed his first work at the young age of 19 (as Lipsius claimed to have done as well). He was bolstering his claims of academic brilliance, while advertising his embrace of a new career.[11]

Unfortunately, 1576 was the wrong year to enter royal service. In the autumn of 1575, Philip II of Spain had declared bankruptcy. Not long after, the Army of Flanders sent to combat a Protestant-led revolt in the Low Countries mutinied for lack of pay. In November 1576, these troops even sacked the splendid city of Antwerp. This horrendous event in which thousands of civilians died, known as the Spanish Fury, inspired Catholic and Protestant factions to put aside their differences and unite against a common Spanish enemy. This left the Delrio family horribly and hopelessly exposed. Both Luís and Delrio's father Antonio had been instrumental in implementing some of the harshest anti-Protestant measures, which were now fully disowned. Worse, they also stood accused of profiting financially from the estates of those executed for heresy. Delrio's tenure as a magistrate from 1576 to 1579 (during which he confronted that magical mandrake root) occurred at a time when royal power in the Low Countries was at an all-time low, while his father facing bankruptcy fled the country and his cousin was imprisoned. For a very short time, it looked like Delrio himself might personally redeem the family honour when a new royal governor, Don John of Austria, took back part of the country, including Leuven, but Delrio's apparently rapid rise (to Vice-Chancellor of the Duchy of Brabant at the age of 27) did not last long. Delrio's lengthy vindication of Don John remained in manuscript after the governor's successor Alexander Farnese adopted a more conciliatory policy.[12] The loyalty of followers who have nowhere left to go can be taken for granted and Delrio's positions were offered instead to those whose support needed to be won back. With his career and his family's fortune in ruins, Delrio left the Low Countries to embrace the religious life. On 9 May 1580, the erstwhile magistrate and humanist scholar entered the Society of Jesus in the Spanish city Valladolid.[13]

## 2 The *Disquisitiones* as a work of Catholic scholarship

Martin Delrio's religious calling thus has somewhat of an air of desperation around it. Yet, his experiences during the Revolt of the Netherlands (1566–1648) also fundamentally shaped his outlook. Historians have spent much ink debating the origins of the Revolt, which ultimately fractured the Low Countries into two Protestant and Catholic entities but for Delrio, the conflict was only ever a religious one. Acknowledging the validity of any other factor, such as the defence of local privileges or Spanish heavy-handedness, would have made Delrio and his family personally responsible for their own misfortunes.

In that sense, Delrio's entry into the Society of Jesus made perfect sense. The Society was one of the youngest religious orders of the period, only founded by Ignatius of Loyola and a group of companions in 1540, but it was at the forefront of the Catholic response to the Protestant Reformation. The Jesuits, in particular, embraced the role of education, founding schools which offered free but high-quality tuition across Catholic Europe to serve as 'Trojan Horses' to re-introduce the faith in areas where Protestants had once gained control. A person with Delrio's educational background and skills made quite an attractive catch to Jesuit superiors. For the remainder of his life, he would teach at Jesuit colleges near the frontlines of Catholic Europe: in Leuven, Liège and Douai in the Low Countries, in Mainz in Germany and in Graz in Austria.[14] Beyond the classroom, Delrio would also engage Protestants and moderate Catholics in print, writing a particularly vicious invective against Joseph Scaliger, probably the most famous Protestant scholar of his day. Scaliger referred to Delrio, among other things, as 'the devil's shit', to which the Jesuit replied with an A-to-Z list of insults to be hurled at the Protestant instead.[15]

All of this raises the question: to what extent was Delrio's *Disquisitiones magicae* (Figure 11.1) a work of Catholic scholarship? Given Delrio's fervent anti-Protestantism this is a more difficult question to answer than one might think. The preface of the *Disquisitiones* took on a strongly apocalyptic undertone, linking the rise of the threat of witches with the onset of Protestantism and both with the approaching end of the world. Delrio offered four links between witchcraft and heresy, which he had taken from his fellow Jesuit (and possibly his teacher) Juan Maldonado°. He argued that heresy unless it returned to the true religion from which it had originated, inevitably 'degenerates into the magical arts or the extreme impiety of atheism.' In a strikingly gendered metaphor, Maldonado and Delrio also maintained that 'demons are wont to use heretics to deceive men as if they are beautiful courtesans' but once they lose their seductive figures, heretics are transformed into witches, just as aged prostitutes become madams and brothel-keepers.[16]

Scattered through the *Disquisitiones* are occasional anti-Protestant outbursts. He claimed that the witches' sabbat was held near Calvinist Geneva's main church and that at Martin Luther's death, demons left the bodies of the possessed to attend his funeral.[17] A wooden Christ statue in the town of Damme, near Bruges, allegedly worked miracles and grew a beard that required shaving every year, 'until the impious and obstinate fury of the Calvinists destroyed the image in flames.'[18] Some of the anecdotes reflect Delrio's personal experiences of the Revolt. He claimed that Protestant iconoclasts had destroyed all the images in Antwerp's cathedral, except one

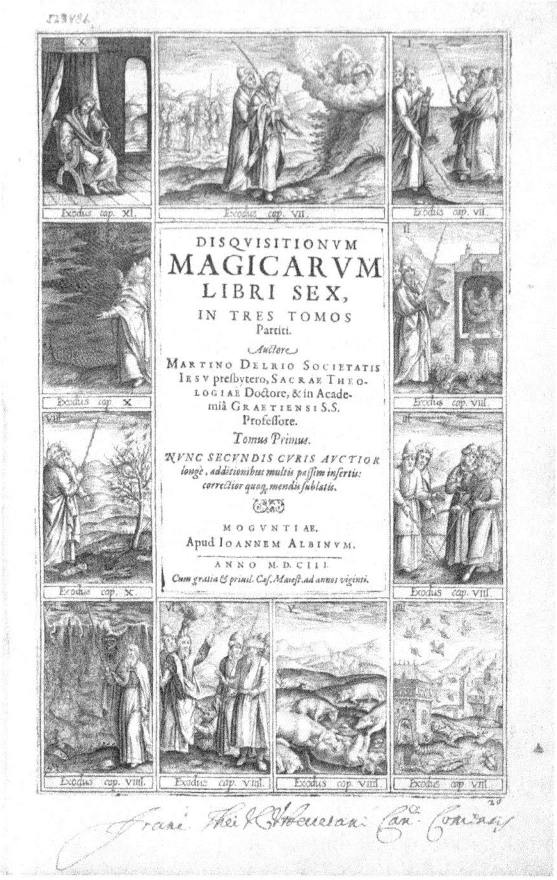

DISQVISITIONVM
MAGICARVM
LIBRI SEX,
IN TRES TOMOS
Partiti.
*Auctore*
MARTINO DELRIO SOCIETATIS
IESV presbytero, SACRAE THEO-
LOGIAE Doctore, & in Acade-
miâ GRAETIENSI S.S.
Professore.
*Tomus Primus.*
*NVNC SECVNDIS CVRIS AVCTIOR*
*longè, additionibus multis passim insertis:*
*correctior quoq; mendis sublatis.*
MOGVNTIAE.
Apud IOANNEM ALBINVM.
ANNO M.D.CIII.
*Cum gratia & priuil. Cæs. Maiest. ad annos viginti.*

*Figure 11.1* Cover page showing Moses combatting the Magicians of Egypt. Martin Delrio, *Disquisitionum magicarum libri sex, in tres tomos partiti*, 3rd ed., Mainz: Johannes Albinus, 1603. Image by permission of the Koninklijke Bibliotheek, The Hague. KB | Nationale bibliotheek [KW 3236 C 3 Disqvisitionvm magicarvm libri sex,: in tres tomos partiti./Auctore Martino Delrio].

statue of the devil, which he had seen himself.[19] He remembered how the pregnant wife of his cousin Luís had been terrified out of her wits when Protestant rebels invaded her home. She gave birth to a child that showed its mother's fear in its eyes even as an adolescent.[20] In the concluding pages of the work, Delrio launched a polemic against Joseph Scaliger – the 'Achilles' of the Protestant camp – on a subject that had nothing at all to do with witchcraft.[21]

We should not, however, judge the *Disquisitiones* by its preface. Polemical outbursts along the lines above were relatively few and far in between. In fact, it is striking how frequently later Protestant authors relied on Delrio as an authority. In the wake of the 1692 Salem witchcraft trials, the Harvard divine Increase Mather cited him approvingly: 'it is rare to see such Words dropping from the Pen of a Jesuit.'[22] He was treated with similar reverence by other Protestant authorities, such as the Anglican theologian Meric Casaubon and the Dutch Calvinist Gijsbert Voet.[23] Although witchcraft had clear potential for confessional polemic, the subject could also transcend such boundaries.

There is, moreover, more to early modern Catholicism then hatred of Protestants, and Delrio had two other aims that we could consider particularly Catholic. The first of these becomes apparent when we consider the title Delrio originally considered until his friend Lipsius suggested *Disquisitiones magicae* to him: *De superstitione et malis artibus*.[24] The fact that one of the most popular demonological texts could have been called 'On Superstition and the Evil Arts' may raise an eyebrow, given the frequency with which the word 'superstition' is bandied about in modern popular culture to describe and belittle pre-modern witchcraft beliefs. Yet, Delrio would readily have agreed that witchcraft belief was 'superstitious.' Superstition, as a concept, goes back to ancient Rome, where it was discussed by such thinkers as Cicero, Seneca, and Plutarch. Although its etymology is unclear, it has always been understood as referring to false belief. Yet while we often define superstition as the opposite of science today, its traditional rival was religion.[25] For Delrio, witchcraft beliefs were superstitious, not because witchcraft and the devil did not exist, but because their practice was not directed at God. Delrio consequently denounced a sceptic who 'thought that magicians who believed [in weather magic] were superstitious. They are superstitious *because* they are magicians.'[26] The opening chapter of the work is similarly called 'on superstition and its subdivisions'.[27]

It is therefore more helpful to consider the *Disquisitiones* not as yet another book on witchcraft but foremost as a taxonomy of superstition, defined as wrong belief. Many later editions include a table of contents that rather resembles a flow chart. The *Disquisitiones* are divided into six different books, three of which tackle different types of wrong beliefs: Book Two is devoted to demonic magic; Book Three is subdivided into two parts – one covering *maleficium*, the other so-called 'vain observances'; Book Four is devoted to the subject of divination. Inevitably, the sections on demonic magic and *maleficium* to some extent overlap but the magic involved differs in focus. Where Book Two in a Q&A format discusses the scope of demonic power – whether demons could raise the dead, change a person's sex, or restore their youth (no, no, and no) – the section on *maleficium* discusses the different types of harm, including insomnia and love magic, inflicted by their human allies.[28]

From a Catholic perspective, the two sections on vain observances and on divination are still more interesting. Delrio, following in the footsteps of Thomas Aquinas and others, defined vain observances as 'superstitious magic'. They were popular rituals or practices aimed at obtaining a cure or some other effect – and they were superstitious because they were not aimed at

God. They are called vain, 'because either the intended effect does not follow or if it does happen it brings more harm than good.'[29] If these vain observances inexplicably were successful, this could well be because of demonic intervention, in which case either an implicit (accidental) or explicit pact with the devil had been made. The Jesuit ridiculed beliefs in the hidden properties of eggs laid on Good Friday, said to have the power to extinguish fire,[30] or those of special cakes, shaped as a triangle ('supposedly in honour of the most sacred Trinity') and offered to beggars, to ward off attacks by wolves.[31] Of course, all religious reformers, both Protestant and Catholic, were forced to confront such popular practices. Pre-modern societies equipped themselves with an arsenal of such rituals to manage the risks and dangers of daily life.[32] Yet, the problem was especially acute for Catholic reformers because, unlike their Protestant counterparts, they had a *legitimate* arsenal of sacraments and sacramentals which needed to be both distinguished and protected from popular abuses. Delrio, therefore, defended the effectiveness of protective charms that had the name of an angel inscribed on them but insisted that only the three angels mentioned in Scripture – Gabriel, Michael, and Raphael – could be used. Any other name could be a demonic invocation.[33] He also attacked women who placed such charms in their vaginas.[34]

The same twin concerns – to distinguish official Catholic doctrine from popular religion and defend it against Protestant assault – shape Book Four of the *Disquisitiones* which was devoted to the subject of divination. Protestants held that the age of miracles had long since ceased, ruling out the possibility of divine prophecy in the present. Yet Catholics had not closed the door to continued divine revelation. The late medieval Church had canonized a number of prominent female mystics, most notably Catherine of Siena (1347–1380) and the more controversial Bridget of Sweden (1303–1373), who provided a role model for early modern Catholic women. Book Four, accordingly, opened with the subject of divine prophecy followed by a discussion as to how it could be distinguished from demonic deception and even demonic possession. Delrio, accordingly, defended the visions of Catherine and Bridget (which seemed to contradict each other on the vexing question of the immaculate conception of the Virgin Mary).[35] Yet, he also devoted a chapter to discussing 'the revelations of women who are not saints.'[36] As Moshe Sluhovsky has shown, female mystics were a particular concern to the Church. Claims of divine revelation, especially by women, had the potential of undermining its authority, and the Church was anxious to regulate popular devotions to so-called *beati moderni*, who had not yet been canonized.[37] Delrio argued that, other things being equal, more faith should be attached to the visions of men than of women, as the imagination of the latter was more easily deceived by the devil.[38] His chapter offered some stark examples of what could happen to would-be female prophets and their male followers who were taken in by the devil.

Demonology as textual scholarship   187

The *Disquisitiones*, then, was much more than a witch-hunter's manual. It sought to map an entire field of approved and forbidden knowledge. I would argue that this encyclopaedic quality constitutes a second way in which the *Disquisitiones* can be seen as a particularly Catholic work of the period. The work cannot only be placed within a corpus of demonological texts, as the present volume seeks to do, but also as a contribution to a particular type of Catholic scholarship which emerged a generation after the closing of the Council of Trent (1545–1563).[39] The 1580s and 1590s had witnessed the publication of a growing number of Catholics works of 'synthesis'. Antonio Possevino's *Bibliotheca selecta* (1593), for instance, provided a bibliographical survey of all the sciences, offering authoritative assessments of the authors, and selecting – as the name suggests – only those works that should be read. Cesare Baronio's *Annales ecclesiastici* (12 vols, 1588–1607) was an ambitious attempt to offer an authoritative year-by-year account of the Catholic Church's history that only ended early – in 1198 – because of the author's death. A prefatory poem by one of Delrio's admirers likened the *Disquisitiones* to Possevino's *Bibliotheca*. Yet Baronio's *Annales* was, if anything, still more important. Delrio was an avid admirer of the historian's work. He included additional examples taken from the *Annales* as new volumes appeared in subsequent editions of the *Disquisitiones*. It was also in defence of Baronio's *Annales* that Delrio launched his attack on Joseph Scaliger. The *Disquisitiones* was part of a wider effort to map Catholic traditions and pin down what Catholics were meant to believe.

### 3 The *Disquisitiones* as a work of textual scholarship

Given the encyclopaedic ambitions we have just ascribed to the *Disquisitiones*, the project could not be undertaken by just about anyone. In fact, Delrio who – whatever his religious vows may have said – was not given to modesty, claimed that no one had satisfactorily discussed magic before him:

> I do not remember reading anyone who thoroughly examined and destroyed all the entrails of the superstitious arts. Philosophers, lawyers, and theologians have written [on the subject], but only as far as their own discipline so that while they may have satisfied their own school and sect, it would certainly appear to be less useful to the others ... [I]f I say that I have dwelled a long time in [all] three faculties, I do not lie because I speak the truth. Neither do I glorify myself, because I do not claim success. I profess the cultivation and the labour, but I leave judgement on the crop to others.[40]

Later editions of the *Disquisitiones* stressed the work's interdisciplinary nature and value (and that of demonology) on their title page, describing it, for instance, as 'exceedingly useful and necessary for theologians, lawyers, physicians and philosophers, especially to preachers of God's Word and to secular and ecclesiastical judges to whom, above all, golden rules are given.'[41] As both Delrio's opening boast and the work's title page make clear, demonology was perhaps the first interdisciplinary science, which theologians, lawyers, physicians, and philosophers all needed to address. Delrio's legal studies and all-too-brief career provided part of the justification for his book project but his later theological studies as a Jesuit did as well. Books Five and Six of the *Disquisitiones*, therefore, were advice manuals for judges and for priests hearing confession. The *Disquisitiones* also marks an interesting halfway point between law and theology and to an extent, its author used his expertise in one field to stake a claim in the other. The Jesuit only obtained his doctorate in theology in 1602 and upon his death, he left a vast project of biblical exegesis unfinished.

At the same time, these different disciplines – in the traditional, orthodox way that our Jesuit conceived of them – shared the same foundations: texts. Delrio's direct experience with witchcraft was rather limited. The *Disquisitiones* lacked the empirical source base of, for instance, Pierre de Lancre's *Tableau* or, less directly, Nicolas Remy's *Demonolatreia*. Those works were built on trial testimony and thus authenticated to a large extent by their author's persona as a judge. As we have seen, Delrio's only personal encounter with magic as a magistrate was with a mandrake root. (If there were others, it is striking that he chose not to mention them and he certainly did not put them centre stage.) While Delrio was completing his manuscript, a friend based in Liège shared the records of one witchcraft trial – the curious 1597 case of the monk and magician Jean Delvaux – with him.[42] Delrio often referred to the Delvaux case, but these references feature in the margins or come at the end of paragraphs. They were added late in the writing process. It was not Delvaux, therefore, that prompted the writing of the *Disquisitiones*, but an encounter with a witch of considerably greater fame, a figure from Greek mythology: Medea.

The figure of Medea leads us back to Delrio's earlier writings. We saw how his 1576 edition of Senecan tragedy provided the budding magistrate with a platform to publicly say goodbye to his life as a student and classical scholar and to embrace another, that of law and government service. The edition contained passages that had to embarrass someone who entered the religious life. For instance, Delrio's annotations surveyed the different types of kisses discussed in classical Latin literature (from chaste to lascivious) and expressed admiration for Protestant or heterodox scholars – like Joseph Scaliger – whom no pious Catholic should praise.[43] Soon after his admission into the Society of Jesus, Delrio embarked on the project which removed – as he put it – 'the stains which infirmity of judgement, nature, and doctrine, or the fervour of [my] inconstant age had strewn' on the original edition.[44] This second edition, which appeared only in 1593–1594 but had been years in the making, was also aimed at a new audience: the students of the Jesuit colleges scattered across Europe and, indeed, beyond. The Society of Jesus had discovered that school theatre, performed by the students, was a perfect venue to educate parents and pupils alike in good Catholic values. The aim of Delrio's new set of notes, therefore, had been to make Seneca's fundamentally pagan plays safe for a Christian audience.

This was no small feat. The ten plays ascribed to the philosopher Seneca (although only eight are likely to have been written by him) tend to describe shockingly evil actions which go entirely unpunished. The *Thyestes*, for instance, involved the butchery of two innocent children so they could be fed to Thyestes, their unsuspecting father. (It was an inspiration for Shakespeare's equally gruesome *Titus Andronicus*.) Almost as problematic, from a Christian perspective, was the use and description of a wide-ranging set of practices of magic, witchcraft, and divination. Particularly important here was Seneca's most famous play, *Medea*. It recounts the witch's revenge on her husband Jason who had abandoned her for the daughter of King Creon of Corinth. Medea used her magic to kill the entire royal family and then in front of Jason, she killed their two sons as a final act of revenge for his betrayal, before flying off on a winged chariot unscathed and scot-free.[45]

Christianizing such nihilistic plays involved considerable ingenuity, and Delrio solved it partly by treating these plays not as myths, as we would now do, but as true history. This allowed him, for instance, to introduce other 'historical' facts in his notes, to excuse characters from blame or to foreshadow punishments not evident from the play itself. Yet, as true history these notes also provided Delrio with his first opportunity – years before the *Disquisitiones* – to comment on witchcraft in print, and he did so at length and with evident relish. Medea's potions and spells provoked extensive commentary, while her escape by air led to a discussion of the reality of demonic flight.[46]

The fact that the origins of the *Disquisitiones* can be traced back to a work of classical scholarship illustrates the extent to which it reflected a world made out of words. Yet, classical texts form only a small but significant part of its source base. Aside from the obligatory biblical and patristic sources, Delrio also drew extensively on medieval saints' lives and contemporary travel accounts. Both provided different types of demonic encounters. Successfully resisting temptation by the devil is an almost essential criteria for sainthood, while the various forms of pagan religion, whether practised by Indians in the New World or Buddhists in China and Japan, was from a Christian perspective nothing but demon worship in disguise. Much of the *Disquisitiones* accordingly is a carefully woven tapestry which brought together evidence of demonic activity from across space and time. In support of the reality of weather magic, for instance, Delrio marshalled the ancient Greek author Pausanias and a letter describing a Peruvian rain dance performed by Inca priests.[47] The garden-variety witch found in the villages of early modern Europe was, in effect, embedded in a much wider web of demonic activity, which made the evidence for their existence all the more compelling. The fact that the *Disquisitiones* was written not by a blinkered

190  *Jan Machielsen*

inquisitor but by a voracious bookworm, one who quite literally read until his eyes gave out, goes a long way to explaining the work's unusual longevity.[48]

## 4 The limitations of success

The textual foundations of the *Disquisitiones* help to explain why it outlasted many of its rivals and continued to be published well into the eighteenth century. The parallels it established between different types of textual sources provided the work with a sense of universality which, in turn, enhanced its overall credibility. The *Disquisitiones*, then, was no simple case study based on the observations of a single judge. As such, its scholarship proved considerably more difficult to dislodge. It was, after all, easier to impugn the credibility of a judge such as Nicolas Remy or Pierre de Lancre – whose credulity could be mocked, for instance – than a work that was, in essence, a compilation of hundreds of examples from many different sources. Like a game of Jenga, removing one example would not cause the edifice of the *Disquisitiones* to collapse. The Anglican theologian Meric Casaubon (1599–1671), thus relied heavily on Delrio's work, even though he was not always convinced: 'I will not say, that I believe every thing that he doth propose as true: it may be his faith doth in some things extend much further than mine: but I would have the quality of his witnesses well considered.'[49]

There are two reasons, though, to suspect that the long-term impact of the *Disquisitiones* on the early modern witch-hunt was something other than what its author had intended. In fact, an – entirely unprovable – case could be made that the *Disquisitiones* hampered rather than promoted witchcraft persecutions. Both reasons evolve around the work's textual origins and its author's expertise as an armchair scholar. Perhaps because its author had no *practical* legal experience, the *Disquisitiones*'s advice to judges struck a rather moderate tone. It claimed that it was better to let ten guilty go free than punish one innocent and argued that many grey (as in, dubious) pieces of evidence did not together make one white (solid) piece.[50] The *Disquisitiones* conveyed the idea that witch-hunting was possible in a measured and considerate fashion – and in that it was very much mistaken. Delrio had not appreciated the extent to which witch-hunting was possible only when rules limiting torture and the collection of evidence were flouted. To his dismay, he discovered that moderates and sceptics had seized on his words and interpreted them in their favour. When in 1602 he was consulted on a case of witchcraft by Duke Maximilian of Bavaria, he abandoned any appearance of moderation. He now defended, for instance, the use of testimony from the witches' sabbat, arguing that God would not permit the devil to deceive such witnesses.[51] He added an appendix to Book Five, his original manual for judges, which permitted a great deal more judicial discretion, but he confusingly also kept the original text. The result meant that later witchcraft sceptics, such as his fellow Jesuit Friedrich Spee, continued to use Delrio's seeming moderation in support of their arguments.[52]

Secondly and finally, the *Disquisitiones* as a work of textual scholarship also gradually became a work of historical scholarship, its examples growing increasingly dated over time. Insufficient attention has been given to those who stopped believing in the urgency of witchcraft as a contemporary problem but felt the need to defend it in the abstract for reasons of religious orthodoxy. As late as 1768, the founder of Methodism, John Wesley, confessed to his journal that witchcraft was 'one great proof of the invisible world' and giving it up was 'in effect giving up the Bible.' A few years later, in 1776, Wesley wrote that he could not give up the existence of witchcraft 'till I give up the credit of all history, sacred or profane.' Similarly, in New England, in 1773, Ezra Stiles, later the president of Yale College, mused in his diary how the 'Antient System is broken up, the Vessel of Sorcery shipwreckt and only some shattered planks and pieces disjoyned floating and scattered on the Ocean of the human Activity and Bustle'. Stiles explicitly believed that witchcraft had once been real: 'When the System was Intire, it was a direct seeking to Satan.'[53] The *Disquisitiones* spoke to an elite audience for whom witchcraft had ceased to be an every-day concern. Like its author, they likely never encountered a real witch, nor did they expect to. Yet, for religious reasons, such as those expressed by Wesley and Stiles, they felt the need to defend the existence of the spirit world and could therefore not give up on witchcraft in the abstract. Far from a call to action, by the eighteenth century the *Disquisitiones* had become a comfort blanket used for protection against the dangerous ideas of those who had little use for spirits or God at all.

## Notes

1. Martin Delrio, *Disquisitionum magicarum libri sex*, 3 vols, Leuven: Gerardus Rivius, 1599–1600, vol. 2, p. 226. Most of the information in this chapter is derived from my biography of Martin Delrio: Jan Machielsen, *Martin Delrio: Demonology and Scholarship in the Counter-Reformation*, Oxford: Oxford University Press, 2015.
2. An abbreviated translation of Delrio's *Disquisitiones magicae* appeared in 2000: [Martin Delrio], *Investigations into Magic*, trans. P. G. Maxwell-Stuart, Manchester: Manchester University Press, 2000. Dr Maxwell-Stuart is currently working on a complete translation of the *Disquisitiones* forthcoming with Brill Academic Publishers.
3. On Binsfeld, see Henry C. Lea, *Materials toward a History of Witchcraft*, Whitefish, MT: Kessinger Publishing, 2004, vol. 2, p. 593; see also the discussion by Thomas Stapleton: Jan Machielsen, 'On the Confessional Uses and History of Witchcraft: Thomas Stapleton's 1594 Witchcraft Oration', *Magic, Ritual, and Witchcraft*, 2018, vol. 13/3, 381–407, at 406.
4. For an example of a social historian being entrusted with a discussion of early modern demonology, see James Sharpe, 'The Demonologists' in Owen Davies, ed., *The Oxford Illustrated History of Witchcraft and Magic*, Oxford: Oxford University Press, 2017, pp. 65–96.

5 Aloïs Gerlo et al., eds, *Iusti Lipsi epistolae*, vol. 1: 1564–1483, p. 194 [ILE 78 03 04].
6 Machielsen, *Martin Delrio*, pp. 10–13.
7 Machielsen, *Martin Delrio*, p. 34.
8 Adrien Baillet, *Des Enfans devenus celebres par leurs etudes ou par leurs ecrits*, Paris: Antoine Dezallier, 1688, p. 196.
9 Machielsen, *Martin Delrio*, pp. 30–32.
10 Martin Delrio, *In L. Annaei Senecae … tragoedias decem … adversaria*, Antwerp: Christophe Plantin, 1576, p. 10.
11 Machielsen, *Martin Delrio*, pp. 128–30.
12 [Martin Delrio], *Mémoires de Martin Antoine Del Rio sur les troubles des Pays-Bas durant l'administration de Don Juan d'Autriche, 1576–1578*, trans. Adolphe C. H. Delvigne, 3 vols, Brussels: Société de l'histoire de Belgique, 1869–71; see also Machielsen, *Martin Delrio*, chap. 1.
13 Machielsen, *Martin Delrio*, p. 51.
14 On the Society of Jesus and its education mission, see John W. O'Malley, *The First Jesuits*, Cambridge, MA: Harvard University Press, 1993; on Delrio's Jesuit career, see Machielsen, *Martin Delrio*, chap. 2.
15 On Delrio's conflict with Joseph Scaliger, see Machielsen, *Martin Delrio*, chap. 13.
16 Delrio, *Disquisitiones* (1599), vol. 1, p. 7.
17 Martin Delrio, *Disquisitionum magicarum libri sex, in tres tomos partiti*, 3rd ed., Mainz: Johannes Albinus, 1603, sig.)()(4v [absent from the first ed.]; Delrio, *Disquistiones* (1599), vol. 1, p. 76.
18 Delrio, *Disquistiones* (1599), vol. 1, p. 247.
19 Delrio, *Disquisitiones* (1599), vol. 1, p. 76.
20 Delrio, *Disquisitiones* (1603), vol. 1, p. 16; on Luís or Louis Delrio (del Río), see Julie Versele, *Louis del Río, 1537–1578: Reflets d'une période troublée*, Brussels: Editions de l'Université de Bruxelles, 2004.
21 Machielsen, *Martin Delrio*, chap. 13.
22 Increase Mather, 'Cases of Conscience Concerning Witchcraft', in *A Further Account of the Tryals of the New-England Witches*, London: J. Dunton, 1693, p. 17.
23 Machielsen, *Martin Delrio*, p. 233.
24 Machielsen, *Martin Delrio*, p. 212.
25 For the history of 'superstition', see Euan Cameron, *Enchanted Europe: Superstition, Reason, and Religion, 1250–1750*, Oxford: Oxford University Press, 2010; S. A. Smith, 'Introduction', in *The Religion of Fools? Superstition*, Past and Present Supplement, 2008, vol. 3, pp. 7–55.
26 Delrio, *Disquisitiones* (1603), vol. 1, p. 121.
27 Delrio, *Disquisitiones* (1599), vol. 1, p. 9.
28 Machielsen, *Martin Delrio*, chap. 10.
29 Delrio, *Disquisitiones* (1600), vol. 2, p. 98.
30 Delrio, *Disquisitiones* (1600), vol. 2, p. 112.
31 Delrio, *Disquisitiones* (1600), vol. 2, p. 113.
32 Ronald Hutton, *The Witch: A History of Fear, from Ancient Times to the Present*, New Haven: Yale University Press, 2017, chap. 1.
33 Delrio, *Disquisitiones* (1599), vol. 1, p. 61.
34 Delrio, *Disquisitiones* (1599), vol. 1, p. 60.
35 Delrio, *Disquisitiones* (1600), vol. 2, p. 174.
36 Delrio, *Disquisitiones* (1600), vol. 2, p. 167.
37 Moshe Sluhovsky, *Believe Not Every Spirit: Possession, Mysticism, and Discernment in Early Modern Catholicism*, Chicago: University of Chicago Press, 2007.
38 Delrio, *Disquisitiones* (1600), vol. 2, p. 167.

39 On the Council of Trent, see in particular: John W. O'Malley, *Trent: What Happened at the Council* (Cambridge, MA: Harvard University Press, 2013).
40 Delrio, *Disquisitiones* (1599), vol. 1, p. 2.
41 See Delrio, *Disquisitionum magicarum libri sex, quibus continetur accurata curiosarum artium, et vanarum superstitionum confutatio*, Venice: Vincentius Florinus, 1616, title page.
42 Jean Fraikin, 'Un Épisode de la sorcellerie en Ardenne et en région mosellane: L'Affaire du moine de Stavelot, Dom Jean del Vaulx (1592–1597)', *Revue d'histoire ecclésiastique*, 1990, vol. 85/3–4, 650–68. The Delvaux case may, however, have inspired Delrio's choice of dedicatee. Ernest of Bavaria, Prince-Bishop of Liège, was ultimately responsible for Delvaux's trial and execution.
43 Machielsen, *Martin Delrio*, pp. 135, 132.
44 Machielsen, *Martin Delrio*, p. 104.
45 Machielsen, *Martin Delrio*, chaps 5–8. See also the classical study by Maturin Dréano, *Humanisme chrétien: La Tragédie latine commentée pour les chrétiens du XVIe siècle par Martin Antoine Del Rio*, Paris: Éditions Beauchesne, 1936.
46 Machielsen, *Martin Delrio*, chap. 8.
47 Delrio, *Disquisitiones* (1599), vol. 1, p. 155. See also Machielsen, *Martin Delrio*, chap. 10.
48 On Delrio's eyesight, see Machielsen, *Martin Delrio*, p. 15.
49 Meric Casaubon, *A Treatise Proving Spirits, Witches and Supernatural Operations by Pregnant Instances and Evidences*, London: Brabazon Aylmer, 1672, pp. 72–73.
50 Machielsen, *Martin Delrio*, p. 283.
51 Machielsen, *Martin Delrio*, pp. 288–89. On Delrio's involvement (from afar) in the Bavarian witch-hunt, see also Wolfgang Behringer, *Witchcraft Persecutions in Bavaria: Popular Magic, Religious Zealotry and Reason of State in Early Modern Europe*, Cambridge: Cambridge University Press, 2002, pp. 247–68.
52 This is a shortened version of the argument developed in Machielsen, *Martin Delrio*, chap. 11.
53 For Wesley and Stiles, see Machielsen, *Martin Delrio*, p. 267. On the decline of witchcraft belief in the later seventeenth and early eighteenth centuries, see also Ian Bostridge, *Witchcraft and Its Transformations, c.1650–c.1750*, Oxford: Clarendon Press, 1997.

## Further reading

Dréano, Maturin, *Humanisme chrétien: La Tragédie latine commentée pour les chrétiens du XVIe siècle par Martin Antoine Del Rio*, Paris: Éditions Beauchesne, 1936.
Fischer, Edda, *Die 'Disquisitionum magicarum libri sex' von Martin Delrio als gegenreformatorische Exempel-Quelle*, Frankfurt: Johann Wolfgang Goethe-Universität, 1975.
Machielsen, Jan, 'Friendship and Religion in the Republic of Letters: The Return of Justus Lipsius to Catholicism (1591)', *Renaissance Studies*, 2013, vol. 27/2, 161–182.
———, 'The Rise and Fall of Seneca Tragicus, c. 1365–1593', *Journal of the Warburg and Courtauld Institutes*, 2014, vol. 77, 61–85.
———. *Martin Delrio: Demonology and Scholarship in the Counter-Reformation*, Oxford: Oxford University Press, 2015.
Nagel, Petra, *Die Bedeutung der 'Disquisitionum magicarum libri sex' von Martin Delrio für das Verfahren in Hexenprozessen*, Frankfurt: Peter Lang, 1995.
Thomas, Werner, 'Martín Antonio Delrío and Justus Lipsius', in Marc Laureys, ed., *The World of Justus Lipsius: A Contribution towards His Intellectual Biography*, Brussels: Institut historique belge de Rome, 1998, pp. 345–366.

# Part 4
# Demonology and theology

## 12 'Of ghostes and spirites walking by nyght'

Ludwig Lavater's *Von Gespänsten*

*Pierre Kapitaniak*

> It is a common custome in many places, that at a certaine time of the yeare, one with a nette or visarde on his face maketh Children afrayde, to the ende that ever after they shoulde laboure and be obedient to their Parentes, afterward they tel them that those which they saw, were Bugs, Witches and Hagges, which thing they verily beléeve, and are commonly, miserablie afrayde. [...] It chaunced once at Tigurine [Zurich] where we dwell, that certayne plesaunt yong men disguising themselves, daunced aboute the Churcheyarde, one of them playing on a beere with two bones, as it were on a drumme. Wich thing when certaine men had espied, they noysed it about the citie, how they had seene dead men daunce, and that there was greate daunger, least there should shortly ensue some plague or pestilence.[1]

Thus wrote the Swiss Reformed theologian Ludwig Lavater, whose *Von Gespänsten* (Of Ghosts, 1569) remains one of the most comprehensive sources on ghost lore in sixteenth-century Europe. Lavater appears here as a champion battling against ancient superstitions that people perpetuated either because of ancestral popular fears or because of more immediate trauma caused by recurrent plague epidemics. Maybe it was one such an outbreak of the plague, which repeatedly afflicted Zurich between 1564 and 1566,[2] that drove Lavater to dwell upon so morbid a subject. Certainly, he must have witnessed an increase in reported cases of haunting and other similar wonders following the high death toll in his city.

Yet Lavater did not set up to write *Von Gespänsten* because he personally experienced visions or apparitions (at least he never alludes to any such episode), nor had he, like many jurists or ecclesiastics writing about witchcraft, been involved in or witnessed a specific witch trial.[3] Although writing in Switzerland, one of the epicentres of the early modern witch-hunt, Lavater did not focus on witchcraft – a subject treated very marginally in his treatise – perhaps because the witch-craze that inflamed that region started only in the early 1580s.[4] In his treatise, he endeavoured a systematic examination of spiritual apparitions, but, as the quotation above suggests, witchcraft was at that time part of a wider network of beliefs in the manifestations of supernatural forces and the possibility of their interaction with human agents. Nevertheless, his treatise soon became very influential and came to be quoted by numerous authors writing on witchcraft in the following decades. What made this possible was the reshaping of the invisible world by the sixteenth-century Reformation and the privileged role that this new theology bestowed on the devil and his minions. 'Bugs, Witches and Hagges' became just some of the devil's appearances among men, while the father of lies inserted himself all the more easily among the falsehoods and deceptions spread according to the reformed preachers by a decayed and decadent Church of Rome.

The following pages will elucidate the various motivations that triggered Lavater's project as well as the reasons for its success, not only as a profuse quarry of stories about marvels and prodigies, but also as a leading voice in the doctrinal debate about the devil's powers and consequently as an authority in the demonological field.

## 1 Lavater's life before the writing of *Von Gespänsten*

Ludwig Lavater was born in Kyburg, in the canton of Zurich, in 1527,[5] only a decade after the onset of the Reformation. His father, Hans Rudolf Lavater was the bailiff of Kyburg and in 1536 the family moved to Zurich, where Lavater's father climbed the administrative ladder from member of the Small Council to mayor.[6] Hans Rudolf Lavater was an early supporter of the Reformation and a close friend of Heinrich Bullinger, Zurich's principal Reformer.[7] Young Ludwig attended school at the Kappel Abbey and then from 1543 at the Carolinum College in Zurich. Like many young men whose families could afford it, he carried on his theology studies during the mid-1540s at several European universities, first in Strasbourg, then in Paris, in the *Collège de Presles* under the famous French humanist Petrus Ramus who later converted to Calvinism, and who kept an epistolary exchange with Lavater until his murder during the 1572 St Bartholomew's Day massacre.[8] From Paris, Lavater moved to Lausanne to study under Pierre Viret, who had been responsible for introducing the Reformation there and who had only recently published a series of dialogues on the souls of the dead.[9] Lavater finished his European tour travelling through the north of Italy and returning through the Canton of Grisons.

Back from his travels in 1550, Lavater married Heinrich Bullinger's daughter Margaretha on 8 May 1550. The same year he was ordained in Zurich to become archdeacon of the Grossmünster, Zurich's principal church. It is also thanks to Bullinger that he started to work with the printer Christoph Froschauer, by translating one of his father-in-law's works into Latin in 1553.[10] In the ensuing decade, Lavater published extensively with the same printer: an explanation of the rites of the Zurich church (1559), two volumes of biblical commentary on the Book of Proverbs (1562) and on Joshua (1565), as well as a short essay on the plague (1564).

After this period of intensive publication (on average one volume a year), there is a four-year gap in Lavater's publishing activities, which suggests that the author took more time in composing his most famous *Von Gespänsten*, first printed in German, early in 1569 in Zurich again by Christoph Froschauer.[11] At the age of 42, Lavater was then an experienced preacher and theologian who had already become something of an authority on biblical exegesis, especially when it came to angels and demons.[12]

## 2 The structure of the treatise

*Von Gespänsten* is a relatively short treatise, a small 15cm octavo of less than 300 pages. The treatise displays continuity with Lavater's previous writings, which all served clear pastoral and devotional aims. Written after the end of the Council of Trent in 1563 which strongly reaffirmed the Catholic belief in Purgatory, it provides a comprehensive synthesis of Protestant beliefs on the apparitions of spirits – be they angels, devils, or souls of the deceased. The dissertation is divided into three parts, devoted respectively to diverse phenomena mistaken for apparitions, to true apparitions of angels or devils, and to the way a god-fearing person is expected to deal with such manifestations and correctly identify them.

The first book may appear quite sceptical as it starts with a review of a wide range of apparitions that are not to be believed. Among them Lavater lists visions experienced by fearful or mentally unstable people, or by those who suffer from impaired senses or melancholy. He also dwells on natural phenomena often mistaken for ghosts of the departed, and devotes several chapters to those who fake apparitions, singling out among them his Catholic adversaries, especially monks and priests. Here we find some of the most celebrated examples of Catholic fraud, such as the four Jacobin monks who staged a false apparition to chase the rival Franciscan order from Bern,[13] the Franciscan monk in Orleans who pretended to be the spirit of a deceased Lutheran lady,[14] and the parish priest in Chiavenna who impersonated the Virgin Mary.[15] After this long catalogue of fraudulent apparitions, Lavater turns to those that cannot be denied, from Antiquity to ecclesiastic and patristic writings to the most recent contemporary authors, founding his demonstrations on the few biblical (and hence irrefutable) examples of spiritual apparitions. Thus, Lavater reads Isaiah's prophecy against the Babylonians (Isaiah 34) in a way that vouchsafes the possibility of spirits sent by God to punish those who strayed away from him:

> In y$^e$ ruinous & tottering Pallaces, Castles, & houses, horrible spirits shal apeare with terrible cries, and the Satyre shal cal unto hir mate, yea & the night hags shal take their rest there. For by the sufferance of God, wicked Devils worke strange things in those places where men have exercised pride and crueltie.[16]

In order to strengthen his evidence, Lavater glosses the wicked '*dæmonia onocentauris*' mentioned in the Vulgate as '*spiritus horrendi*' (dreadful spirits), rendering these biblical monsters closer to ghosts.[17]

In the second book Lavater undertakes to prove that all apparitions are either angels or demons, and he debunks all Catholic beliefs relative to the haunting of the souls of the dead who had escaped from Purgatory. He spends several chapters on a close exegesis of the Old Testament episode of the Witch of Endor, regularly used by Catholic theologians to prove the possibility of the souls of the dead visiting the living. In 1 Samuel 28, Saul consults a Pythoness before a decisive battle, and she conjures the soul of the prophet Samuel to prophesy. For Catholics, the witch conjures up the real soul of Samuel from the dead, but Lavater (like other reformed theologians before him) argues that Samuel was in reality the witch's familiar demon, taking on the appearance of the deceased prophet in order to deceive the king. After a lengthy demonstration Lavater concludes his second book with the idea that a large majority of apparitions are the devil's work.

The third and last book is the most pastoral as Lavater explains why God allows such apparitions and what a good Christian should do when confronted with a spirit claiming to be someone's soul. Above all, he insists on the fact that apparitions are seldom true nowadays as the age of miracles is past and there is no longer any need for such proofs of God's will. Consequently, most apparitions are the devil's deceitful doing and, as the devil cannot work any mischief against the godly without God's permission, the only real remedy is to be firm in one's faith, pray, fast, and amend one's sinful life. The book's conclusion is to reform all good Christians, beseeching the Lord

> to deliver all suche as are still entangled in [Catholic] superstition and errours, and to graunt those whome he hath delyvered hys Heavenly grace, that they be always thankful for so great a benefite, least they be wrapped againe in the same mischiefe.[18]

But, as Bruce Gordon has observed, beyond this avowed aim, Lavater denies lay people any capacity to discern spirits advising them to turn to the Church and its professionals.[19]

## 3 Sources and influences

The book was dedicated to Johannes Steiger (1518–1581), 'Consul of the noble Commonwelth of Berna' since 1562. The preface suggests that he was not a direct acquaintance of Lavater's, but rather that of Georg Grebel (1516–1607), member of the Zurich Council, and '[his] olde companion'. According to the author's preface, *Von Gespänsten* is indebted to the writings of Johann Rivius (1500–1553), Joachim Camerarius (1500–1574), Johann Wier° (1515–1588), Gaspar Peucer (1525–1602), and Ludwig Milich

(1530–1575). These are of course not the only influences of Lavater's treatise and interestingly enough, none of these authors is ever mentioned again in the text, although Lavater quotes them now and then without acknowledging the details of each borrowing. Surprisingly, authors who were geographically much closer to Lavater are not put forward here (though they are mentioned in the course of the text), including Konrad Gesner who lived in the same city as Lavater and displayed a similar curiosity about wonders and prodigies and Johannes Stumpf who settled in Zurich in 1548 to publish a chronicle of Switzerland. Like Lavater, both published with Christoph Froschauer.

In fact, the choice of the authorities mentioned in the preface tells us more about Lavater's doctrinal position than about the genesis of his work. With the exception of Rivius (the only author to have written a whole work on apparitions before Lavater), all these authors were still alive in 1569. They were also all German, with the exception of Wier (the main source of a significant part of the material in the treatise),[20] who was born and educated in the Netherlands but worked as the physician to the Duke of Cleves. All of them were actively engaged in the Reformation and their doctrinal sympathies lay close to Luther and Melanchthon.

Like all other Protestants, Lavater rejects the medieval doctrine of Purgatory on the grounds that Scripture never alludes to any such place and consequently he also discards the possibility for the souls of the dead to return, as those who are already in Heaven would never wish to leave it, while those in Hell would never be allowed to. This is, of course, hardly an original position since such arguments had already been developed by Luther or by Calvin. Yet it is as if Lavater was cautious not to align himself with the two leading figures of the Reformation. He never directly quotes Luther (though he often mentions the ill-treatment of Luther's sect when quoting anecdotes reported by Protestant historians and chroniclers) and he inserts only one short reference to Calvin.[21] When he quotes Melanchthon it is only for the sake of his personal experience of ghostly visions, rather than his theological positions:

> Phillip Malancthon writeth in his booke *de anima*, that he himselfe hathe seene some spirites, and that he hath knowne many men of good credite, whiche have avoutched not only to have séene ghostes them selves, but also y$^t$ they have talked a great while with them.[22]

This relative discretion in using contemporary reformed authorities has led Bruce Gordon to conclude that Lavater's principal aim in writing *Von Gespänsten* was not doctrinal but pastoral.[23] He was hoping to reach as wide an audience as possible.

Lavater's originality is to go beyond biblical and patristic arguments to include pagan as well as contemporary popular stories of apparitions, extracted not only from chronicles and histories but also from works of natural philosophy. The effect is to offer the reader an impressive bulk of evidence whose very volume constitutes its most cogent strength. His choice of authorities also reflects a synthesis between pastoral literature, heavily influenced by the growing fashion of so-called *Teufelbücher* – moralising texts that were using devils to personify diverse sins – that had been circulating in Germany since the late 1540s,[24] embodied by Milich, and a more scholarly dissertation on demonology, whose post-Tridentine revival was foreshadowed by Wier.

## 4 Reformed scepticism?

Because witchcraft is not Lavater's main focus, it is not readily apparent that he in fact shares Wier's scepticism at least to some extent. In *De praestigiis daemonum*, Wier was able to discard most beliefs about witchcraft and witches' skills, because of the great powers which he attributed to the devil.[25] For exactly the same reason, Lavater's scepticism is strongest in the first part of his treatise when he discards everything that is not a real angelic or demonic apparition and specifically targets the machinations of the Catholic clergy bent on extorting money from their credulous flock. To give but one example of a more personal anecdote added by Lavater to the ever-growing corpus of stories about popish clerical deceit, here is one that was aimed at the Society of Jesus, the most prominent Catholic religious order of the time:

> While I was writing these things, it was reported unto me by credible persons, that in Auguste [Augsburg], a noble citie of Germanye, this present yeare 1569. there was a mayde and certeine other men servants in a great mans family, which litle regarded the sect of the Jesuite Friers: & that one of the sayd order made promise to their master, that he would easyly bring them to an other opinion: & so disguising him selfe like unto a Dyvell was hid in a privie corner of y$^e$ house: unto the which place, one of the maides going, either of hir owne accorde to fetch some thing, or being sente by hir master, was by y$^e$ disguised Jesuite made marvellously afrayde: whiche thing she presently declared unto one of the men servants, exhorting him in any wise to take heede of the place. Who shortly after going to the same place, & laying hold on his dagger, sodeynly stabbed in the counterfeit divell, as he came rushing on him.[26]

Such stories had a double objective: on the one hand to attract the reader's attention to the duplicity of the Catholic adversary; on the other to open their eyes to the frequent possibility of human agency in apparently supernatural incidents and thus to offer a reformed version of the Catholic practice of *discretio spirituum* or discernment of spirits.

By contrast, in the second part of his book, which following the rejection of Purgatory transforms ghosts into demons and ghost lore into demonology, Lavater's reformed scepticism vanishes into thin air faced with the belief in the real power of the devil which is ever more firmly reasserted.

Wier and Lavater agreed upon the danger represented by the actions of devils, but whereas for the former this contributed to exonerate powerless, deluded witches, for the latter it only constituted a shift in the supernatural agencies responsible for the apparitions. By removing the possibility of both angelic visitations (as the age of divine miracles had passed) and 'real' ghosts (as there was no Purgatory for them to escape from), demonic deceptions had become both more prominent and more important. As a result, where Wier used the devil's power to weaken the threat that witches represented, Lavater increased the threat posed by apparitions of spirits. The devil's hand was thus increasingly to be found lurking behind each apparition.

## 5 Witchcraft and the Witch of Endor

Even if *Von Gespänsten* does not address the question of witchcraft, it still harbours a few insights on the subject insofar as it is contiguous to that of ghosts. This certainly accounts for its success among various writers on witchcraft in the ensuing decades as is attested by the fact that the treatise was included in a collection of texts on witchcraft as early as 1586.[27] In *Theatrum de veneficis*, a compendium of seventeen treatises in, or translated into German, and gathered by the Frankfurt printer Nicolaus Bassaeus, Lavater stands alongside Ulrich Molitor, Johann Wier, Lambert Daneau, Richard Lutz, Johann Ewich, or Johann Trithemius, all of whom devoted their writings to the discussion of the witches' powers.

If Lavater is deemed a relevant authority on witches, it is because of one biblical episode that combined preoccupations both with ghosts and with witchcraft. In Wier's wake, Lavater denies witches any real power, and more specifically for the purpose of his argument on ghosts, their power to raise the dead. Relying on the authority of the Church Father John Chrysostom, he argues that the devil 'put this false opinion in mens heads, that those persons soules whyche by violent death departed, were turned into Dyvels, & so dyd service unto witches and soothsayers.'[28] Of course, Lavater's main contribution to the demonological debate on witchcraft rested on the sole biblical example of a soul visiting the living, that of the prophet Samuel summoned by the Witch of Endor to prophesy to Saul. Lavater devotes two chapters to the case, first to list all the arguments proving the devil's limited powers and his inability to raise the dead, then to refute all the arguments defending the appearance of the real Samuel in front of Saul.[29]

Judging from those chapters and a few scattered remarks on witches, it is difficult to gauge how much power Lavater grants witches and sorcerers:

> I will speake nothing at this time, of those olde sorcerers, Apollonius and others, of whom the histories report straunge and incredible things. Hagges, witches and inchaunters are sayde to hurte men and cattell, if they do but touche them or stroake them, they do horrible things wherof there are whole bookes extant. Jugglers and tumblers, by

nimblenesse do many things, they will bid one eate meate, which when they spit out agayne, they cast forth ordure and such like. Magitians, jugglers, inchanters, and Necromanciers, are no other than servants of the Divel: do you not thinke their mayster reserveth some cunning unto him selfe?

Howbeit this is not to bée dissembled, y$^t$ the Diuel doth glory of many things whiche in déede he cannot performe: as that he saith, that he raiseth y$^e$ dead out of their graves. &c. He may in very déede by Gods sufferaunce, shewe the shapes of them unto men, but he hath no suche power over the dead bodies.[30]

This passage seems to suggest that Lavater, following in Wier's footsteps, more readily believed in the dangers posed by male magicians rather than female witches but that his overriding concern was the devil's power to deceive. Lavater may also have lacked the incentive to discuss witchcraft as Zurich had experienced very few witch trials and executions compared to other cantons of Switzerland. There had not been a single execution for witchcraft in the city of Zurich, during the period following his return home after completing his studies in 1550 and 1569, when his treatise was published.[31] It is obviously much easier to disbelieve the powers of witches and the danger they may represent when the reports of their exploits are mainly hearsay.

## 6 Success and reception

The German edition of the book was not particularly successful, although it still went through another edition by Froschauer in 1578, before being included in the above-mentioned collection of demonological works in the year of Lavater's death. In the meantime, Lavater immediately aimed at a broader audience by translating it himself into Latin the following year. Publication in Geneva in 1570 with the prominent printer Jean Crespin (most likely recommended to him by his father-in-law) allowed the text to reach a European audience.[32] It proved an inspired move, as this new edition was quickly followed by a French translation, as *Trois Livres de spectres* in 1571, and an English one, as *Of Ghostes and Spirits Walking by Night* in 1572.[33] A Dutch translation followed a few years later in 1591. Taken together, 21 different editions had appeared by 1687.

Unsurprisingly, the Latin and French translations triggered a wave of Catholic refutations from France, as the other languages targeted more exclusively Protestant readers. The earliest riposte came from the Parisian ultra-Catholic academic elite. Juan Maldonado°, a Jesuit theologian from Extremadura, was one of the most erudite scholars of his generation, who at the time was teaching at the *Collège de Clermont* in Paris, where he had been sent from Rome to inaugurate the chair of theology in 1563.[34] Though delivered in Latin, his lessons aimed at a larger audience and met with immense success, if we are to trust the testimonies of his eloquence. In the autumn 1570,[35] in one of his lectures on angels and devils, Maldonado openly attacked Lavater for denying the existence of Purgatory:

> But Jacques [sic] Lavater and other Calvinists wrongly deny that they [i.e. souls] appear, as the consequence of their denying the [existence of] Purgatory, because their Doctor Calvin, in the third book of Institutions, chapter fifteen, denies that souls enjoy a happy life before Judgement Day. Moreover, since Angels, both good and evil, appear, why would souls not appear as well?[36]

Yet Maldonado did not go into any detail about Lavater's arguments and it was only at the moment of Lavater's death in 1586 that the two most virulent and extensive attacks on his treatise saw the day. The author of the first probably attended some of Maldonado's famous lectures. Indeed, Pierre Le Loyer was 20 years old in 1570 and a young student of ancient languages in Paris. It would have been easy for him to attend the Jesuit's open lectures. The following year, Le Loyer left Paris for Toulouse with a brand new ambition of pursuing a law degree.[37] It is even possible that Le Loyer met Maldonado personally, if he is the 'Petrus Lohierius' that Maldonado mentions in a letter of April 1570.[38] Sixteen years later, Pierre Le Loyer published a voluminous treatise on the question of spectres in which his main adversary was Lavater. Ironically, *Quatre Livres des spectres* (1586) was handed to George Nepveu, his Angers printer, only a fortnight before Lavater died in Zurich.[39] Le Loyer's objective was very clearly stated in this thousand-page-long treatise, namely to write:

> agaynst certaine perverse spirits and brainsicke persons of our age, who have invented most strange and variable opinions: as also agaynst some new Dogmatists, who to the intent they might secretly insinuate (as I suppose) into the minds of men, an error of the Epicures: That the soules of men have no being after death) have altogether denied their apparition.[40]

Le Loyer saw Lavater just as such a new Dogmatist and he made it explicit elsewhere in his book: 'Lavater and other new Dogmatists of our century.'[41] For him, Lavater was a heretic, and although he never actually used the term to describe him, because his aim was not overtly polemical, he regularly reminded the reader of the Swiss preacher's reformed views when referring to him as 'Lavater and before him Calvin and some other of the same sect', or 'Lavater and those of his religion.'[42] Although, the first book of his treatise follows a pattern similar to Lavater's, focusing on the apparitions of angels, demons, and diverse misinterpretations of natural phenomena, later Le Loyer's aim is to reaffirm 'the apparition of souls and whether they can return on earth with God's will' against 'whatever Lavater and his kind say to the contrary.'[43] He clearly voices his suspicion of Protestant authors, when just after commenting on an anecdote reported by Lavater, he concludes somehow peremptorily that he himself 'will always be, with the theologians, of the contrary opinion to Wier and Alciato.'[44] The French lawyer was well aware of the highly polemical implications of this demonological debate. When he commented on a story found in Boccacio's *Decameron*, of a monk who pretended to be the angel Gabriel in order to enjoy a Venetian lady's favours, he refused to come to a decision about its veracity, preferring to accuse Lavater and other Protestant authors of deliberately tarnishing the clergy's reputation:

> For my part, I will not assure the same to be true, no more then I will assure many things to this purpose, which Sleydan, Lavater, and other Protestants have set downe in their writings; the which ought so much the more to be suspected, because their intention is alwaies to oppose themselves against the honor of the Clergie, and to spare nothing, (bee it by right, or by wrong) that they thinke may bring them into the scandall and dislike of the world.[45]

A second French voice made itself heard barely a year later. The Franciscan Noël Taillepied, newly promoted as a lector to the convent of Rouen, published *Psichologie, ou Traité de l'apparition des esprits* early in 1588.[46] In fact, Taillepied extensively plagiarised the contents of Lavater's treatise, inverting the arguments against the original author's Protestant views.[47] He seems to have been quite successful in this task as, in the French language at least, *Psichologie* actually superseded Lavater's translation which was never reprinted again after 1581,[48] while *Psichologie* underwent no fewer than 12 more editions by 1667. This can be seen as a Catholic triumph. More likely, the continued popularity shows that readers simply valued ghost treatises for their cornucopia of (entertaining) folk tales.

In England, Lavater's book met with the opposite reception. For obvious doctrinal reasons, the ideas advocated by the Zurich pastor resonated with the Calvinist scepticism of the Church of England towards Catholic superstitions. One of the first English writers to refer to Lavater as an authority on apparitions was John Woolton (c.1537–1594), a reformed priest ordained in 1560, after a short exile during the reign of Mary Tudor, who was later appointed Bishop of Exeter. In his *Treatise of the Immortalitie of the Soule* (1576), he wrote against Purgatory, his main argument being the absence of any biblical evidence, and resting his case with an inevitable analysis of the episode of the Witch of Endor:

> There is no example in the whole bible of any such apparition of the dead. For those thinges which are spoken of Samuel, do nothing strengthen this popish error. That Warwolfe or Maske was not Samuel, but satan him selfe, who partly by the predictions uttered by Samuel yet alyve, and partly by the horror of the whole campe; did divine the ende and event of the battaile the day following.

But I cease to say any more of this matter, & do referre the Readers desirous to reade more of this matter unto that pleasant booke of Lavaterus, translated into our mother toung, and intituled *of the walking of soules & ghostes in the night season*, where that man with great varietie, learning, and judgement, prosecuteth this matter.⁴⁹

But if, for Woolton, Lavater had definitely and successfully argued the case and nothing more needed to be added, a few years later one of the most sceptical voices in England made Lavater his main authority in writing the famous *Discoverie of Witchcraft* (1584).⁵⁰ Reginald Scot°'s denunciation of witch-hunts and 'witchmongers', as he designated those who thrived on the persecution of witches, heavily relied on the opinions and examples of Johann Wier and Ludwig Lavater, while making the authors of the *Malleus maleficarum* and Jean Bodin° the main targets of his derision. Unlike Lavater, Scot rejected any possibility of interaction between the spiritual and the terrestrial worlds thus not only denying the powers of witches over humans but also those of angels and demons over the terrestrial world.⁵¹ His scepticism was most notoriously displayed in his dealing with the inescapable episode of the Witch of Endor for which Scot offered a third interpretation: the Pythoness was a skilled ventriloquist who only made Saul believe in the existence of Samuel's soul.

Although Lavater himself never revisited the subject, history seems to have reserved an ironical coda to his best-selling book. In 1585, after years as archdeacon, he succeeded Rudolf Gwalther as minister (or *antistes*) at the Grossmünster. Lavater would not long enjoy this promotion, as he passed away on 15 July 1586. Yet, it was on his watch that Zurich at long last saw another witchcraft execution. Anna Kaufmann von Oberwil was burned at the stake on 28 May 1586, after her plea for a pardon for the sake of her three starving children was turned down.⁵² Whatever Lavater's role in Kaufmann's trial, her death took place just as his *Von Gespänsten* was given a new lease of life as part of a German compendium of demonological treatises on witchcraft: the *Theatrum de veneficis*.

## Notes

1 Ludwig Lavater, *Of Ghostes and Spirites Walking by Nyght, and of Strange Noyses, Crackes, and Sundry Forewarnynges, Whiche Commonly Happen before the Death of Menne, Great Slaughters, [and] Alterations of Kyngdomes*, London: Henry Benneyman for Richard Watkyns, 1572, pp. 21–22 (bk I, chap. v; all references to this edition).
2 See Edward-A. Eckert, 'Boundary Formation and Diffusion of Plague: Swiss Epidemics from 1562 to 1669', *Annales de Démographie Historique*, 1978, pp. 49–80.
3 For instance, in his *Démonomanie* (1580), Jean Bodin refers to the trial of Jeanne Harvillier in 1578, and in *The Discoverie of Witchcraft* (1584), Reginald Scot refers to the St Osyth trial, instructed by Brian Darcy in 1582.
4 See Brian P. Levack, *The Witch-Hunt in Early Modern Europe*, 2nd ed., 1995, London: Longman, 1987, pp. 22–23.

5 Georg von Wyß, 'Lavater, Ludwig' in Rochus Freiherr von Liliencron et al., eds, *Allgemeine Deutsche Biographie*, Leipzig: Duncker & Humblot, 1883, vol. 18, pp. 83–84.
6 Heinzpeter Stucki, 'Lavater, Hans Rudolf' (20 November 2008), in *Dictionnaire historique de la Suisse*, <www.hls-dhs-dss.ch/textes/f/F18088.php≥ (Last Accessed 23 July 2019).
7 Bruce Gordon, *The Swiss Reformation*, Manchester: Manchester University Press, 2002, p. xvi.
8 See Timothy Chesters, *Ghost Stories in Late Renaissance France: Walking by Night*, Oxford: Oxford University Press, 2011, p. 66.
9 Pierre Viret, *Disputations chrestiennes, en maniere de deviz, divisées par dialogues*, Geneva: Jehan Girard, 1544. Later a dialogue on demons and witches was added to the collection: *Le Monde demoniacle*, Geneva: Jaques Berthet, 1561.
10 Heinrich Bullinger, *De sacro sancta coena domini nostri Iesu Christi, qua forma, quo ritu et in quem finem eam instituerit quomodo item ad ipsam nos praeparari oporteat, Homiliae II*, Zurich: Christoph Froschauer, 1553.
11 Ludwig Lavater, *Von Gespänsten unghüren fälen und anderen wunderbaren Dingen so merteils wenn die Menschen sterben söllend oder wenn sunst grosse Sachen unnd Enderungen vorhanden sind beschähend kurtzer und einfaltiger Bericht*, Zurich: Christoph Froschauer, 1569.
12 For example, in a book published posthumously in 1568, the Lutheran pastor Jodocus Hocker (d. 1566) quoted Lavater on questions related to devils: Jodocus Hocker, *Der Teufel Selbs*, Ursel: Nicholas Heinrich, 1568, vol. 2, chap. 39, p. 237.
13 Lavater, *Of Ghostes*, pp. 28–37 (bk I, chap. vii).
14 Lavater, *Of Ghostes*, pp. 37–41 (bk I, chap. viii).
15 Lavater, *Of Ghostes*, pp. 41–43 (bk I, chap. ix).
16 Lavater, *Of Ghostes*, p. 91 (bk I, chap. xviii).
17 Isaiah, 34:14. Quoted in Lavater, *De spectris*, Geneva: Jean Crespin, 1570, p. 110 (bk I, chap. xix). 'Dæmonia onocentauris' is rendered in English as 'straunge visures & monsterous beastes' (Bishops' Bible), 'demons and monsters' (Douay/Rheims), 'wild beasts of the desert … wild beasts of the island' (King James Bible).
18 Lavater, *Of Ghostes*, p. 220.
19 Bruce Gordon, 'Malevolent Ghosts and Ministering Angels: Apparitions and Pastoral Care in the Swiss Reformation', in Bruce Gordon and Peters Marshall, eds, *The Place of the Dead in late Medieval and Early Modern Europe*, Cambridge: Cambridge University Press, 2000, p. 100.
20 The following authors are quoted at second hand from Wier's treatise: George Agricola, Alessandro Alessandri, Benno, George Buchanan, Philipp Melancthon, Johannes Nauclerus, Bartolomeo Platina, Sulpicius Severus, Johannes Sleidanus as well as some quotations from Augustine and Athanasius.
21 Lavater, *Of Ghostes*, p. 117 (bk II, chap. v).
22 Lavater, *Of Ghostes*, p. 70 (bk I, chap. xv).
23 Gordon, 'Malevolent Ghosts', p. 99.
24 On the *Teufelbücher* tradition, see Kathleen Crowther, 'From Seven Sins to Lutheran Devils: Sin and Social Order in an Age of Confessionalization' in Patrick Gilli, ed., *La Pathologie du pouvoir: Vices, crimes et délits des gouvernants; Antiquité, Moyen Âge, époque moderne*, Leiden: Brill, 2016, pp. 485–524; Keith L. Roos, *The Devil in Sixteenth Century German Literature: The Teufelsbücher*, Bern: Herbert Lang, 1972.
25 See Michaela Valente's chapter on Wier in the present volume.
26 Lavater, *Of Ghostes*, p. 44 (bk I, chap. ix).

27 *Theatrum de veneficis*, Frankfurt: Nicolaus Bassaeus, 1586, pp. 115–92.
28 Lavater, *Of Ghostes*, p. 122 (bk II, chap. v).
29 Lavater, *Of Ghostes*, p. 131–45 (bk II, chaps vii–viii).
30 Lavater, *Of Ghostes*, pp.170–71 (bk II, chap. xviii).
31 Zurich experienced 79 executions between 1487 and 1701, against a total of ca.10,000 executions in Switzerland. See Otto Sigg, *Hexenprozesse mit Todesurteil: Justizmorde der Zunftstadt Zürich*, Zurich: Frick, 2012, p. 13. For the more general picture, see Levack, *The Witch-Hunt*, pp. 21–26.
32 Bullinger had published several books with Jean Crespin in the 1550s: *Consensio mutua in re sacramentaria ministrorum Tigurinae Ecclesiae, et D. Joannis Calvini ministri Genevensis Ecclesiae* (1551), *Resolution de tous les poincts de la religion chrestienne, comprise en dix livres* (1557, 1559), *Cent Sermons sur l'Apocalypse de Jesus Christ, revelée par l'ange du Seigneur* (1558).
33 Lavater, *Of Ghostes*, London: Henry Benneyman for Richard Watkyns, 1572; reprinted London, Thomas Creede, 1596.
34 See the chapter on Juan Maldonado in the present volume.
35 For the chronology of Maldonado's lectures see Paul Schmitt, *La Réforme catholique: Le Combat de Maldonat, 1534–1583*, Paris, Beauchesne, 1985, pp. 413–14.
36 Juan Maldonado, *Traicté des anges et demons*, Rouen: Jacques Besongne, 1616 [first ed. 1605], fols 177v–178v.
37 Célestin Port, *Dictionnaire historique, géographique, et biographique de Maine-et-Loire*, Paris: J.-B. Dumoulin, 1876, vol. 2, p. 492.
38 Jean-Marie Prat, *Maldonat et l'Université de Paris au XVIe siècle*, Paris: Julien, Lanier & co, 1856, p. 582.
39 Note the dedication to Catherine de' Medici dated on 21 June 1586. Lavater died on 5 July 1586.
40 Pierre Le Loyer, *Quatre Livres des spectres*, Angers: Georges Nepveu, 1586, vol. 1, sig. *ijr. Translated by Zachary Jones, *A Treatise of Specters*, London: Matthew Lownes, 1605, sig. A3v.
41 Le Loyer, *Quatre Livres*, vol. 2, p. 91 (bk III, chap. vi). My translation, as only book I was translated by Jones.
42 Le Loyer, *Quatre Livres*, vol. 2, p. 104, 123 (bk. III, chap. viii), but see also vol. 2, p. 91 (bk III, chap. vi), 96, 99, 103 (bk III, chap. vii), 105 (bk. III, chap. viii), 135, 139 (bk. III, chap. ix).
43 Le Loyer, *Quatre Livres*, vol. 2, p. 167 (bk III, chap. xi).
44 Le Loyer, *Quatre Livres*, vol. 1, p. 533 (bk II, chap. v). The anecdote is found in Lavater, *Of Ghostes*, p. 93 (bk I, chap. xviii).
45 Le Loyer, *Quatre Livres*, vol. 1, p. 191 (bk I, chap. vii), trans. Z. Jones, fol. 88v.
46 Noël Taillepied, *Psichologie, ou Traité de l'apparition des esprits, à scavoir des âmes séparées, fantosmes, prodiges et accidents merveilleux qui précèdent quelquefois la mort des grands personnages ou signifient changemens de la chose publique*, Paris: Guillaume Bichon, 1588. The dedicatory epistle is dated 1 December 1587.
47 See Pierre Kapitaniak, 'Noël Taillepied and Ludwig Lavater: Emprunt et adversité au cœur d'un débat démonologique post-tridentin', in Marie Couton et al., eds, *Emprunt, plagiat, réécriture aux XVe, XVIe, XVIIe siècles*, Clermont-Ferrand: Presses Universitaires Blaise Pascal, 2006, pp. 447–65.
48 The last French edition of Lavater's treatise was published in Zurich by Guillaume des Marescz in 1581.
49 John Woolton, *A Treatise of the Immortalitie of the Soule*, London: John Shepperd, 1576, fols 92r–v. A marginal note is added to document the source: '*Ludovicus Lavaterus de spectris.*'
50 See Reginald Scot, *La Sorcellerie démystifiée*, ed. and trans. Pierre Kapitaniak, Paris: Classiques Garnier, 2015, p. 54.

51 See Philip C. Almond's chapter on Reginald Scot in the present volume.
52 Otto Sigg, *Hexenprozesse*, pp. 13, 58–59. I would like to thank Eveline Szarka for this reference. Szarka argues that Lavater took a more supportive position towards witch trials and executions in line with that of Bullinger, which may explain the execution of a witch during his short term as Antistes ('"Mother of Souls" and her helpers: How to get rid of ghosts in sixteenth-century Switzerland', unpublished paper, SCSC, Bruges, 2016).

## Further reading

Bennett, Gillian, 'Ghost and Witch in the Sixteenth and Seventeenth Centuries', *Folklore*, 1986, vol. 97/1, 3–14.

Chesters, Timothy, *Ghost Stories in Late Renaissance France: Walking by Night*, Oxford: Oxford University Press, 2011.

Davis, Natalie Zemon, 'Ghosts, Kin and Progeny: Some Features of Family Life in Early Modern France', *Daedalus*, 1977, vol. 160/2, 87–114.

Gordon, Bruce, 'Malevolent Ghosts and Ministering Angels: Apparitions and Pastoral Care in the Swiss Reformation', in Bruce Gordon and Peters Marshall, eds, *The Place of the Dead in Late Medieval and Early Modern Europe*, Cambridge: Cambridge University Press, 2000, pp. 87–109.

Kapitaniak, Pierre, 'Noël Taillepied et Ludwig Lavater: Emprunt et adversité au cœur d'un débat démonologique post-tridentin', in Marie Couton et al., eds, *Emprunt, plagiat, réécriture aux $XV^e$, $XVI^e$, $XVII^e$ siècles*, Clermont-Ferrand: Presses Universitaires Blaise Pascal, 2006, pp. 447–465.

# 13 A Spanish demonologist during the French Wars of Religion

Juan Maldonado's *Traicté des anges et demons*

*Fabián Alejandro Campagne*

During one of the most violent phases of the French Wars of Religion (1562–1598), the Spanish Jesuit Juan Maldonado made an extraordinarily original contribution to early-modern demonology. This contribution did not originally take on a printed form: rather it started life as a theological course taught at one of the most prestigious and innovative Parisian educational institutions of the period. Although lecture notes circulated widely (and were cited by authors such as Martin Delrio°), they remained unpublished for more than thirty years, a circumstance that perhaps explains the unjust exclusion of Maldonado from the pantheon of the greatest Renaissance demonologists.

## 1 A cosmopolitan Jesuit

Maldonado was born *c.*1533/1534 in Casas de la Reina, in Extremadura, Spain.[1] According to some sources he was a *hidalgo*, a member of the Spanish lower nobility.[2] Other documents insist on his (Jewish) *converso* origins.[3] Between 1551 and 1557 Maldonado studied grammar, Greek, logic, rhetoric and philosophy in Salamanca, devoting the following four years to the study of theology. In 1562 he moved to Rome and became a Jesuit priest the following year. Aware of the unusual intellectual gifts of the young friar, the Jesuit General Diego Laínez sent him to Paris to take part in the foundation of the *Collège de Clermont*. In the French capital, Maldonado began teaching Aristotelian philosophy with extraordinary success.[4] In letters to Rome, his superiors expressed their astonishment with his prodigious memory and his knowledge of the biblical languages.[5] Shortly afterwards he took up the College's professorship in theology.[6]

Given his standing and presence in Paris, the Spanish Jesuit could not avoid being involved in the confessional controversies surrounding the French Wars of Religion (1562–1598).[7] Particularly noteworthy was his contribution to the aggressive missionary campaign in Haut-Poitou organized by the Crown in the aftermath of the Third War of Religion (1568–1570).[8] In recognition of his mission to the city of Poitiers and its hinterland, Maldonado was invited to preach in the presence of king Charles IX at court.[9] Even from the grave Maldonado's skills as a polemicist continued to worry his confessional opponents. Proof of this is the 1599 commission by the Genevan presbytery to the minister and theologian Charles Perrot, to refute the Jesuit's vehement attacks against the evangelical doctrine, sixteen years after his death.[10] The concerns of the Genevan pastors were not the product of mere paranoia. Maldonado, 'a fighting theologian' in Jonathan Pearl's words, saw himself as taking part in the religious warfare ignited in Europe by the Protestant challenge.[11]

However, we should not only place Maldonado's lectures on demonology within this context of religious war and confessional polemics. Just as relevant is Maldonado's permanent conflict with the University of Paris. The unusual success of his classes, his reformist pretensions in didactic matters and his unstoppable propensity to question and correct the established authorities of the discipline, were the main causes of the constant attacks that Maldonado received from his colleagues at the Sorbonne. This conflict reached its crescendo at the end of 1574, on the issue of the Immaculate Conception of the Virgin Mary, a doctrine to which Maldonado subscribed but which he did not consider a definitive article of faith.[12] The idea that Mary had been conceived free from original sin did not become Catholic dogma until the mid-nineteenth century and was highly controversial among early modern Catholics. Maldonado's intervention put an end to his career as professor of theology in the French capital.[13] He found refuge in Bourges, where he dedicated himself to the writing of biblical exegesis, in particular an ambitious commentary on the four canonical gospels. In 1578, the Jesuit Superior General Everard Mercurian appointed him Visitor of the Society's French province, charging him with inspecting its many colleges.[14] In early 1581 Maldonado was chosen to represent the province in Rome at the General Congregation which elected Mercurian's successor. It says much about his reputation that he was assigned the honour of delivering the assembly's inaugural speech.[15] The next Superior General, Claudio Acquaviva, and Pope Gregory XIII decided to retain Maldonado's services in Rome, where he also renewed his acquaintance with the famous French essayist Michel de Montaigne. However, Maldonado died suddenly on 5 January 1583, at the age of only 49.

## 2 A prolific yet unpublished author

In spite of his intellectual gifts and evident productivity, Maldonado never published any of his works. One possible explanation may lie in his obsessive urge to revise the interpretations and conclusions developed in his manuscripts. Publishers may not have dared to edit his courses for fear that the author would discredit them shortly after they had been printed.[16] Maldonado's posthumous *opus magnum* was not his demonological lectures, but the monumental *Commentarii in quattuor evangelistas* (Commentary on the Four Gospels), which were finally published in 1596.[17]

Despite his political influence and intellectual relevance, Maldonado is still a relatively unknown author. In fact, until fairly recently he has been almost entirely forgotten by historians. Although Pierre Bayle still included him in his *Dictionnaire*, by the beginning of the eighteenth century he was otherwise barely remembered beyond a narrow circle of biblical exegetes.[18] Indeed, he was by then becoming a relatively unknown character even for Jesuit intellectuals themselves.[19] A late nineteenth-century revival was mostly confined to Catholic apologists.[20] Even more recent historians have, for the most part ignored him and have continued to underestimate his significance both for his contribution to Catholic theology and demonology, and for his role in the Wars of Religion.[21]

The importance of Maldonado for the evolution of European demonology, however, cannot be exaggerated. This influence is related specifically to the course he taught at the *Collège de Clermont* during the academic year 1571–1572. The preparation of these classes followed Maldonado's anti-Calvinist missionary campaign in eastern Poitou in 1570 and were clearly inspired by his experience there. The classes were given in simple and clear Latin, with the intention of capturing an audience as wide as possible. For the same reason, they were scheduled on Sundays and holidays.[22] It was apparently not unusual for up to 400 attendees to gather to hear him. Nor was it uncommon for the classroom to be filled long before the start time of the course.[23] The novelty of the subject matter should also not be underestimated. By 1571, with the exception of Johann Wier°'s sceptical *De praestigiis daemonum*, the lectures predated most of the late sixteenth-century 'golden age' of demonology, while the first wave of Scholastic treatises had by this stage become a thing of the distant past. These various factors – the context of confessional conflict, the provisional nature of the lectures (subject to further revision), and their early date – combine with the author's originality to place his lecture series well outside the mainstream.[24]

Maldonado had divided his 1571–1572 classes into two parts: a more extensive one, devoted to angelology from a theoretical point of view, and a shorter and more intense one, dedicated to demons. While Maldonado's classes on angels were characterized by surgical precision and astonishing subtlety, those focused on the study of demons took on a coarser and brutal tone and expressed an unashamedly political, openly confessional and inescapably apocalyptical *ethos*. The lectures dedicated to impure spirits also show a trace of bitterness which reflected the anti-Protestant fanaticism of the author, disappointed by the outcome of the Third War of Religion (1568–1570), which made considerable concessions to French Protestants.[25] For anti-Protestant fanatics this agreement reached in August 1570 was a vicious betrayal of the true faith.[26] The return to court of leading Protestants, such as Gaspar de Coligny, the proposed marriage of the king's sister to the Protestant Henry of Navarre (the later King Henry IV), and the fall from grace of the hard-line Catholic Guise family (notable benefactors to the *Collège de Clermont*), all provide the backdrop to Maldonado's decision to devote his theology course for the academic year 1571–1572 to the analysis of angels and demons.

## 3 A demonology for civil war

Although several copies of Maldonado's course notes survive in manuscript, we owe their publication to two men. A former student of Maldonado, François de la Borie, who would later become archdeacon of Perigueux Cathedral, decided to reconstruct the lectures from his notes in Latin and translate them into French.[27] This manuscript, in turn, was discovered by the Franciscan friar Jean Blancone, who published it in Paris in 1605 under the title *Traicté des anges et demons*.[28] The *editio princeps* was published by François Huby, who reissued the book two years later. Further editions appeared in Rouen in 1616 and 1619, and in Paris in 1617. The book follows the two-part organization of the classes taught at the beginning of the decade of 1570 and accordingly is divided into a *traicté des anges* and a *traicté des demons*. The latter is substantially shorter than the first one: 90 pages against 150 in most printed editions. The treatise on angels has two parts and many *quaestiones*, several of them carefully subdivided. Maldonado began by analysing the angels in the abstract, and then moved towards the study of the differences between good and bad angels. Some of the topics addressed are the names of the angels, the debate about their existence, their origin and nature (are they simple or composite creatures? Mortal or immortal beings? Identical or different from each other?), their faculties and actions (how do they know the real world? where are they located? how do they move or change their place?), the circumstances of the fall of the evil angels, the angelic hierarchies, etc. The structure of the treatise on demons is less sophisticated and deals with standard demonological issues, such as how demons differ from each other, the extent of the devil's power, the kind of damage Satan can inflict on human beings, the licit remedies to undo *maleficia*, and so on.

Maldonado's treatise reveals the profound singularity of the author's thought, a claim to originality that impelled him to systematically criticize the interpretations of the most venerated theologians of the past. Maldonado's independent-mindedness, theological and otherwise, reached its zenith between 1570 and 1574, precisely during his second multi-year course of theology at the Jesuit College of Paris of which the classes on angels and demons were a part. By then the Iberian Jesuit had convinced himself that the old syntheses were no longer valid. The new challenges and problems demanded new strategies and solutions. It was no longer useful following or commenting on famous medieval authorities such as Peter Lombard or Thomas Aquinas.[29] In his *De ratione theologiae docendae*, also composed during this time, probably in 1573, the Spaniard made clear his opinion on Aquinas: 'The Church grants his doctrine greater approval than others, but it does not seem that you have to follow him so closely that you cannot disagree on some issues.'[30] In his role as biblical interpreter Maldonado behaved in a similar way: he did not hesitate to criticize Jerome for the faulty Latin translation of many Vulgate fragments, and even Jesus Christ himself for the poor narrative consistency and the incoherent organization of some of His parables![31]

In the treatment that Maldonado grants to angels we detect a similar freedom and audacity. Although his extraordinary erudition allowed him a profound knowledge of almost the entire *corpus* of the Church Fathers and the main figures of Scholasticism, he almost never failed to provide his own personal solutions to the complex controversies raised by a subject as challenging as angelology. Particularly striking are the doubts that Maldonado expressed about Aquinas's science of angels. And this despite the sympathy that Ignatius of Loyola, the founder of Maldonado's order, felt for Thomism, the proclamation of Aquinas as Doctor of the Church in 1567 and the recommendation to privilege his teachings that Pius V sent to Catholic universities around the world. Maldonado does not express the servility with respect to the so-called Angelic Doctor that we find in such canonical works as the *Malleus maleficarum*.

The position of the Spanish Jesuit regarding the question of angelic physicality is a paradigmatic example. How demons got bodies was an especially vexing problem with which the early Scholastics had particularly struggled, because it directly conflicted with Aristotelian philosophy, and which earlier demonologists, such as Gianfrancesco Pico della Mirandola°, had also grappled. As is well known, in order to explain physical interaction between humans and angels (imagined as immaterial and incorporeal beings), Aquinas formulated the theory of aerial virtual bodies, *simulacra* made with portions of condensed or rarefied air, a proceeding similar to the formation of clouds in the atmospheric layer closest to Earth's surface.[32] This theory, soon to be transformed into an orthodox paradigm, was repeated with very few nuances in most demonological treatises from the fifteenth to the seventeenth centuries. Maldonado, however, not only devalued Aquinas's theory, considering it one among many other opinions, but he maintained without hesitation that the assumption of *ad hoc* aerial bodies by angels and demons was a possible but unusual procedure. Only when they needed to maintain a continuous and prolonged contact with men would incorporeal angelic creatures resort to adopting these false aerial bodies.

Furthermore, Maldonado proposed two other strategies used by invisible and purely spiritual angels and demons to acquire visibility in the eyes of men. The first of these consisted of the introduction of images or *phantasmata* into the imagination of the people with whom they wished to interact. The Spanish Jesuit argued, then, that in the majority of cases in which women or men saw angels or demons there were no real angelic bodies of any kind present but merely images projected in their minds. This internalist theory helped to explain many stories in which divine messengers were only seen by some of the people present but not others.[33]

With this first strategy, Maldonado at the same time dismissed two other common solutions to the problem of the communication between angelic creatures and human beings. First, an ancient theory that seems to go back to the Desert Fathers of the third and fourth century and early monastic hagiography, according to which the reason why some people could see angelic creatures and others not, was the supreme purity of certain men as opposed to the sinful nature of the majority.[34] Angels did not need to do anything to be seen: their bodies were naturally visible, but only by those who possessed the virtues and perfection necessary for it. The second explanation that Maldonado relativized was much less ancient. It can be found in the *Malleus maleficarum* and in many other demonologies of the period. According to this alternative interpretation, it could happen that (virtual or real) angelic bodies were not seen by all the people present in a given area because angels or demons resorted to some kind of optical illusion or physical barrier to prevent those with whom they did not want to communicate from seeing them.[35]

According to Maldonado, the second procedure that demons in particular used to interact with humans, was a distasteful practice that some theologians considered possible but exceptional: the possession or animation of corpses.[36] In this case, the impure spirit entered a lifeless human body to animate it and use it as a tool to transmit certain messages.[37]

If Maldonado downplayed the Thomistic theory of angelic virtual bodies, in his teaching on demons he openly rejected the *incubi* and *succubi* theory which Aquinas had developed in the *Summa theologica*. As immaterial beings, fallen angels could not generate offspring but they were able to manipulate human sexuality: under the guise of a succubus demon they could steal semen from a wicked man and then under the guise of an incubus demon proceed to inseminate a woman.[38] After an arduous debate that lasted much of the thirteenth century, Aquinas's solution prevailed among theologians. Centuries later the iconic *Malleus maleficarum* helped to popularize this peculiar Scholastic theory beyond narrow academic circles.[39] Although he accepted the reality of *incubi* and *succubi* (in fact, this was one of the few occasions in which immaterial demons used their virtual aerial bodies), Maldonado drew on biological arguments to deny the possibility that this procedure would generate new individuals of the human species:

> In the first place, because human reproduction is very perfect, and for that reason it is very difficult. Secondly, because I do not see how the semen can preserve its genital virtue and heat if it is not already inside a human body. Thirdly, because all the testimonies alleged were taken either from uncertain stories or characters such as Perseus, Simon Magus and Merlin.[40]

In the analysis of the interrelations between magic and heresy we can clearly appreciate the most blatantly political dimension of Maldonado's intellectual efforts. Away from the abstract subtleties displayed in the sections dedicated to angels, in the chapters dedicated to demons Maldonado openly blames Protestantism for the increase in the number of magicians, sorcerers, and witches typical of the late sixteenth century. In fact, he identifies at least five reasons that explain why the magical arts always follow heresy (an argument that would later be repeated verbatim and popularized by Martin Delrio in his *Disquisitiones magicae*).[41] Unlike the non-confessional demonology of Jean Bodin°, in the hands of this Spanish Jesuit the science of demons became a privileged weapon in the rhetorical war against Calvin's minions. For Maldonado, the main cause of the disproportionate growth of devil worship was the outbreak and spread of the Reformation.

Maldonado based this confessional argument on history. The study of the past proved irrefutably that the power of impure spirits had always been greater at times when the true faith was weak or faced the attack of aggressive heresies. The clearest example was the world before the Incarnation of Jesus Christ. America was another prime example: 'Even today the devils speak familiarly with men, as confirmed by the stories of the New World and the letters that send us the Jesuit Fathers who live there (to whom I grant much credit).'[42] To reinforce his point, the Spaniard reminded his students that the most renowned heresiarchs had been magicians, and that magic and magical schools prevailed for centuries on the Iberian Peninsula as a result of the presence, first of Arian heresy, later because of Islam.[43] In the same way, witchcraft, conceived as a collective crime centred on the sabbat, had begun to grow in Central Europe and in the Holy Roman Empire in the fifteenth century as a result of the emergence of the Hussite movement.[44] But the most brutal attack against the Huguenot party appears in the final paragraph of Maldonado's reflection on the relationship between magic and heresy. He bluntly argued that the witchcraft scourge that was then ravaging France had its origin in the independent Calvinist city-state of Geneva:

> I do not want that Calvinists (whom I would respect more if they were authors of salvation instead of scandals) feel offended by what I'm about to say: I believe that these illusions of the devils that torment us in the present came out of the very same Lake of Geneva, from where their heresies came to us. It has been proven that this city was the first to start being haunted by demons. And given that the small size of Geneva was not appropriate to harbour an increasing multitude of demons, evil spirits, I believe, began entering our own French cities.[45]

This argument, defective and weak from the perspective of the very same angelological doctrine that Maldonado himself had put forth, shows that in the classes dedicated to the devil the dramatic, confessional demands prevailed over the precision and consistency that theoretical reflection *in the abstract* usually required. It should be remembered that in his analysis of angels the Iberian Jesuit had argued that it was factually possible for innumerable angels to simultaneously occupy or inhabit the same place.[46] If this was the case, how could it be possible that the entire jurisdiction of the city of Geneva could not contain the multitude of demons created by its native heresy? Obsessed by the urgency of accumulating rhetorical arguments that helped to radically disqualify Calvinism, Maldonado did not hesitate to include in the second part of his annual course incoherent propositions and failed arguments, borne out of the political expediency. Maldonado prioritized the denigration of his confessional enemies over the logical consistency of his own belief system.

There was, then, nothing implicit or rhetorical about the overlap of heresy and witchcraft in Maldonado's writings: from his perspective, Protestantism necessarily led to a formal alliance and an explicit pact with the devil.[47] Perhaps that is why Professor Maldonado's enthusiastic preaching continued to reverberate. His crowded classes took place in a city of Paris dominated by the most extreme eschatological anguish, a sanguinary imaginary that insisted on the fact that France and the whole world were so tainted by heretical filth that atonement could only come from a divine, universal, and massive punishment.[48] In the words of the successful Catholic publicist Pierre Boaistuau, a clear example of this way of thinking, the universe, poisoned by heretical falsehood, no longer tolerated the enemies of the true faith: the earth, contaminated by their lies, did not want to receive them, and even the sun, out of shame, felt constrained to hide, because it could not keep looking at the heretics.[49] An increasing anxiety affected the Parisian Catholics who perceived in the Calvinists an obstacle to their own individual salvation, a challenge that could only be answered with a holy and merciless crusade: kill to be saved, exterminate to be chosen, annihilate to please God.[50]

Filled with expressions of unconcealed religious hatred, the course on angels and demons taught by Maldonado at the *Collège de Clermont* undoubtedly contributed to aggravate the climate of moral panic that popular preachers fed every day with their violent sermons in the streets of the city. The evidence that the Catholic party in the capital was not willing to accept the new policy of religious tolerance that the Crown sought to impose from above multiplied day by day.[51] No one can be surprised, then, that a few weeks after the end of the academic year, the brutal St. Bartholomew's Day massacre broke out on 24 August 1572, in a city full of fanatics, many of whom, no doubt, had been present in the Jesuit classrooms to hear Maldonado's lectures, subtle and refined when discussing angels, yet polemical and brutal on the subject of demons and their human allies. Without neglecting the fact that there were many factors that contributed to the outbreak of such a complex event as the Massacre of St. Bartholomew, allow me to conclude with a question: is it too much to assume that Maldonado's words still resonated in the minds of the hundreds of Parisian extremists who, a few weeks after the close of the academic year at the

*Collège de Clermont*, came out onto the streets of Paris to annihilate the Huguenots who had dared to hinder their path towards eschatological purification on the eve of the imminent End of the World?[52]

## Notes

1 Jesús Iturrioz, 'Maldonado en Salamanca', *Estudios eclesiásticos*, 1942, vol. 41, 228, 231. All references to Maldonado's *Traicté* are to the 1616 edition. All translations are my own, unless otherwise indicated.
2 Juan Eusebio Nieremberg, *Honor del gran Patriarca San Ignacio de Loyola, fundador de la Compañía de Iesvs*, Madrid: Maria de Quiñones, 1645, p. 453.
3 Robert A. Maryks, *The Jesuit Order as a Synagogue of Jews: Jesuits of Jewish Ancestry and Purity-of-Blood Laws in the Early Society of Jesus*, Leiden: Brill, 2010, p. 167.
4 While biblical exegesis and demonology were the two disciplines in which Maldonado excelled, Aristotle's philosophy was another of his specialties. See Stuart Clark, *Thinking with Demons: The Idea of Witchcraft in Early Modern Europe*, Oxford: Clarendon Press, 1997, p. 224; Charles Lohr, 'Renaissance Latin Aristotle Commentaries: Authors L–M', *Renaissance Quarterly*, 1978, vol. 31, 562–63.
5 Gonzalo Díaz Díaz, *Hombres y documentos de la filosofía española*, Madrid: CSIC, 1995, vol. 5, p. 80.
6 José Ignacio Tellechea Idígoras, 'La nueva educación humanística: Juan Maldonado', in Buenaventura Delgado Criado, ed., *Historia de la educación en España y América*, Madrid: Ediciones Santa María/Morata, 1993, vol. 2, pp. 151–56; Louis Saltet, 'Les leçons d'ouverture de Maldonat à Paris (1565–1576)', *Bulletin de littérature ecclésiastique*, 24, 1923, pp. 327–47; Manuel Mañas Núñez, 'Humanismo y teología en el tratado De ratione theologiae docendae de Juan Maldonado', *Revista de Estudios Extremeños*, 2015, vol. 71, 210; Inos Biffi, 'La figura della teologia in Juan de Maldonado: Tra rinnovamento e fedeltà', in Inos Biffi and Costante Marabelli, eds, *Figure moderne della teologia nei secoli XV–XVII*, Milan: Jaca Book, 2007, pp. 149–55.
7 Jean Céard, 'De L'Hérésie à l'athéisme: La Notion d'hérésie selon le jésuite Maldonat', in Marcel Bataillon, ed., *Aspects du libertinisme au XVI siècle: Actes du colloque international de Sommières*, Paris: Vrin, 1974, p. 59.
8 Paul Schmitt, *La Réforme catholique: Le Combat de Maldonat, 1534–1583*, Paris: Beauchesne, 1985, pp. 336ff.
9 Philippe Lécrivain, *Les Jésuites: Une Synthèse d'introduction et de réference*, Paris: Eyrolles, 2014, p. 52; Schmitt, *La Réforme catholique*, p. 375; Joseph Delfour, *Les Jésuites à Poitiers, 1604–1762*, Paris: Hachette, 1901, p. 13.
10 Scott M. Manetsch, *Calvin's Company of Pastors: Pastoral Care and the Emerging Reformed Church, 1536–1609*, Oxford: Oxford University Press, 2015, p. 246.
11 Jonathan Pearl, 'Demons and Politics in France', *Historical Reflections/Réflections historiques*, 1985, vol. 12, 244.
12 José Ignacio Tellechea Idígoras, *La Inmaculada Concepción en la controversia del padre Maldonado con la Sorbona*, Vitoria: Ed. del Seminario, 1958; Schmitt, *La Réforme catholique*, pp. 421–73; Jean-Marie Prat, *Maldonat et l'Université de Paris au XVI$^e$ siècle*, Paries: Julien, Lanier & Cie, 1856, pp. 349–60; Carolus du Plessis d'Argentré, *Collectio Judiciorum de novis erroribus*, Paris: André Cailleau, 1728, vol. 2, fols 443–48; Richard Simon, *Bibliothèque critique, ou Recueil de diverses pieces critiques*, Amsterdam: Jean Louis de Lormes, 1708, pp. 1–17; Pierre Hurtubise and Robert Toupin, eds, *Correspondance du nonce en France Antonio Maria Salviati, 1572–1578*, Rome: Université Pontificale Grégorienne/École Française de Rome, 1975, vol. 2, p. 473.

13 Henri Lesêtre, *L'Immaculée Conception et l'Église de Paris*, Paris: P. Lethielleux, 1904, p. 93.
14 Prat, *Maldonat et l'Université de Paris*, p. 440, 459–62.
15 Antonio Pérez de Goyena, 'Juan Maldonado', *The Catholic Encyclopedia*, New York: Robert Appleton Company, 1910, vol. 9, p. 1. www.newadvent.org/cathen/09567a.htm (accessed 27 June 2016).
16 Schmitt, *La Réforme catholique*, p. 306.
17 Juan Maldonado, *Commentarii in qvattuor evangelistas*, Pont-a-Mousson: Stephanus Mercator, 1596. See the list of further editions in K. Reinhardt, *Bibelkommentare spanischer autoren, 1500–1700*, Madrid: CSIC, 1999, vol. 2, pp. 17–19.
18 Pierre Bayle, *Dictionnaire historique et critique*, Rotterdam: Reinier Leers, 1697, vol. 2/1, pp. 514–18.
19 *Mémoires pour servir a l'histoire du Père Broet et des origines de la Compagnie de Jésus en France, 1500–1564*, Le Puy: J.-M. Freydier, 1885, p. 592.
20 J. Annat, 'Les Révisions du texte de Maldonat, d'après un document inédit', *Bulletin de littérature ecclésiastique*, 1904, vol. 5, pp. 250–59; Emile Amann, 'Maldonat', *Dictionnaire de théologie catholique*, Paris: Lateouzey et Ané, 1927, vol. IX/2, cols. 1772–75; Romualdo Galdós, 'En el cuarto centenario del nacimiento de Maldonado, 1533–1933', *Estudios eclesiásticos*, 1934, vol. 13, 73–89; J. M. Bover, 'El Padre Juan de Maldonado S.I., teólogo y escriturario', *Razón y Fe*, 1934, vol. 104, 481–504; Romualdo Galdós, '¿Qué año nació Juan Maldonado?', *Estudios eclesiásticos* 15, 1936, pp. 256–63; Romualdo Galdós, ed., *Miscellanea de Maldonato anno ab eius nativitate quater Centenario, 1534?–1934*, Madrid: CSIC, 1947; Jesús Iturrioz, 'Magisterio filosófico de Juan Maldonado', *Pensamiento. Revista de investigación e información filosófica* 4, 1948, pp. 49–59; J. Caballero, 'Introducción general', in Juan Maldonado, SJ, *Comentario a los cuatro Evangelios*, trans. Luis María Jiménez Font, Madrid: BAC, 1950, vol. 1, pp. 1–43; R. Deville, 'Assidua S. Scripturae studiosis theologiae necessaria iuxta Maldonatum', *Verbum Domini*, 1951, vol. 29, 107–111; José Ignacio Tellechea Idígoras, 'Metodología teológica de Maldonado', *Scriptorium victoriense*, 1954, vol. 1, 183–255; José Ignacio Tellechea Idígoras, 'El argumento de los Padres y la Inmaculada Concepción según el P. Maldonado SJ', *Revista de estudios teológicos*, 1954, vol. 14, 3–40; Alaphridus Marranzini, 'De theologica methodo Maldonati', in *Atti del Congresso Internazionale tenuto dalla Pontificia Università Gregoriana in occasione del IV centenario della sua fondazione*, Rome: Gregorian University, 1954, vol. 1: 'Problemi scelti di teologia contemporanea', pp. 133–41; A. Rivera, 'La Virgen en los comentarios evangélicos del P. Juan de Maldonado S.J.', *Estudios Marianos*, 1963, vol. 24, 201–29; Angel Luis Ángel, 'Mt 1–2 en Maldonado', *Estudios Josefinos*, 1976, vol. 30, 41–70; A. Rivera, 'Doctrina y culto mariano en la polémica de Juan de Maldonado S.J. con los Reformadores', in *De cultu mariano saeculo XVI*, Rome: Pontificia Academia Mariana Internationalis, 1984, vol. 5: 'De cultu mariano apud scriptores ecclesiasticos saec. XVI: pars altera', pp. 53–65; Angel Luis Iglesias, 'La paternidad de S. José en la obra de Maldonado', *Estudios Josefinos*, 1985, vol. 39, 63–70. Two doctoral dissertations defended in the twentieth century at the Pontificia Università Gregoriana had Maldonado as their main subject: J. B. Marcano, *La oración de Cristo por los apóstoles (Juan 17, 17–19) según Maldonado*, 1942, and Luigi Cattani, *Il metodo teologico di Giovanni Maldonado nella sua teoria della predestinazione*, 1949. At the Pontificia Università della Santa Croce, Rogello de la Garza defended another PhD dissertation on Maldonado: *Las parábolas en la exégesis de Juan Maldonado*, 1995.
21 For a good example of the continued disregard for Maldonado's importance, see Robert Mandrou, *Magistrats et sorciers en France au XVIIe siècle: Une Analyse de psychologie historique*, Paris: Plon, 1968, p. 143. Passing references to Maldonado are

made in Céard, 'De L'Hérésie à l'athéisme'; Schmitt, *La Réforme catholique*; Reinhardt, *Bibelkommentare spanischer Autoren*, pp. 9–19; Jonathan L. Pearl, *The Crime of Crimes: Demonology and Politics in France, 1560–1620*, Waterloo, ON: Wilfred Laurier University Press, 1999, pp. 59–76; Jonathan L. Pearl, 'Maldonado, Juan (1534–1583)', in Richard M. Golden, ed., *Encyclopedia of Witchcraft: The Western Tradition*, Santa Barbara: ABC-Clio, 2006, vol. 3, pp. 710–11; Alain Legros, 'Maldonat, Jean (Juan Maldonado)', in Philippe Desan, ed., *Dictionnaire de Michel de Montaigne*, Paris: Honoré Champion, 2004, pp. 626–28; Alain Legros, 'Maldonado, Juan (Casas de Reina, 1533/34 – Rome, 1583)', in Colette Nativel, ed., *Centuriae latinae: Cent Une Figures humanistes de la Renaissance aux Lumières*, Geneva: Droz, 2006, vol. 2, pp. 491–98; Timothy Chesters, *Ghost Stories in Late Renaissance France: Walking by Night*, Oxford: Oxford University Press, 2011, pp. 32–34, 83–86.
22 Prat, *Maldonat et l'Université de Paris*, pp. 263–64.
23 Schmitt, *La Réforme catholique*, pp. 336–37; Pearl, *The Crime of Crimes*, p. 62. Although for a long time it was said that both Martin Delrio and Pierre de Lancre attended Maldonado's course on angels and demons, at present it is no longer possible to defend this thesis. See Jan Machielsen, 'Thinking with Montaigne: Evidence, Skepticism and Meaning in Early Modern Demonology', *French History*, 2011, vol. 25, 436–37; Ida Dardano Basso, *Il diavolo e il magistrato: Il trattato Du sortilege (1627) di Pierre de Lancre*, Rome: Storia e Letteratura, 2011, p. 138, especially n. 12. By contrast, there is no doubt that a future adherent to the Holy League, such as the preacher Jean Boucher, and the famous anti-Protestant polemicist Louis Richeome, attended Maldonado's classes. Both Boucher and Richeome were men for whom the fight against witchcraft was inseparable from the fight against heresy. See Le Roux, *Les Guerres de religion*, p. 430.
24 François Lecercle, *Le Retour du mort: Débats sur la sorcière d'Endor et l'apparition de Samuel, XVI$^e$–XVIII$^e$ siècle*, Geneva: Droz, 2001, p. 186. Without directly referencing Wier, Pierre Kapitaniak also agrees with this interpretation in 'Du Progrès et de la promotion des démons: Démonologie et philosophie naturelle dans l'épistémè européenne aux XVI$^e$ et XVII$^e$ siècles', *Études Épistémè*, 2005, vol. 7, 54. In his lectures Maldonado also polemicized against Ludwig Lavater: Chesters, *Ghost Stories*, p. 84.
25 Mack P. Holt, *The French Wars of Religion, 1562–1629*, 2nd ed., Cambridge: Cambridge University Press, 2005, p. 71. For some historians, the Peace of Saint-Germain-en-Laye should be considered 'a Calvinist charter', a kind of Huguenot Magna Carta: Nicola-Mary Sutherland, *The Huguenot Struggle for Recognition*, New Haven: Yale University Press, 1980, pp. 175–77; André Stegman, ed., *Édits des guerres de religion*, Paris: Vrin, 1979, pp. 69ff. In fact, Saint-Germain-en-Laye is more than just an edict of pacification, it is an ambitious edict of toleration, and as such, a direct antecedent to the much better-known Edict of Nantes: Jean-Louis Bourgeon, 'Mieux Q'Un Édit de pacification: Un Édit de tolérance (Saint-Germain, 1570)', *Bulletin de la Societé de l'Histoire du Protestantisme Français*, 2009, vol. 155, 701–3.
26 Nicolas Le Roux, *Les Guerres de Religion, 1559–1629*, Paris: Belin, 2009, p. 112.
27 For a brief biographical sketch on François de la Borie, see F. X. de Feller, *Dictionnaire historique ou Histoire abrégée des hommes qui se sont fait un nom*, Paris: Méquignon fils aîné, 1818, vol. 1, p. 312.
28 Christian Péligry, 'L'accueil réservé au livre espagnol par les traducteurs parisiens dans la première moitié du XVII$^e$ s. (1598–1661)', *Mélanges de la Casa de Velázquez*, 1975, vol. 11, 165.
29 Schmitt, *La Réforme catholique*, p. 365.
30 Schmitt, *La Réforme catholique*, p. 220.

31 J.-P. Delville, 'Les Juifs et les commentateurs: Adversaires imaginaires et adversaires réels dans les exégèses de la parabole des ouvriers à la vigne (Mt 20, 1–16) publiées au XVIe siècle', in Ralph Dekoninck et al., eds, *Controverses et polémiques religieuses: Antiquité–Temps Modernes*, Paris: L'Harmattan, 2007, pp. 161–63.

32 Walter Stephens, *Demon Lovers: Witchcraft, Sex, and the Crisis of Belief*, Chicago: University of Chicago Press, 2002, *passim*; Armando Maggi, *In the Company of Demons: Unnatural Beings, Love, and Identity in the Italian Renaissance*, Chicago: University of Chicago Press, 2006, pp. vii–xii; Gareth Roberts, 'The Bodies of Demons', in Darryl Grantley and Nina Taunton, eds, *The Body in Late Medieval and Early Modern Culture*, Aldershot: Ashgate, 2000, pp. 131–41; Dyan Elliott, *Fallen Bodies: Pollution, Sexuality, and Demonology in the Middle Ages*, Philadelphia: University of Pennsylvania Press, 1999, pp. 127–56. The Council of Lateran IV of 1215 is usually seen as an antecedent of the doctrine of absolute angelic immateriality, even though its decrees lack the demonstrative foundations of any systematized theological discourse: Paul M. Quay, 'Angels and Demons: The Teaching of IV Lateran', *Theological Studies*, 1981, vol. 42, 20–45. For an excellent synthesis of Thomas Aquinas's angelology, see Serge-Thomas Bonino, *Les Anges et les démons: Quatorze Leçons de théologie*, Paris: Parole et Silence, 2007, pp. 115–34.

33 Juan Maldonado, *Traicté des anges et demons*, trans. François de la Borie, Rouen: Jacques Besongne, 1616, fol. 26r–v.

34 David Brakke, *Demons and the Making of the Monk: Spiritual Combat in Early Christianity*, Cambridge, MA: Harvard University Press, 2006, p. 83.

35 [Heinrich Institoris], *Malleus maleficarum*, ed. and trans. Christopher S. Mackay, Cambridge: Cambridge University Press, 2006, vol. 1, p. 420.

36 Maaike van der Lugt, *Le Ver, le démon et la vierge: Les Théories médiévales de la génération extraordinaire*, Paris: Les Belles Lettres, 2004, pp. 232–37, 301.

37 Maldonado, *Traicté des anges et demons*, fol. 28v.

38 Thomas Aquinas, *Summa Theologica*, part 1, q. 51, a. 3. The idea was also defended, with slight nuances, by Albert Magnus, Eudes Rigaud and Bonaventure. See Van der Lugt, *Le Ver, le démon et la vierge*, pp. 273–79.

39 [Institoris], *Malleus maleficarum*, pp. 250–51.

40 Maldonado, *Traicté des anges et demons*, fol. 218r.

41 Maldonado, *Traicté des anges et demons*, fols 157r–58v. See also Martino Delrio, *Disquisitionum magicarum libri sex*, Leuven: Gerard Rivius, 1599, vol. 1, pp. 6–8.

42 Maldonado, *Traicté des anges et demons*, fols 155v–56r.

43 Maldonado, *Traicté des anges et demons*, fol. 156r–v.

44 Maldonado, *Traicté des anges et demons*, fol. 156v.

45 Maldonado, *Traicté des anges et demons*, fols 156v–57r.

46 Maldonado, *Traicté des anges et demons*, fols 92v–93v.

47 Euan Cameron, *Enchanted Europe: Superstition, Reason, and Religion, 1250–1750*, Oxford: Oxford University Press, 2010, p. 238; Linda C. Hults, *The Witch as Muse: Art, Gender, and Power in Early Modern Europe*, Philadelphia: University of Pennsylvania Press, 2005, pp. 111–12.

48 Denis Crouzet, *Les Guerriers de Dieu: La Violence au temps des troubles de religion, vers 1525 – vers 1610*, Paris: Champ Vallon, 1990, vol. 2, pp. 86–87.

49 Pierre Boistuau (also known as Launay), *Histoire des persecutions de l'Eglise chrestienne et catholique … commençant à nostre Sauveur Iesus Christ, et à ses apostres*, Paris: Robert le Mangnier, 1576, p. 113.

50 Denis Crouzet, *La Nuit de la Saint-Barthélemy: Un Rêve perdu de la Renaissance*, Paris: Pluriel, 2010, pp. 490ff.

51 Jean-Louis Bourgeon, 'Sur Un Livre de Denis Crouzet: *La Nuit de la Saint-Barthélémy: Un Rêve perdu de la Renaissance*', *Revue historique*, 1994, vol. 589, 202.

52 See Gary K. Waite, *Heresy, Magic, and Witchcraft in Early Modern Europe*, Houndmills: Palgrave Macmillan, 2003, p. 108, who claimed that 'Catholic preachers influenced by Maldonado harangued their congregants on the dangers of heresy and the need for its extermination, allowing for the spread of the massacres across France.' For a more nuanced view, see Pearl, *The Crime of Crimes*, p. 69.

**Further reading**

Caballero, J., 'Introducción general', in J. Caballero, ed., *Juan de Maldonado SI: Comentario a los cuatro Evangelios*, Madrid: BAC, 1950, vol. 1: 'Evangelio de San Mateo', pp. 1–43.

Céard, Jean, 'De L'Héresie à l'athéisme: La Notion d'héresie selon le jésuite Maldonat', in Marcel Bataillon, ed., *Aspects du libertinisme au XVI siècle: Actes du colloque international de Sommières*, Paris: Vrin, 1974, pp. 59–71.

Crouzet, Denis, *Les Guerriers de Dieu: La Violence au temps des troubles de religion, vers 1525–vers 1610*, Paris: Champ Vallon, 1990.

Idígoras, Tellechea and José Ignacio, 'Maldonado, Juan', in Charles E. O'Neill and Joaquín María Domínguez, eds, *Diccionario histórico de la Compañía de Jesús biográfico-temático*, Rome: Institutum Historicum S.I, 2001, vol. 3, pp. 2484–2485.

Legros, Alain, 'Maldonado, Juan (Casas de Reina, 1533/34 – Rome, 1583)', in Colette Nativel, ed., *Centuriae latinae: Cent Une Figures humanistes de la Renaissance aux Lumières*, Geneva: Droz, 2006, pp. 491–498.

Pearl, Jonathan L., *The Crime of Crimes: Demonology and Politics in France, 1560–1620*, Waterloo: Wilfred Laurier University Press, 1999.

Prat, Jean-Marie, *Maldonat et l'Université de Paris au XVIe siècle*, Paris: Julien, Lanier & Cie, 1856.

Schmitt, Paul, *La Réforme catholique: Le Combat de Maldonat, 1534–1583*, Paris: Beauchesne, 1985.

# 14 Scourging demons with exorcism
## Girolamo Menghi's *Flagellum daemonum*

*Guido Dall'Olio*
*(translated by Jan Machielsen)*

Girolamo Menghi earned his nickname – '*Il Viadana*' – from the city of his birth. He was born in 1529 in Viadana, in the Duchy of Mantua, and he died there in July 1609.[1] During his long life, he witnessed the religious and political transformation of the Italian peninsula. The Italian wars, begun in 1494, were still raging when Menghi was born. They ended only in 1559, when most of the Italian states submitted directly or indirectly to Spanish control. In his youth, Menghi would have seen the books and doctrines of Luther, Zwingli, and more radical religious reformers spread across the peninsula. Religious dissent continued to grow in many Italian cities (Venice, Modena, Lucca, Faenza, among others) even after the establishment of the Roman Inquisition (1542) and the convocation of the Council of Trent (1545), which were intended to stem the Protestant tide. Protestantism failed in Italy, partly because of a lack of political support, partly because of the smallness of the numbers of followers. At Menghi's death, however, Italian religious dissent had evaporated. Only the Waldensians, settled in the alpine valleys near Turin, survived. From the late sixteenth century until the age of the Enlightenment, social, political, and cultural life in Italy were dominated by Roman Catholic institutions, especially the Inquisition and the Congregation of the Index of Prohibited Books. The trials against the freethinker Giordano Bruno and the astronomer Galileo Galilei were only the most notorious examples of this repressive climate.[2]

We know little about Menghi's life, and what we know often derives from his books and from his activities as Italy's best-known exorcist. Even then, the only accounts of Menghi's exorcisms are autobiographical. We do know, however, that he entered the Franciscan order in 1549 and that he resided at the convent of Santa Maria Annunziata in Bologna since at least 1556. Most likely, he spent almost his entire life in that monastery. The city of Bologna had notoriously been reconquered by Julius II, the so-called 'warrior pope', in 1511 and would remain part of the Papal States until Italian unification in 1860. It was governed jointly by a papal legate and a senate, an assembly whose forty members represented the noblest families of the city.[3]

Crucially, Bologna hosted the most ancient and famous university in Europe. The intellectual debates hosted by this venerable institution produced two different kinds of religious heterodoxy. The first originated from the free cultural climate of late fifteenth- and early sixteenth-century Renaissance humanism. Its most significant representative was the radical philosopher Pietro Pomponazzi (a professor at the University from 1511 until 1525). Pomponazzi called into question both the immortality of the human soul and the existence of demons on philosophical, Aristotelian grounds. Therefore, Pomponazzi and his followers considered virtually all of the phenomena attributed to demons to be natural events.[4]

The second form derived from the religious restlessness that was, as we already noted, typical of many sixteenth-century Italian cities, and that turned into open dissent with the spread of Protestantism. Small groups of nobles, merchants, artisans, and intellectuals united around the ideas of the Reformation. Although they were nowhere near as large as similar groupings in Modena or Lucca, the Bolognese religious and political authorities were nevertheless worried. During the second half of the sixteenth century, especially during the pontificate of the former inquisitor Pius V (r. 1566–1572), the Inquisition conducted many trials which resulted in notable public executions and abjurations.[5] By 1580 at the latest, Protestantism in Bologna had been defeated. Yet, scepticism about demons and other occult phenomena still thrived. It had the potential to threaten some of the most sensational features of Counter-Reformation religious propaganda, such as miraculous healings, demonic possessions, and exorcisms. Although particularly widespread among the Bolognese ruling class, such critical attitudes also extended to the lower classes. This was the environment in which Menghi began his work.[6]

## 1 A life spent fighting the devil

According to his own account, Girolamo Menghi became an exorcist in or around 1558.[7] During Easter 1559, he performed an exorcism that took on strong confessional undertones. The demoniac, a young woman called Mattia, – or rather the devil supposedly possessing her – started to declaim a long series of heresies. Through Mattia's mouth, the devil denied the existence of God and declared himself to be the creator of the world. Menghi's exorcism forced him to recant and he eventually left the woman's body. According to Menghi, the event lasted seven hours.[8] The exorcism therefore demonstrated to a wide audience both the existence of the devil and the demonic nature of heresy. Menghi, and possibly other exorcists as well, may have intended to influence the witchcraft trials that were going on in Bologna during the same year – four witches were condemned to death on 27 June 1559.[9] It is possible to argue that exorcism as a means of religious propaganda against Protestantism spread from Italy to France, where it became a notorious weapon against the Huguenots. French Franciscans stopped at Bologna on their way to their order's General Chapter (its general meeting) at L'Aquila. They attended the exorcisms and listened to the demon's discourses. The events they witnessed predated the notorious 'miracle of Laon' of 1566, the first of a long series of exorcisms in France used to expose the demonic origins of Protestantism.[10]

Indeed, it is worth emphasizing that this polemical and public purpose of exorcism was also new to Bologna, as it was to the rest of Italy. This was due partly to the early victory over Protestantism on the peninsula, but also because of the cautious and careful attitude of the city's Bishop (later Archbishop), Gabriele Paleotti (1522–1597, bishop from 1566). Considered one of the most famous post-Tridentine bishops, Paleotti was concerned with issues such as heresy, superstition, and witchcraft, but he never tried to solve those problems with harsh legal persecutions, as his famous contemporary and friend Carlo Borromeo, the Archbishop of Milan and future saint had done.[11] In actual fact, Paleotti's caution did not target Menghi himself but a close ally and friend, Antonio Muccini, the parish priest of the church of Sant'Antonino. In 1569, the bishop forbade Muccini to engage in any exorcisms with the church doors opened. Evidently, Paleotti sought to prevent the sensationalism that would otherwise have accompanied such events. Moreover, during an investigation of a possible case of simulation, the bishop's own tribunal was strongly critical of Muccini's techniques as an exorcist. Paleotti, then, seems to have been highly conscious of the possibility of both public uproar and clerical abuse and was determined to prevent both.[12]

The battle against harmful magic and witchcraft, waged by Menghi and his allies, also made little progress. Even if the 1559 executions for witchcraft were influenced by them, then Pope Paul IV clarified that the decision was taken only because of the exceptional seriousness of the allegations against the defendants. Any hopes that the executions might be the start of a wider campaign against witchcraft were quickly dashed. The ecclesiastical tribunals in Bologna did not engage in any systematic witch-hunting, even though a small number of executions did take place. Although local exorcists (including Muccini) attempted to intervene to prove the danger posed by witches, the judges refused to issue condemnations based on their evidence. This attitude seems consistent with the moderation towards witchcraft displayed by the judges of the Roman Inquisition since the second half of the sixteenth century.[13]

Although the first treatise published by Girolamo Menghi contained, as we shall see, many excerpts from the notorious *Malleus maleficarum*°, that most renowned manual of witch-hunting, he himself scarcely took part in the above-mentioned events. In his works the friar from Viadana mentioned many exorcisms that he performed, but actions promoting the prosecution of witchcraft are noticeably absent. Moreover, in the surviving records of the Bolognese ecclesiastical tribunals, Menghi is mentioned in only a single trial conducted in 1583. A witness testified that the exorcist had advised a woman, who had fallen ill after invoking the devil, to confess her sins to a priest.[14]

While still in Bologna at the start of the 1570s, Menghi was in Reggio Emilia (about 60 km from Bologna) in 1574 and 1575, where he performed a number of exorcisms. We do not know if he moved to that city, or if he was just called in on account of his renown as an exorcist. One sign of his growing reputation was the republication of an older treatise on exorcism originally written by Silvestro Mazzolini in 1502, for which Menghi provided a new introduction. In swift succession, Menghi then released the two books which made his name and for which he is always remembered: the *Compendio dell'arte essorcistica* (Compendium of the Art of Exorcism, 1576), and the *Flagellum daemonum* (The Demons' Scourge, 1577). It was certainly no coincidence that in both books – above all in the *Compendio* – Menghi harshly criticized scepticism regarding witchcraft, demonic possession, and exorcism. Both were publishing sensations, going through a great number of editions and reprints.[15]

Narratives inserted in these and subsequent books in which Menghi recounted being called to exorcize and cure the rich and famous further testify to his growing reputation. In 1582, for example, he healed a priest in Bologna who had repeatedly been attacked by a witch's *maleficia*. At that time, even Bishop Paleotti asked the friar for his opinion. In the same year, Menghi also attempted to cure the seven-year-old son of a senator. After physicians proved unable to heal the boy, his father had found many suspicious maleficent objects hidden in the beds of his home. Although the senator called in Menghi, the by now quite celebrated exorcist could not prevent the child's death.[16]

The following year, Menghi locked horns with Bologna's inquisitor Eliseo Capys. The Dominican friar had put on trial for witchcraft a very young novice from a noble family who had been about to make her profession in the convent of San Lorenzo. Not only did she confess to having performed many curses and spells, she also denounced others, including members of her own family, as her accomplices. The father of the girl, understandably worried about the trial and its possible consequences, called in Menghi, who, together with other exorcists, declared that the girl was possessed by the devil. During the exorcism, the possessing demon confessed that he himself had been responsible for all the misdeeds and accusations. The demon had planned to slander the girl's family in order to trigger a feud between her relatives. The girl was eventually removed from the monastery and the charges against the girl and her family were withdrawn – a resounding victory of the exorcist over the Holy Office.[17]

In 1584, the first edition of Menghi's third treatise, the *Fustis daemonum* (The Rod of Demons), was published in Bologna. In his prefatory letter to Francesco Gonzaga (the minister general of the Franciscan friars), the exorcist repeated what he had already observed many times since the initial publication of his *Compendio*: the art of exorcism was surrounded by suspicion and mistrust, a situation Menghi inevitably attributed to Satan's machinations. A telling episode occurred in 1585 in a nameless city located somewhere in 'Lombardy' (a label which covered much of central and northern Italy). The friar from Viadana was called to heal a 'very important person' and continued to exorcize them over a six-month period. During this time, he or she appeared clearly possessed: the usual signs were observed, such as superhuman strength and demonic speech which sowed discord among the victim's family. Yet, despite Menghi's diagnosis, 'a meeting of Doctors, Theologians, Canonists, Lawyers, and Physicians' was called, and everybody declared that the demonic possession did not exist.[18]

Perhaps, Menghi owed his successful career within his religious order to his reputation as an author and exorcist. In 1587 and in 1589 he was appointed *definitore* of the Bolognese province (that is, advisor of the father provincial), and in 1598 he rose to become provincial himself. He had been handpicked for that role by Pope Clement VIII, who wished to settle some differences that had arisen among the Franciscans. During this time, Menghi continued to publish extensively on the art of exorcism: the *Eversio daemonum* (The Overthrow of Demons, 1588), the *Fuga daemonum* (The Flight of Demons, 1596), and the second part of the *Compendio* (1601). Yet, he also wrote on a range of other subjects: the *Giardino delitioso de i frati minori* (The Delicious Garden of the Friars Minor [i.e. the Franciscans], 1592), dedicated to his religious order, an Italian translation of Angelo da Chivasso's *Summa Angelica* (Venice, 1593), and the *Thesoro celeste della gloriosa madre di Dio* (The Celestial Treasure of the Glorious Mother of God, 1607).

We do not know when or why Menghi decided to return to Viadana, his hometown, only that he died there, between 8 and 10 July 1609.

## 2 Exorcisms in print

By the time that Girolamo Menghi, according to his own testimony, began to practise as an exorcist, the art of expelling demons from the bodies of the possessed had already had a long and storied history, founded upon the exorcisms performed by Christ and the Apostles in the New Testament (*e.g.* Mark 1:21–34; Mark 5:1–20; Mark 9:14–29; Acts 19:11–20). At some point during late Antiquity and the early Middle Ages, exorcism became an official art, and one of the steps of the ladder of clerical ordination that led up to the priesthood. Where the power to expel demons once depended on personal charisma, it was increasingly being founded upon a legal basis and attributed to the Church as an institution. This transition was inevitably accompanied by the development of an official liturgy and formulae for exorcisms, even though extraordinary narratives of deliverance from demons continued to feature prominently in the saints' lives of the period.

Between the thirteenth and fifteenth centuries, amidst the birth of medieval Scholasticism and demonology, speculations about the devil and his power became more and more prominent and complex. The most famous Scholastic theologian Thomas Aquinas, who believed firmly in the incorporeal nature of demons (that is, that demons had no bodies), considered their power to be strictly limited, and therefore concluded that their relationships with human beings were ultimately not very close. By contrast, his Franciscan counterparts, notably Duns Scotus, considered Satan and his minions much closer to mankind, and therefore much more dangerous. Moreover, they transformed *maleficium* into a 'satanic sacrament', therefore implying the presence of the devil in the objects used to create harm.[19] The same period also saw the rise of ritual magic and necromancy, which mixed elements drawn from the Christian liturgy with more occultist inventions. In the eyes of many, the rituals of exorcists must have appeared very similar to those used by necromancers and learned (male) magicians.[20] Finally, the heretical movements of this period, already mentioned by other chapters in this volume, often displayed a strong apocalyptic fervour, while they were accused of devil worship by their opponents.[21]

While these various factors certainly contributed to the development of demonology, exorcism also has an important role to play for many reasons. Perhaps most obviously, the increased presence of the devil in the world demanded a greater commitment from and by exorcists. Increasing attention to the devil's human allies also added to their workload. Exorcists were no longer dealing just with the devil's wickedness, they now also had to repair the damage caused by witches, by expelling demons from their victims' bodies, and by neutralizing the maleficent objects (the 'instrumenti maleficiali', as Menghi called them) they had used. It was no coincidence that one of the first and most famous treatises against witches, the *Malleus maleficarum* (1486) included a short section on demonic possession and exorcism, which even contained a formula to cure the victim of harmful magic (although naturally Heinrich Institoris° considered judicial trials and condemnations much more effective in fighting witches than exorcism). At the same time, however, the exorcists were forced to address the suspicion and the mistrust that accompanied their activities. Not only did their practices appear similar to necromancy, they were often dismissed as charlatans.[22] Exorcists were often the subject of satire. Erasmus lampooned them in his *Exorcism* colloquy, and they were mocked in the short story *Belfagor arcidiavolo* by Niccolò Machiavelli.[23]

We should place Menghi's first writings, although much later in time than the historical developments that we have described, within this context, perhaps because his first foray into the subject was, as we already noted, an edition of a much older work. Silvestro Mazzolini's 1502 *Aureus tractatus exorcismique pulcherrimi et efficaces in malignos spiritus effugandos de obsessis corporibus* (Golden Treatise and Most Beautiful and Effective Exorcisms to Expel Evil Spirits from the Bodies of the Possessed) had been a minor, indeed almost unknown work, but composed by a famous theologian.[24] Mazzolini (or Prierias from the place where he was born, Priero in Piedmont) had been an influential Dominican theologian. As Master of the Sacred Palace, he had been the highest doctrinal authority in the Catholic Church after the pope. (He also went on to write a book against witches called *De strigimagarum daemonumque mirandis* [On the Amazing Deeds of Witches and Demons, 1521].) Mazzolini's short exorcism manual consisted of a set of instructions to help exorcists to clearly distinguish between licit and illicit or 'superstitious' rituals.[25] However, Menghi's 1573 edition added notes about the symptoms of demonic possession and the treatment of the diabolic illnesses which he took from the *Liber sacerdotalis*, written by another Dominican, Alberto da Castello (first ed. 1522). These additions had the effect of considerably widening the range of the exorcist's activities and highlighting the danger of harmful magic. The *Aureus tractatus* ended with several ready-made exorcism rituals, which any priest could use.

In 1576, Menghi published in Bologna, with the same printer, Giovanni Rossi, the *Compendio dell'arte essorcistica*. The purposes of this book were manifold. First of all, the friar from Viadana was again trying to restore the dignity of the art of exorcism, in both philosophical and theological terms. To combat associations with necromancy and superstition, Menghi explained the physiology of demonic possession and of harmful magic with references to authorities such as Augustine, Thomas Aquinas, and Duns Scotus. A second aim, which Menghi declared from the very beginning of the book, was to overcome any and all scepticism about the devil and demonic possession. In addition to Pomponazzi's radical legacy, another form of scepticism had emerged during the sixteenth century, perhaps best exemplified by Johann Wier°'s famous *De praestigiis daemonum* (On the Deceptions of Devils, 1563), which by 1576 had already gone through four Latin editions. Most likely, Menghi resorted to recounting his own experiences, as well as those of other exorcists (including the above-mentioned Antonio Muccini) in order to reject scepticism with eye-witness evidence. He chose to write in the Italian vernacular because he feared that disbelief had spread among the common people.

A third, particularly remarkable feature of the *Compendio*, at least for an exorcism manual, was its firm stance in favour of witch-hunting and, in particular, the reality of the witches' sabbat. References to the *Malleus maleficarum* abound throughout the volume. In fact, about one third of Menghi's treatise consisted of both explicit and hidden quotations from Institoris's manual.[26] This was by no means obvious for a treatise about exorcism and demonic possession. It is not clear, however, whether supporting the witch-hunt was a separate aim of Menghi's, or whether he saw it as another part of a wider struggle against scepticism. Regardless, his attitude contrasted with those expressed by Bologna's judges and the Inquisition in Rome, which during the same period became increasingly sceptical of evidence derived from the witches' sabbat and much more reluctant to condone witch-hunting. Given these circumstances, we can consider the *Compendio*, like the *Malleus* a century earlier, to have its origin in failure.

Despite this side interest in witchcraft, exorcism remained Menghi's main preoccupation. In 1577, he published his *Flagellum daemonum*, again in Bologna, which he had already announced in the *Compendio*. The *Flagellum* consisted of a short treatise divided into fifteen brief chapters (eighteen in later editions), followed by seven long exorcism rituals and various formulaic blessings, that were meant to be used to cleanse the objects (water, bread, salt, and so on) needed during the exorcism. This book was written in Latin, not only because of its liturgical purposes, but also to keep the more technical aspects of exorcism hidden from the laity (who were certainly not meant to try to perform an exorcism at home). The aim of the work, Menghi declared to Paleotti in a dedicatory letter, was to make reliable and orthodox rituals available to the wider community of exorcists. Like the *Compendio*, the theoretical part of the *Flagellum* was hardly original. Many chapters were actually long quotations taken from Mazzolini's *Aureus tractatus*, the *Liber sacerdotalis*, and, again, the *Malleus maleficarum*. One of the few pages that was actually written by Menghi himself contained veiled criticism of authorities who had ordered priests to close church doors during an exorcism. This could well be a comment on what had happened in Bologna some years before.

Still, the prescribed exorcism rituals possess some very interesting features. First of all, Menghi did not bother to reference his sources for these formulae or the accompanying instructions. Curiously, the exorcisms contained lengthy references to the Greek and Hebrew names of God, such as *Hel*, *Heloym*, *Tetragrammaton*, *Adonay*, *Agla*, and so on. Although these can be found in the *Liber sacerdotalis* (though not in Mazzolini's work), they were also frequently used by necromancers. For the healing of the possessed, Menghi proposed – although with some caution – potions and anointings, which would eventually trigger controversy between exorcists and physicians. On 14 January 1583, perhaps because of these more unusual features, the inquisitor of Bologna submitted the *Flagellum* to a censor, fra' Timoteo Pennoni, who like Menghi hailed from Viadana. We do not know the precise outcome but there were evidently concerns about Menghi's sources. Starting with the 1584 edition, the *Flagellum* began listing references in its margins. In some cases, the reference was accurate and well-known, such as the exorcism ritual attributed to St. Ambrose, or Mazzolini's treatise. In many other cases, however, these references were hardly helpful at all, referring only to generic 'ancient exorcisms'.

Menghi's second work was a remarkable success. By one count, it was reprinted 47 times between 1577 to 1727 in Italy, Germany, and France. Many editions also included his later *Fustis daemonum*. Legal records also testify to the widespread use of Menghi's treatise. Almost always, whenever an Italian exorcist was accused of any malpractice committed during their activities, they referred to the *Flagellum daemonum* in their defence.[27] This is significant for two reasons: on the one hand, these exorcist defendants thought that Girolamo Menghi's name and reputation would help their cause; on the other hand, Menghi clearly failed in his mission to restore the dignity of the art of exorcism.

All the subsequent, less famous exorcism works by Menghi follow the structure of the *Flagellum*: they were divided into a theoretical part and another section which contained the text of exorcism rituals. In a certain sense, they were all different versions, of various lengths, of the same book. The titles were: *Fustis daemonum* (1st. ed. 1584, 18 chapters and 8 exorcisms); *Eversio daemonum* (1st ed. 1588, 10 chapters and 17 exorcisms); *Fuga daemonum* (1st ed. 1596, 18 chapters, 7 exorcisms, and an appendix with blessings for the natural elements). All these works discussed demons and their power at length. Menghi inevitably surveyed demonic possession and harmful magic, quoting from the standard philosophical and theological authorities. Sometimes he referred to his own experiences and to his previous writings. He did, however, notably move away from attributing possession to witches, although he continued to hold demons responsible for witchcraft in general. As for his exorcism rituals, from his *Fustis daemonum* onwards Menghi deleted the most ambiguous and mysterious ones, such as the invocation of God's Hebrew names included in the *Flagellum*. The exorcisms proposed in his later works were more like prayers than conjurations.

Menghi's last manual was *La seconda parte del compendio dell'arte essorcistica* (*The Second Part of the Compendium of the Art of Exorcism*, Venice 1601). Although written in the Italian vernacular, it was much less influential and well-known than his other treatises. The author stressed the continuity with the first part of the *Compendio*, which he had published 25 years earlier. That earlier work had contained three books, this 'second part' opened with Book Four. Still, this second volume was more than seven hundred pages long and the topics were partially new. The nature of demons was now considered from their angelic origins. The whole fourth book dealt with the description of the nature of the heavenly beings and the fall of the rebel angels. The fifth book, however, was a reprise of Menghi's earlier works, with almost the same references, such as the *Liber sacerdotalis* and Mazzolini's *Aureus tractatus*, which were repeatedly quoted throughout the volume. Yet, as he approached the end of his life, Menghi also drew significantly more on his personal experiences as an exorcist than he had done before. Inevitably, this led him to defend the art of exorcism still more strenuously, denouncing scepticism even among the clerical elite. The harsh condemnation of witchcraft with which he had begun his writing career was now almost missing, yet Menghi devoted considerable attention to popular superstitions. The sixth and final book dealt almost entirely with the performance of exorcisms. Here Menghi drew on his personal experience with particular frequency and he denounced both sceptics and uneducated exorcists, who helped to sully the reputation of a proud profession with their ineptitude.

Among Menghi's wider corpus, a number are worth singling out. His *Giardino delitioso de i frati minori* (1592) was a collection of sources concerning the Franciscan order, translated into the Italian vernacular. In his *Celeste thesoro della gloriosa madre di Dio Maria Vergine* (1607) demonstrated a great devotion to the Virgin, as other Catholic demonologists, such as Institoris and Delrio° did as well. The book included descriptions of Marian shrines throughout Italy and

Europe. Inevitably, Menghi also discussed instances where the Virgin defeated the forces of the devil.[28] The *Celeste thesoro* was not an outlier. On the contrary, it exemplified his Counter-Reformation religiosity. Like his many exorcism manuals, the work fought elite 'impiety' and scepticism and popular 'superstition' at the same time.

## 3 Girolamo Menghi: founder of the modern art of exorcism?

Girolamo Menghi was undoubtedly one of the most − if not the most − well-known exorcists of early modern Europe. This reputation was due to the publication of his Latin manuals, which combined theory with ready-to-use exorcism rituals. This combination was a significant innovation. Before Menghi, few books contained such liturgical formulae, and fewer still could be considered reliable. The development of exorcism manuals in the fifteenth century oddly did not result in the compilation of authoritative examples. Perhaps this was because many formulae included ambiguous elements that resembled the spells of necromancers.[29] On the other hand, theological treatises, such as Jean Gerson's famous treatise on *discretio spirituum*, were too abstract to be used as practical guides.[30] Possibly the most practical of the early works was Silvestro Mazzolini's 1502 treatise, which was precisely the work that Menghi decided to re-issue on account of its apparently limited circulation.

The *Liber sacerdotalis* (1523) by the Dominican friar Alberto da Castello was, as we have seen, a significant inspiration for Menghi. In fact, it was arguably the most important Catholic contribution to the subject of exorcism, because it provided the basis for the 1614 *Rituale Romanum*, the Church's official compendium of liturgical rites which remained in use until the Second Vatican Council (1962–1965). The *Liber sacerdotalis*, however, was a complex and expensive work, more than 700 pages long, devoted to a whole series of religious rituals. It discussed exorcism almost as an afterthought, at the end of the volume in twenty short pages (nine chapters and three exorcisms).[31] Unsurprisingly, this part of the work was excerpted and translated into Italian, and it appeared in many editions (for example in Venice 1536, 1545, 1560). These editions, however, did not identify the author, although the title page declared that the rituals had been 'revised and emended' by the inquisitor Bonaventura Farinerio. The full title reveals the sensationalism that surrounded sixteenth-century exorcism: *Exorcismo mirabile, da disfare ogni sorte de maleficii e da cacciare li demoni* (Marvellous Exorcism, that Undoes Every Kind of Harmful Magic and Expels the Demons). It is no wonder, then, that Girolamo Menghi provided his *Flagellum* with a boastful subtitle as well: *Exorcismi terribiles, potentissimi, & efficaces, remediaque probatissima in malignos spiritus expellendos* (Terrible, All-Powerful, and Effective Exorcisms, and Very Tested Remedies to Expel Evil Spirits).

Menghi's *Flagellum daemonum*, thus, filled a gap in the market. His book integrated theory and practice. Menghi was no innovator − he simply brought together with what he judged most useful from previous works in a more appealing format. Yet, the work's great success was also due to the growth in the number of demonic possession cases during the second half of the sixteenth century. In fact, Menghi became something of a trendsetter. His *Flagellum* was followed by a boom in exorcism manuals, authored by members from a large number of different religious orders. Many of them were Italian. Indeed, it has been observed that while Italians published few works of demonology, their absence was filled by exorcism manuals. The importance of Italian exorcists can be clearly seen, for example, in a miscellaneous volume published in 1608 in Cologne: the *Thesaurus exorcismorum*, which included, besides Menghi's *Flagellum* and *Fustis*, the *Practica exorcistarum* (Practice of Exorcists) by Valerio Polidoro (first ed. 1587), the *Complementum artis exorcisticae* (Complement to the Art of Exorcism) by Zaccaria Visconti (1600), and the *Fuga Satanae* (Satan's Flight) by Pietro Antonio Stampa (1597).[32]

The great success of the exorcists aroused the suspicions of church authorities in Rome, especially among the inquisitors at the Holy Office. The reasons for this mistrust, as we have already seen, were the growing and bewildering forest of the exorcism formulae, jurisdictional controversies with physicians, and the ongoing risk of scandal. The Inquisition was particularly concerned to avoid witch-hunts on the basis of the denunciations uttered by demoniacs (or deceitful demons!) during their exorcisms. While (mass) possession cases became a frequent occurrence in France during the first half of the seventeenth century, the Roman authorities prohibited Italian inquisitors from using evidence gathered during exorcisms as proof.[33] The publication of the *Rituale Romanum* (1614) was an important step towards the codification of exorcism rituals. The *Rituale* also contained instructions for exorcists, much more sober and cautious than those issued by authors, such as Menghi. It took a long time, however, for the *Rituale* to establish itself as a binding document, partly because the Roman authorities did not prosecute priests who failed to follow it. Texts by Menghi and his followers therefore continued to be used for a long time to come.[34]

Things changed dramatically in the eighteenth century, when the Roman Congregation of the Index of Prohibited Books heavily censored Girolamo Menghi's books – in 1704 the *Flagellum* and the *Fustis* were declared superstitious and they were completely banned (the same happened to Visconti's *Complementum*). Three years later the *Compendio* was also prohibited. The Roman authorities, however, did not behave consistently, and other manuals, including Menghi's lesser known works, escaped sanction.[35]

# Notes

1 On Menghi's life see Guido Dall'Olio, 'Menghi, Girolamo', in *Dizionario Biografico degli Italiani*, vol. 73, Roma: Istituto della Enciclopedia Italiana, 2009 <www.treccani.it/enciclopedia/girolamo-menghi_(Dizionario-Biografico)/> (last accessed 25 July 2019); Vincenzo Lavenia, 'Menghi, Girolamo', in Adriano Prosperi, ed., *Dizionario Storico dell'Inquisizione*, vol. 2, Pisa: Edizioni della Normale, pp. 1022–23. On his role in Counter-Reformation Italy, with special reference to the

prosecution of witchcraft, in addition to what can be found below, see Giovanni Romeo, *Inquisitori, esorcisti e streghe nell'Italia della Controriforma*, Florence: Sansoni, 1990, pp. 109–43.
2 For an overview: John A. Marino, ed., *Early Modern Italy*, Oxford: Oxford University Press, 2002; on the Reformation in the Italian States, see Massimo Firpo, *Juan de Valdés and the Italian Reformation*, London: Routledge, 2016; on the Roman Inquisition and the Counter-Reformation, see Gigliola Fragnito, ed., *Church, Censorship and Culture in Early Modern Italy*, Cambridge: Cambridge University Press, 2001; Christopher F. Black, *The Italian Inquisition*, New Haven: Yale University Press, 2009.
3 Renato Zangheri and Adriano Prosperi, eds, *Bologna nell'età moderna*, 2 vols, Bologna: Bononia University Press, 2008.
4 See Martin L. Pine, *Pietro Pomponazzi: Radical Philosopher of the Renaissance*, Padua: Antenore, 1986.
5 Guido Dall'Olio, *Eretici e inquisitori nella Bologna del Cinquecento*, Bologna: Istituto per la Storia di Bologna, 1999.
6 On the persistence of sceptical attitudes in the Counter-Reformation, see Nicole Reinhardt, 'Sotto il mantello della religione: Camillo Baldi, un proto-libertino nello Stato della Chiesa?', in Guido Dall'Olio et al., eds, *La fede degli italiani: Per Adriano Prosperi*, Pisa: Edizioni della Normale, 2011, pp. 81–96; Nicholas Davidson, 'Unbelief and Atheism in Italy, 1500–1700', in Michael Hunter and David Wootton, eds, *Atheism from the Reformation to the Enlightenment*, Oxford: Clarendon Press, 1992, pp. 55–85.
7 Girolamo Menghi, *Fuga daemonum*, Venice: Heirs of Giovanni Varisco, 1596, fols 59v–60r.
8 Girolamo Menghi, *Parte seconda del compendio*, Venice: Georgio Varisco, p. 336.
9 On this episode see Guido Dall'Olio, 'Tribunali vescovili, inquisizione romana e stregoneria: I processi bolognesi del 1559', in Adriano Prosperi, ed., *Il piacere del testo: Saggi e studi per Albano Biondi*, 2 vols, Rome: Bulzoni, 2001, vol. 1, pp. 63–82.
10 On the French cases see Sarah Ferber, *Demonic Possession and Exorcism in Early Modern France*, London: Routledge, 2004.
11 See Paolo Prodi, *Il cardinale Gabriele Paleotti, 1522–1597*, 2 vols, Rome: Edizioni di Storia e Letteratura, 1959–1967; for Borromeo's harshness towards superstition and witchcraft, see Romeo, *Inquisitori, esorcisti e streghe*, pp. 47–52.
12 See Guido Dall'Olio, 'Antonia: Una storia d'amore, di possessione e di esorcismo', in Gian Paolo Brizzi and Giuseppe Olmi, eds, *Dai cantieri della storia: Liber amicorum per Paolo Prodi*, Bologna: Clueb, 2007, pp. 71–85, esp. 73–74; Guido Dall'Olio, 'The Devil of Inquisitors, Demoniacs and Exorcists in Counter-Reformation Italy', in Richard Raiswell and Peter Dendle, eds, *The Devil in Society in Early Modern Europe*, Toronto: CRRS, 2012, pp. 511–36.
13 On Bologna, see Guido Dall'Olio, 'Alle origini della nuova esorcistica: I maestri bolognesi di Girolamo Menghi', in Giovanna Paolin, ed., *Inquisizioni: Percorsi di ricerca*, Trieste: Università di Trieste, 2001, pp. 81–129, esp. 122–24; and in general, Tamar Herzig, 'The Roman Inquisition and Witchcraft', in Brian P. Levack, ed., *The Oxford Handbook of Witchcraft in Early Modern Europe and in Colonial America*, Oxford: Oxford University Press, 2013, pp. 253–58.
14 Archivio Arcivescovile di Bologna, *Ricuperi Attuariali*, reg. 247, fols 65v–84v.
15 An accurate list can be found in the reprint of the *Compendio*, edited by Ottavio Franceschini: *Compendio dell'arte essorcistica et possibilità delle mirabili et stupende operationi delli demoni et de' malefici*, Genoa: Nuova Stile Regina Editrice, 1987, pp. xxi–xxiii (at the end of the volume).
16 See Menghi, *Parte seconda del compendio*, pp. 367–68 and 665.
17 Dall'Olio, 'The Devil of Inquisitors', p. 522: for a more detailed account see Guido Dall'Olio, 'Il diavolo e la giustizia: Note sugli usi giudiziari della

possessione e dell'esorcismo', in Dinora Corsi and Mattei Duni, eds, *'Non lasciar vivere la malefica': Le streghe nei trattati e nei processi, secoli XIV–XVII*, Florence: Firenze University Press, 2008, pp. 197–212.
18  Menghi, *Parte seconda del compendio*, p. 357.
19  Alain Boureau, *Satan the Heretic: The Birth of Demonology in the Medieval West*, Chicago: University of Chicago Press, 2006.
20  Richard Kieckhefer, *Forbidden Rites: A Necromancer's Manual of the Fifteenth Century*, University Park, PA: Pennsylvania State University Press, 1998, pp. 126–53.
21  For the history of exorcism, see Francis Young, *A History of Exorcism in Catholic Christianity*, London: Palgrave Macmillan, 2016; and focussed on the early modern period: Brian P. Levack, *The Devil Within: Possession and Exorcism in the Christian West*, New Haven: Yale University Press, 2013.
22  See for example Matteo Duni, *Under the Devil's Spell: Witches, Sorcerers, and the Inquisition in Renaissance Italy*, Florence: Syracuse University in Florence, 2007, pp. 46–51.
23  Marco Villoresi, 'Tra possessione ed esorcismo: Divagazioni nella Firenze del Rinascimento', *Paragone*, vol. 57, 2016, pp. 66–98.
24  The title of the original edition was more sober: *Tractatulus, quid a diabolo sciscitari et qualiter malignos spiritus possit quisque expellere de obsessis* (Little Treatise on What One Can Ask Demons, and How to Expel Evil Spirits from the Possessed).
25  On Mazzolini, see Michael Tavuzzi, *Prierias: The Life and Works of Silvestro Mazzolini da Prierio, 1456–1527*, Durham, NC: Duke University Press, 1997.
26  Guido Dall'Olio, 'Esorcistica e caccia alle streghe: Il *Compendio dell'arte essorcistica* e il *Malleus maleficarum*', in Andrea Del Col and Anne Jacobson Schutte, eds, *L'inquisizione romana, i giudici e gli eretici: Studi in onore di John Tedeschi*, Rome: Viella, 2017, pp. 131–43.
27  See for example Romeo, *Inquisitori, esorcisti e streghe*, p. 146.
28  See Jan Machielsen's contribution on Martin Delrio in this volume.
29  Nancy Caciola, *Discerning Spirits: Divine and Demonic Possession in the Middle Ages*, Ithaca, NY: Cornell University Press, 2003, pp. 235–51.
30  Caciola, *Discerning Spirits*, pp. 284–315; Moshe Sluhovsky, *Believe Not Every Spirit: Possession, Mysticism, and Discernment in Early Modern Catholicism*, Chicago: University of Chicago Press, 2007, pp. 175–80.
31  *Liber sacerdotalis nuperrime ex libris Sancte Romane Ecclesie et quarundam aliarum ecclesiarum ex antiquis codicibus apostolice bibliotheca [...] collectus atque compositus ac auctoritate sanctissimi domini domini nostri Leonis Decimi approbatus*, Venice: Melchior Sessa, 1523; on the importance of this treatise, see Davide Righi, *Il 'Sacerdotale' di Alberto da Castello e le sue numerose edizioni, 1523–1603*, PhD dissertation, Istituto di Liturgia Pastorale 'Abbazia di S. Giustina', 2012–13; Sluhovsky, *Believe Not Every Spirit*, pp. 75–76.
32  *Thesaurus Exorcismorum atque conjurationum terribilium, potentissimorum, efficacissimorum, cum Practica probatissima* ... Cologne: Lazarus Zetzener, 1608.
33  It was precisely for this reason that the *Instructio pro formandis processibus in causis strigum, sortilegiorum et maleficiorum*, released by the Holy Office in the 1620s, warned inquisitors not to take words uttered by demoniacs during exorcism as a proof: John A. Tedeschi, 'The Question of Magic and Witchcraft in Two Inquisitorial Manuals of the Seventeenth Century', in his *The Prosecution of Heresy: Collected Studies on the Inquisition in Early Modern Italy*, Binghamton, NY: Center for Medieval and Early Renaissance Studies, 1991, pp. 229–58, at 236.
34  Giovanni Romeo, *Esorcisti, confessori e sessualità femminile nell'Italia della Controriforma: A proposito di due casi modenesi del primo Seicento*, Florence: Le Lettere, 1998, pp. 98–99.
35  Lavenia, 'Menghi, Girolamo'; Vincenzo Lavenia, 'Esorcismo', in Prosperi, ed., *Dizionario Storico dell'Inquisizione*, vol. 2, pp. 549–54.

## Further reading

Balzano, Davide, 'Girolamo Menghi, esorcista viadanese del Cinquecento', *Vitelliana: Viadana e il territorio Mantovano fra Oglio e Po; Bollettino della Società Storica Viadanese*, 2009, vol. 4, 103–124.

Dall'Olio, Guido, 'The Devil of Inquisitors, Demoniacs and Exorcists in Counter-Reformation Italy', in Richard Raiswell and Peter Dendle, eds, *The Devil in Society in Early Modern Europe*, Toronto: CRRS, 2012, pp. 511–536.

———, 'Esorcistica e caccia alle streghe: Il *Compendio dell'arte essorcistica* e il *Malleus maleficarum*', in Andrea Del Col and Anne Jacobson Schutte, eds, *L'inquisizione romana, i giudici e gli eretici: Studi in onore di John Tedeschi*, Rome: Viella, 2017, pp. 131–143.

Lavenia, Vincenzo, '"Tenere i malefici per cosa vera": Esorcismo e censura nell'Italia moderna', in Vittoria Bonami, ed., *Dal torchio alle fiamme: Inquisizione e censura; Nuovi contributi dalla più antica biblioteca provinciale d'Italia*, Salerno: Biblioteca provinciale di Salerno, 2005, pp. 129–172.

Maggi, Armando, *Satan's Rhetoric: A Study in Renaissance Demonology*, Chicago: University of Chicago Press, 2001.

Seitz, Jonathan, *Witchcraft and Inquisition in Early Modern Venice*, Cambridge: Cambridge University Press, 2011.

Watzka, Carlos, 'Interaktionen von Dämonen und Menschen im Wege der Besessenheit', in Steffen Schneider, ed., *Aisthetics of the Spirits: Spirits in Early Modern Science, Religion, Literature and Music*, Göttingen: V&R unipress, 2015, pp. 307–364.

# 15 The ambivalent demonologist

William Perkins's *Discourse of the Damned Art of Witchcraft*

Leif Dixon

William Perkins (1558–1602) was one of the most significant theological and pastoral minds of the English Calvinist tradition. Based throughout his career in Cambridge, Perkins wrote three dozen books, the vast majority of which were penned in the 1590s – a time when godly ministers in England were seeking to embed an already successful Protestant Reformation by rooting out 'popish remnants' in society, and by providing support and guidance for those who sought to deepen their religious commitment. He wrote one work of demonology, *A Discourse of the Damned Art of Witchcraft*, which was first published posthumously by one of his editors, Thomas Pickering, in 1608. Although it is not possible to date the writing of this work with precision, we do know that it was written after 1595, as in one marginal note he cites Nicholas Remy°'s *Daemonolatreiae libri tres* which was first published in that year; and it was probably written after 1597, the year in which King James VI°'s *Daemonologie* went into print.[1] It was penned during the busiest period of Perkins's literary career, and when he was at the height of his powers: at around the time of his *Exposition of the ... Creed* (1595), *Reformed Catholike* (1597), and *Treatise of the Manner and Order of Predestination* (1598). These are all justly famous works, much reprinted at the time, and well-known to students of both English puritanism and continental Calvinism. Perkins's reputation is based partly on his theological rigour, and partly on his clarity of expression and shrewd pastoral judgement. We might expect his *Damned Art*, therefore, to be something of a tour de force: a Calvinist equivalent, perhaps, to the great Catholic demonologies produced on the continent. As we shall see, however, this was not quite the case.

Although the *Damned Art* went on to have a modest influence on later English demonologies, it never rose to the heights of popularity of some of Perkins's other writings.[2] It has also received limited scholarly attention, perhaps because it is too often assumed that the *Damned Art* is 'so perfect an expression' of 'orthodox' Calvinism that 'it needs no extensive analysis'.[3] This is an assumption that needs to be challenged. Indeed, it is even possible to speculate that the *Damned Art* was not written by Perkins at all. The witchcraft sceptic, Thomas Ady, suggested in 1656 that it was concocted by others after Perkins's death and 'put in presse for the benefit of his Wife, who had but small means for her maintenance in her widowhood'.[4] This explanation would help to account for why the *Damned Art* often lacks the singularity of purpose that characterised Perkins's other writings. On the other hand, we must note that it was convenient for Ady to pitch this interpretation – he was seeking to demolish demonological arguments, and by his own admission was nervous about criticising the *Damned Art*, lest readers think 'I go about to defame' such a 'chosen instrument of ... God's word' as William Perkins. A further pinch of salt should be added to Ady's argument because he tried exactly the same trick when it came to James VI's *Daemonologie* which, he concluded with breathtaking insouciance, was written 'by some Scotish man, blinded by some Scotish Mist ... for the upholding of Popish errours'.[5]

Although Ady exaggerated the authorship problems, we should certainly acknowledge that the *Damned Art* may have been pulled together by Pickering's editorial hand, rather than left in its final form by Perkins himself. However, this essay intends to show that the *Damned Art* not only bears the hallmarks of Perkins's deeply committed and uncompromising approach to both Calvinist theology and puritan pastoral endeavour, but also that some of the distinctive elements of the text reveal how the subject of witchcraft interacted – often uncomfortably – with Perkins's wider theological worldview. I thus intend to question the notion that Perkins's demonology represents a wholly consistent system based around covenants and binary inversions, and even that he assumed witches to be reprobates who must be exterminated *en masse*.[6]

The unusual nature of Perkins's approach can be usefully previewed by turning to the five elements that Wolfgang Behringer calls the 'elaborated early modern concept of witchcraft.' These are belief in: 1) the demonic pact; 2) sexual relations with the devil; 3) the witches' sabbat; 4) witches' flight to the sabbat; and 5) *maleficium*.[7] Perkins appears to be ambivalent, in part, because he simply does not buy into this package. In short, Perkins believed strongly and absolutely centrally in the notion of a demonic pact; he believed, with some careful qualification, in the idea of *maleficium*; but he rejected wholesale the package of ideas around the sabbat, including sex and flight. He was much more concerned to attack the demonic spin operation that was so-called 'white witchcraft', and it was this element of the *Damned Art* which, I shall suggest, shows Perkins at his most dynamic and purposeful. I shall also suggest that the ways in which he navigated around structural fashions in contemporary theory underline the extent to which the intellectual scaffolding of the witchcraft phenomenon was contested and destabilised not only from the outside – by 'sceptics' – but also by those who sought to build – or re-build – the edifice of demonology itself.

## 1 Demonic power and *maleficium*

Perkins's primary concern, throughout his writings, was to emphasize the absolute power of God over every situation. Satan was not a major actor within his theology. One of his most popular books, *The Whole Treatise of the*

*Cases of Conscience*, is divided into three parts: humans in regard to his own conscience; humans with respect to God; and humans in relation to each other. Here, the devil represents not structure, but detail. As such, few of Perkins's books place any great stress on the machinations of Satan. Although Ady was not quite correct – in doubting the authorship of the *Damned Art* – to suggest that witchcraft doctrine 'was not taught by him … in his Lifetime', it is nonetheless the case that the reduced role that Perkins usually assigned to the devil had serious implications for his approach to witchcraft.[8]

We can see how carefully Perkins handles demonic power by looking briefly at his one work – aside from the *Damned Art* – that tackles the subject in any depth. This is his *Combat betweene Christ and the Devill*, which focusses on the synoptic gospels' accounts of Christ's temptation in the Judean Desert. The essential posture of the *Combat* is a head-on confrontation between the 'Christian souldier' who is urged to 'dress in the whole armour of God', and the 'strong armed' devil.[9] The lesson that he aims to impart is that this 'armour' is most likely to be weakened through internal degradation rather than external battering, and that it is faith in, and knowledge of, God that will maintain its lustre. While Perkins does discuss witchcraft here, he frames it largely in terms of how man's usually safe existence within a well-ordered world is the product of constant divine intervention. In one short paragraph on the question of whether the elect can be 'bewitched', Perkins uses the phrase 'if God permit' three times. And the focus is less on witchcraft per se than on extremes of providential misfortune, including the devil's ability – with 'permission' – to 'kill the bodie'[10]. He does not, though, wholly ignore the subject of witchcraft. *Pace* the hopeful sceptic Thomas Ady, Perkins argues that Satan's biblical magic establishes a precedent upon which a history and reality of witchcraft must be founded: Scripture proves that the works of 'Sorcerers and Magicians' are 'not mere fancies, as some thinke'.[11] However, Perkins's focus here is telling. He locates demonic activity in 'the manifold complots and treasons … against our Prince and State, by profane men stirred up by the devill', and those who covenant with Satan do so for 'honour, riches … or great renowne'.[12] This does not sound much like the sad reality of the average village witch. His reference to plots against 'our Prince and State' seems in fact to relate demonic activity to Catholic attempts to overthrow Queen Elizabeth. We shall return to Perkins's tendency to see a relationship between Catholicism and witchcraft, but for now it is simply important to underline that his *Combat* showed little or no interest in the actual person of the witch, emphasized the dependence of Satan upon divine permission, and sought to tether demonic magic to the wider purposes of providence.

As such, it should be no surprise that Perkins's *Damned Art* heavily stresses the ways in which demonic activity invariably contributes to God's larger providential plan. The mere existence of witchcraft is a function of divine will. It serves as one spiritual crime among many through which the reprobate might be justly condemned, and 'to proove whether [God's] children will steadfastly beleeve in him, and seeke unto his word'.[13] And, as if thinking about the contrast between the *Combat*'s focus on the devil's desire to 'overturne states' and the everyday harm of village witches to crops and cattle, Perkins draws the lesson that 'the devill can doe so much onely as God permits him, and no more'.[14] This unremitting focus on divine power makes Perkins emphasize, at length, that Satan cannot act within the world in a way which contests – even if the net effect is to complicate – God's ownership and governance of creation and the laws of nature. Thus, the acts of a witch might appear to be

> extraordinarie workes in regard of man, because they proceed not from the usuall and ordinarie course of nature: and yet ... they are done by the vertue of nature, and not above or against nature simply, but above and against the ordinarie course thereof.[15]

In other words, the devil manipulates not nature itself, but our expectations of it. For instance, Perkins's solution to the apparent problem of dead people seeming to return to life is both prosaic and proto-Frankensteinian. Satan 'is able, having gathered together fit matter, to joyne member to member, and to make a true bodie', and then 'to enter into it, to moove and stirre it up and downe' – a 'strange worke' certainly, but, crucially, not one 'above' nature.[16] In a similar vein – and evoking an equally striking mental image – the devil can feign profound predictive knowledge, not through any equivalent to divine omniscience, but because he has demonic minions 'present at all assemblies and meetings, and thereby [they] are acquainted with the consultations and conferences both of Princes and people' – moving at lightning speed, they can then pool and exploit the secrets that they have learned.[17]

Perkins's theologically self-conscious focus on emphasizing the power of his predestinarian deity ensured that he was rigorous in highlighting the devil's inability to transcend the laws of divinely ordained nature. Mocking up pseudo-living bodies and 'speedily convey[ing] himselfe from place to place', the devil looks more like the sole being with access to the internet in an age of the horse and cart, than he does the second most awesome spiritual being in the universe. Stuart Clark is, of course, correct when he points out that there was something close to a consensus among demonologists that 'despite the sheer extent and variety of their powers, devils ultimately obeyed the laws of nature'.[18] And more broadly it might be said that all orthodox demonologists were forced to work within the constraints of a 'metaphysical triangle', which balanced the moral culpability of the witch, the threat of the devil and the ultimate sovereignty of God – for to lay too much stress upon one of these principles inevitably weakened the other two, with potentially heretical consequences. However, demonologists were far from an undifferentiated mass, and the distinctive ways in which they erected their systems might be able to give us some information about the stability of the cumulative structure.

Without question, Perkins's logical impetus entailed a strong centre of gravity away from the witch and toward the devil, and in turn away from the devil and toward God. Where some theorists placed (sometimes voyeuristic) emphasis on the deeds of the witch, Perkins focussed squarely on the top-down mechanics. He called witchcraft a 'wicked Arte'; but whereas in most cases 'the Arts-master is able by himselfe to practise his art', in the case of witchcraft it is 'otherwise' as the 'power' to effect the art 'is derived wholly from Satan'.[19] This power in turn rests upon 'permission' from God, and it is to this important – and slippery – concept that we must now turn.

Contemporaries often understood divine permission in passive terms: as a means of allowing an evil act to happen without it undermining God's omnipotence, but without recourse to His direct agency so as not to impugn His moral goodness. But as a rigorous Calvinist, Perkins did not need the devil to lead people to Hell – God's decree of reprobation had already played the decisive role. As such, while Perkins may have used the language of divine 'permission', what he meant by the term was something more active, contributing unambiguously to God's wider providential pathways. An analogy would be the distinction, in law enforcement, between a sting operation and entrapment – in the former case, police allow a crime to occur, whereas in the latter they facilitate its occurrence, with both enterprises being designed to apprehend those who deserve judgement. Perkins's deity 'permiteth the Arts of Magicke & Witchcraft ... in his providence, either for the triall of his children or for the punishment of the wicked'[20]. The passive concept of permission (the sting operation), in the space of the same sentence is transmuted into the much more active notion of providential entrapment. Power and agency are greedily sucked back into ambit of the predestinarian God, and witchcraft becomes a sub-type of providence rather than a true 'damned art' in its own right. It might be objected that all of this adds up to little more than a shift in rhetorical presentation: Perkins did, after all, accept that malefic witchcraft existed and must be punished. But language matters, and here Perkins was very deliberately avoiding the sort of hysterical, dualistic, and apocalyptic framework which consumed many of those who served to stoke the fires of the European witch-hunts.

We might also add two other ways in which Perkins's demonology was unusual. For one, he was wholly uninterested in the notion of the witches' sabbat, and with its associated concepts of human flight and sex with demons. Perkins is stony in his silence about these increasingly central concepts within contemporary demonology.[21] Given the likelihood that the *Damned Art* was written after James' *Daemonologie*, it is probable that he would have been aware of the Scottish king's argument that witches can be 'carried by the force of the Spirite which is their conductor, either above the earth or above the sea swiftlie.' James went on to say that this flight, being 'violent &

forceable', can only be sustained for 'a shorte bounds' and for as long as the witch can hold their 'breath.' Perkins doubtless steered clear of such arguments both to uphold his metaphysical principles, and to avoid the possibility of ridicule, unprotected as he was by the gravity of kingship. James at least tempered his surreal account by allowing that witches might also fly only in spirit, as it is known that 'witnesses … have seene their bodies lying senseless in the meane time'.[22]

In a formative Protestant demonology of which Perkins would surely have been aware, the Frenchman Lambert Daneau sought to undermine even this sort of pseudo-rationalism, arguing that witnesses who enter the 'chambers and beddes' of witches observe only 'counterfeit bodies placed in their steede by Satan', to mask the true bodily flight that is occurring simultaneously.[23] As we have seen, Perkins also deployed 'counterfeit bodies', but he used them for a completely contrary purpose. That is, where Daneau used them as a type of 'special pleading' for the power of the devil to destroy human confidence in the laws of nature, Perkins's construction of the undead was explicitly geared toward reinforcing God's power to make the devil conform to nature's 'ordinary' laws. All of this might seem, to us, like hair-splitting within an inherently surreal debate, but these were distinctions to which contemporaries were highly attuned. Knowledgeable readers of Perkins would have understood that he sought either to pass over the physically impossible in silence or to repurpose it to confirm God's explicit control over all happenings within nature. For Perkins, James's flying humans and Daneau's napping doppelgangers were not only a bridge too far but in fact a clear step beyond the limits of Calvinist orthodoxy.

Perkins's fidelity to the principles that underpinned his wider theological worldview are equally evident when we turn to the aspect of demonology with which he is most associated – that of the demonic pact. The normative view was that the covenant between a witch and the devil represented an apostasy from which none could return – it was the clearest possible road to perdition. Remarkably, though, Perkins argued that witches could be members of the elect. This claim underpins a legal discussion – an implicit antitype to Jean Bodin°'s notion of witchcraft as a *crimen exceptum* and a uniquely wicked crime against God – which urges high standards of evidence and advises 'all Jurers' that they be 'carefull what they doe', and never convict 'without sound and sufficient proofes', lest their 'rashnesse' leads them to 'shedding innocent bloud'.[24] Entirely inverting the premise behind many continental demonologies, Perkins argues that the devil does not seek to protect his witches – the starting point for claims that extraordinary legal processes are needed – but in fact seeks actively to abandon them. One reason for this is that, much to Satan's chagrin, even some of those 'in confederacie' with him, 'have through the great mercie of God … been reclaimed and … freed from his covenant.' As such, the devil seeks 'to prevent … their conversion, by laying a plot for their discoverie'.[25]

There are two explanations for Perkins's radical claim that 'some one or more [witches] may belong to Gods election'.[26] The first lies in an unusually pure reading of how predestination and providence relate to each other. Although the categories of 'election' and 'reprobation' were created before time began, in the case of each 'elect' person their conversion – the point at which saving faith is imputed into them – occurs at a specific point in their life. Before that time, they may be embroiled in any of the same sins as a reprobate. Salvation is not caused by good works, and neither is damnation caused by bad ones. Perkins and his fellow puritan evangelists argued that no sin was beyond forgiveness: that God sometimes demonstrated His mercy by bringing men to heaven 'by the very gates of hell.' No example of this could have been more breath-taking – and comforting for a troubled sinner – than the potential salvation of a reclaimed witch. In Perkins's hands, witchcraft could usefully serve as a 'lesson for the meaning of predestination as a whole'.[27]

The second reason why Perkins argued that witches could be among the elect was even more central to his theological instincts: simply, the covenant of grace must trump all other forms of contractual relationship. People might appear bad – and might indeed be reprobate – but we can know nothing of the fate of souls in this life. As long as a person has breath in their body, they might be freed by God from the threat of hellfire. As such, Perkins was deeply uncomfortable with the notion – however conventional within some quarters – that there was a diametric opposition, or equivalence, between deals with the devil and covenants with God.[28] This meant that life was messy rather than binary, because for 'causes best knowne to [God] himselfe', the elect may first be 'holden in the snares of Satan' before, 'in mercie he reclaimes them'.[29] Such are the mysteries of providence – the lesson is that true believers must strive to acquire an informed knowledge of both divine power and their own ignorance, and certainly not to seek the death of another based upon superficial considerations.

However, the notion of the elect witch created a practical problem. If the devil sought their discovery and execution, then the judicial procedures must not be stacked toward a presumption of guilt. As such, Perkins insists that 'the forme and order of Law' must be followed, just as it is in the case of 'a theefe or a murtherer', and the verdict determined according to sound evidence and witness testimonies.[30] On the other hand, because witchcraft is a secret crime, it cannot be discovered by ordinary means – as Sir Robert Filmer (c.1588–1653), one of Perkins's shrewdest critics, pointed out, it makes little sense to promote reliance on evidence from witnesses within a covenant-centric understanding of witchcraft, simply because such compacts 'be [so] very secret, that hardly a man can be brought, which upon his own knowledge can aver such things'.[31] Because this sort of evidence cannot be discovered through the usual processes of detection and observation, Perkins is forced to allow that torture may 'lawfully and with good conscience be used', provided that the evidence is already 'strong'.[32] Perkins certainly sought moderation in his approach to witch prosecution, but his views were also hard both to maintain and implement with any degree of consistency. It is difficult to rely upon torture to extract evidence of secret demonic interactions while being sufficiently mild in the use of it that none who are innocent will ever confess their guilt. It remains an open question whether Perkins's 'uneasy accommodations' did more to consolidate the by-and-large professionally administered and evidence-oriented character of English witch trials in the seventeenth century, or to facilitate those such as Matthew Hopkins who sought to exploit legal loop holes and ambivalences within authoritative writings to pursue brutal, systematic hunts.[33]

It would not be entirely fair, though, to dwell on Perkins's failure to develop an assured legal approach to the problems of procedure and evidence: he was, after all, a theologian not a jurist, and he wrote the *Damned Art* not primarily to prescribe the punishment of malefic witches, but instead to redefine how contemporaries understood witchcraft itself. It is to Perkins's focus on diabolic compact that we must now return, and to the ways in which he sought to shift the focus from the practices of black magic to the phenomenon of white witchcraft.

## 2 'Naturall popery' and white witchcraft

It is important to understand that Perkins thought about witchcraft less as a discrete category of crime, and more as a moral and psychological tendency which flowed naturally from the (fallen) human condition itself. He had a similar attitude to Catholicism: it was not only an institutional religion, but more profoundly something that manifested in what he termed 'the naturall Popery of the multitude'.[34] People are naturally prideful and selfish, preferring to pursue their interests through an overestimation of their own abilities: so too popery is 'naturall' because 'there is none by nature free from this thought', that one looks to be saved 'by their own righteousnesse'.[35] Within Perkins's wider oeuvre he wrote relatively little about malefic witchcraft. The same could not be said, though, of white witchcraft. 'In our daies', he says in his *Exposition of the... Creede*,

> the common practise ... when crosses and calamities fall ... is [a] trotting out to that wise man, to this cunning woman ..., that is, from God to the divell; and their counsell is received and practised without any bones making.[36]

And in his *Exposition upon ... Galatians* we are told that, 'in the time of distresse upon extremity, figure-casting, and charming, are overmuch used'.[37] Catholicism functions in much the same way, bringing the 'common sort to yeeld unto them' by 'deluging the outward senses with false apparitions of ghosts and soules of men, walking and ranging abroad after their departure' –

playing upon a predictable human response to 'extremitie of feare and dread', Catholic practices of indulgences and prayers for the purgatorial dead persuade people to 'purchase their owne peace and securitie, by many and great expenses'.[38] In other words, human beings seek easy, reassuring answers — whether in the form of saints, sorcerers or, indeed, scapegoats.

In his *Damned Art*, Perkins elaborates on this theme, showing how white witches administer 'the devills Sacraments' — and, like the priests of old, are thanked for it.[39] He gives the example of a person 'who findes himselfe bewitched' and, seeking a cure, 'he sendeth for the suspected Witch' and 'scratch[es] him or her, thinking by this means to be cured of the witchcraft.' However, they are making a terrible mistake in thinking that there is 'vertue' in this method, as the 'helpe' comes 'by the power of the devill'.[40] The cure may superficially succeed, but only because either it or the original malady resulted from a demonic illusion — 'binding' and 'unbinding' witchcraft work in satanically coordinated tandem. What is striking about Perkins's case study is that the witch who was brought forth to be scratched is made entirely incidental: he does not even bother to pause to condemn — or gender — her or him. Instead, Perkins's critical focus is turned upon the scratcher of witches.

This was not, we should note, a mere generic railing against the popular culture of those who remained blithely untouched by Protestant reform agendas — Perkins's targets rarely resided very far from home. He would certainly have been aware of a well-known possession case from the early 1590s in Warboys, Lincolnshire, a village less than 20 miles from Cambridge. The demoniacs were all children from a family of well-to-do, godly Protestants, the Throckmortons, and the case gained significant exposure through a popular pamphlet, *The Most Strange ... Discoverie of the Three Witches of Warboys* (1593). A detailed account is given in this pamphlet of the numerous occasions upon which the main suspect is brought before the possessed Throckmorton children, at the behest of their desperate parents, and remorselessly scratched in an effort to break the spell.[41] Solid, educated Protestants like the Throckmortons would never have countenanced summoning the devil directly. And this was why, to Perkins, 'of the two, the more horrible & detestable Monster is the good Witch ... [because] they are better knowne [i.e. better reputed] then the bad'.[42] He was cutting through social and confessional boundaries, therefore, when he concluded bluntly that, 'the using of these meanes is plaine Witchcraft'.[43]

The Throckmortons would have objected that they did not intend to compact with Satan and so could not be guilty of witchcraft. Perkins offered this ambiguous response:

> it is to be remembered, that [no witchcraft practices] can be effected, unlesse the partie have made a league with the devill, expresse or secret, or at the least, a preparation thereunto, by a false and erroneous opinion of the meanes.[44]

This distinction between – and indeed conflation of – conscious and unconscious demonic pacts was one of Perkins's more distinctive demonological insights.[45] Through a carefully constructed ambiguity, he was able to underline the soul-threatening seriousness of accidental entanglements with the demonic, while also offering hope that the damage done was not yet irretrievable. This warning was much needed, because when Perkins surveyed widespread superstitions, he found no shortage of beliefs and practices that could be accounted as witchcraft, according to his broad definition of an 'implicite' pact. Everything from astrology to popish exorcism rites to the belief that spilled salt signalled bad luck, and even making the sign of the cross to ward off evil, constituted a form of witchcraft.[46] Robert Filmer objected that according to such criteria, 'then whole Nations are every man of them Witches, which I thinke none will say'.[47] It is true that Perkins would not have quite said this, but he was perfectly happy to imply something close to it: 'naturall popery' did, after all, belong to a 'multitude' rather than a minority, and it was the reprobate not the elect who made up the bulk of humankind.

Perkins, though, was not seeking to describe a static reality, but to counteract a societal trend, and his exaggeration of the proportion of witches among the population constituted a deliberate strategy. He was writing in the 1590s, a third of a century after Protestantism had been declared the national religion of England, when a generation of born-and-bred Protestants were perhaps inclined to think salvation their birth-right: that all you needed to do to be saved was to hate Jesuits and Spaniards, and say three cheers for Good Queen Bess. In his *Combat*, Perkins had warned:

> beware of presumption, [which] is the common snare of the devil wherein he intangles many a soule. It is true indeed that he oft prevailes by bringing men to desperation, but a thousand perish through presumption, almost for every one by desperation: for despaire is a painfull thing to flesh and bloud, and as the devill knowes well … to presume is sweet and pleasant to the flesh, and most agreeable to mans corrupt nature.[48]

Perkins feared less a full-blown Catholic revival than he did the emergence of a nominally Protestant society that sleepwalked its way into worshipping Satan in the name of God. Just as his wider pastoral mission sought to challenge people's assumptions about what 'godliness' truly constituted, so too his 'evangelical demonology' took on a similar set of shapes and priorities.[49] Ignorance was antithetical to salvation: 'without knowledge it cannot be that any should truely beleeve', he wrote in his *Exposition of the … Creede*.[50] Some self-proclaimed Protestants needed to understand that 'their present ungodly practises … may bring them in time to be the ranckest Witches that can be'.[51]

Perkins thus understood witchcraft to be an insidious threat which functioned upon a spectrum of (often well-meaning) error, and he was more concerned by this than any sort of existential threat that malefic witchcraft posed to society. But presumption cut both ways, and Perkins thought it just as dangerous to deny that witches existed as to blithely assume that one could never become entangled with witchcraft oneself. It was for this reason that Perkins developed a clever and distinctive critique of the infamous witchcraft sceptic Reginald Scot°. Although Perkins never references Scot by name, his editor, Thomas Pickering, does: in his preface he calls Scot 'the gainsayer', and states that his views 'grossely erre'.[52] Perkins's refutation of Scot begins – as indeed does the book itself – with the injunction of Exodus 22:18: 'Thou shalt not suffer a witch to live.' 'The patrones of Witches', says Perkins, 'indeavour to delude the true interpretation of that lawe. For by a Witch (they say) we must understand a poisoner'.[53] His initial response to Scot's famous claim looks rather narrow. He says that because elsewhere in the Bible it is stated that murderers (of which poisoners are, of course, a subtype) should be put to death, according to a principle of divine economy it is therefore unlikely that 'there should be one and the same law twice propounded for the same thing.' As such, 'the word used by Moses in [Exodus] signifieth not a poisoner properly, but a Witch'.[54]

This looks like a standard refutation of Scot. But what Perkins does next is important. He goes on to argue that there were numerous biblical witches who would not deserve death if the core criterion was that they used their magic to kill – 'we reade not of any great hurt that was done by the Inchanters of Egypt, or by the Pythonisse of Endor, or by Simon Magus', he says; and yet still they deserve to die. The reason that they must be killed is 'the very making of a league with the devil … For by vertue of this alone … they stand guiltie of horrible impietie before God'.[55] He makes the point again on the last page of the treatise: 'As the killing witch must die by another Lawe, as though he were no Witch: so the healing and harmlesse Witch must die by this Law … onely for the covenant made with Satan'.[56] Startlingly, the white witch becomes the essence of witchcraft itself: it is here that the intrinsic evil of the covenant with Satan is revealed in its purest, simplest form. Scot is refuted, because witchcraft need not be a physical crime, but only one of mental – or even unconscious – allegiance.

## 3 Conclusion

Perkins was not a sceptic when it came to malefic witchcraft, but his account was surrounded with sceptical instincts, and he struggled intellectually to disentangle the category from the ways in which God routinely inflicts providential harm on those who require spiritual correction. This made it impossible for him to buy into the apocalyptic notion that society was somehow under grave threat from black magic. It is no coincidence that he devoted only a fraction of the *Damned Art* to this sort of witchcraft, and it may also explain why he apparently lacked the motivation to decide whether malefic witches should simply be put to death for murder (as implied in his refutation of Scot) or whether more extreme judicial methods were required for teasing out their guilt on the basis of a diabolic pact. These gaps and ambiguities may also be a result of Perkins never writing the book front-to-back himself, and its final form being left to the endeavours of Thomas Pickering's far less subtle theological mind. But we might also say that Perkins only felt able to construct a demonology which he considered to be orthodox by keeping his distance from contemporary fashions.

The *Damned Art* was significantly more ambitious, forthright, and accomplished, however, when it came to the centrality of white witchcraft. Not only did this focus help to pare the phenomenon down to its one irreducible element – the diabolic compact – but it also allowed Perkins to connect the subject back to the theological, pastoral, and indeed psychological, concerns which had animated his entire evangelical career. Salvation depended not upon good intentions, but upon a properly informed devotion to God, which necessarily also entailed a heightened awareness of one's own sinful natural instincts and motivations. The most disturbing thing about witchcraft, properly understood, was less its supernatural origin than its natural appeal – indeed, outside of fallen nature it had no scope to exist whatsoever. It was, at root, a lack of faith in God's power rather than an active appeal to the devil that facilitated witchcraft. As if to prove this point in the most striking way possible, Perkins turned the whole conversation on its head to argue for the possible salvation of witches. There was no more incredible way of showing just how easy it was to fail to place divine power and possibility at the centre of every consideration. Perkins had lessons for people who wanted to hunt witches as well as for those who denied their existence; above all, though, he wrote to enlighten those who actually were witches-of-sorts but did not know it because they did not know their own hearts. His diagnosis was uncompromising, and it may not be a surprise to find that contemporary readers sought easier answers elsewhere.

## Notes

1. Clive Holmes suggests that Perkins's reference to 'learned' proponents of the swimming test for witches may well be an allusion to James VI. Although hardly conclusive, it is hard to think who else Perkins may have had in mind here, as most contemporary demonologists opposed the practice: Clive Holmes, 'Popular Culture? Witches, Magistrates and Divines in Early Modern England', in Steven L. Kaplan, ed., *Understanding Popular Culture: Europe from the Middle Ages to the Nineteenth Century*, New York: Mouton, 1984, p. 104. The same view is taken by Robert Filmer, who says that Perkins 'condemnes point blanke King James' judgement ... in allowing of the triall of a Witch by swimming': Robert Filmer, *An Advertisement to the Jury-Men of England, touching Witches*, London: Richard Royston, 1653, p. 11.
2. Perkins's most popular book, *The Foundation of Christian Religion*, went into 34 editions in England alone. By contrast, *The Damned Art* went into only two editions, one in 1608 and the other in 1610.
3. John L. Teall, 'Witchcraft and Calvinism in Elizabethan England: Divine Power and Human Agency', *Journal of the History of Ideas*, 1962, vol. 23/1, 29.
4. Thomas Ady, *A Candle in the Dark: A Treatise Concerning the Nature of Witches and Witchcraft*, London: Thomas Newberry, 1656, p. 163. With thanks to Clive Holmes for this reference.

5  Ady, *A Candle in the Dark*, p. 140. For Ady's scepticism about the authorship of the *Daemonologie*, see also P. G. Maxwell-Stuart's contribution to this volume.
6  The more distinctive and ambivalent aspects of Perkin's approach are downplayed in Stuart Clark's seminal study, *Thinking with Demons: The Idea of Witchcraft in Early Modern Europe*, Oxford: Oxford University Press, 1997. For Perkins as a 'right-wing' Calvinist who primarily wrote to promote the execution of all witches see, Teall, 'Witchcraft and Calvinism in Elizabethan England', pp. 29–30.
7  Wolfgang Behringer, *Witchcraft Persecutions in Bavaria: Popular Magic, Religious Zealotry and Reason of State in Early Modern Europe*, Cambridge: Cambridge University Press, 1997, p. 14.
8  Ady, *A Candle in the Dark*, p. 162.
9  William Perkins, 'The Combat Betweene Christ and the Devill Displayed', in *The Workes of ... William Perkins*, London: James Boler et al., 1631, vol. 3, p. 379, 385.
10  Perkins, 'The Combat', p. 388.
11  Perkins, 'The Combat', p. 397.
12  Perkins, 'The Combat', p. 382, 401.
13  William Perkins, *A Discourse of the Damned Art of Witchcraft*, Cambridge: Cantrel Legge, 1608, p. 38.
14  Perkins, *Damned Art*, p. 39.
15  Perkins, *Damned Art*, p. 18.
16  Perkins, *Damned Art*, p. 31.
17  Perkins, *Damned Art*, pp. 59–60.
18  Clark, *Thinking with Demons*, p. 163.
19  Perkins, *Damned Art*, p. 12.
20  Perkins, *Damned Art*, p. 38.
21  Perkins does briefly and obliquely state that the devil can 'very speedily ... convay himselfe and other creatures into places farre distant from one another', but makes no mention of the sabbat or of actual flight, and is clear that such 'wonders' can never derive from an alteration in the natural properties of things. Perkins's precision in such matters can be seen in his careful observation that while Satan may be able to generate speech by manipulating the larynx of another, 'beeing a spirit' he cannot speak himself, and must make use of a creature specifically 'as hath the instruments of speech, or such whereby speech may be framed or uttered.' If Satan cannot speak through a 'stone', it seems very unlikely that Perkins would allow that he could make a human fly: Perkins, *Damned Art*, p. 21, 32.
22  James VI, *Daemonologie*, Edinburgh: Robert Waldegrave, 1597, pp. 39, 40.
23  Lambert Daneau, *A Dialogue of Witches*, London: R. Watkins, 1575, sig. H1r (chap. IV).
24  Perkins, *Damned Art*, p. 218.
25  Perkins, *Damned Art*, p. 216.
26  Perkins, *Damned Art*, p. 217.
27  Ian Bostridge, *Witchcraft and its Transformations, c.1650–1750*, Oxford: Oxford University Press, 1997, p. 12.
28  Perkins's editor, Thomas Pickering was, however, guilty of this in his Dedicatory Epistle to the *Damned Art*, listing a crude set of equivalences between the methods of God and the devil; but Perkins himself was much more careful. He certainly would not have agreed with King James that 'the devill is the verie contrarie opposite to God', both because this suggests that their power was comparable, and because Perkins would not have accepted that Satan had any capacities or fundamental attributes which God lacks: Perkins, *Damned Art*, pp. 2–3; James, *Daemonologie*, p. 55.
29  Perkins, *Damned Art*, p. 217.
30  Perkins, *Damned Art*, p. 199.

31 Filmer, *Advertisement*, sig. A3r.
32 Perkins, *Damned Art*, p. 204.
33 Malcolm Gaskill, 'Witchcraft and Evidence in Early Modern England', *Past & Present*, 2008, vol. 198/1, 57 and *passim*.
34 Perkins, 'An Exposition upon ... Galatians', *Workes*, vol. 2, p. 422.
35 Perkins, 'A Treatise of Mans Imaginations', *Workes*, vol. 2, p. 471.
36 Perkins, 'An Exposition of the ... Creede', *Workes*, vol. 1, p. 128.
37 Perkins, 'Galatians', p. 332.
38 Perkins, *Damned Art*, p. 26.
39 Perkins, *Damned Art*, p. 175.
40 Perkins, *Damned Art*, p. 55.
41 For the full story of this case – and the scratching – see, Philip C. Almond, *The Witches of Warboys: An Extraordinary Story of Sorcery, Sadism and Satanic Possession*, London: I. B. Tauris, 2008, esp. pp. 38–43.
42 Perkins, *Damned Art*, pp. 174–75.
43 Perkins, *Damned Art*, p. 55.
44 Perkins, *Damned Art*, p. 56.
45 Richard Bernard made faithful use of Perkins's understanding of demonic pacts in his *A Guide to Grand-Jury Men ... A Treatise Touching Witches*, London: Ed. Blackmore, 1627, p. 124 and *passim*.
46 Perkins, *Damned Art*, pp. 72–77, 150.
47 Filmer, *Advertisement*, p. 14.
48 Perkins, 'Combat', pp. 390–91.
49 This phrase is from Stuart Clark, 'Protestant Demonology: Sin, Superstition, and Society', Bengt Ankarloo and Gustav Henningsen, eds, *Early Modern European Witchcraft: Centres and Peripheries*, Oxford: Clarendon Press, 1990, p. 57.
50 Perkins, 'Creede', p. 123.
51 Perkins, *Damned Art*, pp. 170–71.
52 Perkins, *Damned Art*, sig. 6r.
53 Perkins, *Damned Art*, p. 178. Perkins is referencing Reginald Scot, *The Discoverie of Witchcraft*, London: William Brome, 1584, pp. 111–12 (bk VI, chap. 1).
54 Perkins, *Damned Art*, p. 180.
55 Perkins, *Damned Art*, p. 183.
56 Perkins, *Damned Art*, p. 255.

## Further reading

Breward, Ian, ed., *The Works of William Perkins*, Abingdon: Sutton Courtenay, 1970, introductory essay.
Dixon, Leif, *Practical Predestinarians in England, c.1590–1640*, Farnham: Ashgate, 2014, chap. 2.
Jinkins, Michael, 'Perkins, William (1558–1602), Theologian and Church of England Clergyman', *Oxford Dictionary of National Biography*, (24 May 2007).
Patterson, W. B., *William Perkins and the Making of a Protestant England*, Oxford: Oxford University Press, 2014.
Sharpe, James, *Instruments of Darkness: Witchcraft in England, 1550–1750*, Philadelphia: University of Pennsylvania Press, 1997, chap. 3.
Teall, John L., 'Witchcraft and Calvinism in Elizabethan England: Divine Power and Human Agency', *Journal of the History of Ideas*, 1962, vol. 23/1, 21–36.

# 16 Piety and purification
The anonymous *Czarownica powołana*

Michael Ostling

Although the Commonwealth of Poland and Lithuania was host to well over a thousand trials for witchcraft, including some of the last in Europe,[1] its contribution to 'the science of demons' was modest indeed. The turn of the seventeenth century saw the publication of a polemical attack on Agrippan natural magic and an abridged and bowdlerized translation of the *Malleus maleficarum* – the earliest translation of this work into a vernacular language.[2] In the late eighteenth century, Poland's 'clerical Enlightenment' produced a spate of treatises attacking 'superstitious' belief in witches, the water ordeal, vampires, and demonic possession.[3] But in the decades between, the *Czarownica powołana* (1639, hereafter translated as *Denounced Witch*) stands very nearly alone as an original, local denunciation of the excessive cruelty and peremptory justice of the Polish witch-trials.[4]

Polish historiography has celebrated the *Denounced Witch* without studying it very closely, assigning to its author a heroic, enlightened status such as used to be given to Reginald Scot°, Johann Wier°, and Friedrich Spee. His was a 'skeptical voice',[5] whose protest against a fanatical church constituted 'an extraordinarily dangerous act'[6] he was lucky to find 'a printer brave enough to publish this sort of material.'[7] Such a position is no longer tenable. The *Denounced Witch* enjoyed the full approval of the ecclesiastical hierarchy, receiving official approbation from the Bishop of Poznań and from the director of the respected Lubrański Academy, an organ of the Poznań cathedral chapter-house; its publisher, Albertus [Wojciech] Regulus (1595–1652), had at one time been a professor at that same academy.[8] Bishop Kazimierz Florian Czartoryski's later *Mandatum pastorale* explicitly recommends the *Denounced Witch*, together with Spee's *Cautio criminalis*, as moderate guides to the prosecution of witchcraft.[9] Thus the *Denounced Witch* author is no radical skeptic, still less the ahistorical proto-Enlightened 'voice in the wilderness' of earlier accounts. Rather, I will argue, the author was an orthodox, even a zealous voice for Counter-Reformation. Thus resituated, the text emerges as primarily concerned with Catholic reform in three ways: by educating pious but ignorant Catholic common folk, by caring pastorally for the souls of accused witches and their judges, and by attacking educated heretical Protestants as the true diabolical threat to the Polish-Lithuanian commonwealth.

The *Denounced Witch* does not denounce witches. Instead, its central concern is a denunciation of denunciation – of the practice of torturing an accused witch until she denounces her alleged accomplices, who are in turn 'arrested, tied up, dunked in the river, tortured, and burnt at the stake, lest evil multiply' (39). Although the author also denounces 'false exorcists' and other 'superstitious' witchfinders (23, 53–55, 81), he saves the full force of his denunciatory thunder for the secular-court magistrates of small-town Poland; magistrates whom he calls 'legal ignoramuses ... of small understanding,' 'who hardly know their Our Father and have barely heard of the ten commandments' (7, 52). The text ends with a valedictory blast of pent-up vitriol against judges who, by 'lightmindedly, inordinately passing judgement' against innocent women, have set themselves against God himself:

> He gives life, and you, enlivened by Him, unreasonably kill, yearning for a wretched handful of your neighbor's blood. What will this impetuous and unreasonable curiosity get you? Only eternal damnation for you and your household, here on earth and in that world to come. For after your judgement, the inescapable judgement of God awaits.[10]

One can see why a previous generation of scholars could find in such language a rare voice of humanitarian skepticism. And yet one thing we can be pretty sure of, on closer inspection, is that our author was a fervent and partisan Catholic, attacking the witch-trials in the furtherance of, rather than despite, his faith.

## 1 Authorship

We know nothing about the author of the *Denounced Witch* except what its publisher tells us in the preface to the 1639 edition: he is 'a friend of [the publisher], expert in both ecclesiastical and secular law' (vi). The author could indeed be the publisher himself, Albertus Regulus, a former notary to the Crown Chancellery (the royal office handling legal affairs) who seems to have been active in what Wanda Wyporska characterizes as a 'Poznań circle' of intellectuals worried about the inhumane treatment of accused witches before the court.[11] Regulus oversaw the publication of two other texts highly critical of the Polish witch-trials – Daniel Wisner's *Tractatus brevis de extramagis, lamiis, veneficis aliisque malefactoribus* (1639) and an edition of Spee's *Cautio criminalis* (1647), and he is unquestionably responsible for the bitingly sarcastic preface to the first edition, dedicating the book to the 'illustrious burgomasters, city-counsellors, and other magistrates' of the 'most famous towns of Kościan and Grodzisk' (iii) – the sites of recent witch-trials. Regulus' perspective, if not his tortured, excessively erudite style, resemble that of the *Denounced Witch*, as he goes on to condemn the 'vermin' of ignorant magistrates who

> without any proper evidence [...] not considering whether she is guilty or innocent, whether pregnant or not, sometimes arrest an innocent mother and murder her together with her baby of guilty [i.e. unbaptized] soul, damning it eternally. [...] One cannot remain silent.[12]

The authorial evidence is stronger for a second candidate, Daniel Wisner, whose *Tractatus brevis* issued from Regulus' press just two months after the first edition of the *Denounced Witch*. About Wisner we know little more than that he held a doctorate in philosophy and was a 'candidate for [a degree] in both laws' – canon and secular.[13] Karol Koranyi has demonstrated that seven of the thirteen chapters of the *Denounced Witch* overlap closely with the *Tractatus*, and that a few long passages appear to be verbatim translations into Polish of the Latin work (or *vice versa*).[14] However, Koranyi also notes important differences between the two texts. Whereas the *Tractatus* confines its critique to burgher magistrates, the *Denounced Witch* condemns the inhuman cruelty of noble manor-lords as well – 'ungodly people who would kill a peasant as one swallows a plum' (41).[15] Moreover, the *Tractatus* makes use of just one demonological source – Johann Gödelmann's *Tractatus de magis veneficis et lamiis* (1590) – while extensively citing contemporary compendia of criminal law and a number of primarily Italian jurists.[16] In contrast, the *Denounced Witch* neglects the Lutheran Gödelmann; it draws on an extensive list of Catholic demonological treatises, and it takes its canon and secular law from a different list of Italian and Spanish jurists – Prospero Farinacci, Giulio Claro, Baltazar Gómez, Francisco Suárez, and Guiseppe Mascardi.

These divergent citation practices provide the initial evidence that the *Denounced Witch* may have issued from the pen of a Jesuit. Although I have not yet traced every one of the text's citations, their pattern is clear: the author studiously avoids Protestant authorities and shows a marked favor for Jesuit authors. Of 34 identified sources, all but two are Catholic, of which seven, including many of those most frequently cited, belong to the Society of Jesus: these include Martin Delrio° (14 citations), Paul Laymann (13 citations), Delrio's colleague Leonard Lessius (four citations), and Laymann's contemporary Adam Tanner (three citations). The lay Catholic jurist Prospero Farinacci (1544–1618), whose *Praxis et theorica criminalis* our author cites 13 times, was also a strong influence on Tanner and Laymann (and Spee).[17] Our author cites the aforementioned Lutheran Johann Georg Gödelmann just once (and probably after Wisner), to recount an incident where 'a few real witches [...] were put to the water test, and every one of them sank to the bottom like an axe' (57). In this one instance, our author seems to have found himself unable to avoid making use of a 'heretical' source for so delicious a proof of the water ordeal's falsity.

More telling still are several anecdotes which cast the Society of Jesus in a strongly favorable light. These anecdotes not infrequently divert our author from his main topic, as if our author cannot pass up the opportunity to praise the Jesuits. For example, we learn of a convicted female arsonist who denounced a romantic rival out of 'hidden spite'. Both were brought to the stake, and things looked dire until the mother of the innocent girl, 'cried out "O Stanisław Kostka, I have heard of your strength, now I ask you for help in this unhappy hour for my weeping daughter."' The pious executioner withheld his torch, and the arsonist was moved to confess all, absolving her rival and freeing her to travel to the shrine of 'blessed Stanisław' at the Jesuit church in Lublin (59–61). Thus a story intended to illustrate the danger of denunciation improbably transforms itself into a case supporting the canonization of Stanisław Kostka (1550–1568), the noble Jesuit novice whose short, devout, and virginal life became a model for post-Tridentine devotion in Poland.

If our author indeed belonged to the Jesuit order, this helps explain some details of the text, such as hints of pastoral care for convicted criminals (26, 42–43, 59), evidence for a peripatetic, possibly missionary life in the eastern hinterlands of the Commonwealth (42, 77, 82), and of course his zealous anti-Protestantism. And yet the identification of the author of this 'tolerant' text with the Society of Jesus might seem surprising. The historiography of the Jesuits in Poland, not without justification, portrays them as indefatigably intolerant apologists for a rigid Catholic orthodoxy. Students from the Jesuit academies regularly harassed Protestants in cities such as Lublin and Toruń, leading not infrequently to riots – one such riot led to the destruction of the Lutheran church in Poznań a few years before the *Denounced Witch* was published. Intensive Jesuit promotion of Eucharistic devotion helped foment accusations against Polish Jews for desecration of the Eucharist and for blood libel: as when the remains of young Wojciech, allegedly murdered by the Jews of Łosice in 1598, was given 'to the Jesuit Fathers in Lublin as a jewel,'[18] placed on the altar of the same Jesuit church where our acquitted arsonist prayed in gratitude to Stanisław Kostka. Later historians blamed the Jesuits for the ignorance and superstition of the *ancien regime*: thanks to 'the obscurantism of the Jesuit schools,' claims Józef Łukaszewicz, one finds witch trials on 'nearly every page' of the early modern Polish court-records.[19] Beyond Poland, Jesuits such as Martin Delrio made demonology respectable at the turn of the seventeenth century, updating the late-medieval arguments of texts such as the *Malleus maleficarum* and providing legitimacy to the major witch-hunts of the first decades of that bloody century. But in the 1620s and 30s a new generation of Jesuits – the aforementioned Tanner, Laymann, and especially Spee – reacted to these trials with calls for a humanitarian response. My goal in what follows is to bridge the intra-Jesuit divide between Delrio and Spee, a task attempted by the *Denounced Witch* itself.

Its author explains that he was spurred to write 'out of Christian love in order to rescue the consciences' of people who 'crave that their neighbors lose both their good name and their health' (3). As should be clear by now, the souls thus endangered belong not to maleficent witches but to their accusers and judges. This sets up our author's basic rhetorical strategy. Witches, stereotypically, are enemies of God and humankind, craving the destruction of their neighbors. The *Denounced Witch* author subverts the stereotype, accusing the accusers of alleged witches of antisocial wrath. We shall see this rhetorical reversal used several times: exorcists and magistrates, not accused witches, are prone to superstition; magistrates, not the women accused of witchcraft, are 'light-minded' and 'curious'; Protestants, not accused witches, practice diabolical magic. This inversionary strategy allows our author to have his cake and eat it too: to develop a thoroughgoing attack on witch-trial procedure without straying from Catholic demonological orthodoxy – indeed, in defense of such orthodoxy.

## 2 Three interpretations of the text

### 2.1 As a pastor: against superstitious judges and witchfinders

The *Denounced Witch* repeatedly insists that witches must be tried before ecclesiastical courts, because ecclesiastical judges are better practiced at discerning whether the accused are

> real Witches [*Czarownice*] or only hocus-pocusters [*zabobonice*], which [...] are not the same. For witchcraft includes insult against the Majesty of God and the holy things belonging to Him, together with harm against one's neighbor, [...] whereas hocus-pocustry often does not include those two features, and usually does not fall to the judgement or punishment of the secular law.[20]

The term I have unsatisfactorily translated as 'hocus-pocuster' is *zabobonica*, our author's own back-formation from *zabobon* – a frivolous or silly superstition. *Zabobonica* cannot be satisfactorily translated as 'cunning-woman' (*guślarka, znachorka*), for, as our author makes clear, he means by this term anyone who practices any ritual or prayer or folk practice not officially condoned by the Catholic Church. By this standard, almost everybody – certainly almost every peasant-woman, is a hocus-pocuster, as our author goes on to admit:

> Ba! Sometimes such practices imply no sin at all, for they proceed from a small and frivolous understanding, especially that of women, among whom hocus-pocustry [*zabobony*] are as numerous as grains of sand. And it would be hard to find even one such woman, albeit pious, who does not at least from time to time, out of ignorance, practice such hocus-pocustry and put faith in it: for example spitting three times, with pursed lips; when lifting a child from the bath, taking the child by the nose and giving it a pull; and if someone dies, pouring out the water in which the

body was washed behind those who carry the corpse to the cemetery. Also not looking into a mirror after midnight, or not washing the dishes on Thursday after the evening meal. Why? They know; I know as well but I won't say.[21]

This is extraordinary: among the superstitions judged as 'implying no sin at all' is the feeding of house-demons with the table scraps left over after Thursday-evening meals — as clear an example of Slavic folk-demonolatry as one is likely to find, and a *locus classicus* of Polish anti-superstition polemic since Stanisław of Skarbimierz's early fifteenth-century condemnation of those who venerate 'Satanic' house-demons through offerings of food on Thursdays.[22] Although our author later inveighs at length against idolatry (20–21), he is willing to overlook it when practiced by 'pious' but 'frivolous' women.

Indeed our author finds pious Catholicism in folk practice wherever he reasonably, or even not-very-reasonably, can. Post-Tridentine Catholic reform in Poland was characterized by what Tomasz Wiślicz describes as a '"diabolization" of folk culture' — the reforming village priest Stanisław Brzeżański considered it a form of demonolatry to kneel in church on one knee rather than two.[23] And yet the *Denounced Witch* can find Christian piety even in the peasant Midsummer's Eve celebrations, almost universally condemned by post-Tridentine reformers as diabolical 'Pagan customs'.[24] So whereas Marcin of Urzędów decried the ritual use of mugwort (*Artemisia vulgaris* L.) as an allegedly pagan herb dedicated to the goddess Diana at midsummer bonfires where women 'give worship and prayer to the devil';[25] our author Christianizes both the herbal ritual and the festival — incidentally recapitulating St. John's exorcistic baptism of pagan nature on the feast day that, bearing his name, intends to supersede pagan Midsummer: 'houses, and the entranceways of houses, are decorated devoutly with mugwort from olden times, and garlands worn in sign of celebration, according to Scripture: "Many will rejoice at his [John's] birth"' (22, citing Luke 1:14).[26]

This is not to say that the *Denounced Witch* trivializes superstition. Its legal justification for claiming ecclesiastical jurisdiction over witch-trials relies on an equation between superstition and heresy: because *zabobonice* 'don't believe that the devil is really so vile [...] which smells of heresy' (4), theirs is a religious crime, under church jurisdiction. Indeed our author can be hyper-scrupulous: *any* intermixture of 'holy words [or] pious prayers,' with worldly concerns means those words were 'spoken in the devil's honor, although in themselves pious, because he has hidden his nooses and his words in holy things and in Sacraments' to 'fool pious people and to defame the Majesty of God and of holy things' (28–29). But this scrupulosity undermines itself; if the devil has hidden his nooses in the sacraments themselves, then it is clear that common Catholics are often both demonolatrous and pious simultaneously. This is forgivable, insofar as such people are also *fools*: only fools can worship God and the devil at the same time, and by accident. 'Light-minded' women fulfil this definition, as do the peasantry more generally, especially those of 'shallow understanding,' 'such as one finds without measure in White Ruthenia' (21 – our author thus adds ethnic stereotype to misogyny in his arsenal of exculpatory paternalistic attitudes). Peasants practicing hocus-pocustry are like those who chase after 'what Philosophers call *ignis fatuus*, that is to say stupid fire' (78): they require pastoral instruction not judicial destruction.

Our author cites the *Malleus maleficarum* just once, in a discussion of love charms (34), but his passage answering the question 'Why are there more female witches than male?' (35–38) betrays a close reading of Institoris°'s infamous answer to an almost identical question.[27] Like Institoris, our author reminds the reader that 'the beginnings of sin come from a woman, that is from Eve, our ancestress' (36); like Institoris he recites a list of exceptionally virtuous women to soften the general condemnation of female vice (35–36); like Institoris, he complains throughout against women's unbridled passion and prattling tongues (36–37, cf. 42, 74). But whereas the *Malleus* uses misogyny to explain female demonolatry, a similar misogyny in the *Denounced Witch* functions to explain demonolatry *away*: emotional, 'lightminded' women are acting only as expected, while in contrast 'magistrates should rule by justice, not by affect' (38). In stooping to the depths of womanish emotionalism, our author suggests, magistrates are doing the devil's work.

While the author is willing to turn half a blind eye at least toward the peccadillos of 'light-minded' women or of peasants 'of shallow understanding,' he unleashes his full wrath against a comparable but less excusable 'light-mindedness' among magistrates who use 'witchcraft' themselves in the court of law, 'testing with superstitions who is a witch and who is not' through the water ordeal or other divinatory procedures (67). Ironically it is the magistrate 'who runs to the devil for help' (67) in order to send an allegedly demonolatrous witch to her death. Our author redefines such a magistrate as an 'egregious hocus-pocuster [*zabobonik*] and superstition-worker [*guślarz*]', 'worthy of the stake' himself (53).

Similarly, although one might licitly turn for help against witchcraft to licensed exorcists who follow the official *Rituale Romanum*, false exorcists working as witch-finders should be handed over '*to the secular arm* for charcoal' (77), since they sow 'discord among people: husband against wife, Lord and Lady against their servants and neighbors' (76). Again, while women and peasants are *expected* to be curious, incautious, and light-minded (and are thereby partially absolved of the consequences of such dispositions), magistrates and exorcists are culpably ignorant since they are counted on by society to be wise – our author quotes, on this subject, Psalms 2:10: 'O kings, be wise; be warned, O rulers of the earth' (title page).[28]

### 2.2 As a humanitarian: against diabolically cruel magistrates

Although the traditional humanitarian lens is insufficient by itself for a full understanding the *Denounced Witch*, there can be no doubt that the author does speak out eloquently against the suffering of innocent women accused of witchcraft. Magistrates endanger their own consciences when they fail to 'be wise' in the prosecution of this 'most difficult, most tangled' crime, 'entering into it curiously, or incautiously, or with a light-minded disposition' (4). Insofar as secular judges fail to understand their duty to 'proceed very cautiously,' they 'deserve what the Apostle said [Rom. 2:1]: "by judging others, you have condemned yourself"' (62). When they convict innocent persons by paying heed to such devilish evidence as the water ordeal, testimony recounting the illusory witches' sabbat, or denunciation under torture, they are dupes of the devil – his unwitting servants:

> [A]lthough you do not clearly call on the devil for aid, who is the *accuser of brothers*, nevertheless you assist him in damnation, and in harming humans, which is the purpose and end of all Satanic assistance and agreement.[29]

Our author means this quite literally, noting that innocent women accused of witchcraft 'often hang themselves in their great sorrow,' and thus 'give themselves over to the devil indeed' (71, 42). Others lose their faith in God's justice when faced with the manifest injustice to which the court subjects them: innocent of diabolical witchcraft when arrested, they are incited to diabolism by the very trial procedures ostensibly intended to eradicate witchcraft from the land. The author claims to have been eyewitness to such a process in 'a certain city here in Wielkopolska' where the 'exceptionally venomous wife of [the city's aristocratic] leaseholder' accused an innocent burgher-woman of witchcraft (44). The accused, 'out of great fear, confessed that she is a witch, but not alone': she denounced the wives of the foremost men of the town, hoping 'that their husbands would quickly set her free: for those women were always of good and unblemished reputation' (44). The plan backfired: pressured by the noble leaseholder, the court sentenced several of the denounced to death at the stake, where in desperation the condemned cry out: '"although we are innocent, let the devil take us all, body and soul." And with that commendation or rather desperation, they were burnt alive.' 'The devil', the author concluded the emotional anecdote, 'teaches these judges, as he once taught that malodorous [heretic] Luther, such Jurisprudence' (44). In the next section, we shall return to this curious interjection of Luther, but we must note here the author's artful inversion of categories: the magistrates do Satan's bidding, while the accused witches remain innocent until torture and despair hands them over to the devil.

The *Denounced Witch* sarcastically praises denunciation as 'a beautiful legal procedure, born in Hell!' (58–59). If the denouncer is a real witch, such 'associates of the devil [...] show themselves to be unworthy of trust, because of their hatred and devilish venom against the human race' (65). Alternatively, a confessed witch might honestly denounce her neighbor whom she seems to have seen at the devil's 'ugly banquet;' but this is all Satanic delusion, for the devil 'shapes their fantasy, as if they had attended the banquet, as they lie drunk in their bedding' (58). But most frequently the denouncer, herself no witch, bears false witness when 'broken by torture'

(42), whereupon the innocent women she denounces are 'captured like notorious criminals, tied up, shamelessly stripped naked, tortured, starved, singed with fire' to the point that 'although innocent, they confess everything of which they are accused, just to bring their torment to some sort of end through death' (42). And thus the cycle continues.

To mitigate such chain reaction trials, our author places severe limits on both denunciation and torture.[30] Following Tanner and Farinacci, he insists that a woman cannot be brought to torture on the basis of a single denunciation; moreover, (in a rare explicit disagreement with Delrio) even several denunciations are insufficient in the absence of more substantive evidence (65). Magistrates can send an accused witch to torture only when already convinced of the guilt of the accused by 'proofs and evidence as strong and clear as the noonday sun' (72), and even then, torture is to be kept rigorously within the bounds set out by law. To do otherwise is (in another rhetorical inversion), to become witchlike oneself: 'some cruel, ungodly, wolf-hearted people' transfer alleged witches 'to the forests and the field-borders by night' where they subject them to 'invented tortures of which the law has not even dreamed' (72). Given that 'the forests and the field-borders' were the typical sites of the imagined witches' sabbat, our author is once again suggesting that magistrates are the true servants of Satan.

Nevertheless, our author remains fully orthodox concerning both the reality and the culpability of true diabolical witches, who renounce their baptism, blaspheme against God and the Virgin, and make 'an explicit or open pact with the devil, [thus] murdering their own souls' (25–26). With Satan's assistance and God's permission, such witches aim 'to do the most harm to the greatest number of people': they can cause storms to sink ships at sea, thunder or hail to destroy the crops by land, whirlwinds that knock down houses (30). Such witches are 'worthy of the fire' (14), 'for thus the Lord commanded in Exodus 22: *Maleficos non patieris vivere*: or in our language, thou shalt not suffer a witch to live' (20). But he immediately goes on to emphasize the problem of jurisprudential discernment: 'here's the hole in all that: who is a Witch, and who a Hocus-pocuster? For the courts cannot punish every superstition, nor condemn them all: there would not be enough wood for the pyres' (20). Ignorant secular magistrates are sending too many innocent women to the stake, and if scrupulous care for procedure means a few real witches escape punishment, so be it. Following Tanner (and even Delrio), our author insists that it is 'better to let nine guilty people go free than to allow a tenth, guiltless, to vainly and guiltlessly die with the others' (8).[31] He also finds a similar message in the gospels, reminding readers of Jesus' commandment: 'When pulling out the tares, let them not also pull up the wheat, Let them both grow together' (8, quoting Matt. 13:29).

## 2.3 As a zealot: against the true diabolical threat of Protestantism

And yet. The *Denounced Witch* is inconsistent. Our author's pastoral concern for 'poor skinny women' confessing falsehoods to end judicial torture (71) evaporates entirely when discussing the equally cruel torture of 'malodorous'

Jews, 'avowed enemies of Christendom,' whose torture-induced confessions of poisoning wells he believes uncritically (30). The parable of the tares and wheat, deployed above to advocate for judicial caution, gets a rather different use with respect to Protestant 'heretics.' Our author claims to have interviewed a confessed witch awaiting the stake in the Poznań prison, who explained that witches kill by means of a 'certain herb' known only to themselves, which grows on Bald Mountain: if one sprinkles a decoction of this herb on cattle or human beings, they will instantly die. The author slyly notes that Bald Mountain is located, 'so far as I can learn, where at that time the Heretical [Lutheran] Church still stood.'[32] And he adds: 'Consider, whether this tare [*kąkol*] should not be uprooted, not only for the sake of peace and the common good, but also because it offends against the Majesty of God' (26). The witch's magical herb becomes a weed – specifically the *kąkol* or tare of Matthew 13 – and a description of a witch's methods of malefice slides seamlessly into a discussion of Protestant heresy and the need to root it out.[33]

The *Denounced Witch* is no plea for general tolerance. Any doubt on this score should be removed by the author's praise of a fifteenth-century bishop who raised an army to capture some priests of Hussite tendency, and 'having judged them as notorious heretics, ordered them to be burned like evil vermin' (13). Just as our author cannot stick to his point when an occasion arises to praise the Jesuits, he is easily diverted by opportunities to attack Protestants. In a discussion of illusionary magical arts, we learn that 'we have a clear example from a few-score years ago, when that damned art, together with the new "faith" began to swarm in Poland' (29). He claims that the water ordeal is unheard of in 'decent nations such as Italy, Spain, or France,' but does show up 'in certain corners of Germany, where heresy has become predominant, for, shameless magic or necromancy comes along in heresy's wake, as its cousin. For there in their schools they teach necromancy [...] and treat it as a proper art.' (52). This equation of German (i.e. Lutheran) schooling and diabolical witchcraft is elsewhere used to recommend the rival Jesuit College, where the schoolmasters knew how to beat the mischief out of a boy whose Protestant tutor had taught him 'necromancy along with his grammar' (27).

The correlation of the spread of witchcraft and heresy was of course commonplace among the Jesuits. Martin Delrio's teacher, Juan Maldonado°, made use of this correlation to imply that just as witches are heretics, so too 'the modern Protestant heretics were witches'.[34] Delrio took up this theme in the prologue of his *Disquisitiones*, as did the English Catholic scholar Thomas Stapleton, a colleague of Delrio at Leuven who had flirted with joining the Jesuit order.[35] The *Denounced Witch* makes a structurally similar argument, but with the emphasis shifted: he *distinguishes* hocus-pocustry from true witchcraft by fully conflating witchcraft and heresy. He does so by a further conflation, of *czary* [witchcraft] with *czarnoksięstwo* [necromancy, lit. 'black-bookishness'], which he declares to be 'one and the same, [as] a certain method or science' (25). He thus associates witchcraft with learning –

specifically with German, Protestant, heretical learning – as contrasted both to the ignorant hocus-pocustry of the pious peasantry and to the orthodox learning on offer at the Jesuit schools. Both true witches and Protestants (who are identical) must be weeded out, while pious Catholics (if somewhat ignorant, somewhat superstitious) require education, not the rough justice of the secular courts. In other words, he applies to the Polish situation an argument developed by the Jesuits Paul Laymann and Adam Tanner, both of whom spoke out strongly against the excesses of secular-court witch-trials while being equally 'outspoken in their support of persecution [of Protestants] on religious grounds.'[36]

Our author makes this position clear – so clear as to undercut his main goal of mitigating the cruelty of secular witch-trials – in his repeated, and repeatedly insulting, insistence that secular magistrates have no jurisdiction over such trials under Polish law. He claims that some magistrates think they can ignore standard legal procedure in witch-trials because Polish law is silent on this point (10, 39), and he responds in fury:

> [P]ainted *Jurist*, don't say you find nothing in Polish law concerning Witches, concerning how they are to be tried, or by what procedure treated [...]. You find nothing? Precisely, because Secular Magistrates have been removed from the jurisdiction of such trials: what then should the law describe about things which do not concern you?[37]

The author here invokes the *constitutio* of 1543, a legal declaration of the Polish *Sejm* [Parliament] attempting a compromise between the noble and ecclesiastical estates over the jurisdictions of noble and ecclesiastical courts. As our author points out (18), the *constitutio* assigned witchcraft, together with matters such as heresy, blasphemy, and apostasy, to ecclesiastical courts. But as I have shown elsewhere, the *Denounced Witch* misreads the *constitutio*, which relates to noble and ecclesiastical law and is entirely silent about the Saxon-law town courts where Polish witch-trials overwhelmingly took place. These town courts rightly considered the *constitutio* of 1543 entirely irrelevant to their jurisprudence – so much so that secular-court magistrates never mentioned it in their verdicts or other deliberations.[38] Our author's attempt to apply the *constitutio* of 1543 to the seventeenth-century witch-trials has less to do with witchcraft than with later developments of Polish law at the high tide of Reformation in the Commonwealth: the *constitutio* of 1563 forbidding the Crown from enforcing church-court rulings, and the Confederation of Warsaw which formally wrote religious tolerance into Polish law.[39] Both laws made trials for Protestant 'heresy' impossible – or at least unenforceable wherever local nobles chose to disregard ecclesiastical courts. By awakening sympathy for innocent, 'lightminded' but pious Catholic women cruelly tortured for alleged witchcraft when the true diabolical magicians (learned Lutherans in particular) got away scot-free, our author sought to alleviate the suffering of those women. But he also hoped to reclaim ecclesiastical court jurisdiction not only over witchcraft, but also over heretical Protestantism. The reforming Catholic critique of witch-trials was, thus, also a Counter-Reformation assault on the religious freedoms that Protestant nobility had enjoyed in the sixteenth and early seventeenth centuries. The *Denounced Witch* thus fits well into the growing understanding (illustrated elsewhere in this volume in the chapters on Wier and Scot) that a so-called 'skeptical' critique of the cruelties inflicted on alleged witches need not correlate closely with enlightened, tolerant, Erastian, or even moderate views on religious co-existence.

## 3 Legacy

The *Denounced Witch* did nothing in the short term to dampen the flames. Like Spee, our author seems to have written his polemic 'for those who will not read it, not those who actually will read it.'[40] The powerful rhetoric and indubitable Catholic zeal of the *Denounced Witch* recommended our text to a church hierarchy that, beginning with Bishop Florian Czartoryski's *Mandatum* and extending through the mid-eighteenth century, adopted its dual approach of decrying the cruel excesses of secular courts and advocating for strengthening ecclesiastical courts' power to enforce heresy trials – a movement that had almost no effect on the witch-trials themselves until their very late abatement after 1740.[41] Ironically, the small town of Grodzisk, to which Regulus had sarcastically dedicated the first edition of the Denounced Witch in 1639, hosted one of the largest series of trials in early modern Poland in the early eighteenth century – fourteen trials involving twenty-five accused witches.[42]

Indeed, it is probable that the very strategy which made the *Denounced Witch* so popular among certain factions of the Catholic church hierarchy rendered it anathema to noble or burgher reformers interested in ameliorating the plight of accused witches.[43] As Stanisław Salmonowicz has noted,

> the gentry were not [...] menaced by witchcraft trials before the common law courts, and they feared being tried by ecclesiastical courts, if ecclesiastical jurisdiction were to be restored not only in witchcraft cases but also in such matters as heresy or atheism.[44]

Ironically, by 1639 or not long after, most of the nobility and burghers of Poland, who had flirted with various forms of Protestantism for a century, had returned to the Catholic fold – the Counter-Reformation unequivocally triumphed in the Polish Commonwealth. Yet as P.T. Stolarski argues, general agreement with Tridentine reform co-existed with a strong anticlericalism, and in particular with a strong suspicion of Jesuit attempts to maximize church power at the expense of noble freedoms or burgher privileges.[45] The *Denounced Witch* took precisely this Jesuit line, tying its humanitarian concern to jurisdictional arguments in such as a way as to guarantee the failure of both.

## Notes

1 Małgorzata Pilaszek, *Procesy o czary w Polsce w wiekach XV-XVIII*, Kraków: Universitas, 2008; Michael Ostling, *Between the Devil and the Host: Imagining Witchcraft in Early Modern Poland*, Oxford: Oxford University Press, 2011; Wanda Wyporska, *Witchcraft in Early Modern Poland, 1500–1800*, New York: Palgrave Macmillan, 2013.
2 Stanisław z Gór Poklatecki, *Pogrom: Czarnoksięskie błędy, latowców zdrady i alchemickie fałsze*, Kraków: Jakub Siebeneycher, 1595; Stanisław Ząbkowic, *Młot na czarownice*, Kraków: Szymon Kempini, 1614.
3 E.g. Józef Jędrzej Załuski, *Objaśnienie błędami zabobonów zarażonych* [etc.], Berdychów: Drukarnia Karmelitów Bosych, 1766; Jan Bohomolec, *Diabeł w swojej postaci*, Warsaw: Michał Gröll, 1775–77.
4 For this study, I consulted two versions of the text: the original edition of 1639 (Poznań: Albertus Regulus (Biblioteka Jagiellońska Cim. Qu. 5857)) and the 1714 edition (Gdańsk: Jan Daniel Stoll (Biblioteka Narodowa XVIII.2.296, Mf. 84123)). The Gdańsk edition lacks the dedicatory preface found in the Poznań edition, while it includes, as an appendix, Latin and Polish editions of the famously mild *Instructio circa judicia sagarum* developed by the Roman Inquisition. I follow the pagination of the Gdańsk edition except when quoting the 1639 preface.
5 Wyporska, *Witchcraft in Early Modern Poland*, p. 151.
6 Bohdan Baranowski, *Procesy czarownic w Polsce w XVII i XVIII wieku*, Łódź: Łódzkie Towarzystwo Naukowe, 1952, p. 57.
7 Karol Koranyi, 'Danielis Wisneri *Tractatus brevis de extramagis lamiis, veneficis a Czarownica powołana*. Szkic z dziejów polskiej literatury prawniczej', in K. Koranyi, ed., *Pamiętnik 30-lecia pracy naukowej Przemysława Dąbkowskiego*, Lwów: Kółko Historyczno-Prawne, 1927, p. 146.
8 Jacek Wijaczka, *Kościół wobec czarów w Rzeczypospolitej w XVI–XVIII wieku (na tle europejskim)*, Warsaw: Wydawnictwo Neriton, 2016, pp. 128–30. One of Regulus' students was Krzysztof Opaliński, whose poetic *Satyry abo Przestrogi* (Satires or Warnings, 1650) spoke out eloquently against witch-trials.
9 Kazimierz Florian Czartoryski, *Mandatum pastorale ... de cautelis in processu contra sagas adhibendis* (Kraków: Krzysztof Domański, 1705 [1669]), fol. 12r.
10 *Czarownica powołana*, p. 85.
11 Wyporska, *Witchcraft in early modern Poland*, p. 152.
12 *Czarownica powołana*, pp. v–vi. Regulus' invocation of unbaptised infants damned to Hell by cruel magistrates is a neat inversion of a more common suggestion: that witches prey on unbaptised infants and must therefore be prosecuted without mercy.
13 Daniel Wisner, *Tractatus brevis de extramagis lamiis, veneficis, aliisque malefactoribus*, Poznań: Wojciech Regulus, 1639, title page.
14 Koranyi, 'Danielis Wisneri', pp. 139–40.
15 Koranyi, 'Danielis Wisneri', p. 140.
16 Koranyi, 'Danielis Wisneri', p. 130.
17 William Bradford Smith, 'The Persecution of Witches and the Discourse on Toleration in Early Modern Germany,' in Marjorie Elizabeth Plummer and Victoria Christman, eds, *Topographies of Tolerance and Intolerance*, Leiden: Brill, 2018, pp. 58–59; Friedrich Spee, *Cautio Criminalis, or a Book on Witch Trials*, trans. Marcus Hellyer, Charlottesville: University of Virginia Press, 2003 [1631], pp. xx–xxi.
18 Sebastjan Miczyński, *Zwierciadło Korony Polskiey*, Kraków: Maciej Jędrzeiowczyk, 1618, pp. 16–17.

19 Józef Łukaszewicz, *Krótki historyczno-statystyczny opis miast i wsi w dzisiejszym powiecie krotoszyńskim*, 2 vols, Poznań: Jan Konstanty Żupański, 1869–75, vol. 1, 74–75; cf. Ryszard Berwiński, *Studia o gusłach, czarach, zabobonach i przesądach ludowych*, 2nd ed., 2 vols, Warsaw: Wydawnictwo Artystyczne i Filmowe, 1984 [1862], vol. 2, 177–79. N.b: witch-trial records, in fact, occur very infrequently in the Polish archives.
20 *Czarownica powołana*, p. 5.
21 *Czarownica powołana*, pp. 5–6.
22 Stanisław of Skarbimierz, *Sermones sapientiales Stanisława z Skarbimierza*, ed. Bożena Chmielowska, Warsaw: Akademia Teologii Katolickiej, 1979, p. 90.
23 Tomasz Wiślicz, 'Jak gdyby wśród pogan lub heretyków: Polityka potrydenckiego Kościoła wobec religii ludowej i jej osobliwości w Rzeczypospolitej,' in Robert Kołodziej and Filip Wolański, eds, *Staropolska ogląd świata*, Toruń: Adam Marszałek, 2009, p. 41; Stanisław Brzeżański, *Owczarnia w Dzikim Polu*, Lwów: Drukarnia Kollegium [ ... ] Societatis Jesu, 1717, fol. 23r.
24 E.g. in Cardinal Bernard Maciejowski's seminal *Epistola pastoralis*, 1630, orig. 1601; see Bernard Maciejowski, '*List pasterski*' *kard. Bernarda Maciejowskiego*', ed. S. Nasiorowski, Lublin: Redakcja Wydawnictw Katolickiego Uniwersytetu Lubelskiego, 1992, p. 204.
25 Marcin of Urzędów, *Herbarz Polski*, Kraków: Drukarnia Łazarzowa, p. 32.
26 On mugwort as a supposedly 'pagan' herb, see further Michael Ostling, 'Witches' Herbs on Trial', *Folklore*, 2014, vol. 125/2, 179–201.
27 Heinrich Institoris, *The Hammer of Witches: A Complete Translation of the Malleus Maleficarum*, trans. Christopher S. Mackay, New York: Cambridge University Press, 2009 [1487], pp. 160–70.
28 Cited there as Psalm 3, according to the Vulgate numeration. Note that Friedrich Spee chose this same verse as an 'Epitome or Summary' of his own argument: Spee, *Cautio Criminalis*, p. 5.
29 *Czarownica powołana*, p. 24.
30 It should be noted that Poland experienced no major witch-panics of the type that awakened Laymann's and Spee's protests, and for structural reasons even smaller scale chain-reaction trials were rare. See Ostling, *Devil and the Host*, pp. 95–103.
31 Cf. Smith, 'Persecution of Witches', p. 59; Jan Machielsen, *Martin Delrio: Demonology and Scholarship in the Counter-Reformation*, Oxford: Oxford University Press, 2015, p. 281.
32 Bald Mountain [Łysa Góra] is the traditional site of the witches' sabbat in Poland. See Ostling, *Devil and the Host*, pp. 132–35.
33 Cf. Marcin of Klecko's earlier anti-Protestant pamphlet: Marcin of Klecko, *Procy na ministry i na wszystkie heretyki*, Kraków: Wdowa Jak. Siebeneychera, 1607, p. 87, in which Bald Mountain is similarly located in the Poznań Protestant Churches.
34 Jonathan L. Pearl, *The Crime of Crimes: Demonology and Politics in France, 1560–1620*, Waterloo: Wilfrid Laurier University Press, 1999, p. 68.
35 Martin Delrio, *Disquisitionum magicarum libri sex* (Cologne: Petrus Henningius, 1633), Proloquium (cf. Machielsen, *Martin Delrio*, p. 235); Jan Machielsen, 'On the Confessional Uses and History of Witchcraft: Thomas Stapleton's 1594 Witchcraft Oration', *Magic, Ritual, and Witchcraft*, 2018, vol. 13/3, 388, 407.
36 Smith, 'Persecution of Witches', p. 58.
37 *Czarownica powołana*, p. 10.
38 Michael Ostling, 'Konstytucja 1543 r. i początki procesów o czary w Polsce', *Odrodzenie i Reformacja w Polsce*, 2005, vol. 49, 93–103.

39 Janusz Tazbir and Mirosław Korolko, *Konfederacja warszawska 1573 roku, wielka karta polskiej tolerancji*, Warsaw: Wydawnictwo PAX, 1980; Wijaczka, *Kościół wobec czarów*.
40 Spee, *Cautio Criminalis*, p. 7.
41 Ostling, 'Konstytucja 1543'; Ostling, *Devil and the Host*, pp. 54–57; Wijaczka, *Kościół wobec czarów*.
42 Wyporska, *Witchcraft in Early Modern Poland*, p. 35.
43 Ostling, *Devil and the Host*, pp. 57–59.
44 Stanisław Salmonowicz, 'Witchcraft Trials in Old Poland: Reflections on Małgorzata Pilaszek's book *Procesy o czary w Polsce w wiekach XV–XVIII*', *Acta Poloniae Historica*, 2009, vol. 99, 113.
45 P.T. Stolarski, 'Dominican-Jesuit Rivalry and the Politics of Catholic Renewal in Poland 1564–1648', *Journal of Ecclesiastical History*, 2011, vol. 62/2, 255–72.

## Further reading

Ostling, Michael, *Between the Devil and the Host: Imagining Witchcraft in Early Modern Poland*, Oxford: Oxford University Press, 2011.
———, 'Witches' Herbs on Trial', *Folklore*, 2014, vol. 125/2, 179–201.
Pilaszek, Małgorzata, *Procesy o czary w Polsce w wiekach XV–XVIII*, Kraków: Universitas, 2008.
Salmonowicz, Stanisław, 'Witchcraft Trials in Old Poland: Reflections on Małgorzata Pilaszek's book Procesy o czary w Polsce w wiekach XV–XVIII', *Acta Poloniae Historica*, 2009, vol. 99, 107–124.
Stolarski, P.T., 'Dominican-Jesuit Rivalry and the Politics of Catholic Renewal in Poland 1564–1648', *Journal of Ecclesiastical History*, 2011, vol. 62/2, 255–272.
Wyporska, Wanda, *Witchcraft in Early Modern Poland, 1500–1800*, New York: Palgrave Macmillan, 2013.

# Part 5
# Demonology and law

# 17 An untrustworthy reporter
## Nicolas Remy's *Daemonolatreiae libri tres*

*Robin Briggs*

When Nicolas Remy lay on his deathbed in his country house at Saint-Mard near Bayon in April 1612 he could look back on a notably successful career over a long life (he was at least in his early eighties). His immediate ancestors had held office for the Duke of Lorraine in the small town of Charmes and the surrounding region, but he had risen to be ennobled by Duke Charles III, had become a member of the ducal council, and for fifteen years held the senior legal office in the duchy as *procureur-général de Lorraine*. One reward for his services had been the transfer of that office to his son Claude-Marcel on his own retirement in 1606. Remy might also have congratulated himself on his achievements as an author, writing in both French and Latin. He had displayed his skills as a humanist by composing short Latin encomia for ducal ceremonies, and written a stylish short history in French of the events surrounding the accession of Duke René II, achieved by the defeat of Charles the Bold, whose death outside Nancy in 1477 brought about the collapse of the Burgundian state.[1]

Remy's chief bid for fame as a writer had, however, been his book on witches and their doings, entitled *Daemonolatreiae libri tres* (Three Books on Demon-Worship) and published as a folio volume at Lyon in 1595. Editions in smaller formats from Cologne and Frankfurt quickly followed, then were joined by a German translation. By writing in Latin Remy asserted his status as a humanist intellectual who sought an international readership; he may also have felt that a publication of this kind would do particular honour to his master the Duke of Lorraine. However, he was also limiting his audience quite drastically, in sharp contrast to his obvious model Jean Bodin°, whose *Démonomanie des sorciers* of 1580 plainly sought attention as widely as possible in the Francophone world. It seems rather curious that Remy neither produced his own French version nor encouraged someone else to do so. He could hardly think that the subject matter should be kept away from the vulgar multitude, when Bodin's book was already circulating so widely. In recent times the *Daemonolatreia* has been known almost exclusively through the 1930 English translation by E.A. Ashwin.[2] A French translation by Jean Boës finally appeared in 1998, in a small edition that quickly sold out and remains very hard to find.[3]

## 1 Remy and his sources

If the *Daemonolatreia* quickly established itself as a reference for other writers within the field of demonology, such as Delrio° and De Lancre°, this had less to do with its arguments, which were almost wholly conventional, than with the wealth of new material that Remy provided from the trials of Lorraine witches. In his introduction to 'the courteous reader' he justifiably claimed that no other author had 'adduced so great a number of cases as I have been able to bring forward and at first hand'. The prefatory material to the book gives an account of the circumstances in which it was written, and of Remy's methods and motives, which needs to be read attentively but with some caution.[4] The very first words invoke the miserable calamities of the times, among which the greatest evil is the abjuration of true faith. Two guilty groups are distinguished here, the atheists who are led astray by the abuse of reason, and the ignorant whose credulity leads to their seduction by the devil. The vulnerability of the latter is linked to the failure of the local clergy to preach or teach effectively. Remy then recognises that many, especially in France, see such people as deserving pity rather than punishment; his intention is therefore to show from his own experience just how much real harm witches do, taking advantage of a period of leisure when an outbreak of plague has forced him to stay in the country. Although he knows there has already been much weighty writing on the subject, his friend Thierry Alix, president of the *Chambre des Comptes*, has spoken to the duke and told him the ruler would welcome such a publication.

All this is part of the opening dedication to Cardinal Charles de Lorraine, son of the reigning duke and Bishop of Metz and Strasbourg (1567–1607), one member of the ruling family who would have possessed the linguistic skills to read the book. The cardinal was a suitable choice for a less happy reason, because his short life was to be ruined by some kind of developing paralysis, which was attributed to witchcraft. It was in the vain hope of a cure that he brought the Ambrosian friars, specialists in exorcism, to Nancy from Italy.[5] When addressing the reader Remy adds that during his fifteen years conducting criminal trials his head had been filled with thoughts about the behaviour of witches at the sabbat and elsewhere. He had started by jotting down odd details, then over the last five years had made more systematic notes about his examinations of prisoners. This enabled him to call on the independent testimony of many witnesses, while if he recounted much that was new and unheard of, the reader must remember that the demons have mighty powers inconsistent with the normal operations of nature. Remy, however, claimed to walk a path between excessive scepticism and credulity, rejecting as absurd claims that men can be turned into animals, that souls can be separated from bodies, and that demons can make women pregnant.

This self-presentation clearly seeks to project the image of a practical and trustworthy man, who can appeal to 'the experience and confidence' derived from his 'long judicial practice', as a person who 'has himself seen and heard these things'. Historians have not surprisingly tended to take Remy at his own valuation, seen him as a judge with extensive courtroom experience, and often gone on to describe him as an active witch-hunter. This is where the survival of around 400 witchcraft trials in the Lorraine archives allows one to detect the ambiguities in his text and reach a more realistic understanding of his relationship to the judicial process. The many trials in the duchy were scattered widely and the real action took place in a multiplicity of very local courts. The central court of the *Change de Nancy*, on which Remy sat for the fifteen years from 1576 to 1591, exercised a supervisory role by inspecting the paperwork. The witness testimonies and the preliminary interrogation of the accused were sent up to Nancy with a proposal for further action, almost always the use of torture. The Change normally assented, then a second consultation followed once the record of the questioning under torture was available, to confirm the final sentence. In four cases out of five this was the death sentence that inevitably followed a confession, while the brave minority who resisted could expect a kind of release under licence. The point of the system was to ensure regular proceedings in the local courts, in which it seems to have been relatively successful, whatever distaste a modern observer may feel for the methods employed.

Only on rare occasions did the four to six jurists who staffed the Nancy court act as a court of first instance for the ducal capital itself; in 1593 they tried the remarkable case of the healer and would-be magician Nicolas Noel le Bragard.[6] Just two such trials can be identified from the fifteen years of Remy's membership. One of these, from 1584, involved a woman named Catharine Ouay, evidently released on licence after a first trial before he intervened personally with the duke to have her imprisoned again on account of fresh suspicions against her.[7] The other was the 1582 case of the beggar-woman known as Lasnier, reported in two quite extended passages which show Remy interrogating her personally, and getting a confession from her despite the interventions of her 'Little Master', who appeared to her in strange forms invisible to the judge himself.[8] These were almost certainly the only two witches Remy had encountered in person up to the time he sat down to write his book. All the other details would have passed before him on paper, as part of the normal procedures; in that sense he was behaving almost like the modern historians who base their analyses on reading the legal records. Indeed, it seems likely that he did have many of the trial documents before him as he wrote, as well as the notes he mentions. Of the 140 or so trials he cites, only one can still be found in the archives, the 1591 case of Jean and Didière Bulme. Since his friend Thierry Alix, who had encouraged him to write the book, had recently reorganised the ducal archives that he controlled, the overwhelming probability is that these dossiers were passed over to Remy and never returned. Although it is frustrating that we cannot match up his narratives with the original records, in practice it is quite easy to detect how they have been manipulated by comparisons with the hundreds of other surviving cases.

## 2 Remy and the demonological context

In writing about witches Remy was necessarily entering a controversial field, for if demonologists generally agreed about the need for persecution, there were plenty of vexed issues about the powers of Satan and his relationship to the witches he had effectively enslaved. His text is generally rather sparing in its references to other contemporary opinions, and one cannot assume that he had necessarily read the works that he mentioned. However, there are good reasons to suppose that he made use of the *Malleus maleficarum*, alongside the works of Molitor, Grillando, Cardano, Della Porta, Wier° and Bodin. In an age when the concept of plagiarism was still unformed, it is no surprise to find that he borrowed references to classical, biblical, and Christian sources from his predecessors, complete with their minor errors. There are sections dealing with all the familiar issues of procreation by demons, flight to the sabbat, transformations into animal form, the nature of the diabolical powders, the implicit pacts of magicians, and storm-raising. These discussions hardly add anything worthwhile to existing debates and sometimes suggest uncertainty or confusion on Remy's own part, as we shall see. Our author is not much of a theorist, we must conclude, while the intermittent display of erudition may be something of a smokescreen for the lack of originality, logical rigour, and engagement with deeper issues. The occasional recognition that there are disputes is almost swamped by the general presentation, with its insistence on a broad concordance between pagan, Hebrew, and Christian authors. In this respect Remy seems very close to Bodin, whose shadow does indeed fall much more strongly across his book than the five rather trivial references in the text would imply. Previous writers have taken it as certain that the two men knew one another, although this cannot be definitively proven. When Remy was appointed to his first position in Lorraine (1570) the document stated that he had been studying and teaching in France for twenty years; he is thought to have been in Toulouse before 1563, then in Paris, which would indeed mean a very close overlap with the career of his near contemporary Bodin.[9] In truth the extent, if any, of their early acquaintance does not seem very significant, when the elaborated position laid out in the *Démonomanie* was clearly a product of the late 1570s, and a reading of the book would have been quite sufficient to prompt a complex set of reactions from an author who aspired to a more conventional and traditional stance.

Apart from his final chapter attacking Wier without actually naming him, Remy never engages in a debate with specific antagonists, contenting himself with brief statements that views differ. It may even be that he chose to ignore the startlingly heterodox elements in the *Démonomanie*, hard though that must have been to manage, treating the book as simply another source of information. A more plausible view would be that he shared only those positions compatible with orthodox Christianity and some presentational techniques, without subscribing to Bodin's dramatic worldview or his barely concealed heresies.[10] In effect he was avoiding controversy and returning demonology to a more central stance, in a matter-of-fact text standing at the opposite extreme to Bodin's risky intellectual fireworks. That choice did not have to represent a conscious programme, since it would conform to everything we know about Remy, while also reflecting how different witchcraft must have appeared in Nancy as opposed to Paris. In the small self-sufficient world of the duchy the support of the civil and ecclesiastical powers could be taken for granted, where Bodin had to reckon with the scepticism of the Valois kings and the higher judiciary, with his dedication of the *Démonomanie* to Chrestophle de Thou looking singularly maladroit.[11] In any case an approach contrasting the two books need not presume deliberate interaction to have value, because numerous readers must have known both, bearing in mind that Bodin was translated into Latin, German, and Italian.

In other respects, Remy's opening statements might seem to place him very close to his predecessor, whose key concerns he matched exactly when he evoked a world afflicted by calamities, with heresy and unbelief leading to apostasy, before remarking on the culpable failure of the French elites to take witchcraft seriously. He would of course have witnessed the first decade of the French Wars of Religion at first hand, while independent Lorraine was far too close and too involved for him to ignore the descent of the French kingdom into something approaching anarchy by the time he was writing. Yet once he has offered those brief flourishes in the prefatory sections he seems to forget all about them, never again describing witches and their activities as any kind of existential threat to society at large, as opposed to their unlucky individual victims. We are a world away from Bodin's repeated invocations of a terrifying punitive deity, capable of being sufficiently outraged by the toleration of Satanic apostasy to destroy whole kingdoms. Remy avoids any reference to those exalted conceptions of a harmonic order governing the universe, in which good and bad somehow balance one another, while angels and demons both act as God's enforcers. Nor is it easy to see him accepting Bodin's somewhat variable claims that only one in ten or one in fifty attempted bewitchments actually broke through the barrier of divine protection to take effect.[12]

The *Démonomanie* combines implacable arguments with formidable rhetorical skills to put across an urgent message, demanding a radical change of policy from the political and judicial authorities. There is a striking difference here, because while Remy is no slouch when it comes to rhetoric, he merely employs it to stress the power and cruelty of Satan alongside the wickedness of his human servants, familiar themes that generate none of the same intellectual excitement. His book makes far fewer demands on the reader, who is invited to share a long series of stories and vignettes to illustrate what in their time were largely conventional claims; this comes close to the French genre of *histoires prodigieuses*, scary and fantastic tales to entertain. Nor did this lawyer feel any need to bother with considerations of legal procedure, which in Bodin occupy some 50 rather technical pages of the modern edition.[13] While this rather surprising omission must have reduced the book's appeal to those conducting trials, readability was probably enhanced as a result. Remy may well have thought that Lorraine had already constructed something like the ideal system for eliminating witches, when the duchy saw one of the highest proportions of trials and executions anywhere in Europe. One issue he did confront was that of the appropriate punishment for child witches; like Bodin he favoured the death sentence with some hesitations and suggested that once perverted by the devil it was almost unknown for them to break away from his control.[14]

In his preface and his very first chapter Bodin drummed home his conviction that witchcraft and demonic power had been the same phenomena across the ancient and modern worlds, for him irrefutable proof of their existence. Remy clearly shared this view, drawing heavily on classical sources (sometimes borrowed from his predecessor and indeed from Wier) to back up his contemporary material; at one point he followed Bodin when he identified the Little Masters of the witches with the pagan gods men had once worshipped.[15] Most of the time, however, the assumption of identity across time is merely implicit in his writing, and has nothing of the almost hallucinatory quality of Bodin's declamatory prose. Both authors also collected stories from friends and colleagues, displaying a rather minimal degree of critical spirit in the process. They seemed to agree on a more substantial matter of interpretation, that witches possessed no independent capacity to harm their victims but were merely intermediaries through whom demonic power operated. This had been a key issue for demonology from the start, a fault line created when the friars welded together popular beliefs about *maleficium* by neighbours with the fantasy of a great Satanic conspiracy, with the inevitable result that all accounts were dragged into the insoluble problems of theodicy.

In the *Malleus maleficarum*, Heinrich Institoris°'s attempted solution was to constantly resort to the mantra 'with the permission of God', an evasion that maintained the inferior status of the devil by making God an accomplice to all the evil he did.[16] Bodin's harmonic justice was a bold if ultimately circular attempt to cut the Gordian knot, with evil as the necessary counterpart to good, and somehow a retribution for bad conduct. As Christopher Baxter neatly puts it, this produced a form of daemonic Judaism, in which 'the rewarding and punishing functions of a strictly monotheistic and rigidly transcendent deity are carried out through a complex bureaucracy of good and evil demons'.[17] As a next step Bodin effectively discarded the whole notion of the preternatural, after scornfully pointing out in his preface how little human reason understood about the operations of nature. The standard argument that the devil was just a master of illusion, operating under a divine prohibition that denied him supernatural powers, was by-passed by asserting that God did allow him just such capabilities, selectively, in order to act on his behalf. For Bodin witches really did fly to the sabbat, turn into wolves or other animals, have intercourse with demons, and conceive children by them, all of which was much more in accord with common sense than the elaborate illusions others invoked to explain these well-attested phenomena. Such extreme positions were very unlikely to win support from an orthodox Catholic such as Remy, who clearly preferred the traditional approach stressing the preternatural powers of demons, and whose default position was based on the possibilities of illusion.

## 3 The presentation of the Lorraine trials

Despite their differences, there are many points at which Remy's arguments make sense as a kind of dialogue with Bodin, sometimes edging towards his stance while trying to preserve the conventional limitations, with constant references to the Lorraine trials. Few difficulties arose with transport to the sabbat, where Remy took the quite common option of insisting there was plentiful evidence such assemblies really happened, while allowing that they might sometimes be dream experiences. It was the demons who carried the witches into the air, often making use of the wide chimneys found in Lorraine peasant cottages. This could be classified under the preternatural because demons were known to possess enormous strength and speed, perhaps more an appeal to common opinion than a compelling piece of logic.[18] The canon *Episcopi* was dismissed just as Bodin had done, as the product of a marginal local Council controverted by many weightier authorities.[19] Examples from the confessions of witches were cited on such topics as the awfulness or the illusory character of the food, the discordant music and dancing, the attempts to keep identities secret, and the homage to the devil. Promiscuous sexuality did not feature at all in this account of the Lorraine sabbat, and it is indeed a very rare theme in the 300 or so surviving confessions; Bodin also downplays the theme in his quite restrained reports of the sabbat.

In two other respects, however, Remy makes claims that are seriously at variance with the archival material. According to him witches were unanimous in claiming that great numbers attended the meetings, in fact a very exceptional feature in surviving confessions, which characteristically describe rather furtive gatherings of a few individuals. Then he relates how the witches are obliged to list their crimes at each sabbat, adding the rather quaint detail that their master holds classes instructing them in the best ways to harm the crops and use their poisons.[20] Again the reporting of crimes is very uncommon in the confessions, only appearing a handful of times, while there is no sign at all of those diabolical evening classes. It is not really surprising to find Remy generalising from the particular in this fashion; he will have had preconceived notions and like so many people then and now simply not bothered to think about typicality.

Remy does not wholly neglect sexual issues, because after five relatively brief chapters he suddenly devotes fifteen pages to the question of intercourse between demons and humans, with the related question of procreation.[21] Here the reader is treated to a great medley of evidence from every type of source, with all the typical material about huge freezing cold penises and horribly painful couplings, although it is implied that these are private encounters between the witches and their Little Masters. Remy then moves on to the idea that children may be born from such unions, noting that the authorities who argue for this differ about the means, and coming down against the idea that monstrous births should be explained in this fashion. It is predictable that he should invoke the conventional explanation in terms of the impact of the mother's imagination during pregnancy and go on to suggest that women who keep company with demons will be highly susceptible to such a fate.

Where Remy finds himself in much greater perplexity is with his discussions of shape changing, in another substantial chapter that begins with instances from the trials and stories told him by trustworthy witnesses.[22] At this point he suggests that the devil could not possibly have the power to effect such transformations:

> It is, therefore, absurd and incredible that anyone can truly be changed from a man into a wolf or any other animal. Yet there must be some foundation for the opinion so obstinately held by so many: the countless stories that are circulated about such happenings cannot be entirely without warrant. Nearly all those who have deeply examined this whole question are convinced that such transformations are magical portent and glamours, which have the form but not the reality of their appearances; and that they can be caused in two ways.

The first of these is by confusing the imagination of a man so that he believes himself to have been changed and behaves like the animal. The second is causing an actual object to assume the shape of the animal. Now Remy really starts to waver, since he sees the problem that according to the accounts 'Satan does actually so empower them', because they leave traces of their activities and are sometimes caught in the act.

> It must then be admitted that these things are actually what they appear to be; but that they are done through the agency of the demon, who, by virtue of his immense preternatural powers, makes their accomplishment possible. ... We will admit, therefore, that witches so well imitate the faculties, powers and actions of the beasts whose appearance they assume that they differ but little from actuality; but that they are in very truth actual will not easily be believed by anyone who will ponder on the dignity and excellence of man ...[23]

Ultimately Remy steps back from the precipice to assert that belief in complete transformation 'cannot be consistent with true religion', but the reader may be forgiven for wondering just what these passages mean.

One of Remy's problems in any of the above debates would have been his own inconsistency. He was clearly very struck, as the modern historian must be, by the very specific and different witchcraft beliefs found in the German-speaking eastern fringe of the duchy. Here the confessions told how little groups of witches worked together at night, to attack victims who were off their guard or asleep. Their masters gave them the power to penetrate houses in other shapes, changing themselves into mice, cats or locusts to squeeze in, before they resumed their normal form to immobilise their victims with drugs. Remy himself described this shape-changing ability as a reward for those who had served the demon for a long time, without expressing any doubts about its reality.[24]

This discussion illustrates a crucial characteristic of the whole book, for although the reservations and more cautious views found in a few chapters would have allowed the author to defend his own orthodoxy, only the most careful reader would have taken these messages away afterwards. Along that old fault-line between popular beliefs and demonological theory the scissors and paste technique Remy employed, with its lengthy narratives of bewitchments interspersed with tall stories from the literary sources, allowed the popular elements to swamp the confusing excursions into theory. One must admit that despite the much higher intellectual quality of the *Démonomanie* the same effect is sometimes visible there, with the barrage of instances getting somewhat out of step with the central thesis, so that one loses sight of the total inefficacy of demonic magic in Bodin's system. As his recent editors remark, that book was also marked by a singular level of carelessness in citing recent authorities, to whom Bodin might even attribute the opposite of their true meaning, which surely tells us something about his state of mind.[25] Any attempt to turn witchcraft into a logically watertight theory was of course doomed to failure, but most demonologists were hardly attempting anything so ambitious; they knew beyond any question that witches were the ultimate traitors to Christian society and were not much bothered about the different levels on which they made their case against them. These were rhetorical rather than logical exercises, sweeping over problems without much hesitation, and often exposing their flanks in the process.

Remy does attempt to distance himself from popular behaviour in the case of defences and cures against witchcraft. He was well aware of the belief that only the witch could cure an illness he or she had inflicted, and cited instances where this seemed to have proved true. However as usual he took the standard view that since such healing was diabolical those who sought it endangered their own souls; he further suggested that the illness might be transferred to another person, and that the cures might only be temporary. He also condemned the routine local practice of taking substances from the house and garden of the suspected witch to make a soup. Those who asked suspects to heal them were actually making witches more vindictive and confident, while to take this course was to 'purchase a brief and uncertain bodily health at the price of sure and eternal damnation to our souls'. The best defence against bewitchment was to live a good Christian life, saying prayers and washing your hands every morning.[26] With some hesitation he allowed that it might be permissible to threaten a suspect with violence, on the very dubious grounds that this did not involve a pact with the devil.[27] On the other hand he denounced resorting to the local *devins* (popular healers), three of whom he named with complaints that they were untouchable by justice, although one of them had in fact been convicted and executed before his book appeared.[28] It was equally wrong to allow the cunning folk, suspected witches, or anyone else to seek healing by pilgrimages to local shrines, especially if they attributed illnesses to the malign influence of the saints concerned. A particular concern was with the healing shrine of *le beau Bernard* at Metz, where Remy hoped the duke might put a stop to the abuses; he cannot have been too happy when an attempt in this direction was frustrated by the local Jesuits, who intervened to keep this very popular pilgrimage centre open.[29]

Although the issue is never confronted directly, the third book of the *Daemonolatreia* in particular provides a great deal of evidence for the therapeutic role of witchcraft beliefs in local culture, when identifying the witch responsible was the obvious first step towards obtaining a cure. Of course, Remy is at pains to explain how the demons are the real agents who both inflict and relieve sickness; in most of his stories he makes sure to reinforce the point by including the negotiations between the witch and Little Master. This is certainly a skewed presentation of the evidence from the trials, where confessing witches described the great majority of their crimes and healings as committed on their own initiative. However, one must admit that there were quite frequent accounts that did fit Remy's model, with the devil encouraging the crime, even offering to perform it, and either agreeing or refusing to allow a cure. This element had therefore penetrated to the popular level and might be used as a kind of excuse. What one suspects very few villagers would ever have believed was that witches were incapable of doing them very direct harm by their own agency. That would have negated all the powerful symbolic logic of the diabolical pact, where what the devil offered above all was power to harm and to heal, as represented by the coloured powders to inflict types of sickness and the white ones to remove it. Remy did not actually want to let witches off from responsibility either, of course. A long chapter is nominally devoted to the question of why the devil often demands their consent when plotting evil.[30] The two possibilities suggested are that God took away from the devil any power to do evil by his own will – otherwise the entire human race would have perished long ago – and therefore he needs human agency in order to harm mankind. The second is that he simply wants to make the witches accomplices, although he nearly always works independently. To this effect

> whenever something happens to offend a witch there is always a demon ready to revenge her wrongs even more drastically than she herself had wished ... Thus they lead in one unbroken chain from the original wrong to resentment, from resentment to revenge, and from revenge to a sacrilegious and detestable cult which is by far the worst of the abominations into which they try to seduce mankind.[31]

The question is never actually resolved in the chapter, because Remy slides off into examples of witches' curses that were fulfilled and a lengthy collection of classical sources on the power of curses. Perhaps he thinks that both are true, and his stories often imply that the witch has an essential function in providing the devil with opportunities; in the next chapter a witch is reported testifying 'that she rarely had asked the demon to bring misfortune on anyone without the deed following immediately upon her word: so eager and assiduous is he to seize every opportunity of ill-doing.'[32] Another chapter title includes the statement that 'the demons cast headlong down those whom they have had licence from witches to injure'.[33]

In the trials one can see that the witnesses much preferred explanations that might be called mechanical, by the use of powders, poisoned food, and touching or breathing on the victim. Remy seems to be following Bodin very closely when he insists that the powders had no inherent power, arguing that they did not affect the witches themselves or anyone against whom they were not specifically directed. He claimed that they owed something to the hidden ministry of the demon, and that the unguent was merely the outward symbol of the wretched witch's complicity in the crimes committed under the guidance and advice of the demon. However Remy then goes on to describe jars of unguent that flared and spluttered when put on the fire, saying these were the true poison.[34] The meaning here is extraordinarily slippery, as in those sections on German-speaking Lorraine where human corpses were allegedly used to make spells and potions.[35] As on other occasions the presentation virtually allows Remy to have it both ways, sliding between the popular beliefs he pretends to disallow and assertions of more orthodox positions.

It is no surprise that he should have followed Bodin in ending his book with a formal attack on Wier, because for all his inadequacies the Rhenish doctor had found some real targets. One was to question the possibility of distinguishing between the real and the imaginary, linked to the idea that witches were deluded by Satan, an argument the demonologists themselves exploited in a dangerously loose fashion. Another was the powerlessness of the witch according to orthodox demonology, on just that fault-line that has already been so apparent. This second point obviously struck home for Bodin, who responded with a rather unconvincing argument for the proposition that neither the witch nor Satan could perform alone those acts they could accomplish together.[36] Similarly Remy argued that the demon was deceiving witches into believing in their own powers in order to increase their complicity and 'make them more prone to do evil and injury'. To spare old women, as Wier wanted, would be like allowing mad dogs to live, when they were 'a danger by reason of the evil bewitchments which inevitably follow upon their threats, and finally would be revered on account of the miraculous power of healing with which they alone are said to be endowed!'[37] The evidence from the witnesses and the confessions is a sufficient answer to the suggestion 'that it is against all law and justice to give such weight to a popular fear or a scare bred of an uncertain rumour, as to think it necessary to put a fellow-creature to an ignominious death in order to allay that fear'.[38]

This last quotation represents an unusually sharp insight from Remy, because there is good reason to think that elite judges in several parts of Europe did think along just such lines, and often displayed great scepticism in handling witchcraft accusations. They were very far from being fools and knew all about village hatreds and the dangers of torture. Remy himself cannot have been ignorant of these concerns, so he must have made a conscious decision to ignore them; like other advocates of persecution he probably believed that God always made sure that only the guilty were punished. His younger colleague from the *Change de Nancy*, Claude Bourgeois, was much more concerned about the possible abuses when torture was used on suspected witches.[39]

## 4 Conclusion

It is surely a mistake for modern historians to turn writings about witchcraft into a contest in which the 'best' arguments were going to win, because many members of the literate audience had preconceived ideas of their own and reacted more instinctively than intellectually to what they read. Remy exploited that situation to preach to the converted, primarily by adding masses of material to the existing common stock (fruitfully exploited, for example, by Martin Delrio), and only very secondarily through his rather feeble attempts to make the evidence cohere. He was certainly going to provide reinforcement for those who wanted tough action against the Satanic menace, but one may reasonably doubt whether his book made any significant difference to a persecution that was already at peak levels when it appeared. Nor can he be held responsible for the exceptional levels of persecution in Lorraine. He greatly exaggerated the number of trials that passed before him and made an even wilder claim that as many accused had escaped condemnation or fled.[40] As I have explained elsewhere, in his later judicial capacity as *procureur-général* he simply operated within the system, with a concern to prevent abuses offsetting the odd case where he sought additional torture. The claims made about his activities as a witch-hunter are remarkably flimsy and cannot be matched to any archival evidence.[41] Historians of an older generation often exaggerated here, where a more nuanced view would not only reflect Stuart Clark's analysis of a demonology that was wholly congruent with accepted views of natural philosophy but also show awareness of just how far the trial records can almost persuade even a sceptical modern historian of the malevolence attributed to the accused. Yet a less sensational approach does not render this mediocre demonologist uninteresting, because both his misrepresentations and his confusions are so revealing of the problems that might arise in matching up popular beliefs and demonological theory.

# Notes

1 Useful biographical and bibliographical details (pp. 16–57) are just about the only value of Lucien Dintzer, *Nicolas Remy et son oeuvre démonologique*, Lyon: Université de Lyon, 1936. For other historical literature about Remy see the footnotes to Robin Briggs, *The Witches of Lorraine*, Oxford: Oxford University Press, 2007, pp. 20–21. A 1998 Nancy thesis by Mary-Nelly Fouligny, *Les sources antiques dans la Démonolâtrie de Nicolas Remy*, has never been made available in the normal fashion on line; the thesis abstract and her useful article 'Sorcières de Lorraine à la Renaissance: Sorcières de partout, sorcières de toujours', in Gérard Giuliato et al., eds, *La Renaissance en Europe dans sa diversité*, Nancy: Université de Lorraine, 2015, vol. 1, pp. 79–98 suggest that her approach is very marginal to the issues discussed in this chapter.
2 Nicolas Remy, *Demonolatry*, trans. E.A. Ashwin, London: John Rodker, 1930.
3 Nicolas Remy, *La Démonolâtrie*, trans. Jean Boës, Nancy: Presses Universitaires de Nancy, 1998.
4 Remy, *Demonolatry*, pp. v–xiv.
5 Briggs, *Witches*, pp. 80–81.
6 For the legal system Briggs, *Witches*, pp. 59–91, and for Le Bragard, see ibid., pp. 210–13. Abstracts of the trials can be consulted at <http://witchcraft.history.ox.ac.uk>.
7 Remy, *Demonolatry*, p. 160.
8 Remy, *Demonolatry*, pp. 130–31, 174–75.
9 Dintzer, *Remy*, pp. 19–20.
10 Jean Bodin, *De la Démonomanie des Sorciers*, ed. Virginia Krause et al., Geneva: Droz, 2017 is the admirable new scholarly edition, to which all references will be made.
11 See the editors' introduction to Bodin, *Démonomanie*, pp. 43–45.
12 Bodin, *Démonomanie*, p. 280, 319 for these different estimations.
13 Bodin, *Démonomanie*, pp. 353–402.
14 Bodin, *Démonomanie*, pp. 428–29; Remy, *Demonolatry*, pp. 92–99.
15 Remy, *Demonolatry*, p. 123; Bodin, *Démonomanie*, pp. 114–17, 203–5.
16 Sydney Anglo, 'Evident Authority and Authoritative Evidence: The *Malleus Maleficarum*', in Sydney Anglo, ed., *The Damned Art. Essays in the Literature of Witchcraft*, London: Routledge, 1977, pp. 1–31, esp. pp. 20–21.
17 Christopher Baxter, 'Jean Bodin's *De la Démonomanie des Sorciers*: The Logic of Persecution', in Anglo, ed., *The Damned Art*, pp. 82–83.
18 Remy, *Demonolatry*, pp. 47–55.
19 Remy, *Demonolatry*, pp. 83–84; Bodin, *Démonomanie*, p. 486.
20 Remy, *Demonolatry*, p. 56, 68.
21 Remy, *Demonolatry*, pp. 11–27.
22 Remy, *Demonolatry*, pp. 108–14.
23 Remy, *Demonolatry*, p. 113.
24 Remy, *Demonolatry*, pp. 104–5.
25 Bodin, *Démonomanie*, p. 29.
26 Remy, *Demonolatry*, pp. 142–58.
27 Remy, *Demonolatry*, pp. 152–54.
28 Remy, *Demonolatry*, p. 150; the conviction was of Nicolas Noel Le Bragard, see n. 6 above.
29 Remy, *Demonolatry*, pp. 137–42.
30 Remy, *Demonolatry*, pp. 120–30.
31 Remy, *Demonolatry*, p. 130.
32 Remy, *Demonolatry*, p. 123.
33 Remy, *Demonolatry*, p. 132.

34 Bodin, *Démonomanie*, pp. 276–80; Remy, *Demonolatry*, pp. 3–7.
35 Remy, *Demonolatry*, pp. 100–1.
36 Bodin, *Démonomanie*, pp. 464–67.
37 Remy, *Demonolatry*, pp. 185–86.
38 Remy, *Demonolatry*, p. 186.
39 Claude Bourgeois, *Pratique civile et criminelle pour les Justices inferieurs du duché de Lorraine*, Nancy: Jean Garnich, 1614, fols 38v–44v.
40 Remy, *Demonolatry*, p. 56.
41 Briggs, *Witches*, pp. 78–80.

**Further reading**

Briggs, Robin, *Witches and Neighbours*, 2nd ed., Oxford: Blackwell, 2002.
———, *The Witches of Lorraine*, Oxford: Oxford University Press, 2007.
Cabourdin, Guy, *Histoire de la Lorraine: Les Temps modernes*, vol. 2, Nancy: Presses Universitaires de Nancy, 1991.
Dintzer, Lucien, *Nicolas Remy et son oeuvre démonologique*, Lyon: Université de Lyon, 1936.
Pfister, Christian, 'Nicolas Remy et la sorcellerie en Lorraine à la fin du xvie siècle', *Revue Historique*, 1907, vol. 93, 225–239, and 1907, vol. 94, 28–44.

# 18 The mythmaker of the sabbat

Pierre de Lancre's *Tableau de l'inconstance des mauvais anges et démons*

*Thibaut Maus de Rolley and Jan Machielsen*

It is the summer of 1609, and an observer watches the children of Saint-Jean-de-Luz and Ciboure play. The two seafaring communities on opposing banks of the river Nivelle were connected by a bridge, and the observer may well have stood on it. At least, he saw naked children play in the water below. Their ability to swim as the river water crashed into the Atlantic Ocean amazed him, disappearing as they did 'a hundred thousand times in these great heaps, which were white like snowflakes, and by their very whiteness were like a headband which blinded us' (46).[1] So rough was the sea that its movements were 'capable of drowning the strongest courage of the most constant philosopher of the world' (46). Yet, some children even dived head-down from the bridge in pursuit of some small piece of coin, only to emerge five hundred feet from where they went in. To us this scene may appear idyllic, perhaps even glistening in the summer sun, but our observer, the Bordeaux judge Pierre de Lancre (1556–1631), saw something dark and sinister stirring underneath the surface with children at the very root of an evil conspiracy.[2]

The witch-hunt De Lancre conducted, together with his colleague Jean d'Espaignet (1564–after 1643), during the summer and autumn of 1609 in the Pays de Labourd, a Basque-speaking territory on France's border with Spain, is justly ranked among the most famous and notorious of the early modern period. It was, perhaps, the only hunt in the kingdom of France to have led to mass executions, and certainly the only one explicitly sanctioned – at least at the outset – by the central authorities.[3] It is unclear, however, how many women and men died. The number may be as high as eighty, and higher still if we look beyond the activities of De Lancre's and D'Espaignet's 1609 commission.[4] The traditional figure of 600 executions, used well into the 1970s, was based on a misreading that, as we shall see, can be traced back to the seventeenth century. Inquisitors on the Spanish side of the border, among them Alonso de Salazar Frías°, were facing a witchcraft panic of their own for which they also blamed De Lancre and his royal commission.[5] De Lancre's sensationalist 1612 account of his experiences – one historian has described it as a work of 'scholarly pornography' – includes the most detailed description of the witches' sabbat of the early modern period.[6] The elaborate fold-out engraving of the sabbat, included in the second 1613 edition of the *Tableau de l'inconstance des mauvais anges et démons* (Tableau of the Inconstancy of Evil Angels and Demons), remains one of the most iconic and most frequently used images of the early modern witch-hunt (See Figure 18.1). In a poem prefacing De Lancre's *Tableau*, his colleague D'Espaignet rightly predicted, perhaps with a sign of unease, that his colleague's pen would give the witches burned eternal life (sig. āāā2r). The testimony of children and teenagers played a central role in securing their fate.

For all its renown, the witch-hunt that took place in the Pays de Labourd remains deeply misunderstood. With the original trial documents destroyed

*Figure 18.1* Children being flown to the sabbat/A child being offered to a demon. Fragment from Jan Ziarnko's 'Description et figure du sabbat des sorciers' included in Pierre de Lancre, *Tableau de l'inconstance des mauvais anges et démons*, 2nd ed., Paris: Nicolas Buon, 1613. Sp Coll Ferguson Al-x.50. Image by permission of University of Glasgow Library, Special Collections.

by fire, the 1612 *Tableau* furnished historians with the archetype of a witch-hunt imposed on an unfortunate territory by elites from the outside.[7] In the most extreme version articulated by Josane Charpentier, Pierre de Lancre was held solely responsible 'for these crimes', although he has also shared responsibility with King Henry IV of France, who had authorized the witchcraft commission.[8] Blame has also been shifted onto elite fears and actions.[9] Because this was a witch-hunt that was effectively 'done' to the Pays de Labourd, very little attention has been paid to the territory's social and political geography.

Yet, De Lancre too has been misunderstood. Historians, even when they recognized that he was extremely unusual among French magistrates, attributed to him whatever mind-set they expected a wicked witch-hunter to possess. Hugh Trevor-Roper, accordingly, described him as the 'gleeful executioner of the Pays de Labourd', while for Robert Muchembled and Jonathan Pearl he was the personification of the 'cleric-magistrate acting as a missionary for reformed Catholicism in the French countryside'.[10] Such portrayals of religious bigotry or zeal bypass obvious biographical questions. How did the Bordeaux judge end up in the Basque territory? How did this experience fit in with his wider career? How did the *Tableau* fit in with his other (demonological and non-demonological) writings? Why was he so fascinated by the witches' sabbat? And why did he take the testimony of children and teenagers so seriously?

## 1 Pierre de Lancre before the Pays de Labourd

Pierre de Rosteguy de Lancre was born in or near Bordeaux in 1556. His family was of Basque origin but De Lancre's conduct in the Pays de Labourd showed no recognition of shared roots or language; as we shall see, his *Tableau* reported on local customs in ways that at once exoticized and dehumanized the territory's inhabitants. Mid-sixteenth-century Bordeaux had seen the emergence of a new political class. Bordeaux's merchants had invested new-found wealth in both titles and political offices (which, at the time, were bought and sold as property) to establish dynasties. Étienne de Rosteguy, the son and grandson of wine merchants, bought the title of Sieur de Lancre (a fictitious place) shortly after the birth of his son Pierre. Another noble title was found for Pierre's younger brother and both obtained offices within the Bordeaux Parlement; both of their two sisters also married into the institution. Although not as old or prestigious as the parlements of Paris and Toulouse, it was the highest court of appeal for much of the south-west of France. The Bordeaux Parlement was central to the city's intellectual milieu and counted among its members a notable number of famous authors. One of De Lancre's brothers-in-law, Florimond de Raemond (*c.*1540–1601), had penned celebrated invectives against the Protestants. De Lancre's colleague on the witchcraft commission, Jean d'Espaignet, was a noted alchemist. In 1588, De Lancre himself had married Jeanne de Mons, the daughter of yet another member of the Parlement and a relative of perhaps the most famous French author of the sixteenth century (and yet one more *parlementaire*), the essayist Michel de Montaigne (1533–1592).

Surrounded by such prominent literati, De Lancre himself made a first hesitant literary foray in 1607. His *Tableau de l'inconstance et instabilité de toutes choses* (Tableau of the Inconstancy and Instability of All Things) first appeared only with his initials on the title page. The author likened the book – in what certainly would not be his last gendered metaphor – to 'a young girl who was rather ashamed to come out into the light'.[11] Montaigne, like him the ennobled son and grandson of merchants, formed a particular inspiration. Inconstancy was a popular theme in the early seventeenth century, largely because of the essayist. The title of De Lancre's book paid homage to one of Montaigne's famous *Essays* ('Of the inconstancy of our actions', 1580), and both works appeared with the same Paris printer.[12] De Lancre's admiration for his relative by marriage has been an uncomfortable topic for historians and literature specialists. Montaigne, whose motto was 'Que sçay-je?' (What do I know?), was a well-known sceptic who transformed the questioning of received wisdom into a virtue, once declaring 'presumption' to be humanity's 'natural and original malady'.[13] This scepticism, not just of knowledge but of the *possibility* of knowledge, caused Montaigne to be critical of witchcraft persecutions: 'it is putting a very high price on one's conjectures to have a man roasted alive because of them'.[14]

De Lancre's scepticism in this first *Tableau* did not apply to witchcraft, a topic absent from this inaugural work. But it led the Bordeaux judge down avenues similar to Montaigne's, questioning the reliability of the senses and the mind, even noting that 'someone who does not recognize that he is ill can neither find a doctor nor accept any cure'.[15] One scholar went so far as to declare De Lancre Montaigne's 'spiritual son' until, in 1609, the 'witchcraft bug' of the Labourd infected him.[16] This was a strange inversion of the traditional blame game – as we have seen, it is usually De Lancre who is accused of harming the Pays de Labourd. There is some truth, however, to the idea that a preoccupation with witchcraft never left him after 1609. De Lancre would author two further books on the topic – the last of these, his 1627 *Du Sortilège* (On Witchcraft), was even printed in a very limited print run of 40 copies for its author's 'personal contentment'.[17] And yet, as the similarity in their titles suggests, De Lancre himself saw no radical break between his 1607 and 1612 *Tableau*. In fact, he styled the latter work as a case study, pointing out that 'there is nothing more inconstant and fickle than demons' (sig. ĩ1r). Where the inconstancy of all things led Montaigne towards scepticism, for De Lancre it legitimated a form of acceptance of all evidence, no matter how contradictory. In his 1622 *L'Incredulité et mescreance du sortilège plainement convaincue* (The Incredulity and Misbelief of Witchcraft Clearly Disproven), which he presented as a theoretical follow-up to the 1612 *Tableau*, De Lancre rhetorically asked sceptics: 'For is there anything that the Evil Spirit cannot do?'[18] His only – and entirely orthodox – caveat was that demons could not contravene the laws of nature. Still, this willingness to entertain the possibility of demonic interference was obviously a dangerous attitude in a judge, and in De Lancre's case, it was also self-serving in more ways than one. He would apply it successfully not only to the accused witches he interrogated in the Pays de Labourd but to the entire territory and all its inhabitants as well.

## 2 The Pays de Labourd

One may get a sense from reading De Lancre's 1612 *Tableau* that the Pays de Labourd, as a border region on the sea coast, caught between the Pyrenees and the Atlantic Ocean, was on the very edge of civilisation. In reality, the territory was a veritable crossroads of cultures. The Labourd played host to some of the most seminal moments in Franco-Spanish relations: the release from Spanish captivity of King Francis I in 1526, the exchange of the princesses that marked the Franco-Spanish marriage alliance in 1615, and the marriage of Louis XIV to the Spanish Infante, Maria Theresa, in Saint-Jean-de-Luz in 1660. Yet many ordinary overland travellers to and from Spain, including the many pilgrims to Santiago de Compostela, also passed through. A twelfth-century travel guide for those making the *camino* to Santiago already warned of the lack of wine, bread, and food, 'but one can find apples, cider, and milk by way of compensation'.[19] The evident sterility of the soil prompted Basque maritime exploration across the North Atlantic from the 1540s onwards. Cod fishing and whaling contributed greatly to the wealth of Saint-Jean-de-Luz, the main town – economic activity which even led the Basques to trade with indigenous tribes in what are now Canada's maritime provinces.[20]

As already noted, historians studying the witch-hunt have tended to overlook the social and political context of the Pays de Labourd itself, but Pierre de Lancre himself never did. The Bordeaux judge linked the witch-hunt explicitly to the territory's geography. Fascinated by the Labourd's customs and especially its women, De Lancre approached the territory as an ethnographer exploring a remote and alien country. To be sure, he was no unbiased observer, even leaving aside his special receptiveness to the 'bewitching' eyes, 'beautiful' hair, and 'immodest' dress of Basque womenfolk (42). (Nor was he strictly speaking an outsider, as we shall see.) To the second, 1610 edition of his *Tableau* on the inconstancy of all things, De Lancre had added an extra section to vindicate the special constancy of the French over all other nations.[21] Keen to demonstrate the French stiff upper lip still further, De Lancre rooted the inconstancy of the Basques in the liminal position of their homeland. With the exception of the local nobility 'raised in the French manner', the people of the Labourd had been infected by Spanish customs, especially Spanish pride, arrogance, and deceitfulness (37, 33). The sterility of the soil also caused their surrender to the sea, 'this restless element', which in turn affected their behaviour: 'they entrust all their good fortune and possessions to the waves that toss them about night and day' (31). De Lancre described them as constantly affected, in their souls and in their bodies, by a 'maritime' inconstancy, a frenzy physically expressed, beyond seafaring, in the Basque taste for abrupt and turbulent dancing, for acrobatics, for swimming, and for running. As we saw at the beginning of this chapter, De Lancre was particularly struck by the frantic energy of Basque children, whom he also describes as running races that sent them hurtling into doors and windows.[22] As playthings of the elements and contaminated by Spanish vices, the inhabitants were a product of their geography. Even the fact that the Labourd was a 'land of apples' caused its women 'to eat only apples and drink only apple juice', making them into earthly Eves 'who willingly seduce the sons of Adam' (43).

In the judge's mind, it was the liminal status of the border region that the devil exploited. (Suspected witches did so as well, fleeing across the border with Spain or departing for fishing grounds across the Atlantic (40–41).) With demons chased out of the New World and the Far East through the good efforts of Christian missionaries, the exotic and remote Pays de Labourd (described by De Lancre as a New World of sorts) became an ideal new home within Europe. Not only did the devil take advantage of these different jurisdictions when organizing his sabbats, he also exploited the absence of the men who were away from home on long sea journeys. These long journeys caused the men to feel indifferent towards their women – treating them like 'half-year wives' – and uncertain about whether their offspring were really theirs. The result was that women, abandoned by their husbands, chose another father for their children: Satan (38). The devil thus transformed the Labourd into a 'nursery' of witchcraft with no family left untouched by the crime (30).

What should we make of this argument? It is, of course, primarily of interest for the insight it offers into De Lancre's mindset. He may well have provided the most fascinating analysis of failing patriarchy within the corpus of early modern demonology – fascinating especially because while it was the *men* who failed in their assigned role as providers it was their wives who became witches. The gulf that separates De Lancre as an elite male, who as a member of a royal commission quite literally embodied the French crown, from the inconstant Basque women he encountered could not be wider and yet their 'bewitching' qualities of seduction puts that distance (and De Lancre with it) in constant peril. In the preface, he even worried that he might seem to 'play the magician or witch' for revealing too much information (sig. ē2v). Still, as an analysis of the real social and political conditions of the territory, it is severely limiting though by no means completely worthless. The Spanish border posed a real threat to the inhabitants and recent Spanish raids seem to have destabilized the territory.[23] Yet, the analysis is also contradictory and problematic for De Lancre's own argument: its geographical determinism could have excused the inhabitants from any responsibility for their crimes. De Lancre thus also put blame on Basque moral failings for good measure:

'Although nature has provided the whole world with land for sustenance, they prefer (fickle and inconstant as they are) that of the stormy seas over that provided by that sweet and peaceful goddess [of agriculture], Ceres' (32).

## 3 De Lancre's *Tableau*

De Lancre's *Tableau*, then, was not a straightforward chronological narrative of a witch-hunt (some crucial details, such as the commission's end date on 1 November 1609, are only mentioned, as if accidentally, in passing (451)), nor was it quite like any other demonological treatise discussed in this volume. Deeply personal, it was at the same time a scholarly demonology, a travel narrative, an ethnography, and a philosophical meditation on inconstancy shaped by De Lancre's reading of classical texts. Because it was written according to De Lancre's interests, much of what we would like to know about the 1609 witch-hunt has been left out. We may safely guess, for instance, that much of the harm that the witches were alleged to have caused was centred on the dangers of the sea, but mundane *maleficia* did not interest De Lancre much.[24] It was the hidden yet flighty demonic underworld and everything that happened there that enthralled him. As Margaret McGowan observed long ago, the judge used a 'fevered accumulation of words' to convey his fascination and excitement to the reader:

> Dancer indecemment, festiner ordement, s'acoupler diaboliquement, sodomiser execrablement, blasfemer scandaleusement, se venger insidieusement, courir aprés tous desirs horribles, sales et desnaturez brutalement, tenir les crapaux, les viperes, les lezards et toute sorte de poison precieusement, aymer un bouc puant ardamment, le carresser amoureusement, s'acointer et s'acoupler avec luy horriblement et impudemment: ne sont-ce pas des traicts desreglez d'une legereté non pareille, et d'une inconstance execrable?
>
> (sig. ĩ1v)

> [To dance indecently, to feast filthily, to have sex diabolically, to sodomize atrociously, to blaspheme scandalously, to avenge themselves insidiously, to pursue all horrible, nasty and unnatural desires brutishly, to keep toads, vipers, lizards, and all sorts of poison preciously, to love a stinking goat ardently, to caress him lovingly, to familiarize and have sex with him horribly and shamelessly: are these not the unruly traits of a fickleness without equal and an execrable inconstancy?][25]

Given the richness of such baroque prose, it is no wonder that in France today the *Tableau* is principally studied within literature departments. The passage shows how the book's aim to instruct the reader sits alongside a desire to titillate. It also underscores the aspects of witchcraft that most appealed to De Lancre, notably the witches' sabbat and everything that went on there. The

*Tableau* offered perhaps the most detailed and explicit account of the sabbat in early modern literature, and was one of the very first printed works to describe the sabbat in such detail as a Black Mass – that is, as a systematic inversion and parody of the Catholic Mass. De Lancre also devoted an entire chapter to the 'incestuous' Spanish dances that were performed with 'even more liberty and insolence' at the sabbat (202, 203). Not only did he describe these in considerable detail, he also had the children he interrogated dance in front of him 'in the same fashion as they dance at the sabbat, to deter them from such filth and to make them recognize how even the most modest movement was filthy, ugly and unbecoming an honest girl' (207–8). Strikingly, the judge also relates how, as a youth, he himself had impressed an Italian visitor to Bordeaux with his own dance moves, suggestive evidence of De Lancre's own inconstancy (204–5; the subject this chapter shall end with).

With his professed prowess on the dance floor, De Lancre could have made quite the entry at the witches' sabbat, and perhaps he secretly wanted to. Indeed, the *Tableau* was presented as an eye-witness account, the very opposite of the type of book-based learning put forth by Jean Bodin° and Martin Delrio°. Yet, visual evidence of the sabbat was impossible to obtain. The sabbat was so tantalisingly within De Lancre's reach but, as the principal realm of demons, also utterly inaccessible to a Christian judge. When seventeen-year old Marie Dindarte told him that the devil had flown her to the sabbat, the judge asked her to fly away right in front of him. (Unfortunately, the young woman did not have the right ointment with her but promised to bring some back from her next trip to the sabbat (97).) In July 1609, not long after his arrival in the region, De Lancre assembled an expedition for a failed attempt to climb to the top of a rock where the sabbat had taken place, near the village of Hendaye. During a second, more successful effort, the party was able to discern the site where witches had kept the pot during the previous night's sabbat from the mark left by its base (139). Unable to attend the sabbat, De Lancre seems delighted to learn that a sabbat, complete with a Black Mass, was held in his own bed chamber. On 24 September 1609 around midnight, a troupe of witches entered his room and even climbed under his bed curtains with the intent of poisoning him. Try as they might, they could not harm him as they told the devil waiting by the door (142–43). The alleged episode illustrated how De Lancre as a Christian magistrate was inviolate, protected by God against demonic assault, yet it also conveys a sense of proximity and the danger of possible corruption.

## 4 De Lancre's witches and witnesses

De Lancre, of course, was fast asleep while these events were said to have unfolded in his bedchamber. He discovered them in the same way as he learned an almost infinite amount of other details about the sabbat: not through visual evidence, but through stories – those told by the persons he and his colleague, Jean d'Espaignet, interrogated. Here De Lancre's preoccupation with inconstancy intersects with the *Tableau*'s other notable feature: his claim to offer a 'simple account of the depositions of witnesses and the confessions of accused' (sig. ẽ3v). Later, he would even describe the *Tableau* as the 'written record of the proceedings [*procés verbal*]'.[26] The contrast between these two themes is noteworthy, as is the way De Lancre's own rich ornate prose is interspersed with long extracts from legal depositions, immediately identifiable by formulaic markers of indirect discourse such as 'asked if' [*interrogé si*] and 'said that' [*dict que*]. In some respects, De Lancre's *Tableau* resembles a collage, where relevant legal testimonies and confessions drawn from the archives were slotted in according to the subjects or themes that the judge was trying to develop.

The *Tableau* thus offers a striking example of the importance given to legal depositions in demonology, and of the ways witchcraft confessions helped shape early modern demonological thought. Demonologists, and perhaps especially French ones, gained much of their knowledge, as Virginia Krause observed, 'from the witch's mouth'.[27] However, it must be noted that the testimony in this case passed through at least three filters before it reaches us: first that of the Basque interpreter (who, according to De Lancre, felt more shame posing the judge's sexually explicit questions than the witnesses showed in answering them (216)), then that of the legal scribe, and finally De Lancre himself as he sorted through the material for publication in the *Tableau*. Yet, those filters notwithstanding, the seemingly raw nature of these confessions retained a strong aesthetic appeal, both for De Lancre and for his readers, as the author knew well: 'they are so strange in and of themselves that they will not fail to please the reader, even though I leave them in their original, naive form [*en leur naïveté*]' (sig. ẽ3v).[28]

De Lancre's handling of this testimony, which removed it from its original context, has caused severe misunderstanding of the witch-hunt of the Pays de Labourd, though it probably also served to obscure areas of the judge's own inconsistency (if not inconstancy) from view. In his preface, De Lancre stated that the commission had interrogated 'sixty or eighty notable witches and five hundred witnesses' (sig. ẽ3r). It was the combination of these figures (five hundred plus eighty) that by the end of the seventeenth century was rounded up to the figure of 600 executions – a figure that remained widely accepted until the 1970s.[29] This confusion is easily enough understood as the 'witnesses' in question all possessed the devil's mark and 'go to the sabbat everyday' but, being witnesses, they were evidently not punished (sig. ẽ3r). The lower figure of 'sixty or eighty' also included witches who had been banished or transported to Bordeaux for further examination after the commission ended.

The identity of these witnesses is no mystery: they were the children and teenagers that the commission interrogated. The real puzzle, perhaps De Lancre's greatest act of inconstancy, was why these witnesses were not apparently persecuted. The format of the *Tableau*, devoted to uncovering a demonic underworld rather than describing criminal procedure, meant that De Lancre could avoid answering that question. By his own logic, they should have been executed. For De Lancre, attendance at the sabbat alone was sufficient for a death sentence (566–67). Elsewhere, he acknowledged that age was no excuse and in this harsh view, he was by no means alone.[30] The judge's detailed description of the children's induction into the devil's service – at the age of nine – included a voluntary profession of faith and a demonic Creed (390–91; after which the children were given a speaking toad to take care of). Without a rare 'special grace from God', no one in the devil's clutches could hope to escape (398). Yet, he seems to bestow this grace on his teenage witnesses, claiming that they were 'already on the road to salvation before our commission. Some had completely left and had not been to the sabbat for some time, others were struggling and still had one feet in' (208).

Perhaps the most straightforward solution to the puzzle was simply that they served a purpose: they testified against the 'notable witches' (mostly older women, although the commission also executed a number of priests) who had taken them to the sabbat and provided De Lancre with access to the demonic underworld in vivid detail that would otherwise have remained out of reach. He needed these teenagers as witnesses and even declared that 'two girls bearing the devil's mark who have gone through puberty should count as one good witness' (553). They offered intimate details of every aspect of the sabbat. De Lancre's star witness, sixteen-year old Jeannette d'Abadie, who had sex at the sabbat more than a hundred times, told him about 'the tremendous pleasure' she felt just describing her sexual experiences at the sabbat, 'calling everything by their rightful name more freely and shamelessly than we ever dared to ask her, which wonderfully confirms the reality of the sabbat' (134). Marie Dindarte, whom we already met briefly, told De Lancre that the devil changed her into something else during sex so as to avoid the public embarrassment (216). Jean d'Aguerre, age unknown, claimed that the devil appeared as a goat and had his penis attached to his back side (217). According to Abadie, the devil's organ was scaled 'like a fish' (224). Fifteen-year old Marie de Marigrane claimed that it was half made of metal (225). Another girl named Margueritte, aged sixteen or seventeen, said that it resembled that of a mule, which led De Lancre to conclude that 'all the female witches of the Labourd are better served by Satan than those of the Franche-Comté', studied by the judge Henri Boguet (224–25).

What are we to make of this testimony? How did it come about? And what does it tell us about our judge? It is the second question that is the most vexing on every level. The role played by children within the European witch-hunt, as accused witches but especially as accusers, has rarely been addressed in the historiography.[31] At no other point is transcending De Lancre's perspective – which historians must do to make sense of the witch-hunt – as difficult as it is on this issue. The answer is heavily dependent on how much agency one is willing to grant these witnesses. De Lancre's supposed credulity can be a particularly useful cover by shifting attention away from the testimony of teenagers to De Lancre's willingness to believe them. There is no doubt that the witnesses were mistreated. The fact that they were searched for the devil's mark shows us as much. Yet, their fantastical testimony was based on lived experience and popular culture. At least two of the witches executed were musicians, included in the Ziarnko engraving, who had performed at weddings and festivals such as the sabbat (131; see also Figure 18.2). For De Lancre, Marie de Marigrane's 'shameful' comment that the devil had sex with pretty witches from the front and ugly ones from behind had to be true – 'her youth was incapable of so sordid an invention' (217). Yet, this could be precisely the sort of crude sexual comment in a world without much privacy that she could easily have picked up.

To be sure, De Lancre formed an extraordinarily receptive audience. Beyond his sexual curiosity, his fascination and preoccupation with inconstancy made him likely to accept almost everything that he was told. Consistency, as we have seen, was no prerequisite for credibility. If inconstancy was the devil's hallmark, variety in testimony, rather than disqualifying, provided additional *proof* of his demonic presence. The devil's penis, we might say too glibly, could come in all shapes and sizes. Unable to understand the Basque testimony first-hand, De Lancre scrutinized the bodies and faces of his witnesses for their emotions, commenting how instead of 'going red and crying' they took 'a singular pleasure' in recounting their sexual activities with the devil (216). These descriptions must be, at least in part, projection on De Lancre's part – the pleasure his witnesses supposedly took from describing the sabbat certainly seems equal to his own pleasure in writing the *Tableau*. His apology in the preface for discussing sex 'a little bit too openly' can neither masque his fascination with the Basque women he encountered nor his lurid attention to sexual detail (sig. ē4v). As a subject, the sabbat would never let De Lancre go. The preface of his 1622 *L'Incredulité* opened with the promise to describe 'the orgies and nocturnal assemblies of the magicians and witches'.[32] His 1627 *Du Sortilège*, printed, as we saw, for his 'personal contentment', opened with a chapter defending the discovery and publication of the 'abominations' of witches that others thought should be kept secret.

## 5 Pierre de Lancre: a rock and an anchor

As far as names go, there could hardly have been a more appropriate bulwark against inconstancy than 'Pierre de Lancre', a name which encapsulates both a rock [*pierre*] and an anchor [*l'ancre*; a spelling used in some of his writings].[33] His coat of arms featured three anchors – a number and figure which he claimed represented the Holy Trinity.[34] The image was prominently included (on the *verso* side of the title page) of his 1612 *Tableau*. The only truly constant entity, of course, was God. (The motto of his 1607 *Tableau* was taken from Malachi 3:6: 'I am God, I do not change'.) Yet, in a symbolic way Pierre de Lancre was not far behind. Not only was 'the anchor ... the hieroglyph of the constancy of God', it was also associated with St Peter [*Pierre*] 'who represents the Church'.[35] By

*Figure 18.2* Village musicians performing at the sabbat/nude dancing at the sabbat. Fragment from Jan Ziarnko's 'Description et figure du sabbat des sorciers', in Pierre de Lancre, Tableau de l'inconstance des mauvais anges et démons, 2nd ed., Paris: Nicolas Buon, 1613 [Sp Coll Ferguson Al-x.50]. Image by permission of University of Glasgow Library, Special Collections.

1622, when De Lancre completed his second witchcraft treatise, he had fully become his name. Already well into his sixties he had retired to his country estate, where he invited visitors who 'will certainly find, at the top of my Mountain, an old ANCHOR, which I am myself, ready to receive him'.[36]

As we have already seen, De Lancre had not always embodied constancy to such a perfect degree. Writing about inconstancy, he was worried about being infected by it in a way that mirrors his interest in witchcraft: 'Writing about inconstancy, I can hardly avoid its taint'.[37] Yet, De Lancre's inconstancy was not confined to the written word. We have explored some of the reasons for his pre-occupation with inconstancy and we have seen how it may account for his willingness to believe his witnesses. Yet, we have also noticed how his writings purposely obscured certain issues from view. From what we know so far, the traditional depiction of De Lancre as a 'cleric-magistrate' does not seem overly plausible, even if we were to accept the claim that he 'constantly emphasized the distastefulness of the task in which he was engaged'.[38] Strikingly, the *Tableau* shows no concern about the spread of heresy in the Labourd. (The adjacent territory of Béarn had been officially Protestant.) Instead, his fascination for the topic of witchcraft, in particular its sexual aspects, and his gendered use of language suggest that this was only a pious facade. The fact that De Lancre left his personal library to an illegitimate son provides further support for this.[39]

Sex, however, was only one form of De Lancre's inconstancy. Another aspect illustrates the difficulty of interpreting De Lancre's work and demonstrates the extent to which our knowledge of the witch-hunt of the Pays de Labourd remains incomplete. Scholars, to our knowledge, have never properly considered why it was Pierre de Lancre, of all people, who was nominated to serve on the witchcraft commission. The royal decree was issued in response to a petition from within the Pays de Labourd itself.[40] It seems improbable that the French crown would identify and select a Bordeaux judge for a time-consuming mission on its own initiative. It is much more likely that his name was put forth by the local sponsors. In 1612, De Lancre identifies the two leading noblemen of the Labourd, the Lords of Urtubie and Amou, only once in passing (141). Only in the preface of the (slightly expanded) 1613 edition are they mentioned by name.[41] What De Lancre never mentioned, however, was his close family relationship to one of these men. In 1598, Tristan de Gamboa d'Alzate, *Seigneur* of the castle of Urtubie, had married Catherine Eyquem de Montaigne, the daughter of a Bordeaux magistrate and a cousin of De Lancre's wife.[42] Far from an impartial judge, De Lancre was a local partisan. If we wish to understand the witch-hunt of the Pays de Labourd, we must investigate the agency and actions of all those involved, including not only Urtubie and Amou but also De Lancre's child witnesses. Such a study may tell us a great deal about Pierre de Lancre, the mythmaker of the sabbat, in turn.

## Notes

1 All in-text references are to Pierre de Lancre, *Tableau de l'inconstance des mauvais anges et démons*, Paris: Nicolas Buon, 1612. All translations are by the authors. A modern French critical (and abridged) edition was published by Nicole Jacques-Chaquin in 1982. The English translation needs to be used with care: Pierre

de Lancre, *On the Inconstancy of Witches: Pierre de Lancre's Tableau de l'inconstance des mauvais anges et demons* (1612), ed. and trans. Gerhild Scholz Williams et al., Tempe, AZ: Arizona Center for Medieval and Renaissance Studies, 2006.
2 For Pierre de Lancre's biography, combine Armand Communay, *Le Conseiller Pierre de Lancre*, Agen: Lamy, 1890, with Jan Machielsen, 'Lancre, Pierre de (1556–1631)', in Luc Foisneau, ed., *Dictionnaire des philosophes français du XVIIe siècle*, Paris: Classiques Garnier, 2015, pp. 984–88. The latter establishes, among other things, De Lancre's year of birth.
3 For a recent overview of witch-hunting in France, see William Monter, 'Witchcraft Trials in France', in Brian P. Levack, ed., *The Oxford Handbook of Witchcraft in Early Modern Europe and Colonial America*, Oxford: Oxford University Press, 2013, pp. 218–31.
4 Pierre de Lancre references the confessions of 'soixante ou quatre vingts insignes Sorcieres' and had very little incentive to understate the number: De Lancre, *Tableau* (1612), sig. ẽ3r. '[P]lusieurs' witches were banished rather than executed: ibid., p. 382.
5 On the response of Spanish Inquisition officials, see Lu Ann Homza's contribution to this volume.
6 Robin Briggs, *Witches and Neighbours*, 2nd ed., Oxford: Blackwell Publishing, 2002, p. 26, also p. 70.
7 The building and archives of the Bordeaux Parlement were destroyed by fire in 1710.
8 Josane Charpentier, *La Sorcellerie en Pays basque*, Paris: Librairie Guénégaud, 1977, p. 27.
9 Beñat Zintzo-Garmendia, *Histoire de la sorcellerie en Pays basque: Les Bûchers de l'injustice*, Toulouse: Privat, 2016, avertissements.
10 Jonathan L. Pearl, *The Crime of Crimes: Demonology and Politics in France, 1560–1620*, Waterloo, ON: Wilfrid Laurier University Press, 1999, pp. 129–30.
11 Pierre de Lancre, *Tableau de l'inconstance et instabilité de toutes choses*, 2nd ed., Paris: widow of Abel L'Angelier, 1610, sig. a2r.
12 See the entries in Jean Balsamo and Michel Simonin, *Abel L'Angelier et Françoise de Louvain, 1574–1620* Geneva: Droz, 2002. The authors describe De Lancre's first *Tableau* as 'un ouvrage imité des *Essais*' (p. 360).
13 Michel de Montaigne, 'Apology for Raymond Sebond', in *The Complete Works: Essays, Travel Journal, Letters*, trans. Donald M. Frame, London: Everyman Guides, p. 401.
14 Montaigne, 'Of Cripples', in *The Complete Works*, p. 962.
15 De Lancre, *Tableau* (1610), fol. 149v.
16 Henri Busson, 'Montaigne et son cousin', *Revue d'histoire littéraire de la France*, 1960, vol. 60/4, 481–499, at 484.
17 See the 12 April 1627 contract printed in Jules Delpit, 'Pierre de L'Ancre et la sorcellerie: À propos d'une rareté bibliographique', *Bulletin du bibliophile et du bibliothécaire*, 1885, vol. 28, 81–89, which must relate to the appearance of Pierre de Lancre, *Du Sortilège*, s.l.: s.n., 1627.
18 Pierre de Lancre, *L'Incredulité et mescreance du sortilège plainement convaincue*, Paris: Nicolas Buon, 1622, p. 834.
19 Philippe Veyrin, *Les Basques de Labourd, de Soule et de Basse Navarre: Leur Histoire et leurs traditions*, [Grenoble]: Arthaud, 1955, p. 41.
20 For a good introduction, see Brad Loewen and Claude Chapdelaine, eds, *Contact in the 16th Century: Networks among Fishers, Foragers and Farmers*, Ottawa, ON: University of Ottawa Press, 2016.
21 The 1610 edition, evidently finished after his return from the Labourd, included a preface addressed to 'the French'.

22 Thibaut Maus de Rolley, 'Of Oysters, Witches, Birds, and Anchors: Conceptions of Space and Travel in Pierre de Lancre', *Renaissance Studies*, 2018, vol. 32/4, 530–46.
23 This aspect will be explored in Machielsen's forthcoming book on Pierre de Lancre and Basque witch-hunt.
24 One of the rare references to *maleficia* relates to the sinking of a ship: De Lancre, *Tableau* (1612), p. 95.
25 Margaret M. McGowan, 'Pierre de Lancre's *Tableau de l'Inconstance des Mauvais Anges et Demons*: The Sabbat Sensationalised', in Sydney Anglo, ed., *The Damned Art: Essays in the Literature of Witchcraft*, London: Routledge & Kegan Paul, 1977, pp. 182–201, at 196.
26 De Lancre, *L'Incredulité*, p. 11.
27 Virginia Krause, *Witchcraft, Demonology, and Confession in Early Modern France*, Cambridge: Cambridge University Press, 2015, p. 43.
28 On the aesthetic appeal of these confessions, see Maus de Rolley, *Elévations: L'Écriture du voyage aérien à la Renaissance*, Geneva: Droz, 2011, pp. 486–92.
29 *Factums et arrest du Parlement de Paris contre des bergers sorciers executez depuis peu dans la province de Brie*, Paris: Rebuffé, 1695, p. 64; McGowan, 'Pierre de Lancre's *Tableau de l'Inconstance des Mauvais Anges et Demons*', p. 183 still accepted the figure. It was first challenged by Gustav Henningsen, *The Witches' Advocate: Basque Witchcraft and the Spanish Inquisition, 1609–1614*, Reno, NV: University of Nevada Press, 1980, pp. 24–25.
30 De Lancre, *L'Incredulité*, p. 41. Jean Bodin, for instance, took a similarly harsh view.
31 A good starting point, however, is Lyndal Roper, '"Evil Imaginings and Fantasies": Child-Witches and the End of the Witch Craze', *Past & Present*, 2000, vol. 167/1, 107–39.
32 De Lancre, *L'Incredulité*, p. 9.
33 This alternative spelling was used on the title page of his 1622 *L'Incredulité*.
34 De Lancre, *Tableau* (1610), fol. 492v.
35 De Lancre, *Tableau* (1610), fols. 492v–93r.
36 De Lancre, *L'Incredulité*, p. 41. The capital letters are De Lancre's. On De Lancre's symbolic interpretation of his own name, and the contrast between De Lancre's country estate of Loubens and the Pays de Labourd, see Maus de Rolley, 'Of Oysters, Witches, Birds, and Anchors'.
37 De Lancre, *Tableau* (1610), sig. a2v.
38 Pearl, *The Crime of Crimes*, p. 143.
39 See Jan Machielsen, 'Lancre, Pierre de (1556–1631)', p. 988.
40 See the 'Lettres patentes' transcribed in Roland Villeneuve, *Le Fléau des sorciers: Histoire de la diablerie basque au XVIIe siècle*, [Paris]: Flammarion, 1983, pp. 221–22.
41 Pierre de Lancre, *Tableau de l'inconstance des mauvais anges et démons*, 2nd ed., Paris: Nicolas Buon, 1613, sig. õ1r.
42 See the data on Geneanet. The marriage is not mentioned in Théophile Malvezin, *Michel de Montaigne: Son Origine, sa famille*, Bordeaux: 1875.

# Further reading

Communay, Armand, *Le Conseiller Pierre de Lancre*, Agen: Lamy, 1890.
Dardano Basso, Isa, *L'ancora e gli specchi: Lettura del* Tableau de l'inconstance et instabilité de toutes choses *di Pierre de Lancre*, Rome: Bulzoni, 1979.
Houdard, Sophie, *Les Sciences du diable: Quatre Discours sur la sorcellerie, XV$^e$–XVII$^e$ siècle*, Paris: Éditions du Cerf, 1992.

Machielsen, Jan, 'Thinking with Montaigne: Evidence, Scepticism and Meaning in Early Modern Demonology', *French History*, 2011, vol. 25/4, 427–452.

———, 'Lancre, Pierre de (1556–1631)', in Luc Foisneau, ed., *Dictionnaire des philosophes français du XVIIe siècle*, Paris: Classiques Garnier, 2015, pp. 984–988.

Maus de Rolley, Thibaut, 'Of Oysters, Witches, Birds, and Anchors: Conceptions of Space and Travel in Pierre de Lancre', *Renaissance Studies*, 2018, vol. 32/4, 530–546.

McGowan, Margaret M., 'Pierre de Lancre's *Tableau de l'inconstance des Mauvais Anges et démons*: The Sabbat Sensationalised', in Sydney Anglo, ed., *The Damned Art: Essays in the Literature of Witchcraft*, London: Routledge & Kegan Paul, 1977, pp. 182–201.

# 19 An expert lawyer and reluctant demonologist
## Alonso de Salazar Frías, Spanish Inquisitor

*Lu Ann Homza*

Alonso de Salazar Frías was born in 1564. Like thousands of other Spanish men, he became a lawyer, and he specialized in the decrees of the Catholic Church. Salazar's legal expertise was significant, and while still young, he acquired important benefactors, the most renowned of which was Don Bernardo de Sandoval y Rojas, who became the Archbishop of Toledo in 1599.[1] Though he could not have known it at the time, Sandoval eventually placed Salazar in a position in which he would become celebrated by modern historians. Sandoval was named Inquisitor-General in 1608; Salazar was the first inquisitor he appointed, on 23 March 1609. Sandoval assigned Salazar to the inquisition tribunal in Logroño, which monitored heresy in the former kingdom of Navarre, in northern Spain. When Salazar arrived there in late June 1609, he joined two other inquisitors, Alonso de Becerra and Juan de Valle Alvarado, and became part of their massive investigation into witchcraft that they had started the previous January.[2]

Initially, Salazar worked in the tribunal, conducting interrogations, hearing confessions, and voting on verdicts throughout 1609–1610. At the end of those two years, he and his associates convicted 31 witches, and handed out punishments ranging from death at the stake to light abjurations of heresy. The verdicts were read publicly at a famous *auto de fe* in early November 1610.[3] As the most junior member of the tribunal, Salazar was next in line to visit Navarrese territory, should the need arise. Because accusations of witchcraft continued after the *auto de fe*, he was sent out the following year with an edict of grace. That edict allowed him to reconcile to the Catholic Church those individuals who had confessed to witchcraft but had not yet been absolved of their sin. Witchcraft was such a serious heresy that absolution was reserved to higher religious authorities than ordinary priests or friars.

Salazar's trip through northern Navarre lasted from May 1611 to January 1612. He returned to Logroño with more than 5,000 folios of evidence; he then locked himself in a room and began to write a report for the Royal General Council of the Inquisition, the so-called *Suprema* based in Madrid. The document he finished on 24 March 1612 relayed how the witches reached the devil's assemblies, what their witchcraft entailed, and whether their activities took place in real life, or in hallucinations and dreams. But Salazar also appended a fourth category of inquiry, which addressed 'the testimonies or proofs that can result from all of the above, to punish the guilty.' There, he confirmed that he had been unable to find witnesses to witchcraft who were not witches themselves. He also declared that the suspects he had interviewed in the field could not be punished for witchcraft because there was no sustainable proof that they were heretics.

The other two inquisitors, who were senior to Salazar, took issue with his statements. Over the next year and a half, or through October 1613, the three inquisitors sent defenses of their positions to the *Suprema*. The *Suprema* ultimately invited Salazar to Madrid, and after five months of work, the Spanish Inquisition issued revised guidelines on witchcraft prosecutions in 1614. Those instructions became binding on every inquisition tribunal in Spanish imperial territory.[4]

No longer should inquisitors believe witch suspects who said that they had visited the devil in their dreams. The new instructions told inquisitors they could only prosecute witch suspects if the latter had been awake during the alleged heresy; the accused had to have committed apostasy during the day, and persisted in demonic worship. Inquisitors were told to look for signs that witch suspects had been coerced into confessing. Remarkably, the 1614 guidelines also stated that the individuals who had been executed or reconciled for witchcraft in Logroño's 1610 *auto de fe* would no longer lose their property, have to wear the penitential garment called the *sanbenito*, or see their descendants labeled infamous. Alonso de Salazar Frías was the force behind these revisions. It is for this reason that he has become known to history as 'the witches' advocate'.[5]

## 1 Similarities between Salazar and De Lancre

In many respects, Salazar can be imagined as Pierre De Lancre's Spanish twin.[6] Both men were investigating the same sort of witchcraft, which involved diabolical veneration and harmful magic. They both catalogued many details about the devil's reunions, which in Salazar's territory were called *aquelarres*. In those gatherings, men and women renounced their baptismal vows, pledged their allegiance to the devil, engaged in various sexual acts with each other and the devil himself, and promised to injure people, animals, and crops to the best of their ability.[7] Some facets of the witchcraft on the Spanish side of the border inverted aspects of Christianity, to the point that witches were given individual toads that functioned like guardian angels, and the devil asked his witches to confess the evil they had failed to do.

For both De Lancre and Salazar, the chief victims and witnesses of these diabolical activities were children and teenagers.[8] Salazar listened attentively as girls and boys, many as young as five, relayed how older witches had snatched them from their beds while they slept and carried them through the air to the devil's gatherings, where they watched the horrific activities and sometimes took part in the same. Salazar heard teenage girls attest that they had engaged in sexual intercourse with the devil.[9] Young children told Salazar that they had guarded the toads that later would be distributed to more mature witches; the toads vomited the unguent that allowed the witches to fly to the devil's gatherings.[10]

Another commonality to both witch-hunts is that all of the accused testified in Basque, which neither Salazar nor De Lancre understood; they had to employ translators.[11] The aura of otherness was compounded by the fact that Salazar and De Lancre had been taught to expect an alien world before they moved into the suspected witches' territories. In Salazar's case, members of the *Suprema* and the other inquisitors from Logroño repeatedly pointed out the poverty and fearsome topography of northern Navarre.[12]

Another similarity, albeit an unfortunate one, is that key sources from De Lancre's and Salazar's experiences no longer exist. The original trial documents generated by De Lancre's investigations were destroyed by fire. The entire inquisition tribunal in Logroño was burned to the ground by Napoleon's forces in the early nineteenth century. Nevertheless, scholars can still examine multiple editions and variations of De Lancre's writings, and an enormous number of documents relating to Salazar's activities do survive. This cornucopia makes it all the more strange that modern assessments of De Lancre and Salazar tend to be thoroughly one-dimensional. If, as Thibaut Maus de Rolley and Jan Machielsen point out in this volume, De Lancre has been dismissed as a credulous producer of 'scholarly pornography', then modern assessments of Salazar have turned him into a forward-looking skeptic. There are significant benefits to examining these figures' current portraits.

## 2 Salazar's devil as a liar

Salazar turns out to have been more complex than ruling studies allow because of his sense of legal limits, his esteem for obedience, and his attention to the *cura animarum*, or care of souls. He was a reluctant demonologist, especially after he left on visitation in 1611.[13] Unlike De Lancre, who delighted in pondering what the devil might do, Salazar had no interest in the hypothetical contemplation of demonic powers. Simply put, Salazar thought the devil was a liar, which means he had absorbed one of the messages of the Christian New Testament. John 8:44 explained that the devil 'was a murderer from the beginning, not holding to the truth, for there is no truth in him. When he lies, he speaks his native language, for he is a liar and the father of lies.'

Salazar's vision of the devil had a great deal in common with the images summoned by clerical authors in Spain in the sixteenth century.[14] Salazar and his fellow inquisitors did not distinguish between the devil and demons, but consistently referred to the former as *el Demonio*. The devil engaged in both explicit and tacit pacts with human beings; he wanted to be revered as a god, and delighted in enticing persons to overthrow their baptismal vows. Finally, the devil could transport individuals through the air in reality – as he had done with Jesus in Matthew 4:1-11 – or he could trick individuals into believing that they had flown, as confirmed by the canon law text called the canon *Episcopi*.[15]

The evidence that Salazar heard in the field confirmed his vision of the devil as mendacious. He was told that suspected witches could be in two places at the same time, but no onlooker could discern which of the two was a *figura*, put in place by the devil, and which was real. Parents tied their offspring to beds to prevent them from being taken to the devil's gatherings, but in the morning, the children identified the witches who had snatched them. Some suspects even insisted they had simultaneously attended Mass and the devil's reunions, though no one in church had seen them disappear.[16]

Questions of deceit continued. Defendants and their child victims testified repeatedly that the witchcraft here involved ointments and powders that allowed the witches to fly and to work harmful magic against their enemies. Throughout 1609 and 1610, Salazar and his colleagues eagerly collected samples of such materials, and submitted them to doctors and apothecaries for testing; findings were inconclusive. On the road in 1611, Salazar continued amassing samples, and again came up empty; everything was counterfeit.[17]

From the field, Salazar also heard claims that seemed unbelievable. Witch suspects contended they had given birth to toads through their throats. They insisted that a whole troop had invaded Salazar's office and stayed there, suspended and invisible, while he was hearing depositions. Several stated they had set fire to Salazar's chair as he held an audience; some declared they had dropped poison into his mouth while he slept.[18] Salazar told the *Suprema* in 1612 that there was no tangible evidence for any of these claims, and he personally had sensed nothing; the rooms in which he conducted business could barely accommodate three persons, much less forty.[19] Similar puzzles occurred with the devil's reunions. As they traveled, Salazar and his assistants went to the sites of those alleged gatherings, but failed to discover signs that crowds had been there; the vegetation was fresh, not flattened.[20]

After returning to Logroño, Salazar concluded that the Spanish Inquisition could not convict the witch suspects he had heard on visitation because of this gap between assertions and perceptions. No one could provide one of the two pillars of inquisitorial procedure, both of which had to arise from the human senses: a believable confession, or two eyewitnesses to the same events. The persons confessing very often could not explain how they arrived at the diabolical assemblies, or how they returned home. Salazar had gone so far as to examine 36 persons from nine covens, all of whom contradicted each other.[21] Witnesses outside the witches' sect were unique and rarely saw anything substantial: if they glimpsed in the distance a crowd, they inevitably exclaimed *Jesús!*, whereupon the assembly disappeared. Because the devil's nature was to prevaricate, Salazar thought it was much more likely that he was tricking people into thinking they were at his assemblies, or saw their neighbors there.[22] Thus the Father of Lies fulfilled the description of 1 Peter 5:8, where he was compared to a prowling lion, 'seeking whom he may devour.'[23]

## 3 Salazar's legal values

Earlier scholars believed that Salazar must have had a prescient skepticism about the reality of witchcraft, given his stand in March 1612, and his subsequent emendations to the rules about the Inquisition's prosecution of witches. I disagree. The surviving documentation does not contain any assertions by Salazar that the devil, demons, and witches did not exist. Instead, it illuminates three primordial values that were often entwined in his thinking and operations: fidelity to the law, as laid out in the inquisitorial system; obedience to higher authorities, and concern with the salvation of souls.

Salazar understood that his job was to find conclusive proof of heresy. Such proof had to rest on either a confession – called the 'queen of proofs' [*regina probationum*] in the inquisitors' world – or two eyewitnesses whose testimony matched. Salazar possessed only dubious confessions. He had no consistent eyewitnesses who were outside the witches' sect. What made matters even more confusing from the standpoint of proof was that numerous persons appeared before Salazar in 1611 to revoke the confessions to witchcraft that they had previously made. Revocations of confessions given under oath should have qualified as heresy, because the oath had been contravened. Nonetheless, theorists for the Inquisition occasionally maintained that a confessed heretic who wanted to alter testimony for a just reason could go on to make credible statements.[24] When Salazar was in the field, he learned of one 'just reason' that could make revocations acceptable: physical and emotional violence. Confessed witches appeared before him and his employees to relay that their confessions had been false, and only had been achieved through verbal threats and physical abuse, carried out by family members, neighbors, and local village justices.[25]

When Salazar finished his visitation and returned to Logroño, he made one unusual decision, namely, not to share his working papers – all 5,000 folios of them – with his fellow inquisitors while he was writing up results. Instead, he only gave them his 24 March 1612 summary once it was completed and destined for the *Suprema*, though they were allowed to sift through it for two months.[26] The other inquisitors were offended, and followed suit. From March 1612 through September 1613, they worked on their own summary of proof. They refused to show it to Salazar until it was finished, when they read it aloud to him.[27]

## 4 The tribunal's errors

Salazar quickly responded, with damning evidence. His October 1613 reply illuminates his values and what he believed the *Suprema* would find most telling. Obedience was at the top of the list, for Salazar first addressed the ways in which the tribunal had neglected to follow instructions from the *Suprema*. He reported that in March 1609, before he arrived, the *Suprema* had specifically asked the inquisitors in Logroño to search their archive and forward any precedents for coping with witchcraft cases. Salazar then revealed that in July 1609, his colleagues had only sent on materials that seemed to encourage witch-hunting, though they knew that the tribunal's records also contained much more cautious instructions. For example,

> on 14 December 1526, a letter from the *Suprema* about the sect of witches was written to the tribunal ... and it said that through the statement and confession of suspected witches, no one should be imprisoned, nor should others be condemned on the suspects' word, until investigations are carried out regarding these errors ... the inquisitors should perform, with all possible care, the proceedings and investigations that may be necessary regarding the suspects who have gone or continue to go to the devil's gatherings. The point is to ascertain whether they really go, as they confess, or if on those nights that they say they were with the devil, they remain in their houses, without leaving. This can be known from the other persons who live in those houses.[28]

In 1531, the *Suprema* told inquisitors in Logroño not to trust the depositions of alleged witches if their statements could not be verified by non-witches. In 1538, it warned that witch suspects could be mistaking dreams for reality.[29] The same letter admonished them not to trust the *Malleus maleficarum*, and counseled them to conduct thorough investigations into homicides purportedly caused by witchcraft. In 1555, the *Suprema* told the tribunal that no witch suspect was to be imprisoned without its permission. It reiterated that warning in 1595. Finally, in 1596 the *Suprema* had freed and imposed no penances on witch suspects who revoked their original confessions.[30]

According to Salazar, by ignoring these mandates and precedents, his associates revealed their unwillingness to be prudent where suspected witches were concerned. In early modern Europe, the accused always were presumed guilty in both the inquisitorial and secular legal jurisdictions, but the Inquisition's system also rested on its officials' discretion.[31] Immovable inquisitors were not exercising judgment.

Salazar attempted to cement his accusations by taking up next the ways in which his tribunal had violated procedure as it pursued accused witches. His colleagues failed to record contradictions.[32] They pressured defendants into saying exactly what they needed to corroborate other cases. They brought suspects face-to-face to achieve confessions.[33] They promised repeatedly to free anyone who confessed. They declined to record revocations of confessions made in their presence, and then ignored revocations and contradictions overheard and relayed by one of their prison wardens. They disregarded pleas to revoke made by individuals who were dying in their jails.

In a clear contravention of proper procedure, Logroño's inquisitors had persuaded defense attorneys not to offer defenses. (The defense attorneys were employees of the inquisition tribunal.) Sometimes, they told those attorneys that a defendant's attempt to stain [*tachar*] a prosecution witness was not likely to reveal capital enmity: if proven, capital enmity would have disqualified a witness and that witness's testimony. On other occasions, they said defense witnesses would not be capable of affirming a truth that already was established.[34]

One of the most inflammatory charges to come out of Salazar's October 1613 polemic was the accusation that the Logroño tribunal had been complicit in the torture of witch suspects between 1609 and 1612:

> And as for the notorious suspicion, which I've already mentioned, that the people [of northern Navarre] suffered such violent and wrongful humiliations from their own relatives and even secular justice, and from inquisitorial commissioners who should have prevented the mistreatment, it now turns out that we inquisitors agreed to it. Beyond the fact that we failed to stop it, I have learned through various means that we actually encouraged it. Note the letter that we wrote to the Viceroy of Navarre, on 17 May 1611, which praised such mistreatment [of accused witches] …[35]

Salazar was correct. His colleague Valle Alvarado did write to the Viceroy of Navarre on that date, to demand that investigations into possible harassment of alleged witches be stopped immediately. Valle's letter expressed shock that the royal court would even contemplate acting in defense of such accursed persons.[36]

As for the charge that inquisition employees – the commissioners – were encouraging violence against witch suspects, that too was true for certain locales. Commissioners were hired by inquisitors to take witness testimony; they typically were local clerics. Commissioners allowed the Spanish Inquisition to reach distant places, and they were especially valuable in Navarre because they were bilingual in Basque and Spanish.[37] While on visitation, Salazar discovered that the parish priest and commissioner in the village of Vera had encouraged children to name particular individuals as witches. Unsurprisingly, the named suspects then suffered the wrath of the children's parents.[38]

In 1613, Salazar stated that his colleagues were so full of hatred toward the witch sect that they were determined not to allow anyone to escape the label of witch once it was applied. They had not acted prudently, and had not used their discretion. Instead, Salazar charged that their actions were directed toward a single outcome, to find every witch suspect guilty. In 1613, Salazar contended that his associates' bias had governed the advice they had sent him two years earlier. In late May 1611, just as he had started on visitation, he had written to the tribunal to ask whether he could hear persons who wished to revoke their previous confessions and testimony. His colleagues had swiftly replied on 6 June:

306  *Lu Ann Homza*

> The matter of persons who have been reconciled by the Holy Office, and now wish to ask to revoke their confessions, is most serious. Those who have such nerve should be brought as prisoners to Logroño, where they will be heard according to law, in order to be punished as they deserve for wrongful revocations, and impenitence, and relapse, and for having deceived the Holy Office ...[39]

The upshot was that Salazar could not see such persons; that mandate only changed on 28 June 1611, when the *Suprema* told Logroño that all its inquisitors and their employees should hear revocants. From Salazar's perspective in 1613, his colleagues originally had constrained him in an imperious manner, and he hated the fact that he had obeyed them.[40]

## 5 Salazar's obedience

In all other respects, and throughout his career, Salazar was happy to follow instructions. For example, in March 1611, the *Suprema* sent a detailed letter to the Logroño tribunal about the impending visitation and potential interviews with witch suspects. The inquisitor who left was to publicize everywhere the edict of grace, which would allow him to absolve persons if they confessed. The *Suprema* clearly wanted absolution to be accessible; its members opined that persons who wished to confess should find the inquisitor on visitation, or come to the Logroño tribunal, or locate an inquisition commissioner. It stipulated that witchcraft confessions should be brief, and focused only on the essential, which was defined as 'the matter of going to the devil's assemblies, and how that is accomplished; and adoration of the devil, and apostasy, without getting into the matter of accomplices.'[41] The inquisitor in the field should investigate all the details about flying through windows, doors, and so on, 'to clarify the doubt in this matter as to whether persons go physically to the devil's gatherings, or not.' Male suspects under 14 and female ones under 12 should be absolved *ad cautelam*, or as a precaution. The tribunal as a whole, and its various employees, should publicly make plain that 'no one, not even a relative, shall threaten or punish anyone regarding a confession to witchcraft.'[42] For the time being, persons who said they had relapsed should not be reconciled to the Church, but they also should not be imprisoned; such cases should be referred to the *Suprema* for adjudication.

Salazar followed these directions to the letter.[43] When he had two cases of relapse, he awaited the Suprema's advice on how to handle them: in neither instance did the confessants know how they were being taken once more to the devil's assemblies, and they were going most unwillingly. Salazar pursued the question of whether people were attending the sabbat in fact or in dreams, but because he was receiving contrary evidence, and his trip was not over, he told the *Suprema* from the field that he could not yet answer that inquiry.

Salazar, then, took his profession, and its hierarchies, seriously. He was not a professional or intellectual rebel; in fact, he spent years explaining and defending his actions where the witch suspects were concerned. He was not insubordinate toward the law, either: in fact, he belonged to a long tradition of legal diligence where witch suspects were concerned. In the field in 1611, he did not hesitate to chase, chastise, and issue penances for fornicators, popular healers, priests who made sexual advances toward female penitents, and so-called *moriscos* and *conversos*, who had lapsed from Christianity into Islam and Judaism, respectively.[44] He worried actively about English ships and their Protestant sailors, and lamented that he had been unable to locate the suspicious Portuguese whose names he carried on a list.[45] As for the question of confession versus revocation, Salazar did not throw out one or the other, but simply muted the legal weight of confessions when it could be proven that violence had produced them.

## 6 Salazar and the care of souls

We might well ask why Salazar believed the people who appeared before him and told him they had been tortured into confessing to witchcraft. It is true that as the secular and episcopal jurisdictions were looking into accusations that suspects had been mistreated by their neighbors, those authorities apprised Salazar of their findings.[46] But Salazar also knew that the theoretical justification for the Spanish Inquisition was to reconcile to the Catholic Church those persons who were found guilty of heresy. The formulas and vocabulary of inquisition practice was full of this concern with souls, which is why the phrase 'holding God before our eyes' preceded verdicts in trials, and why punishments were called 'penances.'

Salazar understood the pastoral aspect of the Inquisition's mission, and he was deeply affected by what he heard and saw on visitation.[47] In his report from March 1612, he declared that the *revocantes* 'by revoking, demonstrated much more peace and conviction in their souls than those persons who confessed to witchcraft and were reconciled.'[48] He described for the *Suprema* what had happened in the field when one particular witch, aged 80, sobbed and expressed her tremendous sorrow that she was being taken against her will to the devil's meetings. The Basque translators who attended the interview had started a long argument with the woman, and in the process, they and Salazar had become convinced that she had only dreamed it.[49] Salazar relayed as well a story he had heard from a 36-year old woman, whose mother had drowned herself in a river after confessing to witchcraft and naming accomplices in the Logroño tribunal. Before her suicide, the mother told her daughter that 'her soul was taxed by those whom she had unjustly denounced;' when the daughter then tried to find a solution from an inquisition commissioner, he had threatened to prosecute her mother as a perjurer.[50]

Salazar cared enough about the care of souls to continue to write about the topic. In his 1613 polemic, he lamented the appearance of Don Martín de Alcoz, parish priest of Iraycoz, who came to the tribunal on 9 June 1612 to tell the inquisitors about the spiritual upheaval that was occurring in his own village and in Pamplona. There, persons who had confessed to witchcraft were suffering tremendously, searching in vain for a spiritual remedy for their lies about themselves and others. They wandered astray, consulting confessors and other religious, who failed to steer them toward what they should do. Because Alcoz had not written down a statement, Salazar did so, and had Alcoz sign it; Salazar then insisted upon reading it to his colleagues.[51]

Salazar lamented the turmoil of souls [*confusión de las almas*] that ensued from false accusations and confessions to witchcraft. What compounded the situation was that persons who had confessed to that heresy or had been publicly accused of the same, had been prevented for years from receiving the ecclesiastical sacraments of Penance and the Eucharist, as well as Extreme Unction, putting their souls still further at risk. The *Suprema* had insisted since 1609 that such individuals had to be absolved by an inquisitor rather than local religious clergy. Once he had witnessed first-hand the spiritual agony of Navarrese villagers who were kept from the sacraments, Salazar condemned the practice as another form of violence. He was grateful he was carrying an edict of grace that would enable reconciliation.[52] Still, what would happen to those villagers when he returned to the tribunal? He knew how difficult and expensive it could be to reach Logroño. His commissioners already had told him and his colleagues how reluctant villagers were to incur the stigma of traveling there. In January 1611, one commissioner wrote:

> I know that Your Lordships would use your customary mercy with witches who want to confess, and would reconcile them in secret if they made a spontaneous confession. But the shame of going in person to the Inquisition tribunal is the greatest obstacle the devil employs to keep them from leaving him and returning to God. And here such travel would be publicly known, as would be its purpose. I beg Your Lordships to think about this matter. Perhaps you could allow them to make their spontaneous confessions to me. If such were the case, I am certain that many would come to make spontaneous and very complete confessions, and with this, many souls would be saved.[53]

The Spanish Inquisition never gave the lower employees of the Logroño tribunal the power to reconcile witch suspects. Those suspects had to appear before an inquisitor; they did not know if the Inquisition would welcome them; they especially feared what would happen to them if they appeared before inquisitors to revoke an earlier confession. As late as 1614, Salazar continued to worry that there were accused witches in northern Navarre whose salvation was threatened because they desperately needed to be reconciled to the Church, but no one was offering them a spiritual remedy there.

Salazar's legal diligence, respect for authority, and pastoral values eventually turned him into a wary witch-hunter. His priorities have gone unrecognized by scholars eager to turn him into a modern skeptic. Still, his thoughts, actions, and reputation as a witches' advocate become that much more intelligible and fascinating when we allow him to be an inhabitant of the early seventeenth century, bound by the structural, procedural, and even pastoral norms of the Spanish Inquisition.[54]

## Notes

1 Archivo Histórico Nacional [AHN], Madrid, Sección de la Inquisición [Inqu.], Legajo [Leg.] 2220, n. 21, contains a *Relación de los inquisidores y oficiales que ay en esta Inquisición del Reyno de Navarra que reside en esta ciudad de Logroño*, dated June 1622, in which Salazar described his career. Also see Gustav Henningsen, ed., *The Salazar Documents: Inquisitor Alonso de Salazar Frías and Others on the Basque Witch Persecution*, Leiden: Brill, 2004, pp. 21–23. Sandoval y Rojas was the uncle of the Duke of Lerma, who was the court favorite of King Philip III. Sandoval y Rojas also had served as the Bishop of Pamplona from 1588–1596; Pamplona was the capital of Navarre, which was the territory which Sandoval y Rojas assigned Salazar to oversee as an inquisitor.
2 This Spanish witch-hunt coincided with De Lancre°'s prosecutions in France, which was pushing numerous French suspects across the Spanish border. AHN Inqu., Libro 794, fols 457r–458r, 459r–462r, for comments on French witches in Navarre in 1609.
3 At the *auto*, eleven witches were sentenced to death, and eighteen received penances. A number of the convicted were burned or penanced in effigy because they had died in prison. A priest and a friar, who were first cousins, were sentenced to exile in a private ceremony. See the chart in Gustav Henningsen, *The Witches' Advocate: Basque Witchcraft and the Spanish Inquisition (1609–1614)*, Reno, NV: University of Nevada Press, 1980, pp. 199–200.
4 The new instructions are reprinted in Miguel Jiménez Montserín, *Introducción a la inquisición española: Documentos básicos para el studio del Santo Oficio*, Madrid: Editora Nacional, 1980.
5 The leading scholar on Inquisitor Salazar is ethnographer and folklorist Gustav Henningsen. See his *Witches' Advocate* and *The Salazar Documents*. Before Henningsen, Julio Caro Baroja produced important work on Salazar, especially *De nuevo sobre la história de brujería*, Pamplona: Diputación Foral de Navarra, 1969.
6 Salazar was on the job much longer: whereas De Lancre returned to Bordeaux by the end of 1609, Salazar pursued witchcraft in Navarre through 1614, and then handled witchcraft accusations in Vizcaya, a Basque province, between 1616–1623. Salazar's actions in Vizcaya have never been studied, though some thirteen documents about his work there are contained in AHN Inqu., Leg. 1679, exp. 2.
7 See the pamphlet based on the 1610 *auto de fe* and printed immediately afterwards: Manual Fernández Nieto, *Proceso a la brujería: en torno al auto de fe de los brujos de Zugarramurdi, Logroño, 1610*, Madrid: Editorial Tecnos, 1989.
8 Florencio Idoate, *La brujería en Navarra y sus documentos*, Pamplona: Institución Principe de Viana, 1978, p. 63, asserted that early modern witch-hunting in Navarre almost inevitably began with statements from children. Also see Lu Ann Homza, 'When Witches Litigate: New Sources from Early Modern Navarre', *The Journal of Modern History*, 2019, vol. 91/2, 245–75.
9 AHN Inqu., Leg. 1679, exp. 2 (21), fol. 7r.
10 A number of adults whom Salazar and De Lancre interviewed insisted that they and their cohort had attempted to work harmful magic against both men.

11 There consequently was a substantial degree of mediation between testimony as it was uttered and recorded. For the prevalence of Basque in early modern Navarre, Peio Monteano Sorbet, *El iceberg Navarro: Euskera y castellano en la Navarra del siglo XVI*, Pamplona: Pamielo, 2017, pp. 47–50, 60–69, 193–203.
12 For example, in August 1609, Inquisitor Valle Alvarado, who was on visitation, commented on the 'very uncomfortable terrain' he encountered on the border with France; there were mountains everywhere. AHN Inqu., Libro 794, fol. 459r. In February 1610, the inquisitors referred to 'that poverty-stricken land' they were supervising: AHN Inqu., Libro 795, f. 84. In August 1610, the *Suprema* described Navarre as 'full of poor people and poor land': AHN Inqu., Libro 333, fol. 87r.
13 The extent to which Salazar changed over time is controversial. Henningsen and Caro Baroja believed he was fundamentally skeptical, always. Yet the evidence suggests that Salazar participated fully in the Logroño tribunal's witch-hunting until he was in the field in June 1611, and was given permission to hear the revocations of witchcraft confessions; he then began to doubt whether he had proof of heresy. Years later, Salazar read his doubts of 1611–1613 backwards into his opinions of 1609–1610.
14 Martín de Castañega, *Tratado de las supersticiones y hechicerías* (1529), ed. Juan Robert Muro Abad, Logroño: Instituto de Estudios Riojanos, 1994; Pedro Ciruelo, *Reprobación de las supersticiones y hechicerías* (1530), ed. Alva V. Ebersole, Valencia: Albatros hispanofila, 1978. Homza, *Religious Authority in the Spanish Renaissance*, Baltimore: The Johns Hopkins University Press, 2000, chap. 6.
15 The canon *Episcopi* originally was attributed to the Council of Ancyra in 314 CE. Its supposed antiquity explains why medieval and early modern authors treated it with such authority. The canon reported that certain women believed they could fly with the goddess Diana but were only deluded by the devil. The canon was included in Gratian's twelfth-century, canon law collection, called the *Decretum*.
16 AHN Inqu., Leg. 1679, exp. 2 (21), fols 2v–3r for these details.
17 AHN Inqu., Leg. 1679, exp. 2 (21), fol. 10r–v. Salazar's associates insisted in 1611 that the ointments and powders they were collecting in the tribunal were authentic: AHN Inqu., Libro 795, fols 152v–53r, 159r.
18 AHN Inqu., Leg. 1679, exp. 2 (21), fol. 4r–v.
19 AHN Inqu., Leg. 1679, exp. 2 (21), fol. 4r–v.
20 AHN Inqu., Leg. 1679, exp. 2 (21), fol. 8v.
21 AHN Inqu., Leg. 1679, exp. 2 (21), fols 9v–10r, 10v–11r.
22 AHN Inqu., Leg. 1679, exp. 2 (21), fols 11v, 14r.
23 For the social and emotional devastation that came with this witch-hunt, see Homza, 'When Witches Litigate.'
24 Diego de Simancas, *Enchiridion iudicum violatae religionis*, Venice: Officinia Iordani Ziletti, 1573, tit. 31, 'De retractione testium', fols 51v–52r.
25 From 1609–1612, families throughout northern Navarre pressured their relatives to confess to witchcraft if they were publicly accused; they believed quick confessions would save the accused from having to appear before the Inquisition. At the same time, village constables and even parish priests were imprisoning and torturing the accused in order to force confessions. Some of those suspected witches later sued their torturers, successfully, in secular court. See Archivo Real y General de Navarra [AGN] 100,796 (Elgorriaga 1612), and AGN 072902 (Arráyoz 1613), as well as Homza, 'When Witches Litigate.'
26 AHN Inqu., Leg. 1679, exp. 2 (29), fol. 10r–v.
27 Their written response to Salazar's 1612 report is not extant, but the appendix is: see Florencio Idoate, *Un documento de la inquisición sobre brujería en Navarra*, Pamplona: Ediorial Aranzadi, 1972.
28 AHN Inqu., Leg. 1679, exp. 2 (29), fol. 1r.

29  AHN Inqu., Leg. 1679, exp 2 (29), fol. 2r.
30  AHN Inqu., Leg. 1679, exp 2 (29), fols 2r, 3r.
31  Kimberly Lynn, *Between Court and Confessional: The Politics of Spanish Inquisitors*, Cambridge: Cambridge University Press, 2015.
32  AHN Inqu., Leg. 1679, exp. 2 (29), fol. 3r.
33  In fact, the tribunal asked the *Suprema* in July 1610 for permission to put in the same room those who had confessed, and those who remained *negativo*: AHN Inqu., Libro 795, f. 41r–v.
34  AHN Inqu., Leg. 1679, exp. 2 (29), fol. 4v.
35  AHN Inqu., Leg. 1679, exp. 2 (29), fol. 4v.
36  For references to the correspondence between the tribunal and the royal court, which had no effect in 1611, AHN Inqu., Libro 795, fol. 157r–v. In 1609, the tribunal stopped the secular jurisdiction from pursuing defamation cases over the label of 'witch': AHN Inqu., Libro 794, fol. 448r–v. It seems clear from the evidence that individual inquisitors could post letters to other authorities without the knowledge of their associates.
37  For the importance of the commissioners' role, Sara T. Nalle, 'Inquisitors, Priests, and the People during the Catholic Reformation', *Sixteenth Century Journal*, 1987, vol. 18, 557–87.
38  AHN Inqu., Leg. 1679, exp. 2 (29), fol. 4r.
39  AHN Inqu., Leg. 1679, exp. 2 (29), fol. 4r.
40  AHN Inqu., Leg. 1679, exp. 2 (29), fols 3v–4r. Salazar was already questioning his obedience to his associates in September 1611. In a letter to the *Suprema* from Fuenterrabia, he commented on the violence that had occurred with villagers' interrogations of witch suspects. He suspected that the number of revocants would be high, not least because he had been told to repulse this category of penitent when he first left on visitation: AHN Inqu., Leg. 1679, exp. 2 (31), fols 2v–3r.
41  AHN Inqu., Libro 333, fol. 145r.
42  AHN Inqu., Libro 333, fols 145v–46r.
43  Another sign of Salazar's diligence is that he also investigated whether it would be feasible to build two new monasteries near the locations of the witch epidemic; the *Suprema* had asked him to check. AHN Inqu., Libro 333, fol. 147r. After consulting with locals, Salazar reported that it would be perilous to put new monasteries near the French border, 'because there would not be enough income, for it was hard to stay solvent, given the poverty of the land, and the continuous invasions of the French, who harass the friars': AHN Inqu., Libro 795, fol. 358r.
44  Moriscos were Christians who descended from Muslims; conversos were Christians who descended from Jews.
45  See his initial comments in his 24 March 1612 report, AHN Inqu., Libro 795, fols 354r–60v. It is important to note that Salazar divided that March 1612 summary into two parts. One, which covered his general activities on visitation, is contained in AHN Inqu., Libro 795, fols 357r–68r. Another is devoted purely to questions about witchcraft posed by the *Suprema*, in AHN Inqu., Leg. 1679, exp. 2 (21).
46  For the interactions of Salazar with the episcopal and secular legal jurisdictions, see Homza, 'When Witches Litigate.'
47  Elsewhere, I have contended that Salazar came to his new awareness about proof because he was willing to believe what was relayed to him in the field, rather than holding onto experiences that had occurred in the past: Homza, 'Local Knowledge and Catholic Reform in Early Modern Spain', in Thomas Mayer, ed., *Reforming Reformation*, New York: Ashgate, 2012, pp. 81–102.
48  AHN Inqu., Leg. 1679, exp. 2 (21), fol. 13r.

49 AHN Inqu., Leg. 1679, exp. 2 (21), fol. 6v. In all his extant writings from the 1609–1614 witch-hunt, Salazar portrayed his Basque translators as his colleagues.
50 AHN Inqu., Leg. 1679, exp. 2 (21), fol. 13v.
51 AHN Inqu., Leg. 1679, exp. 2 (29), fol. 3v.
52 AHN Inqu., Leg. 1679, exp. 2 (21), fol. 12v.
53 This quote is from correspondence by Leon de Aranibar, who wrote to the tribunal on 29 January 1611: AHN Inqu., Leg. 1679, exp. 2 (11), fols 2v–3r.
54 Significantly, Salazar's priorities also have never been examined vis-à-vis the Council of Trent and its spiritual objectives.

## Further reading

Caro Baroja, Julio, *De nuevo sobre la história de brujería*, Pamplona: Diputación Foral de Navarra, 1969.

Henningsen, Gustav, *The Witches' Advocate: Basque Witchcraft and the Spanish Inquisition (1609–1614)*, Reno: University of Nevada Press, 1980.

———, ed., *The Salazar Documents: Inquisitor Alonso de Salazar Frías and Others on the Basque Witch Persecution*, Leiden: Brill, 2004.

Homza, Lu Ann, 'When Witches Litigate: New Sources from Early Modern Navarre', *The Journal of Modern History*, 2019, vol. 91/2, 245–275.

———, 'Local Knowledge and Catholic Reform in Early Modern Spain', in Thomas Mayer, ed., *Reforming Reformation*, New York: Routledge, 2016 [first published 2012], pp. 81–102.

Idoate, Florencio, *La brujería en Navarra y sus documentos*, Pamplona: Institución Principe de Viana, 1978.

Lynn, Kimberly, *Between Court and Confessional: The Politics of Spanish Inquisitors*, Cambridge: Cambridge University Press, 2015.

# Critical editions and English translations of demonological texts

[Anonymous], *Forbidden Rites: A Necromancer's Manual of the Fifteenth Century*, ed. and trans. Richard Kieckhefer, University Park, PA: Pennsylvania State University Press, 1998.

[Anonymous], 'Errores Gazariorum, seu illorum qui scopam vel baculum equitare probantur, *c*.1437', critical ed. and French trans. Martine Ostorero, in Martine Ostorero et al., eds, *L'Imaginaire du sabbat: Édition critique des textes les plus anciens, 1430c.–1440c.*, Lausanne: Université de Lausanne, 1999, pp. 277–299.

[Anonymous], 'La Vauderye de Lyonois en brief, *c*.1439–1441', critical ed. and French trans. in Martine Ostorero and Franck Mercier, eds, *L'Énigme de la Vauderie de Lyon: Enquête sur l'essor des chasses aux sorcières entre France et Empire, 1430–1480*, Florence: SISMEL-Edizioni del Galuzzo, 2015, pp. 60–93.

Anonymous of Arras, 'A History of the Case, State, and Condition of the Waldensian Heretics (Witches) (1460)', in Andrew Colin Gow et al., eds. and trans., *The Arras Witch Treatises*, University Park, PA: Pennsylvania State University Press, 2016, pp. 19–80.

Bodin, Jean, *On the Demon-Mania of Witches*, ed. Jonathan L. Pearl, trans. Randy A. Scott, Toronto: Centre for Reformation and Renaissance Studies, 1995.

———, *De La Démonomanie des sorciers*, critical ed. Virginia Krause et al., Geneva: Droz, 2016.

Boguet, Henry, *An Examen of Witches Drawn from Various Trials of Many of This Sect in the District of Saint Oyan de Joux, Commonly Known as Saint Claude, in the County of Burgundy, including the Procedure Necessary to a Judge in Trials for Witchcraft*, ed., Montague Summers, trans. E. Allen Ashwin, London: J. Rodker, 1929 [many reprint editions].

De Lancre, Pierre, *Tableau de l'inconstance des mauvais anges et démons où il est amplement traité des sorciers et de la sorcellerie*, ed. Nicole Jacques-Chaquin, Paris: Aubier, 1982.

———, *On the Inconstancy of Witches: Pierre de Lancre's 'Tableau de l'inconstance des mauvais anges et démons', 1612*, ed. and trans. Gerhild Scholz-Williams et al., Tempe, AZ: Arizona Center for Medieval and Renaissance Studies, 2006.

[Delrio, Martin] Del Rio, Martín, *Investigations into Magic*, trans. P. G. Maxwell-Stuart, Manchester: Manchester University Press, 2000.

Guazzo, Francesco Maria, *Compendium Maleficarum, Collected in Three Books from Many Sources … Showing the Iniquitous and Execrable Operations of Witches against the Human Race, and the Divine Remedies by Which They May Be Frustrated*, ed. Montague Summers, trans. E. Allen Ashwin, London: J. Rodker, 1929 [many reprint editions].

Hartlieb, Johannes, 'The Book of All Forbidden Arts', in Richard Kieckhefer, ed. and trans., *Hazards of the Dark Arts: Advice for Medieval Princes on Witchcraft and Magic*, University Park, PA: Pennsylvania State University Press, 2017, pp. 21–92.

## 314  Critical editions and English translations

Institoris, Henricus [and Sprenger, Jacobus?], *Malleus maleficarum*, critical ed. and trans. Christopher S. Mackay, 2 vols, Cambridge: Cambridge University Press, 2006.

———, *The Malleus Maleficarum*, trans. P. G. Maxwell-Stuart, Manchester: Manchester University Press, 2007.

———, *The Hammer of Witches: A Complete Translation of the Malleus Maleficarum*, trans. Christopher S. Mackay, Cambridge: Cambridge University Press, 2009.

James VI, 'Daemonologie' in James Craigie and Alexander Law, eds, *Minor prose works of King James VI and I: Daemonologie, The True Lawe of Free Monarchies, A Counterblaste to Tobacco, A Declaration of Sports*, Edinburgh: Scottish Text Society, 1982, pp. 1–58. (text), 147–92 (notes).

———, 'Text of Demonology', in Lawrence Normand and Gareth Roberts, eds, *Witchcraft in Early Modern Scotland: James VI's 'Demonology' and the North Berwick Witches*, Exeter: University of Exeter Press, 2000, pp. 353–426.

Lavater, Ludwig, *Of Ghostes and Spirites Walking by Nyght*, ed. J. Dover Wilson and May Yardley. Oxford: Printed for the Shakespeare Association at the University Press, 1929.

Menghi, Girolamo, *The Devil's Scourge: Exorcism during the Italian Renaissance*, trans. Gaetano Paxia, Boston: S. Weiser, 2002.

Molitor, Ulrich, 'On Witches and Pythonesses, in German "Unholden" or "Hexen"' in Richard Kieckhefer, ed. and trans. *Hazards of the Dark Arts*, University Park, PA: Pennsylvania State University Press, 2017, pp. 93–153.

Nider, Johannes, *Formicarius*, [Book II, chap. 4 and Book V, chaps 3, 4 and 7, *c*.1436–38], critical ed. and French trans. Catherine Chène, in Martine Ostorero et al. eds, *L'Imaginaire du sabbat*, 122–199.

Pico Della Mirandola, Gianfrancesco, *La Sorcière: Dialogue en trois livres sur la tromperie des démons*, critical ed. and trans. Alfredo Perifano, Turnhout: Brepols, 2007.

Poeton, Edward, *The Winnowing of White Witchcraft*, ed. Simon F. Davies, Tempe, AZ: Arizona Center for Medieval and Renaissance Studies, 2018.

Remy, Nicolas, *Demonolatry*, ed. Montague Summers, trans. E. Allen Ashwin, London: John Rodker, 1930 [many reprint editions].

Salazar Frías, Alonso de, *The Salazar Documents: Inquisitor Alonso de Salazar Frías and Others on the Basque Witch Persecution*, ed. and trans. Gustav Henningsen et al., Leiden: Brill. 2004.

Scot, Reginald, *The Discoverie of Witchcraft*, ed. Montague Summers, London: John Rodker. 1930. [many reprint editions].

———, *La Sorcellerie démystifiée*, critical ed. and trans. Pierre Kapitaniak and Jean Migrenne, Grenoble: Jérôme Millon, 2015.

———, *The Discoverie of Witchcraft*, ed. Brinsley Nicholson. London: Elliot Stock, 1886. [Reprint, Charleston, SC: Bibliolife, LLC, on demand through Amazon. This ed. is complete: Summers's edition has excisions.].

Spee, Friedrich, *Cautio criminalis, or A Book on Witch Trials*, trans. Marcus Hellyer, Charlottesville: University of Virginia Press, 2003.

Stapleton, Thomas, 'Why Has Magic Grown Today Together with Heresy? An Oration Given before the Academic Assembly of Leuven', trans. Jan Machielsen, in 'On the Confessional Uses and History of Witchcraft: Thomas Stapleton's 1594 Witchcraft Oration', *Magic, Ritual, and Witchcraft*, 2018, vol. 13/3, 381–407, at 389–407.

T.P., *Cas Gan Gythraul: Demonology, Witchcraft and Popular Magic in Eighteenth-Century Wales*, ed. and trans. Lisa Tallis, Newport: South Wales Record Society, 2015.

Tholosan, Claude, 'Ut magorum et maleficiorum errores', critical ed. Pierrette Paravy, French trans. Martine Ostorero, in Martine Ostorero et al. ed., *L'Imaginaire du sabbat*, pp. 362–415.

Tinctor, Johannes, 'Invectives against the Sect of Waldensians (Witches) (1460)', in Andrew Colin Gow et al. ed. and trans. *The Arras Witch Treatises*, University Park, PA: Pennsylvania State University Press, 2016, pp. 81–144.

[Wier, Johann] Weyer, Johann, *Witches, Devils, and Doctors in the Renaissance: Johann Weyer, De praestigiis daemonum*, ed. George Mora and Benjamin G. Kohl, trans. John Shea, Binghamton, NY: Medieval & Renaissance Texts & Studies, 1991.

———, *On Witchcraft: An Abridged Translation of Johann Weyer's De praestigiis daemonum*, ed. Benjamin G. Kohl and H. C. Erik Midelfort, trans. John Shea, Asheville: Pegasus Press, 1998.

# Index

Note: The main entries for authors and works discussed in the chapters of this volume have been highlighted in bold.

Abadie, Jeannette d' 292
Acquaviva, Claudio 212
Adeline, Guillaume 39
Ady, Thomas 177, 238–39, 240
Africa 2
Agrippa von Nettesheim, Heinrich Cornelius 104–6, 120, 123, 252; love of pet dog 105
Alberti, Leandro 88, 95
Alciato, Andrea 72, 114, 125, 206
Alembert, Jean le Rond d' 20
Alexander IV, Pope 25
Alexander VI, Pope 60
Alix, Thierry 270, 271
Alsace 57
Ambrose of Milan 231
Ambrosian friars 270
Angers 205
Anglo, Sydney xvi–xvii, 8, 53, 145
Anne of Denmark, Queen of Scotland 1, 165, 167
Antwerp 156, 180–83
apocalypticism 6, 36, 38, 55, 92, 139, 174, 183, 213, 218, 229, 242, 248
Aquinas, Thomas 26, 42, 54, 55, 58, 73, 92–94, 123, 128–29, 144, 185, 214–16, 228–29, 230; *see also* Aristotle, Aristotelianism; Scholasticism
Aragon 19, 21, 25
Aristotle, Aristotelianism 86–87, 94, 105, 143, 225; *see also* Aquinas, Thomas; Scholasticism
Armellini, Girolamo 88, 89, 91–92
Arnhem 106
Arras 37–38, 45

astrology 20, 28, 104, 122, 169–70, 247
Avignon 20, 21, 30
Augustine 26, 110, 230
Augsburg 57, 60, 202

Barcelona 19, 20
Baronio, Cesare 187
Basel 37, 108, 115; Council of 35, 36–7, 86
Basque Country 5, 283, 287, 288, 291, 293, 301, 305, 307; *see also* Navarre; Pays de Labourd
Bassaeus, Nicolaus 39, 203
Bavaria 161, 190
Bayle, Pierre 213
Becerra, Alonso de 299, 300, 303
Bekker, Balthasar 112
Benzi, Sozzino 75
Berengar of Tours 60
Bern 199
Bernard of Clairvaux 93
Bernardino of Siena 41
Berni, Benedetto 89–92
Bible 5, 94, 189, 212, 272; Old Testament 2, 4, 29, 44, 92–93, 111, 124, 127–28, 136, 143, 169, 199–200, 203, 206, 248, 258, 260; New Testament 2–3, 8, 70–71, 72, 85, 129, 228, 248, 257, 260, 261, 301, 302, 303
blasphemy 19, 24, 27, 29–30, 42, 56, 121, 152, 157, 159, 256, 260, 262, 289
**Binsfeld, Peter** 6, 149–54, 179; *Commentarius in titulum codicis lib. 9 de maleficis & mathematicis* 152, 159, 161; early life and education 151–52;

*Enchiridion theologiae pastoralis et doctrinae neccessariae sacerdotibus* 152; *Liber receptarum in theologia sententiarum et conclusionum* 152, 153–54; *Tractatus de confessionibus maleficorum et sagarum* 152, 153, 155–57, 159, 161; *Tractatus de tentationibus et remediis* 152; victory over Cornelius Loos 158–60
Blancone, Jean 214
Bodeghemius, Bartholomeus 155, 159
Boccacio, Giovanni 206
**Bodin, Jean** 8, 90, 111–12, 115, **119–32**, 156–57, 168, 207, 217, 243; advocating *lectio difficilior* 124–26; attacked by Reginald Scot 135, 139–40, 143; comparison with Nicolas Remy 269, 272–77, 279; *De La Démonomanie des sorciers* 2, 5, 40, 119–30; definition of witchcraft 120–21; guardian angel of 11, 104, 127–28, 130; refutation of Wier 112, 114, 119, 124; *The Six Books of the Republic* 119; use of the Old Testament 124
Boguet, Henri 6, 12, 180, 292
Bohemia 36, 60
Boaistuau, Pierre 218
Bologna 69, 73, 76, 224–27, 230, 231
Bordeaux 6, 283, 285–86, 290, 291, 295
Borromeo, Carlo 226
Bothwell, Earl of *see* Stewart, Francis, Fifth Earl of Bothwell
Bourges 212
Bourgeois, Claude 280
Bridget of Sweden 186
Brocadelli, Lucia 61–62
Bruno, Giordano 224
Brussels 39, 150, 155, 159
Brzeżański, Stanisław 257
Bucholtz, Arnold of 154
Bullinger, Heinrich 198, 204
Burgundy 35–39, 45, 269
Byron, George Gordon (Lord) 10

Calvin, John, Calvinism 9, 127, 139, 176–77, 183, 185, 198, 201, 205–6, 213, 217–18, 238–39, 242–43; *see also* Perkins, William
Cambridge 238, 246
Camerarius, Joachim 200
Canon *Episcopi* 8, 40, 41–42, 56, 69, 70–71, 72, 74, 76–77, 85–86, 94, 141, 275
Capys, Eliseo 227

Cardano, Girolamo 104, 272
Carmelite Order 39, 127–28
Casaubon, Meric 185, 190
Cassini, Samuele 69, 71, 77
Castelló d'Empúries 24, 27–28, 30
Catalonia 19, 21, 27, 30
Catherine of Siena 38, 62, 186
Charles V, Holy Roman Emperor 107, 181
Charles IX, King of France 212
Chrysostom, John 203
Ciboure 283
Cicero 83, 84, 185
Clark, Stuart xvi–xvii, xviii, 9, 241, 280
Claro, Giulio 254
Cleves, Duchy of 103, 107–8, 113, 201
Colette of Corbie 38
Cologne 55, 57, 154–55, 180, 234, 269
Colomba of Rieti 61–62
Constance, Council of 36
Counter-Reformation *see* Binsfeld, Petrus; *Czarownica powołana*; Delrio, Martin; Jesuits; Maldonado, Juan; Menghi, Girolamo; Trent, Council of
Crespin, Jean 204
***Czarownica powołana* 252–66**; antisemitism of 255; Catholicity of 253, 254–58, 260–63; possible authorship of 253–56; misogyny of 256–58
Czartoryski, Florian 252, 263

Da Castello, Alberto 230, 233
Daneau, Lambert 40, 139, 140, 176, 203, 243
Della Porta, Giambattista 141–42, 272
**Delrio, Martin** 11, 76, 114, 122, 129, 154, 161, **179–94**, 254–55, 260, 270, 280; *Disquisitiones magicae* 156, 159, 179, 261; *Disquisitiones* as a work of Catholic scholarship 183–87; editor of classical texts 181–82, 188–89; early life 180–82; glee at Cornelius Loos's fate 155, 156, 159; self-fashioning of 180, 182, 187; threatened by a mandrake root 179–80; use of Juan Maldonado 183, 211, 217, 261
Delvaux, Jean 188
demon, demons *see* devil, devils
Denmark 1, 165, 167
*Denounced Witch, see Czarownica powołana*
Descartes, René 10, 114
demonology: as entertainment 11, 273, 289; an interdisciplinary science 10,

187–88; source base 5–6, 11, 75, 85, 112, 121–23, 135, 144, 156, 180, 187–90, 200–202, 214–15, 271–72; a spectrum of beliefs 9
Diana see canon Episcopi: pagan gods
devil, devils: corporeality of 40, 42–43, 69, 75, 93–96, 140–41, 144–46, 156, 158, 160, 215–16, 228–29, 241, 243; mark by 137, 140, 171, 174, 175, 291–93; pact with 4, 5, 6, 42, 43, 55, 56, 61, 77, 105, 110–11, 122, 139–40, 156, 159, 186, 218, 239, 243, 246, 248, 260, 272, 278, 301; demonic possession 3–4, 107, 129, 138, 150, 157, 173, 225–28, 230, 232, 234, 246, 252, *see also* exorcism; as familiar 105; as God's ape 6–7, 39, 70, 171, 301; as God's hangman 7–8, 38; powers of deception of 8–9, 36, 39, 41, 71, 72, 75, 85–86, 88, 107, 109–11, 113, 156, 173, 186, 203–4, 215–16, 259, 279, 301–3; reality of 36, 37, 40, 41, 42–43, 58, 69, 74, 93–96, 151, 160, 173, 189, 214, 277; sex with 4, 5, 6, 35, 42, 43, 58, 90–94, 122, 125, 144, 156, 239, 242, 272, 275–76, 292, 300, *see also* sabbat; temptations of 72, 76, 92, 94, 145, 152, 160, 189, 240; worship of 3–4, 25, 26, 30, 35, 36, 37, 40–41, 43, 44, 56, 70, 72, 77, 85, 86, 87, 92, 121, 139, 171, 173, 189, 217, 229, 247, 257, 274, 300, 306; *see also* demonology; witchcraft; witches
Dijon 36, 37
Dindarte, Marie 6, 290, 292
discernment of spirits, *discretio spirituum* 59, 128–30, 146–47, 186, 200, 202
divination 2, 20–21, 25–27, 29, 135–36, 170, 172, 179, 185–86, 189
Dodo, Vincenzo 69
Dominican Order (O.P.) 4, 5, 19, 20, 25, 35, 36, 37, 38, 54, 59, 68, 72, 73, 88, 139, 227, 229, 230, 233
Douai 183
Du Bois, Jacques 45
Duns Scotus 229, 230
Dworkin, Andrea 58

Elizabeth I, Queen of England 240, 247
Erasmus, Desiderius 105, 107–8, 112, 229
Erastus, Thomas 40, 113–14, 263
Ermengol, Bernat 20

*Errores gazariorum* 36, 37
Espaignet, Jean d' 283–85, 291
Este, Ippolito d' 62
Eucharist 27, 44, 56, 60, 62, 88–90, 93, 143, 153, 255, 308
Ewich, Johann 203
exorcism 4, 12, 39, 93, 107, 111, 129, 150, 224–34, 247, 256, 258, 270; lampooned by sceptics 229; *see also* devil, devils: demonic possession; Menghi, Girolamo
**Eymeric, Nicolau** 4, **19–34**; duplicity and bad faith of 21–22, 31; *Contra astrologos imperitos atque nigromanticos* 20, 28; *De iurisdictione Ecclesi[a]e et inquisitorum contra infideles demones invocantes* 20; *De iurisdictione inquisitorum in et contra christianos demones invocantes* 20, 25–26, 28; *Dialogus contra lullistas* 21; *Directorium inquisitorum* 20, 26, 28, 31; epitaph of 30; funeral sermons by 23–24; interrogation techniques of 22–23; inquisitorial activity of 27–30; read by Institoris 54, 57; vision of ideal inquisitor 23–24; youth 21

Fairies 4, 5, 9, 65–66, 173
Family of Love 108
Farinacci, Prospero 254, 260
Farinerio, Bonaventura 233
Fernel, Jean 106
Ferrara 61–62, 74–76, 83, 95
Fian, John 172, 175
Ficino, Marsilio 84–86; *see also* Plato, (neo-)Platonism
Filmer, Robert Sir 177, 244, 247
Flade, Dietrich 150, 156–58, 161
France 6, 35, 37, 44, 45, 140, 179, 204, 211, 213, 217–18, 225–26, 231, 234, 261, 270, 272–73, 283, 285–86, 289; *see also* Wars of Religion, French; subjectively superior to all other nations 287–88
Franche-Comté 6, 292
Francis I, King of France 106, 287
Francis of Assisi, Franciscans 19, 35, 36, 41, 62, 69, 199, 206, 214, 224, 225, 227, 228, 229, 232
Frangipani, Ottavio 155, 158–59
Frankfurt 39, 203, 269
Freud, Sigmund 114
Froschauer, Christoph 198–99, 201, 204

Galen 113, 138
Galilei, Galileo 224
Geneva 106, 183, 204, 212, 217–18
Germany 37, 54, 104, 160, 161, 183, 201, 202, 231, 261
Gerson, Jean 129, 233
Gesner, Konrad 201
Ghent 38, 181
ghosts 4, 9, 86, 92, 129, 197–207, 245
Gibbons, John 151
Gifford, George 136, 172, 174–75
Girona 19, 24, 27, 28, 30
Giovio, Paolo 105
Glanvill, Joseph 12
God: all powerful 110, 136, 239, 241, 242; anger with humanity 76; divine permission 7–8, 9, 40–41, 55, 69, 110, 156, 171, 172, 173, 200, 240–41, 242, 274; divine revelation 61–62, 186; God's goodness 8, 74, 90, 95, 242
Gödelmann, Johann 254
Gómez, Baltazar 254
Gouda 154
Grave 104
Graz 183
Gregory XIII, Pope 212
Grillando, Paolo 156, 272
Grodzisk 253, 263
guardian angels 11, 104, 127–28, 130, 300
Guazzo, Francesco 30
Gui, Bernard 21
Graham, Richard 170, 171

Harvillier, Jeanne 120, 122, 130
Hell 4, 8, 9, 55, 90, 141, 145, 201, 242, 244, 259
Hendaye 290
Henry IV, King of France and Navarre 213, 285, 295
Hondorff, Andreas 105
Hopkins, Matthew 245
humanism 83–84, 87, 95, 96, 104–5, 111, 115, 119, 124, 130, 158, 160, 179–80, 182, 198, 225, 269
Huby, François 214
Hussites 36, 38–39, 60, 95, 217, 261

*incubi* and *succubi* 58, 75, 91, 92–94, 173, 216, 276; *see also* devil, devils: sex with
Innocent VIII, Pope 54, 85
Inquisition 78, 88; Aragon 19, 20, 31; Papal 44, 54; Roman 224–25, 227, 230, 234; Spanish 20, 283, 299–309; Venetian 20
Innsbruck 54, 57
**Institoris, Heinrich** 41, **53–67**, 76, 232; *Epistola contra quendam conciliistam archiepiscopem videlicet Crainensem* 59; hatred of male heretics 59–60; involvement in witchcraft persecutions 54; *Malleus maleficarum* 2, 5, 35, 37, 39, 54–59, 68, 83, 86, 88, 90, 92, 104, 109, 112, 119, 124, 135, 139, 144, 156, 180, 207, 215, 216, 226, 255, 258, 272, 274, 304; misogyny of 57–59, 62–63; *Malleus* translated into Polish 252; obtains papal bull for the *Malleus* 54, 85; relationship with holy women 59, 61–62; *Opusculum in errores 'Monarchie'* 60; *Sancte Romane ecclesie fidei defensionis clippeum adversus Waldensium seu Pikardorum heresim* 60; sole authorship of the *Malleus* 53; *Stigmifere virginis Lucie de Narnia aliarumque spiritualium personarum feminei sexus facta admiracione digna* 62; *Tractatus novus de miraculoso eucharistie sacramento* 60; *Tractatus varii contra errores adversus eucharistie sacramentum exortos* 60; view on exorcism 229
Islam 29, 30, 37, 38, 54, 84, 217, 307
Italy 5, 35, 54, 61, 68, 69, 73, 74, 76, 79, 83, 114, 140, 198, 224, 225, 226, 228, 231, 261, 270, 290

Jacob III of Eltz, Elector of Trier 151
**Jacquier, Nicolas** 4, **35–50**, 61 76, 77, 86; and canonization proceedings 38; *De calcatione demonum* 37, 38–39; diabolical realism of 40, 42, 43; *Flagellum hereticorum fascinariorum* 36, 37, 39–46; at the Council of Basel 36–37; mission for Philip the Good 37; success of 44–46
**James VI of Scotland and I of England** 114, **165–78**; attacked by witches 1, 165, 167; criticism of Reginald Scot 133, 141, 168; *Daemonologie* 1–2, 5, 6–9, 10, 11, 142, 144, 167–77, 238–39, 242–43; hatred of smoking 11; intended audience of the *Daemonologie* 169; youth and education 165; personal reasons for writing the *Daemonologie* 167–68, 171,

174, 175; use of the vernacular 168–69, 171, 172
Jamometić, Andrea 59
Jesuits 150, 151, 152, 153, 182–83, 188–89, 202, 204–5, 211–12, 215, 217, 254–55, 261, 263
John I, King of Aragon 19
John VII of Schönenberg, Elector of Trier 153
John XXII, Pope 21, 26
John of Austria, Don 182
John of the Cross 128
Judaism 19, 27, 35, 54, 84, 85, 89, 127, 211, 255, 260–61, 274, 307
Julius II, Pope 224

Kaufmann von Oberwil, Anna 207
Kent 133, 135
Kościan 253
Kostka, Stanisław 255
Kyburg 198

Lacha, Guido 60
Laínez, Diego 211
La Borie, François de 214
Landshut 57
**Lancre, Pierre de** 6, 74, 190, 270, **283–98**; comparison with Alonso de Salazar Frías 300–1; description of the Pays de Labourd 287–89; *Du Sortilège* 286, 293; fascination with the sabbat 289–92; inconstancy of 293–95; *L'Incredulité et mescreance du sortilège plainement convaincue* 286, 293–94; use of child witnesses 291–93; *Tableau de l'inconstance des mauvais anges et démons* 2, 180, 188, 284–86, 289–98; *Tableau de l'inconstance et instabilité de toutes choses* 286, 287, 293
Laon 122, 129, 226
**Lavater, Ludwig 195–210**; attacked by Juan Maldonado 204–5; attacked by Pierre Le Loyer 205–6; early life 198–99; influence of Johann Wier 200–4; *Von Gespänsten* 195, 199–207
Lausanne 198
Laymann, Paul 151, 160, 254, 255, 262
Le Franc, Martin 37
Le Loyer, Pierre 205–6
Léry, Jean de 5–6
Lessius, Leonard 254
Leuven 154, 179–80, 181, 182, 183, 261
Liège 183, 188

Lille 38
Lipsius, Justus 180, 181, 182, 185
Lleida 19, 27, 30
Llull, Raymond 19, 20
Logroño 299–308
Lombard, Peter 214
**Loos, Cornelius** 6, 11, 146, 149–51, 154–55, 160; a patron of witches 150, 155, 156, 160; *De vera et falsa magia* 157–59, 161; forced recantation by 158–59; peripatetic existence of 154–55
Lorraine 11, 149, 269–75, 279–80
Lorraine, Cardinal Charles de 270
Louis XIV, King of France 287
Lublin 255
Lucca 224, 225
Luther, Martin, Lutheran 89, 104, 108, 151, 183, 199, 201, 224, 254, 255, 259, 261, 262
Lutz, Richard 203
Luxembourg 149, 181
lycanthropy *see* witches: animal transformations of
Lyon 36, 37, 39, 45, 269

MacCalzean, Euphame 171, 175
Machiavelli, Niccolò 229
Maimonides 127, 128
Mainz 154
Majorca 30
Maldon 175
**Maldonado, Juan** 12, 124, 156, **211–23**, 261; attack on Ludwig Lavater 204–5; career as a Jesuit 211–12; *Commentarii in quattuor evangelistas* 212–13; *De ratione theologiae docendae* 214–15; lectures on angels and demons 204–5, 213–14, 218; negative views of Thomas Aquinas 214–16; *Traicté des anges et demons* 214–19; use by Martin Delrio 183, 211, 217
Mantua 224
Marigrane, Marie de 292, 293
Mascardi, Giuseppe 254
Mather, Increase 185
Maximilian I, Duke (later Elector) of Bavaria 190
Mazzolini, Silvestro 73, 227, 229–30, 231, 232, 233
melancholy 110–11, 115, 119, 136, 138, 142, 156, 171
Melanchthon, Philip 108, 201

**Menghi, Girolamo** 12, 73, **224–37**; activities as an exorcist 225–28, 232; *Compendio dell'arte essorcistica* 227, 228, 230, 232, 234; early life 224; *Eversio daemonum* 228, 232; *Flagellum daemonum* 227, 230–31, 232, 233–34; *Fustis daemonum* 227, 231–32, 234; *Fuga daemonum* 228, 232; *Giardino delitioso de i frati minori* 228, 232; *Thesoro celeste della gloriosa madre di Dio* 228, 232
Mercurian, Everard 212
Metz 105, 270, 278
Meusvoet, Vincent 176
Milich, Ludwig 106, 200–1, 202
Mirandola 76, 83, 87–90, 91
misogyny 5, 57–59, 62–63, 72, 93, 135, 136–37, 257–58; *see also* witchcraft: gendering of
Modena 73, 78, 224, 225
Molitor, Ulrich 5, 77, 203, 272
Molitoris, Johannes 60, 68
Montaigne, Michel de 114, 125, 130, 212, 286
More, Henry 12
Morellet, André 20
Muccini, Antonio 226, 230

Nancy 269–71, 273, 280
Napier, Barbara 168, 171
Navarre 299, 301, 305, 308; *see also* Basque country
necromancy 19, 21, 24, 25, 27–28, 92, 169, 170, 171, 204, 229, 233, 261; *see also* ritual magic
Nepveu, George 205
New World 5–6, 161, 189, 217, 287, 288
*Newes from Scotland* 1, 7
Nider, Johannes 37, 54, 56, 61
North Berwick 7, 165, 167, 176

Olomouc 62
Orleans 199
Oslo 1

pagan gods 3, 5, 40, 41, 56, 71, 74, 85, 87, 95, 257, 274, 289
Paleotti, Gabriele 226, 227, 231
Pamplona 308
Paris 45, 181, 204–5, 211, 214, 218–19, 272, 273, 286; Parlement of 45, 124, 285; University of 21, 106, 114, 198, 212
Paul IV, Pope 226
Pays de Labourd 283–84, 287–89, 291, 292, 295; *see also* Basque country
Peña, Francisco 20
**Perkins, William** 9, 136, **238–51**; *Combat betweene Christ and the Devill* 240, 241; *A Discourse of the Damned Art of Witchcraft* 238, 242, 245, 246, 248, 249; *Exposition of the … Creed* 238, 245, 247; *Exposition upon … Galatians* 245; focus on white witchcraft 239, 245–49; places some witches among the Elect 243–44; *Reformed Catholike* 238; *Treatise of the Manner and Order of Predestination* 238; *The Whole Treatise of the Cases of Conscience* 239–40
Peter III, King of Aragon 19, 25, 27
Perrot, Charles 212
Peucer, Gaspar 200
Philip II, King of Spain 179, 181, 182
Philo 123, 127, 128
Piacenza 69, 70, 73
Pickering, Thomas 238–39, 248–49
**Pico della Mirandola, Gianfrancesco** 76, **83–100**, 215; anti-Aristotelianism of 86–87; *Examen vanitatis* 87; *Strix* 2, 83, 87–96
Pico della Mirandola, Giovanni 84, 85, 96, 123
Pierozzi, Antonino 54
Pius V, Pope 215, 225
Plato, (neo-)Platonism 83, 84, 86, 105, 123, 127
Poland 5, 252, 253, 255, 257, 261, 262, 263
Polidoro, Valerio 234
Pomponazzi, Pietro 225, 230
**Ponzinibio, Giovanfrancesco** 10, 12, 69, 77; attacked by Bartolomeo Spina 73, 76, 78–79; influence on Andrea Alciato 72; and the superiority of law over theology 70, 78; *Tractatus subtilis et elegans de lamiis et excellentia utriusque iuris* 69–72
Possevino, Antonio 187
Poznań 252, 253, 255, 261
Prague 36
Protestantism *see* Calvin, John, Calvinism; Luther, Martin, Lutheranism
Puigcerdà 29, 30

Purgatory 4, 129, 152, 199–206; see also Lavater, Ludwig

Quinzani, Stefana 61

Raemond, Florimond de 285
Ramus, Petrus 198
Rategno, Bernard 44
Ravensburg 54
Reggio Emilia 69, 227
Reiser, Friedrich 60
**Remy, Nicolas 269–82**; as *procureur-général* 269, 271, 280; attack on Johann Wier 272, 279; *Daemonolatreia* 2, 11, 159, 180, 188, 190, 238, 269–80; comparison with Jean Bodin 269, 272–77, 279
Reuchlin, Johann 105
Regulus, Albertus [Wojciech] 252–54, 263
Revolt of the Netherlands 113, 154, 160, 179–80, 182–84
ritual magic 29, 105, 106, 111, 120, 123, 169–170, 171, 172, 173, 229, 262; see also Agrippa, Heinrich Cornelius; necromancy
*Rituale Romanum* 233, 234, 258; see also exorcism
Rivius, Johann 200–1
Rome 20, 57, 151, 153, 204, 211, 212, 230, 234
Rokycana, Jan 36
Roselli, Antonio de' 60
Rouen 206, 214

sabbat 4–5, 6, 8, 35, 36, 43–44, 68, 70, 75, 77, 93, 120, 122, 125, 150, 157, 171, 190, 230, 239, 242, 270, 274–75, 283, 288, 291–92, 302, 306; as a Black Mass 290; an illusion 39, 41, 69, 71, 125, 139–40, 156, 159, 307; evening classes at 275; known as *aquelarre* 300; known as *cursus* or *ludus* 74; known as synagogue 35, 43–44; see also devil, devils: sex with; witches: flight of
Saint-Jean-de-Luz 283, 287
**Salazar Frías, Alonso de** 11, 283, **299–312**; comparison with Pierre de Lancre 300–1; legal values and diligence of 303, 304, 307, 309
Salzburg 57
Sandoval y Rojas, Bernardo de 299

Santiago de Compostela 287
Scaliger, Joseph 183, 184, 187, 188
Scandinavia 1, 161; see also Denmark
Scepticism see demonology; Loos, Cornelius; Ponzinibio, Giovanfrancesco; Salazar Frías, Alonso de; Scot, Reginald; Wier, Johann
**Scot, Reginald** 114–15, **133–148**, 168, 207, 248, 252; anti-Catholicism of 135–36; criticism of the demonic pact 139–40; possible Sadduceeism of 140–45; response to Jean Bodin 135; *The Discoverie of Witchcraft* 2, 9, 10, 133–47; use of Johann Wier 136, 138, 143–44; use of melancholy 137–39
Scientific Revolution 12
Scholasticism 42, 55, 83, 89, 92, 94, 95, 119, 156, 215–16; see also Aristotle, Aristotelianism
Scotland 1, 166–77
Seneca 113, 180, 181, 185, 188–189
Servetus, Michael 106
Shakespeare, William 189
Sixtus IV, Pope 54
Skarbimierz, Stanisław of 257
Socrates 120
Spain 5, 113, 180–82, 211, 217, 261, 283, 287, 288, 299–309
Spee, Friedrich 6, 12, 151, 160, 191, 252, 253, 254, 255, 263
Speyer 53, 57
**Spina, Bartolomeo** 73–79, 95, 156; attacks Giovanfrancesco Ponzinibio 73, 76, 78–79; *Quaestio de strigibus* 68, 73, 77, 78, 79, 139; *Tractatus de preeminentia sacre theologie super alias omnes scientias et precipue humanarum legum* 73, 78; *Quadruplex apologia de lamiis contra Ponzinibium* 73, 78
Spinoza, Baruch 10, 114
St Maximin, Imperial Abbey of 149–50, 154–55, 157–61
Stampa, Pietro Antonio 234
Stapleton, Thomas 261
Steiger, Johannes 200
Stewart, Francis, Fifth Earl of Bothwell 167, 170, 176
Stiles, Ezra 191
Strasbourg 198, 270
Stumpf, Johannes 201
Suárez, Francisco 254
superstition 58, 107, 111–12, 145, 151–53, 156, 185–86, 197, 200, 206,

226, 230, 232, 233, 234, 247, 252, 256, 257, 258, 262
Swabia 57
Switzerland 35, 37, 45, 89, 197, 201, 204

Tacitus 180
Taillepied, Noël 206
Tanner, Adam 151, 160, 254, 255, 260, 262
Tasso, Torquato 96
Tecklemburg 113
Terrena, Gui de 25, 31
Thou, Chrestofle de 124, 273
Tinctor, Jean 41
Tholosan, Claude 36, 44, 46
Toledo 299
Toulouse 21, 205, 272, 285
Tournai 38
Torrentius, Laevinus 156
torture 6, 22–23, 24, 28, 46, 68, 95, 113, 114, 122, 138, 150–51, 153, 156, 157, 158, 159, 171, 190, 244–45, 253, 259–60, 261–62, 271, 280, 305, 307; *see also* witchcraft: a *crimen exceptum*; witches: confessions of
Trent, Council of 151–52, 160, 187, 199, 202, 224, 226, 255, 257, 263
Trier 39, 149–61
Trithemius, Johannes 40, 203
Turin 224
Tyrol 57

Urtubie, Tristan d' 295
Urzędów, Marcin of 257

Valencia 19
Valladolid 182
Valle Alvarado, Juan de 299, 300, 303, 305
Valtellina 72
vampires 252
*La Vauderye de Lyonois en brief* 36, 37, 39, 44, 45
Venice 20, 38, 180, 206, 224, 228, 232, 233
Vesalius, Andreas 106
Viadana 224, 228, 231
Vic 27, 28
Vinet, Jean 39, 43
Vignati, Ambrogio 46, 68, 76

Virgin Mary 27, 30, 136, 186, 228, 232–33, 260; immaculate conception of 212; impersonation of 199
Visconti, Girolamo 68
Visconti, Zaccaria 234
Voet, Gijsbert 185
Voltaire 20

Waldensians 21, 37, 45, 60–61, 95, 224
Warboys 246
Wars of Religion, French 124, 211–12, 213, 217–19, 273
werewolves *see* witches: animal transformations of
Wesley, John 12, 94, 191
White Ruthenia 258
Wielkopolska 259
**Wier, Johann 103–118**, 154–55, 168, 207, 213, 230, 252, 272; attacked by Nicolas Remy 272, 279; career as dog walker 105; *De praestigiis daemonum* 2, 5, 9, 10, 11, 103–4, 108–13, 114, 135; formation of 104–7; influence on Ludwig Lavater 200–4; medical works by 113; refuted by Jean Bodin 112, 114, 119, 124; religious views of 107–8
William V, Duke of Cleves 107, 113
Wisner, Daniel 253–54
witchcraft: a *crimen exceptum* 57, 119, 150, 243; as heresy 20–21, 25, 40, 43, 44, 55–56, 156, 183, 217, 240, 261; as treason 44, 119, 157, 167, 168, 240, 277; gendering of 35, 57–59, 61, 62–63, 90, 93, 120, 135, 136–37, 150, 172, 183, 186, 204, 246, 256–58, 279, 287–88; novelty of 1, 41–42, 56, 86, 92, 110–12; *see also* demonology; devil; witches
witches: animal transformations of 56, 68, 74, 75, 113, 142–43, 157, 173, 272, 274–75, 276–77; cannibalism of 35, 56, 90, 95, 110, 122, 125; causing impotence 57, 120, 144; charms, curses, and spells of 29, 40, 41, 44, 55, 56, 57, 71, 88, 89, 92, 95, 120, 123, 169, 170, 257–58, 279; confessions of 6, 25, 41, 70, 75, 78, 87, 89, 122, 138–39, 141, 150, 157, 171, 190, 259, 271, 275, 278, 291, 302–5, 308; criminal intent of 120–21; delusions of 9, 11, 71, 72, 74, 77, 85, 110–11, 113,

135–37, 172, 203, 259, 276, 279, 304; flight of 4–5, 8, 30, 36, 41, 56, 68, 69, 70–71, 74, 86, 90, 140, 142, 156, 159, 171, 175, 189, 239, 242, 274, 275, 301, 302; *maleficia* of 2, 4, 7–8, 11, 30, 35, 36, 40, 41, 55, 77, 90, 142, 156, 172, 185, 227, 229, 239, 240, 242, 270, 275, 289, 300; ointments, powders, and salves of 6, 74, 90, 92, 95, 139, 142, 175, 272, 279, 290; scratching of 246; swimming of 8–9, 157, 174, 249, 252, 254, 259, 261; white witches 9, 29–30, 57, 136, 172, 175, 185–86, 239, 245–49, 256, 271, 277–78; *see also* demonology; devil, devils; witchcraft

Woolton, John 206–7

Zurich 197, 198–99, 201, 204–5, 207

For Product Safety Concerns and Information please contact our EU representative GPSR@taylorandfrancis.com
Taylor & Francis Verlag GmbH, Kaufingerstraße 24, 80331 München, Germany

www.ingramcontent.com/pod-product-compliance
Lightning Source LLC
Chambersburg PA
CBHW071153300426
44113CB00009B/1184